AF739322

Protection of the Environment under International Law during Occupation

This book examines the relationship between International Environmental Law and Human Rights Law regarding the protection of the environment in times of occupation.

Times of occupation create a tangible threat to the environment, alongside human, animal, and plant rights. This book uses international law to grapple with unprecedented environmental challenges, from water, air and soil pollution and severe damage to natural resources to the complexities of regulating emerging environmental challenges during extraordinary situations. Using international case studies alongside the prominent and evolving role of international law agreements, in particular Multilateral Environmental Agreements (MEAs), this book offers a comprehensive analysis of the legal tools available to navigate environmental challenges under occupation. The book also discusses occupying power obligations under public international law and the demands of protecting the environment in occupied territory.

The book provides a valuable resource for researchers in the field of environmental law, human rights law, and humanitarian law.

Waad Abualrob is currently a visiting lecturer in Law at the University of Westminster in the United Kingdom, where he also previously completed his PhD in International Law. He earned his LLB from An-Najah National University, followed by a Diploma in Business, Law, and Social Science from Kaplan College London and LLM in International Law from the University of Westminster. Dr Abualrob's research interests focus on the protection of the environment and natural resources in times of armed conflict and occupation.

Routledge Research in International Environmental Law

Sustainable Fisheries Management and International Law
Marine Fisheries in Bangladesh and the Bay of Bengal
Abdullah Al Arif

Marine Conservation and International Law
Legal Instruments for Biodiversity Beyond National Jurisdiction
Sarah Louise Lothian

Nature Law and Policy in Europe
Edited by Andrew L.R. Jackson

Environmental Liability and the Interplay between EU Law and International Law
Dr Emanuela Orlando

Implementing International Environmental Law and Policy
An Interactive Approach to Environmental Regulation
Joanna Miller Smallwood

Environmental Law and Governance in India
Sairam Bhat and Centre for Environmental Law, Education, Research, and Advocacy (CEERA)

Environmental Law and Policy in India
Sairam Bhat and Centre for Environmental Law, Education, Research, and Advocacy (CEERA)

Protection of the Environment under International Law during Occupation
International Humanitarian, Human Rights and Environmental Law
Waad Abualrob

https://www.routledge.com/Routledge-Research-in-International-Environmental-Law/book-series/INTENVLAW

Protection of the Environment under International Law during Occupation

International Humanitarian, Human Rights, and Environmental Law

Waad Abualrob

Routledge
Taylor & Francis Group
LONDON AND NEW YORK

First published 2025
by Routledge
4 Park Square, Milton Park, Abingdon, Oxon OX14 4RN

and by Routledge
605 Third Avenue, New York, NY 10158

Routledge is an imprint of the Taylor & Francis Group, an informa business

© 2025 Waad Abualrob

The right of Waad Abualrob to be identified as author of this work has been asserted in accordance with sections 77 and 78 of the Copyright, Designs and Patents Act 1988.

All rights reserved. No part of this book may be reprinted or reproduced or utilised in any form or by any electronic, mechanical, or other means, now known or hereafter invented, including photocopying and recording, or in any information storage or retrieval system, without permission in writing from the publishers.

Trademark notice: Product or corporate names may be trademarks or registered trademarks, and are used only for identification and explanation without intent to infringe.

British Library Cataloguing-in-Publication Data
A catalogue record for this book is available from the British Library

ISBN: 978-1-032-85082-5 (hbk)
ISBN: 978-1-032-85419-9 (pbk)
ISBN: 978-1-003-51806-8 (ebk)

DOI: 10.4324/9781003518068

Typeset in Times New Roman
by Deanta Global Publishing Services, Chennai, India

To my Parents
Eman and Waleed

Contents

Foreword

Dr Waad Abualrob's book *Protection of the Environment under International Law during Occupation: International Humanitarian, Human Rights, and Environmental Law* is a welcome addition to scholarship on the law of occupation. The book is a great example on how research on international law and the administration of occupied territory is evolving in order to address new challenges and advance the protection of human interests in occupied territory.

Exploring the legal regulation of occupied territory is far different today than it was in the past. Albeit the rights and duties of occupying powers are still today governed by rules of international humanitarian law codified in 1907, 1949, and (to a less extent) 1977 – the so-called law of occupation – it is increasingly accepted that other branches of international law apply in occupied territory along with international humanitarian law. This shift is likely caused by the realisation that international humanitarian law only applies to certain conduct in armed conflict, while other activities are not regulated by it.[1] In situations of occupation, the occupying power is tasked with administering the occupied territory during an armed conflict: during occupations, people are born and die, they marry and they divorce, they go on strike and they go on holidays. From this perspective, the administration of an occupied territory is as complex as the peacetime administration that a government undertakes over the territory of a state. The law of occupation struggles to address all the issues that might affect human life in occupied territory. Some of these issues were not perceived as relevant at the time of the codification of international humanitarian law and were left out. Other issues involving long-term actions were neglected because the drafters of the law of occupation had in mind short-term occupations. Yet, practice has demonstrated that, contrary to this assumption, occupations can last several decades, and the human needs to be addressed in occupied territory are broader than the traditional understanding of the scope of the law of occupation.

The protection of the environment is one of the issues that is not directly addressed by the law of occupation. Indeed, when the 1907 Hague Regulations and the 1949 Fourth Geneva Convention were adopted, states assumed that they had more pressing concerns than the protection of the environment in relation to the

1 International Court of Justice, *Legal Consequences of the Construction of a Wall in the Occupied Palestinian Territory*, Advisory Opinion, I.C.J. Reports 2004, para 106.

administration of occupied territory. Thus, international humanitarian law does not provide any specific rule on the environment in occupied territory. Even the subsequent codification of the 1977 Additional Protocol I is applicable to occupied territory only in relation to the employment of means and methods of warfare, which are typical of the conduct of hostilities rather than of occupations.

However, these considerations did not discourage Dr Abualrob, who explores in this book the topic of the protection of the environment pursuant to a rigorous and effective analysis. First, the book tries to apply to the protection of the environment rules of international humanitarian law that were adopted with different issues in mind. Dr Abualrob considers both specific rules binding the occupying power, for instance, in relation to the protection of property; and general principles governing the administration of occupied territory, such as the duties to restore and ensure civil life in occupied territory and to preserve the legal framework that existed before the occupation. Dr Abualrob demonstrates that international humanitarian law can offer some protection to those elements of the environment that can be considered to be either private or public property, advancing at the same time a compelling argument that the occupying power must restore and ensure environmental protection in occupied territory as part of its obligations in relation to civil life. In doing so, the occupying power must apply the local legislation in force prior to the occupation, which can include rules protecting the environment.

Is this enough to protect the environment in occupied territory? Of course not, since the rules of international humanitarian law that form the law of occupation were not drafted with the protection of the environment in mind and are often framed as obligations of diligent conduct. Correctly, then, Dr Abualrob moves on to analyse the impact on the application of international human rights law in occupied territory. Indeed, the enjoyment of many human rights is strictly linked to the availability of a clean environment. Accordingly, after having recalled the consistent approach of international judicial decisions on the application of international human rights law conventions in occupied territory, the book argues that within the framework of the law of occupation, applicable international human rights law can contribute to the protection of the environment in occupied territory. This is a correct and farseeing conclusion, which is reached also paying due consideration to the current debate on whether a new and autonomous human right to a clean environment has emerged.

Finally, Dr Abualrob analyses whether international environmental law conventions apply in occupied territory and to what extent they may contribute to the protection of the environment in occupied territory. This is quite a novel question that deserves attention. Why should we integrate the law of occupation with international human rights law conventions only? The variety of situations that an occupying power must address in relation to the protection of human interests in occupied territory justifies enquiry into whether other branches of international law may apply as well. Correctly, Dr Abualrob argues that international environmental law conventions may apply in occupied territory if their scope of application is not limited to peacetime and to the territory of the contracting states. Even though, currently, there is no international judicial decision on this point, the announcement of some litigations pertaining to the application of international environmental law treaties in formerly occupied Nagorno-Karabakh – which Dr Abualrob has analysed in previous publications[2] – demonstrates how topical is the analysis of this book.

Overall, when Dr Abualrob told me that his PhD dissertation had been accepted to be published in book form, I was not surprised. This book fills a lacuna of international law scholarship by bringing together the different fields of international humanitarian law, international human rights law, and international environmental law. The approach that the reader will find here should be applied in the future to other issues pertaining to the protection of human interests in occupied territory, which should be addressed taking into account international humanitarian law, international human rights law, and the specific international law branch at stake case by case (here, international environmental law; in other contexts, other branches such as international health law or international labour law).

We live in a time when new occupations are becoming more and more frequent, as demonstrated by the 2022 invasion and occupation of Ukraine by Russia, and when old occupations are becoming increasingly brutal for the local population, as shown by the 2023 and 2024 atrocities in the Gaza Strip. The study of the law of occupation needs rigorous and future-looking analysis as the one in the present book. I am sure that Dr Abualrob's work will be of interest for both experts of international humanitarian law and of international environmental law. The reader might disagree with some of the findings presented here, but no future discussion on the protection of the environment in occupied territory could prescind engaging with this work.

London, 13 June 2024

Dr Marco Longobardo
Reader in International Law
University of Westminster, London

2 Waad Abualrob, Marco Longobardo, and Ruth Mackenzie, 'Applying International Environmental Law Conventions in Occupied Territory: The Azerbaijan v. Armenia Case under the Bern Convention', *EJIL:Talk!*, 12 May 2023, https://www.ejiltalk.org/applying-international-environmental-law-conventions-in-occupied-territory-the-azerbaijan-v-armenia-case-under-the-bern-convention

1 Introduction

The protection of the environment in times of occupation has gained increased consideration in the last few years. The international community, the United Nations, and international law have all given more attention to the consequences of occupation on the environment in the occupied territory, the consequences resulting from environmental harm in such situations, and how these consequences will impact in the future.[1] While the importance of the protection of the environment in times of occupation has been globally acknowledged, there is still a lack of clarity in scholarly writings and legal decisions under international law regarding such situations.

Several binding and non-binding instruments have been adopted in the last few decades, with the aim of providing sufficient protection to the environment and asking all governments to respect and protect the environment at all times in peace and in war.[2] International awareness of the need to include environmental protection started to increase considerably after some occupations occurred,[3] for example, the prolonged Israeli occupation of the Occupied Palestinian Territories (OPT), the Indonesian occupation of East Timor, the Iraqi occupation of Kuwait, the United States of America's (USA) and the United Kingdom's (UK) occupation of Iraq, the Armenian occupation of Azerbaijan, and the Russian occupation of Georgia and Ukraine.

Notably, environmental damage during occupations is not on the same scale as that caused during the conduct of hostilities, but still, damage during such times can be substantial and have a grave impact on the occupied territory, its population, their health, their sustenance, and their survival needs.[4] Environmental damage

1 Chee Ling, *The Rio Declaration on Environment and Development: An Assessment* (Third World Network 2012) 1–2, 12, 53–55.

2 Naqish Lakhdar, 'Preserving the Environment in Times of Armed Wars in the Light of International Humanitarian Law', (2023) 16 *Journal of Law & Humanities Sciences*, University of Djelfa, Algeria 1163, 1164–1174.
نقيش لخضر، "المحافظة على البيئة في أوقات الحروب المسلحة على ضوء .ما قرره القانون الدولي الإنساني"، مجلة الحقوق والعلوم الإنسانية، المجلد16/ العـــدد:01، (2023)،ص116

3 Rosemary Rayfuse and Britta Sjöstedt, 'Workshop on the Protection of the Environment in Relation to Armed Conflict', (Lund University 2012) 4–5.

4 Karen Hulme, 'Enhancing Environmental Protection During Occupation Through Human Rights', (2020) 10 Goettingen Journal of International Law, 203, 205; Karen Hulme, 'Using a Framework of Human Rights and Transitional Justice for Post-Conflict Environmental Protection and Remedia-

DOI: 10.4324/9781003518068-1

during occupations can even cause degradation of the ecosystem of the occupied territory, with long-lasting effects.[5] The environmental damage that can be caused by an occupying power during occupation includes looting, the pillage and excessive utilisation of natural resources, a loss of habitat and species, the destruction of agricultural areas and forests, and the pollution of water sources (such as groundwater, wells, and rivers that are vital for human survival in the occupied territory), along with environmental injuries and harm caused by the neglect of maintenance and safeguard of nature reserves, forests, and coal mines.[6] For example, the destruction of water wells, hundreds of thousands of olive trees, and thousands of acres of arable land in the OPT and the severe cutting of forests in the Democratic Republic of the Congo (DRC) indubitably led to grave impacts on the environment and caused agrobiodiversity loss.[7]

More recently, an essential reference to environmental protection in times of armed conflict and occupation was offered by Marja Lehto in her 2018, 2019, and 2022 reports for the International Law Commission (ILC) on the protection of the environment in relation to armed conflicts.[8] These reports offer an overview of the obligations to protect the environment in occupied territory[9] and demonstrate the legal consequences of such harm against the environment.[10]

This study focuses on deliberate harm to the environment caused by an occupying power to the occupied territory, the extreme utilisation of an occupied territory's natural resources in an unsustainable manner by an occupying state, and the environmental harm resulting from the lack of oversight and/or disrespect of the environmental laws and regulations applicable in the occupied territory. For example, the occupying state might deliberately cause harm to the environment, such as the Iraqi destruction of hundreds of Kuwait's oil wells and the grave environmental consequences for the land, marine life, vegetation, and the atmosphere along with the environmental consequences for neighbouring countries and areas out of the national jurisdiction of Kuwait – all caused by the Iraqi occupying forces.[11] It observed that the Iraqi occupation of Kuwait

tion', in Carsten Stahn, Jens Iverson, and Jennifer Easterday (eds), *Environmental Protection and Transitions from Conflict to Peace: Clarifying Norms, Principles, and Practices* (Oxford University Press 2017) 131–134; UN International Law Commission, 'First Report on Protection of the Environment in Relation to Armed Conflicts by Marja Lehto, Special Rapporteur', (A/CN.4/720) (30 April 2018), para 13.

5 ILC, 'First Report', para 13; David Jensen, Steve Lonergan (eds), *Assessing and Restoring Natural Resources in Post-Conflict Peacebuilding* (Routledge 2012), 109, 112.

6 ILC, 'First Report', para 13; Hulme, 'Enhancing Environmental Protection', 205; Jensen and Lonergan, *Assessing and Restoring Natural Resources*, 109, 112, 125, 313.

7 Hulme, 'Using a Framework of Human Rights', 131–134.

8 ILC, 'First Report'; ILC, 'Second report on protection of the environment in relation to armed conflicts by Marja Lehto, Special Rapporteur', (A/CN.4/728) (27/March/2019); ILC, 'Third report on protection of the environment in relation to armed conflicts, by Marja Lehto, Special Rapporteur', (A/CN.4/750) (16 March 2022).

9 Ibid.

10 Ibid.

11 The United Nations: General Assembly, Resolution (47/151), (A/RES/47/151) (1992); Anne Dienelt, *Armed Conflicts and the Environment: Complementing the Laws of Armed Conflict with Human*

entailed transboundary environmental harm and is, therefore, a matter of *erga omnes*.[12] Due to the Iraqi occupation of Kuwait, the United Nations Economic and Social Council (UNESC) has adopted a report regarding the human rights situation in Kuwait, in which the Special Rapporteur expressed his concerns about the severe environmental damage and the grave consequences resulting from that damage to the environment when Kuwait was still under Iraqi occupation.[13] He also set out how these environmental consequences caused by the occupation had impacted on the population of Kuwait, in particular, on their health.[14]

Interestingly, the above report confirmed the occupant's responsibility towards public health and hygiene in the occupied territory, particularly when the Special Rapporteur stated that "such behaviour, however, contradicted basic tenets of the duty of the Occupying Power to ensure and maintain public health and hygiene as it is embodied in Article 56 of the Fourth Geneva Convention",[15] noting that, in recent years, the relationship between environmental protection and public health had become closer.[16] More details about the relationship between the occupant's responsibility to protect the environment and the public health of the people in the occupied territory will be discussed in detail in the following chapters, together with the issue of the environment in the occupied territory from a number of relevant perspectives.

Another example of deliberate harm to the environment caused by an occupant can be seen in the case of occupied Iraq by both the USA and the UK in 2003, and how the environment has suffered from severe harm, caused intentionally by both occupants there.[17] The intentional damage caused by the USA and the UK to the Iraqi environment was considered a grave breach of international law treaties and customs and was seen as being a war crime.[18] Furthermore, in 2008, Russia occupied and deliberately destroyed areas of Georgia with large-scale fires in the occupied forests, which in turn, had grave consequences for wildlife there.[19]

Rights Law and International Environmental Law (Springer International Publishing 2022) 2; Abdul Aziz Abdul Hadi, 'The Iraqi Aggression against the Environment in the State of Kuwait in Light of the Provisions of International Law' (1991) 15 *The Law Journal*, Kuwait University, 237, 243–256.

12 Christopher Stone, 'The Environment in Wartime: an Overview', in Jay Austin and Carl Bruch (eds), *The Environmental Consequences of War: Legal, Economic, and scientific Perspectives* (Cambridge University Press 2000) 32.

13 The United Nations: Economic and Social Council, 'Situation of Human Rights in Occupied Kuwait: Report on the Situation of Human Rights in Kuwait under Iraqi Occupation, Prepared by Mr. Walter Kalin. Special Rapporteur of the Commission on Human Rights, in accordance with Commission Resolution 1991/67', (E/CN.4/1992/26), (16 January 1992), paras 201–209.

14 Ibid, para 201.

15 Ibid, para 208.

16 Joel Trachtman, *The Future of International Law: Global Government* (Cambridge University Press 2013) 146.

17 Hesham Bashir and Alaa Sbeita, *The Occupation of Iraq and Violations of the Environment and Cultural Property* (Al Manhal/The National Centre for Legal Issues 2013) 7–9, 13–17.

18 Ibid.

19 Hulme, 'Enhancing Environmental Protection', 238; International Law and Policy Institute, 'Protection of the Natural Environment in Armed Conflict: An Empirical Study' (2014), 29–30.

The Russian occupation of Ukraine since 2014 is another example of deliberate harm to the environment by the occupying power against the occupied territory. For example, Russia as an occupying power in Ukraine has caused several injuries to the Crimean environment, particularly in the regions where the Tatar minorities are living. For instance, in 2015, the occupying power started a new construction project, the so-called "Crimean Bridge", in relation to establishing a new railway. The building of this bridge, as some studies have shown, has had a negative direct impact on the ecosystems of the Azov and Black Seas.[20] Furthermore, the construction of the bridge constitutes a flagrant violation of the ecosystem of the Crimean Mountains. For example, in relation to building the bridge, the occupying power has destroyed the local landscape, and half of the top of Mount Aharmysh has been demolished too, which led to disruption of the functioning of groundwater.[21] In addition to this, and regarding a more recent event, the COP14 of the Ramsar Convention confirmed the application of that Convention to situations of armed conflict and occupation, demanding that Russia avoid harming protected Ramsar sites and wetlands under the Convention in the territories of Ukraine under its occupation and military control.[22]

The second environmental issue that will be addressed throughout the book is the utilisation of natural resources in an unsustainable manner by the occupying power in the occupied territory, where such excessive exploitation can lead to the degradation of the environment and long-term impacts on the ecosystem and biodiversity of the occupied territory.[23] Furthermore, excessive natural-resources exploitation by an occupying power might contribute to environmental contaminants and pollution, especially the utilisation in an unsustainable manner of mineral resources, such as oil.[24] For example, this was the case in the Russian occupation of Estonia, which led to severe and subsequent damage to the Estonian environment.[25] Furthermore, Russia was responsible for transboundary harm caused to

20 Susan Power and Doug Weir, 'Stress-testing the ILC's Draft principles on Environmental Protection during Occupation': 'The revisions to the draft principles on environmental protection in situations of occupation have improved them considerably but gaps remain that should be addressed', (September 19, 2018) 8; Borys Babin, Andrii Chvaliuk, Olexiy Plotnikov, 'Attempted Annexation of Crimea and Maritime Environment Legal Protection', (2021) 7 *Lex Portus* 31, 39, 43.

21 Crimean Tatar Resource Center, 'Contributions for the Study on Right to Land under the UNDRIP: A Human Rights Focus', (No.01/02), (15/January/2020), 6; Crimean Tatar Resource Center, 'Contributions for the Study on Indigenous Peoples' Rights in the Context of Borders, Migration and Displacement', (No. 26/02), (1 February 2019).

22 The 14th Meeting of the Conference of the Contracting Parties to the Ramsar Convention on Wetlands, 'Wetlands Action for People and Nature', Geneva, Switzerland, and Wuhan, China, 5–13 November 2022. Resolution (XIV.20), 'The Ramsar Convention's Response to Environmental Emergency in Ukraine relating to the Damage of its Wetlands of International Importance (Ramsar Sites) stemming from the Russian Federation's Aggression', paras 12–17.

23 Hulme, 'Enhancing Environmental Protection', 238.

24 Ibid, 211, 238–240.

25 Lisa Kaplan, 'International Responsibility of an Occupying Power for Environmental Harm: The Case of Estonia' (1999) 12 *Transnat'l Law*, 153, 155–157, 159.

the neighbouring states of Estonia throughout the Baltic Sea, with the harm being caused by Russia's occupying forces situated in Estonia at that time.[26]

Another example can be seen in the Japanese occupation of Sumatra, as addressed in the *1956 De Bataafsche Petroleum v. War Damage Commission*, where the Singapore Court of Appeal denounced the seizure and plunder of oil resources in Sumatra by Japanese armed forces, "systematically and ruthlessly, throughout the whole period of occupation".[27] The Singapore Court of Appeal stressed that the Japanese seizure of oil resources in Sumatra was a breach of the laws and customs of war, as well as constituting economic plunder.[28] It was noted that, and as mentioned above, the overexploitation and overextraction of natural resources, particularly of mineral ones, could have grave consequences for the environment of the occupied state.[29]

Another similar example to the abovementioned was when the Azerbaijani territory of Nagorno-Karabakh was occupied by Armenia. Armenian occupying forces deliberately destroyed the natural resources there, specifically polluting water sources, along with the extreme utilisation of these resources in an unsustainable manner,[30] which impacted on the biodiversity and the ecosystem of the occupied region.[31] Similarly, there was exploitation of natural resources, especially the production and exploration of oil in the Sinai and Suez areas in Egypt,[32] which were occupied by Israel, together with the exploitation of other mineral and natural resources in other Arab territories, such as the OPT, in particular of the Dead Sea's minerals and natural resources, such as phosphate; and the occupied Syrian Golan Heights, also occupied by Israel.[33] The Israeli policy towards the environment and the overexploitation of natural resources in the occupied Arab territories is described as a racist policy that promotes privileged access to Israeli citizens,

26 Ibid, 159, 200–201.

27 Singapore *(Bataafsche Petroleum v. The War Damage Commission)* (1956), 22 Malayan Law Journal 155, Court of Appeal, Singapore, (April 13, 1956).

28 Ibid.

29 Hulme, 'Enhancing Environmental Protection', 238.

30 Yegane Bakhshiyeva, 'Threats and Provocations Originating from The Republic of Armenia Towards The Water Resources of The Republic Of Azerbaijan', (2019) 40 *Review of Armenian Studies* 113, 113–116.

31 Ibid, 113–116; Administrative Department of the President of the Republic of Azerbaijan: Presidential Library, 'Armenia-Azerbaijan Nagorno-Karabakh Conflict', at: 15, 24. Available online at: < http://files.preslib.az/projects/azerbaijan/eng/gl7.pdf>. Accessed date: 17 December 2020.

32 Brice Clagett, Olin Johnson, 'May Israel as a Belligerent Occupant Lawfully Exploit Previously Unexploited Oil Resources of the Gulf of Suez?' (1978) 72 *AJIL*, 558, 575.

33 Nico Schrijver, *Sovereignty over Natural Resources: Balancing Rights and Duties* (Cambridge University Press 2008) 143, 268; Vaios Koutroulis, 'The Application of International Humanitarian Law and International Human Rights Law in Situation of Prolonged Occupation: Only a Matter of Time?' (2012) 94 *International Review of the Red Cross* 165, 183; Walid Mustafa, *Natural Resources in Palestine: Determinants of Exploitation and Mechanisms for Maximizing Benefit* (MAS/The Palestinian Economic Policy Research Institute 2016) 33, 43–47, 109–111; Aeyal Gross, *The Writing on the Wall: Rethinking the International Law of Occupation* (Cambridge University Press 2017) 199–201.

including illegal settlers, to the natural resources and prevents the local population of the occupied territories from enjoying the benefits arising from their own natural resources.[34] Hence, the overexploitation of natural resources in the occupied territory might lead to further environmental consequences and therefore affect the local society of the occupied state.[35]

Another example is the Moroccan occupation of Western Sahara,[36] where the overexploitation and extraction of natural resources by the occupant caused environmental degradation in the occupied territory, which in turn, impacted on the ability of inhabitants to exercise and enjoy their fundamental rights under International Human Rights Law (IHRL) conventions.[37] It is further argued that there is potential criminal responsibility on the part of individuals and some Moroccan companies involved in unlawful exploitation of the Western Sahara's natural resources, which might attract individual criminal responsibility as war crimes.[38] In 1979, the United Nations General Assembly (UNGA) deemed Morocco as being an occupying power over the territory of Western Sahara and asked it to terminate the occupation.[39] Similar scenarios can be found in other occupied territories, such as East Timor and Northern Cyprus.[40] Arguably, "when an occupying state exploits the natural resources of occupied territory for its own benefit, rather than that of the local population, it appears as colonialism rather than occupation".[41] Even though most of the previously mentioned examples are discussed from the economic and commercial point of view, it still shows that the occupying state has obligations and cannot exploit the natural resources located in the occupied territory in an unsustainable manner.

The third issue the book will address is the environmental harm resulting from the occupying power refusing to implement and respect the environmental laws and regulations applicable in the occupied territory (domestic regulations), which would legally protect the environment. The occupying power has a legal obligation under the norms

34 Rouba Al-Salem, *Security, Rights and Law: The Israeli High Court of Justice and Israeli Settlements in the Occupied West Bank* (Routledge 2019) 109, 156; Waad Abualrob, 'Environmental Racism in Situations of Occupation', *International Law* Blog (2023). Available online at: < https://internationallaw.blog/2023/07/10/environmental-racism-in-situations-of-occupation/>. Accessed date: 19 August 2023.

35 Eliav Lieblich and Eyal Benvenisti, *Occupation in International Law* (Oxford University Press 2022) 172, 197, 221.

36 'Western Sahara is non-self-covering territory, akin to Spanish colonies there, however, that does not change its status as occupied by Morocco'. For more information about Western Sahara see generally: Pal Wrange, 'Occupation/Annexation of a Territory: Respect for International Humanitarian Law and Human Rights and Consistent EU Policy', Directorate General for External Policies/Policy Department, (European Union 2015) 40.

37 Ben Saul, 'The Status of Western Sahara as Occupied Territory under International Humanitarian Law and the Exploitation of Natural Resources', (2015) 27 *Global Change, Peace & Security* 301, 301–304, 315–319, 321–322; Abualrob, 'Environmental Racism in Situations of Occupation'.

38 Ibid.

39 The United Nations: General Assembly, 'Question of Western Sahara', Res. (34/37), (21/Nov/1979), paras 5–6.

40 Gross, *The Writing on the Wall*, 50, 118, 164, 199–201, 259.

41 Ibid, 200.

of the law of occupation to respect the laws and regulations of the occupied territory unless absolutely prevented.[42] Regarding this, there are some multilateral environmental agreements (MEAs) that might be incorporated into the domestic legislation of the occupied state.[43] Such agreements have attracted a number of state ratifications, where the occupied state and/or the occupying power are also parties.[44] All the above environmental issues during times of occupation will be addressed and analysed in detail throughout the chapters, with the aim of bringing them into the spotlight.

The International Court of Justice (ICJ) has discussed the issue of natural resources and the right of permanent sovereignty over those in the occupied territory. However, the issue of the environment itself has not been given any particular attention by the court. For example, the ICJ in the *Congo v. Uganda* case declared that the occupant has a responsibility to "take appropriate measures to prevent the looting, plundering and exploitation of natural resources in the occupied territory".[45] Therefore, the ICJ has recognised the importance of the principle of permanent sovereignty over natural resources in occupied territories, by putting obligations on the occupant to protect them.[46] Moreover, Judge Koroma, in the same case, confirmed that this right is considered effective at all times – including times of occupation.[47] Furthermore, such a principle has been described as a peremptory one applicable to occupations,[48] as it is also emphasised that rights of sovereignty, such as the freedom of enjoyment and exploitation of national natural resources by the local population, do not pass to the occupant.[49]

It has been added that generated limitations of the occupant's power in terms of using immovable property in occupied territory could prevent the occupying power from violating the right of occupied people to enjoy the benefits arising from their natural resources.[50] For example, regarding the right to water usage by

42 Laws and Customs of War on Land (The Hague, IV), Convention (signed at The Hague October 18, 1907), (Entered into force January 26, 1910), Article 43; The Fourth Geneva Convention 1949, Article 64; ILC, 'First Report', para 49; ILC, Draft Principles on Protection of the Environment in relation to Armed Conflicts (2022), Draft Principle 19(3); Mara Tignino, 'Principle 23: The Environment of Oppressed Peoples' in Jorge Viñuales (ed), *The Rio Declaration on Environment and Development: A Commentary* (Oxford University Press 2015) 561–562.

43 ILC, 'First Report', para 49.

44 Ibid.

45 Armed Activities on the Territory of the Congo (*Democratic Republic of the Congo v. Uganda*), Judgment, I.C.J. Reports 2005, p. 168, para 244–248.

46 Ibid, para 244.

47 Declaration of Judge Koroma, ICJ Reports 2005, para 11.

48 Alexander Orakhelashvili, 'The Post-War Settlement in Iraq: the UN Security Council Resolution 1483 (2003) and General International Law', (2003) 8 *Journal of Conflict & Security Law* 307, 311–313.

49 Nico Schrijver, *Sovereignty over Natural Resources: Balancing Rights and Duties* (Cambridge University Press 2008) 266–269.

50 Antonio Cassese, '*Powers and Duties of an Occupant in Relation to Land and Natural* Resources'. In: Emma Playfair (ed), *International Law and the Administration of Occupied Territories: Two Decades of Israeli Occupation of the West Bank and Gaza Strip* (Oxford University Press 1992) 425–426.

the occupant, this right is restricted to use only for military needs in the occupied territory or to serve the needs of the local population.[51] Further, the occupant is not allowed to own water sources or sell them as these are considered a public immovable property situated in occupied territory. This means that an occupying power cannot expropriate water sources and deprive the entire population of the occupied territory of their water needs or natural resources.[52]

It is noteworthy to mention that, during the 1970s and 1980s, UN organs, such as the UNGA and the United Nations Security Council (UNSC), showed some concern regarding the issue of the protection of the natural resources in occupied territories, where they discussed the right to permanent sovereignty over natural resources to people living under occupation or colonial and racial domination.[53] For instance, an UNGA resolution adopted in 1973 confirmed the right of Arab states and all other people living under occupation to have permanent sovereignty over their natural resources.[54] It also reaffirmed that all measures taken by the Israeli authority as the occupying power regarding the utilisation of the natural recourses in these territories were illegal,[55] emphasising also the right of the occupied people to "the restitution of and full compensation for the exploitation and looting" of their natural resources by the occupant.[56] Furthermore, the issue of the environment in times of occupation received particular attention from both the UNGA and UNSC after the Iraqi occupation of Kuwait and the grave environmental consequences resulting from that occupation. Regarding this, both bodies adopted resolutions as a result of Iraq's unlawful invasion and occupation of Kuwait in 1991, and the severe damage caused to the environment as a result of the occupation.[57] According to the UNSC, in Resolution No. 687 adopted in 1991, Iraq was responsible under international law for the environmental harm and depletion of Kuwait's natural resources during the time of its illegal occupation there.[58] Notably, this Resolution was a call to all member states of the UN, not only Iraq and Kuwait. It further confirmed that environmental considerations are one of the occupying power's obligations.[59] Moreover, the UNGA expressed its concern about and condemned Iraq's severe

51 Ibid, 431–432.

52 Ibid.; Abdallah Abu-Eid, 'Water as a Human Right: The Palestinian Occupied Territories as an Example', (2007) 23 *International Journal of Water Resources Development* 285, 289, 290–291, 294.

53 Nico Schrijver, *Sovereignty over Natural Resources: Balancing Rights and Duties* (Cambridge University Press 2008) 8.

54 The United Nations: General Assembly, 'Permanent Sovereignty over National Resources in the Occupied Arab Territories, (A/RES/3175), (XXVIII), (17 December 1973).

55 Ibid.

56 Ibid.

57 Jean-Marie Henckaerts and Louise Doswald-Beck, *Customary International Humanitarian Law* (Cambridge University Press 2009), 147.

58 The United Nations: Security Council, Resolution (687) Iraq-Kuwait (1991), Section E, para 16.

59 Ibid, Philippe Sands and others, *Principles of International Environmental Law* (4th edn, Cambridge University Press 2018) 828, 835–836; Natia Kalandarishvili-Mueller, *Occupation and Control in International Humanitarian Law* (Taylor & Francis 2021), 123.

injuries to Kuwait's environment,[60] particularly in relation to the destruction of hundreds of its oil wells and the grave environmental consequences for the land, sea, and atmosphere of that country as well as that of other nearby states.[61] The resolutions of the UNGA and the UNSC can be also used as legal sources for defining the rights and obligations of both the occupying powers and the people living under occupation.

The ILC, in the Draft Principles on Protection of the Environment in relation to Armed Conflicts, confirmed the responsibility of the occupying power towards the environment in the occupied territory.[62] For example, it stated that the occupant "shall respect and protect the environment of the occupied territory in accordance with applicable international law and take environmental considerations into account in the administration of such territory".[63] Moreover, it declared that the occupying power has a due diligence obligation "to ensure that activities in the occupied territory do not cause significant harm to the environment" of areas beyond the occupied territory.[64] Arguably, as the occupant has a due diligence obligation not to cause harm to the environment in other territories outside of the national jurisdiction of the occupied territory, it is perhaps accordingly also obliged to protect the environment in the occupied territory. According to the Al-Haq Defending Human Rights Organisation, the ILC Draft Principles directly address the legal responsibility of the occupying power in relation to any environmental damage and any unsustainable utilisation of natural resources in an occupied state.[65]

In this work, the interplay between different rules of public international law applicable to situations of occupation that do offer some protection will be discussed. Hence, it is deemed to be crucial that environmental issues need to be identified and explained clearly in order to bring them into the spotlight and to fill the existing gap under international law. This will be achieved by examining the role of the law of occupation as a branch of the *Jus in Bello* (International Humanitarian Law [IHL]), IHRL, and International Environmental Law (IEL) altogether in relation to addressing the abovementioned environmental issues in the occupied territory. The book confirms the notion that IHL is no longer the only legal framework regulating situations of occupation, for nowadays, other frameworks are also applicable, such as IHRL and IEL.[66]

60 The United Nations: General Assembly, Resolution (46/216) (1991); The United Nations: General Assembly, Resolution (47/151) (A/RES/47/151) (1992).

61 Ibid.

62 ILC Draft Principles on Protection of the Environment in relation to Armed Conflicts, (2022), Draft Principles 19–21.

63 Ibid, Draft Principle 19(1).

64 Ibid, Draft Principle 21.

65 Al-Haq Defending Human Rights Organisation, 'ILC Draft Principles on the Protection of the Environment in Relation to Armed Conflicts, (25/July/2019). Available online at: < http://www.alhaq.org/advocacy/14746.html>. Accessed date: 22 February 2020.

66 Lieblich and Benvenisti, *Occupation in International Law*, 15, 197, 221.

According to the norms of the law of occupation, there is no single article that directly protects the environment as such. Moreover, the law of occupation has never mentioned the word "environment". However, the book will explore the applicability of the rules of the law of occupation – such as Article 55 of the Hague Regulations – and discuss the extent and limits of the protection offered by similar rules. For instance, by considering the interpretation rule of Article 31 of the Vienna Convention on the Law of Treaties (VCLT), and "in accordance with the ordinary meaning of the terms to safeguard the capital, as mentioned under Article 55 of The Hague Regulations, any exploitation of mineral resources should be prohibited".[67] Furthermore, the law of occupation gives some support to the principle of permanent sovereignty, which in turn, can reinforce the right of occupied people to enjoy their natural resources and might provide some protection to the environment.[68]

Notably, both IHL and IHRL are intertwining with the possible legal protection of the environment, using various international law treaties that focus on the vulnerability of the people caused by pollution and human activities as well as that caused by the actions during military occupation or any other type of armed conflict.[69] For example, the environmental damage resulting from the occupant's troops' activities during the duration of occupation could be linked, *inter alia*, to the use of "chemicals weapons, inappropriate disposal or dumping of toxic or hazardous waste",[70] or to the mismanagement and unsustainable utilisation of natural resources in the occupied territory.[71] The contamination of groundwater and agricultural lands by the occupant's dumping or moving hazardous waste can cause grave consequences for human health, which could be considered as being a crime against humanity.[72] Hence, the occupant is prohibited from dumping or moving hazardous waste into the occupied territory; otherwise, it will be abusing its status as an administrative power there.[73] Moreover, such dangerous activities may have negative consequences for plants and animals, which in turn, will have an impact on biodiversity and the whole ecosystem of the occupied territory. In other words, these activities are likely to contribute to the

67 Blaine Sloan, The United Nations: General Assembly: Economic and Social Council, 'Implications, Under International Law, of the United Nations Resolutions on Permanent Sovereignty over Natural Resources, on the Occupied Palestinian and Other Arab Territories and on the Obligations of Israel Concerning its Conduct in these Territories: Report of the Secretary-General', (A/38/265) (E/1983/85) (21 June 1983), para 32.

68 Ibid, para 52.

69 Yoram Dinstein, *The Conduct of Hostilities under the Law of International Armed Conflict* (3rd edn, Cambridge University Press 2016) 230–250.

70 ILC, 'First Report', para 12.

71 Ibid, paras 12, 13, 31, 32; Dinah Shelton, Isabelle Cutting, 'If You Break It, Do You Own It? Legal Consequences of Environmental Harm from Military Activities', (2015) 6 J. *Int'l Human. Legal Stud.*, 201, 206.

72 Benjamin Pontin, Vito De Lucia, Jesus Gamero Rus, 'Environmental Injustice in Occupied Palestinian Territory: Problems and Prospects', (Al-Haq Organization 2015) 37, 42, 52–53.

73 Adam Aloni, 'Made in Israel: Exploiting Palestinian Land for Treatment of Israeli Waste', (B'tselem December 2017)16.

extreme degradation of the environment.[74] A safe, clean, and healthy environment is integral to the fulfilment of a wide range of human rights, including the right to life, health, property, water, food, and sanitation. Thus, the occupant is legally responsible for respecting and protecting human rights,[75] including protecting the population, their resources, and the territory from any environmental harm that might affect the enjoyment of such rights.[76]

Under IEL, there are some fundamental instruments that provide protection to the environment in times of armed conflict and occupation, such as the 1972 United Nations Conference on the Human Environment (Stockholm Declaration)[77] and the 1992 United Nations Conference on Environment and Development (Rio Declaration). Regarding these, Principle 23 of the Rio Declaration provides that "the environment and natural resources of people under ... occupation shall be protected".[78] The Rio Declaration was the first universal legal instrument to emphasise the rights of people living under occupation "in relation to both the use of natural resources and the protection of the environment".[79] Notably, both the Rio and Stockholm Declarations, although not legally binding, still asked states to show minimum respect to the international law provisions by not causing harm to the environment during times of armed conflict and occupation.[80] Likewise, the 1977 Mar Del Plata Declaration of the United Nations Water Conference contains references to the protection of the environment, human health, and natural resources during armed conflict and occupation.[81]

It is argued that IEL, both conventional and customary, continues to be applicable in situations of armed conflict and occupation.[82] Furthermore, "applying general principles of international environmental law is necessary to deter an occupying power from causing environmental harm to the occupied territory".[83] This book further

74 Z. Brophy and J. Isaac, 'The Environmental Impact of Israeli Military Activities in the Occupied Palestinian Territory', (Applied Research Institute – Jerusalem 2009) 23.

75 Eyal Benvenisti, *The International Law of Occupation* (2nd edn, Oxford University Press 2012) 14.

76 Ibid, 14, 18; Tristan Ferraro, 'The Law of Occupation and Human Rights Law: Some Selected Issues', in Robert Kolb, Gloria Gaggioli (eds), *Research Handbook on Human Rights and Humanitarian Law* (Edward Elgar 2013) 282.

77 The United Nations Conference on the Human Environment 'Stockholm Declaration' (1972).

78 The United Nations Conference on Environment and Development 'The Rio Declaration' (1992). Principle 23.

79 Tignino, 'Principle 23', 557.

80 The United Nations: Reports of International Arbitral Awards, 'Eritrea Ethiopia Claims Commission, Final Award – Pensions: Eritrea's Claims 15, 19 & 23' (19 December 2005), vol. XXXVI, 471.

81 The United Nations: 'Report of the United Nations Water Conference' Mar del Plata Declaration, Resolution X, 'Water Policies in Occupied Territories', (Mar del Plata, 14–25 March 1977), (E/CONF/70/29), 80–81.

82 ILC, 'First Report', para 80; Britta Sjöstedt, *The Role of Multilateral Environmental Agreements: A Reconciliatory Approach to Environmental Protection in Armed Conflict* (Hart Publishing 2021) 137–174.

83 Lisa Kaplan, 'International Responsibility of an Occupying Power for Environmental Harm: The Case of Estonia', (1999) 12 *Transnat'l Law*, 153, 195.

contends that IEL and IHL should be envisaged together with IHRL;[84] that is, the application of IEL to situations of armed conflict and occupation will ensure better protection of the environment and will complement and harmonise with IHL and IHRL in this regard.[85] Consequently, the book examines the applicability of IEL in times of occupation, with discussion on the extent and limits of the protection provided for the environment in times of occupation being provided in Chapter 4.

The Rome Statute of the International Criminal Court (ICC) also contributes to protecting the environment during times of occupation. There is no doubt that this Statute applies to situations of occupation.[86] The ICC has jurisdiction over international crimes pursuant to the rules on jurisdiction embodied in the Statute.[87] These rules do not mention situations of occupation as an obstacle to the prosecution of international crimes. Whilst the Rome Statute does not provide a definition of occupation, its "Elements of Crimes" equates situations of occupation to armed conflicts in relation to the definition of war crimes: "The term international armed conflict includes military occupation. This footnote also applies to the corresponding element in each crime under Article 8 (2) (a)".[88] It is evident that, in times of armed conflict and occupation, the environment can be seriously damaged.[89] Thus, there is an absolute need to hold committed perpetrators fully accountable for ecological crimes, as required by the rules of international law, particularly under the rules of International Criminal Law (ICL), IHL, and IHRL.[90] It is argued that any acts committed by a state against another with the intention of causing severe injuries to the environment, with destruction to the natural environment as well as contamination of, water, air, and soil with long-term consequences for the ecosystem of the injured state, must be considered an ecological crime and a violation of international law.[91] For example, the ongoing war in Gaza in the OPT

84 Raphael Steenberghe, 'The Interplay between International Humanitarian Law and International Environmental Law: Towards a Comprehensive Framework for a Better Protection of the Environment in Armed Conflict', (2022) 20 *JICJ* 1123, 1124–1129, 1132, 1146–1150, 1154.

85 Ibid.; see also, Sjöstedt, *The Role of Multilateral Environmental Agreements,* 137–174; Dienelt, *Armed Conflicts and the Environment.*

86 Waad Abualrob, 'The Protection of the Environment in Situations of Occupation under the Rome Statute', *International Law Blog* (2023). Available online at: < https://internationallaw.blog/2023/12/11/the-protection-of-the-environment-in-situations-of-occupation-under-the-rome-statute/#_ftn2>. Accessed date: 4 April 2024.

87 Rome Statute of the International Criminal Court, 'Official Records of the Assembly of States Parties to the Rome Statute of the International Criminal Court (ICC-ASP/1/3 and Corr.1)', (First Session, 3–10 September 2002), Part II-B, 'Elements of Crimes', Article 8 (2) (a) (i). F.n (34) at.126; Michail Vagias, *The Territorial Jurisdiction of the International Criminal Court* (Cambridge University Press 2014) 214–215.

88 Rome Statute of the International Criminal Court, 'Official Records of the Assembly', 126.

89 Yusef Bougalim, *Accountability for Environmental Crimes under International Law* (Arab Studies Centre for Publishing, Egypt 2015) 12–13, 24–28, 31–32.
يوسف بوغالم، *المساءلة عن الجرائم البيئية في القانون الدولي* (مركز الدراسات العربية للنشر والتوزيع، مصر ٥١٠٢);
Abualrob, 'The Protection of the Environment in Situations of Occupation'.

90 Bougalim, *Accountability for Environmental Crimes*, 12–14, 31–32

91 Ibid.; Rome Statute, Article 8 (2)(b)(iv).

and the severe damage to the environment may amount to a potential war crime of ecocide because of its scale and long-term impact.[92] The extensive destruction of trees and farmlands, and the huge amounts of munitions and toxins that have contaminated the air, soil, and water, all pose significant threats to Gaza's ecosystems and biodiversity, and therefore such harm to the environment may amount to an ecological crime.[93] Whilst the primary focus of this book will be on the protection of the environment under IHL, IHRL, and IEL, however, protection under ICL will be mentioned where it is necessary.

As mentioned earlier, the three important reports that were authorised by the ILC and written by the Special Rapporteur Marja Lehto in 2018, 2019, and 2022, together with the Draft Principles, have all confirmed the importance of the protection of the environment in occupied territory. While the reports are not purely scholarly works, they still represent the most relevant work that has been done so far in relation to addressing environmental issues in this context. Specifically, Lehto has clarified the issue of the environment in occupied territory from different perspectives – including international law of occupation, IHRL, and IEL – and how periods of intense hostilities either before or during occupation, "or resumption of armed conflict, may further add to and exacerbate existing environmental problems".[94] Additionally, the ILC 2019 second report gave a wider definition to the "natural environment", particularly when it addressed the comments that were made by Switzerland and Malaysia about the use of terms, stating that "natural environment" might be unnecessarily restrictive, since environmental issues are "not limited solely to the natural environment; they also include human rights, sustainability and cultural heritage".[95] More about the issue will be addressed in detail throughout the book chapters.

The following chapter will demonstrate environmental protection in occupied territory through the norms of the law of occupation. Following this, Chapter 3 will illustrate the issue of the environment in occupied territory from the IHRL point of view, whilst Chapter 4 will discuss the issue from the IEL perspective.

92 Eyal Weizman and others, 'No Traces of Life': Israel's Ecocide in Gaza 2023–2024'. Available online at: <https://forensic-architecture.org/investigation/ecocide-in-gaza>. Accessed date: 2 May 2024.

93 For further details about the ongoing war in Gaza and the environmental destruction, see Kaamil Ahmed, Damien Gayle, and Aseel Mousa, 'Ecocide in Gaza: Does Scale of Environmental Destruction Amount to a War Crime?' *The Guardian* (2024). Available online at: <https://www.theguardian.com/environment/2024/mar/29/gaza-israel-palestinian-war-ecocide-environmental-destruction-pollution-rome-statute-war-crimes-aoe>. Accessed date: 15 April 2024.

94 ILC, 'First Report', para 12; The United Nations Environmental Programme (UNEP), 'Environmental Assessment of the Gaza Strip, following the Escalation of Hostilities in December 2008–January 2009', (2009); The United Nations: United Nations Environment Programme (UNEP): 'Protecting the Environment During Armed Conflict: An Inventory and Analysis of International Law', (United Nations 2009), 17–18.

95 ILC, 'Second Report'. para 5. See also, The United Nations: General Assembly: Summary record of the 29th meeting (A/C.6/73/SR.29) (10 December 2018), Switzerland, para 102; The United Nations: General Assembly: Summary record of the 30th meeting (A/C.6/73/SR.30) (6 December 2018), Malaysia, para 67.

2 The Protection of the Environment under the Law of Occupation

This chapter explores whether the rules of the law of occupation can be used to protect the environment in times of occupation, and additionally, it ascertains whether specific rules on property (both public and private) could provide protection to the environment. Furthermore, this chapter will assess other rules that protect public health and hygiene in occupied territory under the provisions of the law of occupation, along with further rules under the same law, aiming to fill the existing void regarding the protection of the environment in such situations.

For many years, scholarly attention has been given to environmental issues regarding scenarios before, during, and post armed conflict; however, the same concern has not been given to the situations of occupation.[1] As mentioned in the introductory chapter, occupation law has never made express reference to the word "environment" as such. Therefore, a more comprehensive analysis is needed.

Whilst, generally, situations of occupation are not characterised by active hostilities, clashes may happen between the occupying power and some armed groups or with the local population of the occupied territory.[2] In those situations, where there are active hostilities, environmental damage could be considerable.[3] Furthermore, some activities conducted by the occupant's armed forces in the occupied territory can cause severe damage to the environment with long-term consequences.[4] For instance, the occupant's armed forces and the military infrastructure supporting it might cause environmental harm, and it can be expected to leave an environmental footprint.[5] This is the case in particular if such activities are resulting from or related *inter alia* to the use of dangerous weapons, the inappropriate disposal or dumping of hazardous waste, or the misuse of natural resources.[6] Thus, the provision of effective protection to the environment in times of occupation is essential.

According to what was mentioned in the previous chapter, there is a clear legal obligation on the part of the occupying power under the norms of the law of

1 ILC, 'First Report', para 12. For an exception, see Hulme, 'Enhancing Environmental Protection', 203–241.

2 Ibid, para 17; The Fourth Geneva Convention, Article 2(2).

3 Hulme, 'Enhancing Environmental Protection', 205–207.

4 ILC, 'First Report', para 12.

5 Ibid.

6 Ibid.

DOI: 10.4324/9781003518068-2

occupation in relation to preventing any kind of pillage or looting, or any act that can merge with the crime of plunder[7] of local natural resources or any other kinds of properties in the occupied territory, either "public or private".[8]

The law of occupation has provided precise rules considering the seizure of property.[9] While it forbids, without exception, all forms of pillage,[10] it allows for some property to be requisitioned by the occupying armed force. Since the relevant rules on the protection of public and private property are different, a distinction needs to be made between the two and the protection provided to each of them under the law of occupation.[11] In particular, there are several instances concerning the protection of public or private property in times of occupation that could be seen from the environmental point of view.[12] The current provisions of the law of occupation are flexible enough to cover these specific issues, and they are still adequate to meet the challenges of today's contemporary occupations.[13] Hence, this chapter will explore whether, and if so to what extent, the law of occupation offers any protection to the environment in occupied territory.

The subsequent sections examine to what extent the provisions of the law of occupation can protect the environment in occupied territory. Particular attention is devoted to the rules protecting property, which are embodied in the Hague Regulations 1907,[14] the Geneva Convention Four(GCIV) 1949, and the Additional Protocol One (API) 1977 to the Fourth Geneva Conventions 1949.

2.1 The Law of Occupation as a Part of *Jus in Bello:* A Brief Overview

The law of occupation is a specific subset of the *jus in bello*, also known as IHL or the law of armed conflict,[15] and it applies to international armed conflict only.[16] The provisions of the law of occupation are mainly contained in the Hague Regulations 1907 and the GCIV.[17] The rules embodied in the Hague Regulations are considered to

7 *Prosecutor v. Delalic et al.* (ICTY, Trial Chamber, 1998), (Case No.: IT-96-21-T), para 591.

8 Benvenisti, *The International Law of Occupation,* 81–82. For more information about pillage in occupied territory, see Yoram Dinstein, *The International Law of Belligerent Occupation* (2nd edn, Cambridge University Press 2019) 224–226.

9 Vité, 'The Interrelation of the Law of Occupation', 645.

10 Note that pillage is prohibited under all circumstances under the Hague Regulations, such as Article 28 and Article 47. Furthermore, pillage is prohibited under the GCIV, such as Article 33/2. It is a war crime under the Rome Statute, Article 8(2)(b)(xvi).

11 Vité, 'The Interrelation of the Law of Occupation', 645.

12 Ibid, 646–648.

13 Philip Spoerri, 'The Law of Occupation', in Andrew Clapham, Paola Gaeta (eds), *The Oxford Handbook of International Law in Armed Conflict* (Oxford University Press 2015) 186–187.

14 Laws and Customs of War on Land (The Hague, IV), (Convention signed at The Hague October 18, 1907), (Entered into force: January 26, 1910); Dinstein, *The International Law of Belligerent Occupation*, 6; H.A. Smith, 'The Government of Occupied Territory', (1944) 21 BYBIL 151.

15 Dinstein, *The International Law of Belligerent Occupation*, 3.

16 Hans-Peter Gasser, 'Protection of the Civilian Population: Belligerent Occupation', in Dieter Fleck (ed), *The Handbook of International Humanitarian Law* (2nd edn, Oxford University Press 2009) 272.

17 ILC, 'First Report', para 27.

reflect customary international humanitarian law, and thus, they bind all states worldwide.[18] Furthermore, the API is applicable during times of occupation as long as the states are parties to it.[19] However, some rules of the API correspond to customary international humanitarian law, and the ones that do so bind non-contracting states.[20]

The law of occupation determines the rights and obligations of an occupying state.[21] The rights of local people living in an occupied territory have been greatly improved under the norms of law of occupation, particularly after the Second World War and the adoption of the GCIV in 1949, which significantly widened the rights of the local population, as well as the moment when the Nuremberg Military Tribunal declared the Hague Regulations part of customary law.[22] Before discussing the specific issue of the environment in occupied territory, it is worth explaining the concept of occupation and the general principles governing such situations. This will be useful for understanding to what extent the law of occupation protects the environment.

2.1.1 The Concept of Occupation

The legal definition of occupation is provided by Article 42 of the Hague Regulations 1907. Moreover, the notion of occupation is also mentioned in the field of applicability of the GCIV 1949 (Article 2), and of API 1977 (Article 1(3)).[23]

From a *jus ad bellum* perspective, a situation of occupation is normally created after the use of armed force by one state or more against another. Article 42 of the Hague Regulations provides that "Territory is considered occupied when it is actually placed under the authority of the hostile army. The occupation extends only to the territory where such authority has been established and can be exercised".[24] This is considered to be the most widely accepted definition of occupation.[25] The definition is applied by international courts and tribunals routinely. For instance, for the International Tribunal for the Former Yugoslavia (ICTY) in the case of *Prosecutor v. Naletilic and Martinovic*, the Trial Chamber adopted the Hague Regulations definition.[26] Additionally, the ICJ in the 2004 *Wall Opinion*[27] and in the *2005 DRC v. Uganda* case[28] also referred to the same definition as Article 42 of

18 'The Legal Consequences of the Construction of a Wall in the Occupied Palestinian Territory', Advisory Opinion. I.C.J. Reports 2004, para 89.
19 ILC, 'First Report', para 27; the API 1977, Article 1(3).
20 For further details about the customary nature of the API 1977 of the Fourth Geneva Conventions 1949, see Henckaerts and Doswald-Beck, *Customary International Humanitarian Law.*
21 Hans-Peter Gasser, 'Protection of the Civilian Population: Belligerent Occupation', 270.
22 Ibid, 270–271; *Trials of the Major War Criminals before the International Military Tribunal*, Nuremberg, Vol. XXII, 497.
23 Gross, *Writing on the Wall: Rethinking the International Law of Occupation*, 57.
24 The Hague Convention 1907, Article 42.
25 Marco Longobardo, *The Use of Armed Force in Occupied Territory* (Cambridge University Press 2018) 2.
26 *Prosecutor v. Mladen Naletilic aka 'Tuta', Vinko Martinovic aka 'Stela'* (Trial Judgment), IT-98-34-T, International Criminal Tribunal for the former Yugoslavia (ICTY), 31 March 2003, (IT-98-34-T). Paras 214–216.
27 ICJ, Wall Advisory Opinion, para 78.
28 ICJ, '*DRC v. Uganda*', para 169.

the Hague Regulations. The definition of these regulations covers situations when a sovereign territorial state loses its control over its territory and the authority is transferred to the occupying power without its consent.[29] Bearing that in mind, the occupation must be a temporary situation.[30]

Whilst the GCIV does not include a definition of the concept of occupation itself, it still deals with the legal status of occupied territory by providing protection to it and endorses obligations upon the occupying power in such situations. For example, Article 2(2) common to the Four Geneva Conventions declares that "The Convention shall also apply to all cases of partial or total occupation of the territory of a High Contracting Party, even if the said occupation meets with no armed resistance".[31] The occupation under Article 2(2) specifically includes occupation with no armed resistance. According to the ICRC, Article 2(2) of the GCIV does not change the widely accepted definition of occupation under Article 42 of the Hague Regulations, but rather, it should be interpreted in light of Article 42 of the Hague Regulations.[32] Indeed, Article 154 of the GCIV states that the GCIV is supplementary to the Hague Regulations and does not replace them, especially for the purposes of defining the notion of occupation.[33] Thus, it seems appropriate to refer to Article 42 of the Hague Regulations for a definition of occupation. Lastly, Article 1(3) of the API 1977 confirmed the applicability of the common Article 2 of the Geneva Conventions when it provided that "this Protocol, which supplements the Geneva Conventions of 12 August 1949 for the protection of war victims, shall apply in the situations referred to in common Article 2 to those Conventions".[34]

Scholars have elaborated upon the definition of occupation embodied in Article 42 of the Hague Regulations. According to Dinstein, the main element in determining the situation of occupation is principally the excercise of effective control by an occupant over an occupied territory.[35] Kalandarishvili-Mueller agreed with Dinstein and also argued that control as such can be different from one occupation to another, since in such situations it can take different forms. It can be direct or indirect, all depending on each situation of the occupation itself, and the way the occupying power establishes such a control.[36] According to the definition given by Roberts, occupation occurs when the armed forces of a state, or several states, are

29 ILC, 'First Report', para 20.

30 Daragh Murray, *Practitioners' Guide to Human Rights Law in Armed Conflict* (Oxford University Press 2016) 238, 241.

31 The Fourth Geneva Convention 1949, Article 2(2).

32 ICRC, 'Convention (I) for the Amelioration of the Condition of the Wounded and Sick in Armed Forces in the Field. Geneva, 12 August 1949', Commentary of 2016: Article 2: Application of the Convention, paras 294–296.

33 Marco Sassòli, 'The Concept and the Beginning of Occupation', in Andrew Clapham, Paola Gaeta, and Marco Sassòli (eds), *The 1949 Geneva Conventions: A Commentary* (Oxford University Press 2015) 1393; Malcolm N. Shaw, *International Law* (9th edn, Cambridge University Press 2021) 1038–1039.

34 The Additional Protocol (I) to the Geneva Conventions 1949. Article 1 para 3.

35 Dinstein, *The International Law of Belligerent Occupation*, 43, 48.

36 Kalandarishvili-Mueller, *Occupation and Control in International Humanitarian Law*, 172–176.

exercising authority temporarily over another inhabited territory outside their own recognised international frontiers.[37]

It is important to note that, traditionally, case law and scholars have maintained that there is a distinction between "invasion" and "occupation". This distinction is important in relation to knowing when the law of occupation starts to apply. Generally speaking, it is accepted that the law of occupation would become relevant and start to apply after a minimum level of stability has been reached in an area that has been invaded.[38] This is clearly expressed in the wording of Article 42 of the Hague Regulations 1907, as noted above. "Invasion" means "the movement of military units into an area belonging to another state".[39] In this context, the term "invasion" has been used by the UNGA as a definition of aggression, which provides that "the invasion or attack by the armed forces of a State of the territory of another State, or any military occupation … resulting from such invasion".[40] It is clear from the UNGA resolution that occupation is a situation that arises after an invasion or comes into being as a result of an invasion.[41] Furthermore, the Oxford Manual of 1888 provides that occupation occurs as a result of invasion by hostile forces.[42] Therefore, to trigger the law of occupation in a situation, some degree of control is required, which is the essence of the application of the law of occupation as noted above, while the mere presence of armed forces on another state's territory does not trigger such an application.[43] For example, the US military manual provides that "military occupation is a question of fact. It presupposes a hostile invasion, resisted or unresisted, as a result of which the invader has rendered the invaded government incapable of publicly exercising its authority, and that the invader has successfully substituted its own authority for that of the legitimate government in the territory invaded".[44] The question that might arise here is when the invading forces are in a position to exercise control and, therefore, trigger the law of occupation. That, of course, depends on different circumstances, that to be identified require further analysis that is outside of the main focus of this book.

Another issue pertains to the possibility that active hostilities occur in occupied territory, and how active hostilities should be defined in light of the lack of an explicit definition in IHL rules. Active hostilities can occur during invasion or even during occupation. Active hostilities in occupied territory might occur between

37 Adam Roberts, 'What is a Military Occupation?', (1985) 55 *British Yearbook of International Law*, 249.

38 Marten Zwanenburg, Michael Bothe, and Marco Sassòli, 'Is the Law of Occupation Applicable to the Invasion Phase?' (2012) 94 *International Review of the Red Cross* 29, 31.

39 Ibid, 37.

40 UNGA, Resolution 3314 (XXIX), 14 December 1974, Annex, Article 3(a).

41 Ibid.

42 *The Laws of War on Land*, Manual adopted by the Institute of International Law (Oxford Manual 1880). Oxford, 9 September 1880. Article 41.

43 Zwanenburg, Bothe, and Sassòli, 'Is the Law of Occupation Applicable to the Invasion Phase?' 39.

44 The US Military Manual, 'The Law of Land Warfare' (FM- Field Manual No. 27-10, 1956) para 355.

the occupying power and the occupied population and/or between the occupying power and the ousted sovereign.[45] Local people of the occupied territory may establish and organise resistance/armed groups to fight against the occupant, aiming to expel its armed forces from the occupied area.[46] For example, during the Soviet occupation of Afghanistan, Afghani resistance was fighting against the occupation forces to restore the independence of that nation.[47] It should be noted that hostilities in the occupied territory can vary depending on specific circumstances, such as its scale, goals, origins, and effects.[48] IHL does not include a particular literal definition of the phrase "active hostilities" or "hostilities". However, the ICRC included the definition of hostilities as presented in the 2009 Interpretive Guidance on the Notion of Direct Participation of Hostilities under International Humanitarian Law. The ICRC Interpretive Guidance defined the concept of hostilities as "the (collective) resort by the parties to the conflict to means and methods of injuring the enemy".[49] International state practice shows that active hostilities may occur during situations of occupation without its termination. For example, the situations of the OPT under the Israeli occupation and in DRC during the Ugandan occupation were clear examples of how active hostilities may occur during occupations.[50]

To sum up the above discussion, the law of occupation requires the exercise of actual authority and having control over the occupied territory in relation to allowing the occupying power to comply with its legal obligations under IHL, namely the provisions of the law of occupation. Therefore, it is safe to conclude that there should be a distinction between a situation of occupation where it clearly triggers the application of the law of occupation, and an invasion that does not trigger such an application to the provisions of the law of occupation. Whilst the issue of when exactly the phase of invasion ends and occupation starts is still problematic, the distinction between the two is rooted in international law.[51]

2.1.2 General Principles Governing Situations of Occupation

From the ensemble of rules of the law of occupation, it is possible to identify three main general principles that govern the situation of occupation: the first is called the "conservationist principle"; the second is that the situation of occupation must be temporary, transitory, and provisional; and the third is that the occupying power must administer the occupied territory with respect, bearing in mind the welfare and interests of the occupied people.

45 Longobardo, *The Use of Armed Force in Occupied Territory*, 166–167.
46 Ibid.
47 Ibid.
48 Ibid, 167–168.
49 ICRC, Interpretive Guidance on the Notion of Direct Participation in Hostilities under International Humanitarian Law, Geneva, May 2009. Available online at: < https://casebook.icrc.org/case-study/icrc-interpretive-guidance-notion-direct-participation-hostilities>. Access date: 29 November 2023.
50 Longobardo, *The Use of Armed Force in Occupied Territory*, 197–199.
51 Ibid, 198–204.

According to the "conservationist principle", the occupying power must maintain the *status quo ante* in the occupied territory.[52] In order to comply with this principle, it must respect the domestic laws and regulations of the occupied territory.[53] The conservationist principle sets the general limits for the occupant in the occupied territory, and it must consider this principle while applying the other rules of the law of occupation.[54] As Schrijver stressed: "A basic rule of the law of belligerent occupation is that rights of sovereignty do not pass to the occupier".[55] Consequently, the occupant is not allowed to introduce any permanent or fundamental changes to the occupied territory.[56]

Nevertheless, some legislative changes, such as modifying the institutions or government of an occupied territory instigated by the occupant, are, to some extent, essential and could even be seen as an improvement.[57] However, the main purpose of allowing the occupant to make such changes to the local laws or to modify the occupied state's government and institutions is to protect and safeguard human beings and not to protect the government of the occupied state, as such.[58]

Article 43 of the Hague Regulations and Article 64 of the GCIV have confirmed that the occupant has obligations under the rules of the law of occupation with respect to the domestic laws in the occupied state.[59] According to Article 43 of the Hague Regulations 1907, the occupying power "shall take all the measures in its power to restore, and ensure, as far as possible, public order and civil life, while respecting, unless absolutely prevented, the laws in force in the country".[60] This Article has been interpreted in way that it can allow the occupant the competence to legislate when it is crucial for the maintenance of public order and civil life in the occupied state and to change any local laws that are contrary to established human rights standards.[61]

In addition to this, Article 64 of the GCIV provides that

> the occupying power may, however, subject the population of the occupied territory to provisions which are essential to enable the occupying power to fulfil its obligations under the present Convention, to maintain the orderly government of the territory, and to ensure the security of the occupying power, of the members and property of the occupying forces or administration, and likewise of the establishments and lines of communication used by them.[62]

52 ILC, 'First Report', para 44.
53 Ibid.
54 Ibid, para 46.
55 Nico Schrijver, *Sovereignty over Natural Resources: Balancing Rights and Duties* (Cambridge University Press 2008) 267.
56 ILC, 'First Report', paras 44, 46.
57 Jean Pictet, 'The Geneva Conventions of 12 August 1949, Commentary: IV Geneva Convention Relative to the Protection of Civilian Persons in Time of War, Article 47, (International Committee of the Red Cross 1958)', 274.
58 Ibid, 274.
59 The Hague Regulations 1907, Article 43, and the Fourth Geneva Convention 1949, Article 64.
60 The Hague Regulations 1907, Article 43.
61 ILC, 'First Report', paras 43–46.
62 The Fourth Geneva Convention, 1949, Article 64.

Accordingly, the occupying power is allowed to make some changes to the local laws only to enable the occupant to comply with its duties under the Convention, to maintain the orderly government of the territory, and to ensure the security of occupying forces and to its administration bodies.[63] This is the case when Iraq was under US and UK occupation in 2003, where the occupying powers made some changes to the Iraqi domestic laws and regulations and/or adopted new orders under the so-called coalition provisional authority legislation.[64] However, the occupant is not allowed to change or modify the domestic laws for its own ideals or interests,[65] and it must stick to these specific expectations under the law of occupation; otherwise it will violate its position as an administrator of the occupied state.

According to the second principle, the occupying power does not acquire any sovereignty over the occupied territory, but rather, has temporary, transitory, and provisional control over it, which means it merely exercises *de facto* authority there.[66] This principle reflects the content of Articles 42 and 43 of the Hague Regulations 1907,[67] Article 47 of the GCIV,[68] and Article 4 of the Additional Protocol 1.[69] Furthermore, there are several other rules from the law of occupation supporting the argument that occupation is a temporary and provisional situation,[70] such as the "prohibition of population transfers, prohibition against requiring allegiance to the occupant, limitation on the use of the resources of the occupied territory etc.".[71] In addition to this, the occupying power has the aforementioned obligation to respect the domestic laws and regulations of the occupied territory,[72] and this obligation is consequential to the occupier's status as a provisional and transitory authority.[73]

The third principle affirms that the occupying power must administer the occupied territory in a way that respects the benefit and interests of the occupied population, while preserving its own security and military needs at the same time. The occupying power has a duty to strike a balance between these two parameters at

63 Ibid.; ILC, 'First Report', paras 43–50.

64 See, for example, the list of the 'CPA Official Documents', which includes several regulations and orders that refer to where some of the Iraqi domestic laws were amendments or/and some new regulations and orders have been adopted. < https://govinfo.library.unt.edu/cpa-iraq/regulations/>.

65 ILC, 'First Report', para 46.

66 Antonio Cassese, 'Powers and Duties of an Occupant in Relation to Land and Natural Resources'. In: Emma Playfair (ed), *International Law and the Administration of Occupied Territories: Two Decades of Israeli Occupation of the West Bank and Gaza Strip* (Oxford University Press 1992) 420; Hans-Peter Gasser, 'Protection of the Civilian Population: Belligerent Occupation', 273, 274, 277.

67 The Hague Regulations 1907, Articles 42 and 43.

68 The Fourth Geneva Convention 1949, Article 47.

69 The Additional Protocol 1 to the Fourth Geneva Conventions 1949, Article 4.

70 The Hague Regulations 1907, Articles 53 and 55; The Fourth Geneva Convention 1949, Articles 49 and 55; The Additional Protocol 1 to the Fourth Geneva Conventions 1949, Article 85(4)(a).

71 Tristan Ferraro, 'Occupation and other Forms of Administration of Foreign Territory', (ICRC Report 2012) 36.

72 The Hague Regulations 1907, Article 43; the Fourth Geneva Convention 1949, Article 64.

73 Cassese, 'Powers and Duties of an Occupant in Relation to Land and Natural Resources', 420.

all times, unless there is an unavoidable military necessity.[74] In that case, solely military needs can gain the upper hand, though that should never result in total disregard for the local people's needs and interests.[75]

Moreover, this principle can lead to an important point, which is that the occupying power must not exercise its authority in the occupied territory to serve its own interests or to meet the needs of its own population. For example, in no case is the occupying power allowed to exploit the natural resources of the occupied territory for the benefit or needs of its own citizens.[76] As an example from international practice, the Japanese occupation of Sumatra and the illegal exploitation of the natural resources there were found unsustainable. In particular, this was so because of the unlawful transfer of resources from occupied Sumatra to the territory of Japan for the benefit of the Japanese people.[77]

The abovementioned principles support the argument that the occupying power only exercises a temporary authority over the occupied territory, that it is only administering the occupied state and can never own it,[78] and that it has responsibilities and obligations that must be respected while it continues to administer the occupied state.[79] It needs to keep, respect, protect, and ensure that the status of the occupied territory will continue to be the same as it was before the occupation, and that undoubtedly includes respecting the domestic laws and regulations that are already in place.

Against this background, general principles governing situations of occupation have reached the point where the occupying power is only an administrator in the occupied state, and it has a responsibility towards the population and their properties, where providing protection to the environment can be indirectly counted too, through the protection provided to civilians and to property. In the following paragraphs, the extent to which the law of occupation can provide protection to the environment through the provisions applicable to property rights in the occupied territory is examined.

2.2 Property Rights Approach to Environmental Protection in Occupied Territory

Generally speaking, the main concern of the law of occupation is the safety of local people and their property in the occupied territory in question. As much as the

74 The Hague Regulations 1907, Articles 43,46, 53; the GCIV, Article 55; API, Article 69; the ICRC, 'Contemporary challenges to IHL – Occupation: overview', (11 June 2012); *The Jerusalem District Electricity Company Ltd v. (a) Minster of Energy and Infrastructure, (b) Commander of the Judea and Samaria Region* 35(23) (H.C 351/80), 35(2) Piskei Din 673, in Fania Domb, 'Judgments of the Supreme Court of Israel Relating to the Administered Territories', (1981) 11 Isr YB Hum Rts 344, 354–358; Benvenisti, *The International Law of Occupation*, 76–77, 81–82.

75 Cassese, 'Powers and Duties of an Occupant in Relation to Land and Natural Resources', 420.

76 Tignino, 'Principle 23', 562.

77 Singapore, *(Bataafsche Petroleum v. The War Damage Commission)* (1956) 22 Malayan Law Journal 155, Court of Appeal, Singapore, (13 April 1956); Tignino, 'Principle 23', 562; Cassese, 'Powers and Duties', 420–421.

78 Cassese, 'Powers and Duties', 420–421.

79 Ibid, 420.

law of occupation places constraints on the occupying state in protecting property rights in that territory, the environment can also be indirectly protected, if property can be perceived as a component of it. Hence, in this section, the extent to which the protection of property rights under the provisions of the law of occupation can provide protection to the environment in such situations is examined.

The law of occupation contains provisions that aim to protect property rights in occupied territories from abusive acts by an occupying power, such as the unjustified destruction and pillage of property located there. Moreover, the prohibition of unjustified destruction of property in occupied territory is considered part of customary international law.[80] Therefore, all states are bound by such norms.

Importantly, property rights provisions may be interpreted to provide protection to some elements of the environment in times of occupation.[81] Despite the word "environment" not appearing in any of the property rights provisions in any of the abovementioned conventions, those provisions can be interpreted to cover the environmental issue in times of occupation through the prohibition of wanton or unjustified damage to property.[82] For example, the UN Secretary-General provided that "a party to a conflict that destroys … property protected by the Fourth Geneva Convention and in so doing causes damage to the environment violates that Convention".[83] Furthermore, the formulation of Article 55 of the Hague Regulations, which considers forests and agricultural areas as properties, is very clear.[84]

The ILC report in 2018 stressed that the occupying power has a responsibility towards inhabitants, properties, and natural resources in the occupied territory, arguing that each of these has its environmental dimension.[85] For example, the occupying power has the accountability to protect public and private properties located in the occupied state, which includes the indirect protection of the environment as well.[86] Furthermore, Article 147 of the GCIV provides that the acts "committed against persons or property protected by the present Convention", including any "extensive destruction and appropriation of property, not justified by military necessity and carried out unlawfully and wantonly",[87] are considered

80 *Prosecutor v. Fofana and Kondewa* (Appeals Judgment), (Special Court for Sierra Leone) (Case No. SCSL-04-14-A), (28 May 2008). Para 390. (*CDF Case*)*;* Wall Advisory Opinion, para 89; The Hague Regulations 1907, Article 23(g).

81 The United Nations: General Assembly, 'Report of the Secretary-General on the Protection of the Environment in Times of Armed Conflict', (A/48/269) (29 July 1993), paras, 28,30 pp. 5–6; Daniella Dam-de Jong, 'International Law and Resource Plunder: The Protection of Natural Resources during Armed Conflict', (2008) Yearbook of International Environmental Law, Vol. 19, Issue 1, pp. 27–57. At: 44–47, 51–52.

82 The United Nations: General Assembly, 'Report of the Secretary-General on the Protection of the Environment in Times of Armed Conflict', paras 28, 30.

83 Ibid, para 29.

84 Daniella Dam-de Jong, 'International Law and Resource Plunder', 44.

85 ILC, 'First Report', paras 15, 28.

86 Ibid.

87 The Fourth Geneva Convention 1949, Article 147.

as being grave breaches to the Convention. The ICRC Commentary of 1958 on the GCIV provided that such destruction and appropriation must be extensive to be considered as a grave breach of the convention, and "an isolated incident would not be enough" for this to be the case.[88] The preoperatory work of the Geneva Conventions (Diplomatic Conference of 1949, Geneva, 21 April–12 August 1949) indicated that grave breaches to the convention shall involve any acts committed against property, which includes the "extensive destruction of property, not justified by military necessity and carried out unlawfully and wantonly".[89] Furthermore, the Geneva Conventions introduced the concept of "universal jurisdiction" for grave breaches within the Geneva Conventions.[90] Therefore, the occupant is prohibited from engaging in any illegal spoliation, exploitation, pillage, or destruction of the land in an occupied territory, including, of course, all public and private property.[91]

The following paragraphs will examine the issue in detail and put forward the possible protection that can provide to the environment in the occupied territory from a property rights perspective.

2.2.1 The Relationship between Prohibition of Pillage and Protection of the Environment in Occupied Territory from the Property Rights Provisions Point of View

The prohibition of pillage is applicable to the territory of a party to the conflict as well as to occupied territories, and it guarantees all types of property, whether private or public.[92] The crime of pillage is prohibited in all circumstances under IHL. For example, Article 28 of the Hague Regulations provides that "The pillage of a town or place, even when taken by assault, is prohibited".[93] Since the Hague Regulations are part of customary international humanitarian law, the occupant must be bound by them as has been confirmed by the ICJ in the Wall Advisory Opinion in 2004.[94]

Accordingly, the pillage of property by an occupying power in an occupied territory is a prohibited act under the rules of the law of occupation. In addition to this, the ICJ demanded that the occupying power not only desist from engaging in pillage in an occupied territory, also extending its responsibility to ensure the properties in the occupied territory are protected from looting by private persons, along

88 Ibid. See also the ICRC Commentary of 1958, 'Convention (IV) Relative to the Protection of Civilian Persons in Time of War. Geneva, 12 August 1949', 'Article 147 – Penal Sanctions II. Grave Breaches'.

89 Final record of the Diplomatic Conference of Geneva of 1949. Vol III, Annexes, at: 42–45.

90 Ibid.; ICRC: 'The Relevance of Preparatory Work and Archival Materials in Updating the ICRC Commentaries', (2017).

91 'The Ministries Case', *Trials of War Criminals Before the Nuernberg Military Tribunals Under Control Council Law No. 10.* (Volume XIV), (Nuernberg 1949), pp. 9, 210, 339, 725, 738, 1103–1104.

92 Jean Pictet, *The Geneva Conventions of 12 August 1949*, (1958), 226–227.

93 The Hague Regulations 1907, Article 28.

94 ICJ, Wall Advisory Opinion, para 89.

with occupying armed forces.[95] Accordingly, the duty of vigilance of an occupying power to prevent other actors from exploiting or plundering the propriety, including natural resources, along with its armed forces in the occupied state, can strengthen the occupant's responsibility towards the environment during the occupation.

According to case law, the excessive and abusive exploitation of natural resources may amount to plunder or pillage.[96] For instance, the ICJ declared that the extreme exploitation of a foreign country's natural resources may be regarded as "pillage".[97] In particular, dealing with Uganda's responsibility as an occupying power for "looting, plundering and exploitation of natural resources in the territory of the DRC",[98] the ICJ affirmed that both Article 47 of the Hague Regulations 1907 and Article 33 of the Fourth Geneva Convention of 1949 prohibit pillage.[99] Accordingly, it seems safe to argue that the prohibition of pillage is applicable to utilisation of natural resources in a situation of occupation.

The International Military Tribunal determined that Germany had abusively exploited its occupied territories during the Second World War. The Tribunal added that the extreme utilisation of the natural resources by Germany amounted, in reality, to a plunder of public and private property of the occupied territories.[100] For instance, the illegal exploitation of Polish agricultural lands by Germany's occupation, *per se*, was considered as a war crime and a crime against humanity.[101]

As Dam-de Jong has pointed out, the exploitation of natural resources has a considerable impact on the environment, because "the extraction of natural resources often takes place in ecologically fragile areas, which are rich in biological diversity".[102] Dam-de Jong supported her claim by giving an example from the DRC, namely, the Okapi Wildlife and the Kahuzi-Biega reserves, where both had suffered from the illegal and excessive exploitation of natural resources.[103]

Another example is the Armenian–Azerbaijani occupation, where Armenia as an occupying power in some Azerbaijani regions cut down and damaged massive amounts of forests and even illegally moved and transported them from occupied areas to neighbouring countries, such as Iran.[104] This constituted a crime of pillage and economic plunder of the occupied territory, which was contrary to several

95 Armed Activities on the Territory of the Congo (*Democratic Republic of the Congo v. Uganda*), Judgment, I.C.J. Reports 2005, p. 168. Para 244–253.

96 Dam-de Jong, 'International Law and Resource Plunder', 51.

97 ICJ, '*DRC v. Uganda*', paras 245–246.

98 Ibid, para 245.

99 Ibid.

100 *Trial of the Major War Criminals before the International Military Tribunal, Nuremberg*, (14 November 1945 –1 October 1946), (1947). Vol. I, Nuremberg, pp. 238–239.

101 'The Ministries Case', *Trials of War Criminals Before the Military Tribunals Under Control Council Law* No. 10. (Volume XIV), (1949), pp. 9, 210, 983.

102 Dam-de Jong, 'International Law and Resource Plunder', 28.

103 The United Nations, 'Interim Report of the Panel of Experts on the Illegal Exploitation of Natural Resources and Other Forms of Wealth of DR Congo', (S/2002/565) (22 May 2002), para 52.

104 Administrative Department of the President of the Republic of Azerbaijan: Presidential Library, at: 12,15.

provisions under the law of occupation, as mentioned above. As argued above, the excessive exploitation of natural resources in an unsustainable manner in an occupied state by an occupying power is considered a crime of pillage.

Arguably, such acts can be considered as excessive destruction and abusive and extreme exploitation of the natural resources of the occupied territory, which might leave an environmental footprint and have an impact upon the biodiversity and the ecosystem functions of the occupied state. Thus, these kinds of acts are clearly beyond the normal use of immovable property in the occupied territory and contrary to the rules of good husbandry.

Interestingly, the Appeals Chamber of the Special Court for Sierra Leone regarding the "*CDF Case*" noted that pillage is distinct from seizure, since the latter is appropriation for public purposes, while the former is for private purposes.[105] At the same, the Appeals Chamber confirmed the customary nature of the prohibition of pillage and that of destruction of property that is not justified by military necessity.[106] Therefore, the occupant is prohibited from engaging in any illegal spoliation, exploitation, and pillage of the land in an occupied territory, including, of course, all public and private property.[107]

2.2.2 The Protection of the Environment throughout the Prohibition of Unjustified Destruction, Seizure, and Confiscation of Public and Private Property in the Occupied Territory

Besides pillage, other rules on the protection of property in occupied territory under the Hague Regulations, the GCIV, and the API are generally seen as applicable to protect the environment, mainly through the provision of restrictions on how the occupying power can exploit or use the natural resources that have been conceived as being property.[108] In particular, the overexploitation of natural resources has a considerable impact on the environment,[109] where the ownership of these could be public or private, depending on how they are classified in the national legislation of the occupied state.[110]

The law of occupation allows the occupying power to seize or damage property in the occupied territory, though this can be done only and solely for military reasons and when there is an absolute military need to do so.[111] Article 23(g) of the Hague

105 *Prosecutor v. Fofana and Kondewa* (Appeals Judgment), (Special Court for Sierra Leone) (Case No. SCSL-04-14-A), (28 May 2008). Para 392, note 770 (*CDF Case*).

106 Ibid, (*CDF Case*), para 390.

107 'The Ministries Case', *Trials of War Criminals Before the Nuernberg Military Tribunals Under Control Council Law* No. 10. (Volume XIV), (Nuernberg 1949) pp. 9, 210, 339, 725, 738, 1103–1104.

108 ILC, 'First Report', para 29.

109 Dam-de Jong, 'International Law and Resource Plunder', (2008) 28.

110 ILC, 'First Report', para 36; Antonio Cassese, 'Powers and Duties of an Occupant in Relation to Land and Natural Resources', 431.

111 The Hague Regulations 1907, Article 23(g) and Article 53(2); the Fourth Geneva Convention 1949, Article 53.

Regulations is considered one of the oldest provisions regarding the protection of the environment through property rights in such situations.[112] According to Article 23(g) of the Hague Regulations, it is prohibited to "destroy or seize the enemy's property, unless such destruction or seizure be imperatively demanded by the necessities of war".[113] Notably, Article 23(g) of the Hague Regulations covers both categories of property: public and private.[114] However, the ICJ, in 2004 in the Wall Advisory Opinion, dismissed the applicability of Article 23(g) to the West Bank.[115] When it dismissed the application of Article 23(g), the ICJ only referred to a specific exclusive time frame and specific territory of the West Bank and did not provide that Article 23(g) was not applicable to the whole situation of occupation.[116] Moreover, it would be also difficult to dismiss the applicability of Article 23(g) to situations of occupation if the ICJ had not provided a clear statement in this regard. Otherwise, there are more benefits of applying such an article to the environment in situations of occupation, rather than dismissing the applicability without a clear statement from the ICJ itself.

Furthermore, this point could be argued from a different perspective, by assuming that the ICJ dismissed the applicability of Article 23(g) of the Hague Regulations to the West Bank's situation since there were no hostilities at that time between the occupying power's armed forces and the occupied population or other armed groups. That does not mean that the situation of occupation in the West Bank is not a belligerent one. According to the ICRC, the fact that an occupation does *not* include armed resistance does not prevent it from being a hostile situation.[117] The ICRC added that a lack of military opposition in an occupied territory against the occupying power should never be interpreted as a form of consent to the foreign forces' presence.[118] Furthermore, "military occupation is by definition an asymmetric relationship: the existence of an occupation implies that foreign forces are imposing their authority over the local government by military or other coercive means",[119] and the hostile nature of an occupation derives from the unconsented-to invasion or presence of a state's armed forces in the territory of another state.[120]

The imposition of occupation authority by military means does not require the use of extreme power or open hostilities to gain such authority over an occupied

112 Antoine Bouvier, 'Protecting the Natural Environment in a Period of Armed Conflict' in Mofeed Shehab, *Studies in International Humanitarian Law* (The Arab Future Publishing House, Cairo 2009) 195; Daniella Dam-de Jong, 'International Law and Resource Plunder' (2008), at: 45–48.

113 The Hague Regulations 1907, Article 23 (g). Note that Article 23(g) applies also to the situations of occupation as a part of customary international humanitarian law.

114 Jean Pictet, *The Geneva Conventions of 12 August 1949*, 300–301.

115 ICJ, Wall Advisory Opinion, para 124.

116 Ibid.

117 ICRC, 'Convention (I) for the Amelioration of the Condition of the Wounded and Sick in Armed Forces in the Field. Geneva, 12 August 1949', Commentary of 2016: Article 2: Application of the Convention. Para 288.

118 Ibid.

119 Ibid.

120 Ibid.

territory, as it could be gained by the mere show of power. In this sense, the occupant armed forces' presence in an occupied territory obviously results from military coercion and is to be considered as a hostile situation, providing evidence of the belligerent character of the occupation.[121] Moreover, whenever civilians and their properties are controlled by an occupying power, even without active hostilities, there is a risk of arbitrariness and abuse. Thus, the rationale for the application of IHL still exists when occupation is established, even without armed resistance and/or hostilities.[122]

It might be argued that, from a broader perspective and by considering stronger protection to the components of the environment in times of occupation, the applicability of Article 23(g) of the Hague Regulations can strengthen the protection provided, particularly by adding more legal limitations on the occupying power regarding the prohibition of destruction or seizure of property, whether public or private movable or immovable property is in question.[123] Consequently, it could be argued that it seems irrational to exclude the applicability of Article 23(g) of the Hague Regulations to the situations of occupation only because the ICJ had not applied it to the situation of the West Bank at the time.

Furthermore, the GCIV 1949 includes specific provisions under Section III in relation to the protection of civilians living under occupation.[124] Some of these provisions protect property rights. For example, Article 53 of the GCIV addressed that "Any destruction by the Occupying Power of real or personal property belonging individually or collectively to private persons, to the State, other public authorities, or to social or co-operative organizations, is prohibited".[125] More details about the rule will be demonstrated in the following paragraphs.

However, the law of occupation has never explained what exactly the environmental obligations of the occupying power are. It could be argued that this could be the case, because when the law of occupation's provisions were adopted and developed, especially under both the Hague Regulations 1907 and the GCIV 1949, there were no concerns about environmental issues or they were not been prominently prioritised as such by the international community at that time, with the main concerns being about the protection of civilians and their properties. This is also clear from the preparatory work of both conventions, where states mainly focused on issues related to civilians, property and other issues related to the maintenance of public order in occupied territory.[126] Nevertheless, the law of occupation still

121 Ibid.
122 Ibid, para 289.
123 ILC, 'First Report', para 40.
124 The Geneva Convention IV, Section III, 'Occupied Territories'.
125 GCIV, Article 53.
126 See, for example, 'The Proceedings of the Hague Peace Conferences'. Translation of the official texts, prepared in the Division of International Law of the Carnegie Endowment for International Peace under the supervision of J. B. Scott. The Conferences of 1899 and 1907; preparatory work of the GCIV 1949: Final Record of the Diplomatic Conference of Geneva of 1949, Vol. I; Final Record of the Diplomatic Conference of Geneva of 1949, Vol. II-A, at: 672, 771, 833; Final Record

provides indirect and varied protection to the environment through the provisions that address the prohibition of destruction or seizure of property, whether classified as public or private, movable or immovable,[127] unless as mentioned above, the destruction or seizure of property is absolutely necessary for military operations.[128] In what follows, it is argued that the provisions of the law of occupation that protect public and private property in the occupied territory can provide protection to the environment as well, starting with considering public property and then, private.

2.2.2.1 Prohibition of Unjustified Destruction and Seizure of Public Property in the Occupied Territory

The main article under the law of occupation that provides protection to public property and has been linked to the protection of the environment in the occupied territory is Article 55 of the Hague Regulations. The Article considers the public immovable property in occupied territory and the limitations and obligations of the occupying power in this regard. Article 55 of the Hague Regulations provides that "The occupying State shall be regarded only as administrator and usufructuary of public buildings, real estate, forests, and agricultural estates belonging to the hostile State, and situated in the occupied territory. It must safeguard the capital of these properties and administer them in accordance with the rules of usufruct".[129]

It is pointed out that the occupying power has a right to use the natural resources of the occupied territory. However, this is only in accordance with the rules of usufruct. Hence, enjoying that right in a wasteful or negligent way is prohibited and therefore, the occupying power is forbidden from cutting down whole forests in the occupied territory unless it is proven to be absolutely necessary.[130] It is argued that the duty of an occupying power in relation to the administration of the occupied territory must always comply with the rules of usufruct.[131] That is, any overutilisation of public immovable property is contrary to the law of occupation, and to the rule of usufruct, as mentioned under Article 55 of the Hague Regulations, which applies to all buildings, forests, and agricultural estates belonging to the occupied territory.[132]

---

of the Diplomatic Conference of Geneva of 1949, Vol. II-B, at: 434, 462-463; Final Record of the Diplomatic Conference of Geneva of 1949, Vol. III; Final Record of the Diplomatic Conference of Geneva of 1949, Vol. III, Annexes; Doris Graber, *The Development of the Law of Belligerent Occupation 1863–1914: A Historical Survey* (Columbia University Press 1949).

127 ILC, 'First Report', para 38; Benvenisti, *The International Law of Occupation*, 81–82; Cassese, 'Powers and Duties of an Occupant in Relation to Land and Natural Resources', 431; Dinstein, *The International Law of Belligerent Occupation*, 239.

128 The Hague Regulations. Article 23(g); GCIV, Article 53 and Article 147.

129 The Hague Regulations. Article 55.

130 Lassa Oppenheim, *International Law. A Treatise, Volume II. War and Neutrality* (2nd edn, Longmans, Green and Co 1912) 175.

131 Robert Kolb and Richard Hyde, *An Introduction to the International Law of Armed Conflicts* (Hart Publishing 2008) 232.

132 Sylvain Vité, 'The Interrelation of the Law of Occupation and Economic, Social and Cultural Rights: The Examples of Food, Health and Property', (2008) 90 *International Review of the Red Cross* 629, 646–648.

In relation to the interpretation of the concept of the word "usufruct" under Roman law, it means the benefactor has the right to enjoy the fruits of property, including the use of assets belonging to others, and to receive the raised benefits resulting from these fruits without altering their substance.[133] As Glahn pointed out, the rights of the occupying power are limited to the rights of use (*jus utendi*) and consumption of fruits (*jus fruendi*).[134]

Accordingly, the occupying power has two main limitations under Article 55, in relation to the use of public immovable property. The first limitation is the extent of the use, which mainly relates to the rules of usufruct.[135] The second limitation is concerning the purpose of the use, which means that the occupant is allowed to use the property located in the occupied territory to meet their security needs and to meet the fundamental needs of the local people living in the occupied territory.[136] Hence, the occupant is prohibited from exploiting such proprieties for the benefit of its own civilian population needs.[137] That is, a failure to respect public immovable property, such as the natural resources during occupation, will eventually lead to environmental harm, which might threaten the viability and usefulness of these resources.[138]

The traditional view of the usufruct right generally applies "to the exploitation of all kinds of natural resources, including non-renewable ones".[139] The usufructuary rule under Article 55 of the Hague Regulations has been seen as the main basis for allowing the occupying power in the occupied territory to "lease or utilize public lands or buildings, sell all crops, cut and sell timber, and work the mines"[140] as well as any other rising benefits of the "fruits" of local public property in the occupied territory.[141] However, as Schrijver stressed, the word "usufruct" in Article 55 means that the occupying state may use the immovable properties in the occupied territory, which includes the natural and mineral resources, but it cannot own them.[142] As Schrijver added, the occupant must protect the capital of these properties, and it has a legal obligation to do so.[143]

133 ILC, 'First Report', para 30.
134 Gerhard Von Glahn, *The Occupation of Enemy Territory: A Commentary on the Law and Practice of Belligerent Occupation* (The University of Minnesota Press 1957) 176–177.
135 Eyal Benvenisti, *The International Law of Occupation* (2nd edn, Oxford University Press 2012) 80–82; Mara Tignino, 'Principle 23: 'The Environment of Oppressed Peoples', in Jorge Viñuales (ed), *The Rio Declaration on Environment and Development: A Commentary* (Oxford University Press 2015) 559–562; The Hague Regulations 1907, Article 55.
136 Ibid.
137 Ibid.
138 Ibid, 559.
139 ILC, 'First Report', para 30.
140 Ibid.
141 Ibid.
142 Nico Schrijver, *Sovereignty over Natural Resources: Balancing Rights and Duties* (Cambridge University Press 2008) 268.
143 Ibid.

Moreover, it is generally accepted that the occupying power may not use the natural resources located in the occupied state for its own domestic purposes. For example, in *1956 De Bataafsche Petroleum* V. *War Damage Commission*, the Singapore Court of Appeal denounced the Japanese occupation for unlawfully transferring resources from the occupied Sumatra to the territory of Japan for the benefit of its own citizens.[144] This constituted a clear violation of Japan's obligation as an occupying power over Sumatra at that time, and in particular, a violation of Article 55 of the Hague Regulations, specifically to the rules of usufruct.[145]

Another example is the Israeli occupation of Palestine, according to the *El Nazer* case from the Israel Supreme Court. The Court per Justice Shamgar set out three main elements from Article 55 of the Hague Regulations, including the occupants' rights and obligations in that regard: firstly, the occupying power should never own public immovable property that exists in the occupied territory; secondly, the occupants can only administer the immovable property and reap its fruits; and thirdly, the occupying power must keep the property safe and ensure it continues to exist.[146] Accordingly, the occupying power is limited by the purpose of the use of the immovable property in the occupied territory.[147]

The "usufructuary rule" under Article 55 of the Hague Regulations limits the occupant's ability to use and administrate the natural resources located in the occupied state. The rule still allows the occupying power to lease or utilise public immovable property.[148] However, the occupant is prohibited from being wasteful with these properties' values[149] and, what is more, it must safeguard the capital of these properties.[150] Thus, the occupying power has a duty under Article 55 to prevent any abuse and overexploitation, contrary to the usufructuary rule.[151] Otherwise, the occupying power will abuse its position as an administrator over the occupied territory and therefore violate its obligation under Article 55 of the Hague Regulations. Notably, the protection provided under this Article is not exhaustive, but it does apply to all immovable public property that is not used for any military purposes.[152]

Furthermore, the enjoyment of the right to self-determination by the occupied people is linked to the occupant's duty under Article 55 and namely, to the respect of the rule of usufruct. For instance, the principle of self-determination

144 Singapore, *(Bataafsche Petroleum v. The War Damage Commission)* (1956), 22 *Malayan Law Journal* 155, Court of Appeal, Singapore, (13 April 1956).

145 The Hague Regulations 1907, Article 55; *(Bataafsche Petroleum v. The War Damage Commission)* (1956); Benvenisti, *The International Law of Occupation*, 82.

146 *El Nazer et al. v. Commander of Judea and Samaria et al.* (HCJ 285/81), (1983) 13 IYHR 368, 704.

147 Benvenisti, *The International Law of Occupation*, 82.

148 ILC, 'First Report', paras 29–30.

149 Benvenisti, *The International Law of Occupation*, 82.

150 ILC, 'First Report', paras 29–30.

151 The Hague Regulations 1907, Article 55; Benvenisti, *The International Law of Occupation*, 82; ILC, 'First Report', paras 29–30.

152 ILC, 'First Report', para 30; UK Ministry of Defence, *The Manual of the Law of Armed Conflict* (Oxford University Press 2004) 303, paras 11, 86.

"assumes special importance in respect of investments relating to use of land, and to the exploitation of natural resources in occupied territory".[153] In the case of the exploitation of natural resources, the underlying rationale of the usufructuary rules embodied in Article 55 of the Hague Regulations is bolstered by the principle of self-determination, which is geared towards maintaining natural resources in occupied territories.[154]

It is evident that the excessive exploitation of natural resources could lead to the degradation of the environment and have a long-term impact on the ecosystem and biodiversity of the occupied state.[155] Furthermore, the excessive exploitation of natural resources by an occupying power might contribute to environmental contaminants and pollution, particularly the utilisation in an unsustainable manner of mineral resources, such as oil.[156]

For example, Russian's abusive acts against some parts of Georgia in 2008 and its cutting and burning of forest in the occupied areas in the North[157] all constitute a violation of the Article 55 of the Hague Regulations. That is, they constitute a breach of the occupying power's responsibility under the usufructuary rule, particularly owing to the destruction of the capital value of the immovable property of the occupied territory.

As Sloan argued, the importance of taking into account the "interpretation rule of Article 31 of the Vienna Convention on the Law of Treaties"[158] and "in accordance with the ordinary meaning of the terms", to "safeguard the capital", as mentioned under Article 55 of the Hague Regulations, any exploitation of mineral resources should be prohibited.[159] It could be assumed that the excessive and abusive utilisation (the utilisation in an unsustainable manner) of the natural resources situated in the occupied territory by an occupying power is an illegal act and contrary to its obligation under Article 55 of the Hague Regulations. Moreover, such acts against the natural resources in the occupied territory would have consequences on all kinds of creatures living there, such as animals, plants, and the local population.[160] The ICJ declared in the case *DRC v. Uganda* that the occupying power must take

153 Yutaka Arai-Takahashi, *The Law of Occupation: Continuity and Change of International Humanitarian Law, and its Interaction with International Human Rights Law* (Martinus Nijhoff Publishers 2009) 171.

154 Ibid, 216; Alaja Manna, 'The Duties of the Occupant in Protecting the Natural Resources of the Occupied Territory under International Humanitarian Law', (2015) *The Research Journal*: University of Palestine, Majallat Jamiat Filastin lil-Abḥath, 6.

155 Hulme, 'Enhancing Environmental Protection', 238.

156 Ibid, 238–240.

157 Ibid, 238; International Law and Policy Institute, *Protection of the Natural Environment in Armed Conflict: An Empirical Study* (2014), 29–30.

158 Vienna Convention on the Law of Treaties (1969), (adopted on 23 May 1969, in force 27 January 1980), Article 31, in Malcolm Evans, *International Law Documents* (13th edn, Oxford University Press 2017).

159 Sloan, The United Nations: General Assembly: Economic and Social Council, 'Implications, under International Law', para 32.

160 See Hulme, 'Enhancing Environmental Protection'.

into account all possible measures to prevent the illegal exploitation of natural resources in the occupied territory.[161]

2.2.2.1.1 SEIZURE OF PUBLIC PROPERTY

Seizing public property for military purposes, such as military exercises, a military vehicle-park, or troop accommodation, might leave an environmental footprint on the seized land.

The environmental harm resulting from such requisition could be related, *inter alia*, to the use of military vehicles, chemicals, weapons, and troop exercises. It might involve the damaging of crops if the land was agricultural land or the contamination of the soil and/or the water by inappropriate disposal or dumping of military waste or the burning or cutting of trees, if the land was a part of forest. Hence, the requisition of public land for military purposes in an occupied territory might have consequences for the ecosystem's functions and on biodiversity, including the loss of habitat and species.

It could be argued that the occupying power must take environmental considerations into account when it seizes public property for military purposes, thereby complying with its obligation under Article 55 of the Hague Regulations. Moreover, in accordance with the "usufructuary rule" stressing that the occupying power is only a beneficiary owner of such assets and it has a duty at all times to maintain and to protect it, "safeguarding the capital" of the property, as argued above, this duty must extend to cover environmental conservation as well.

An example can be given from the Azerbaijani territory Nagorno-Karabakh that was occupied by Armenia.[162] Armenian occupying forces deliberately destroyed natural resources there, specifically by polluting water sources along with the extreme utilisation of these resources in an unsustainable manner.[163] This caused environmental degradation in the Nagorno-Karabakh territory and affected the local people living there. In particular, the acts engaged in by Armenia were against the water resources in the occupied territory along with the deliberate damaging of other natural resources.[164] Thus, the state of the environment worsened in the occupied territory of Nagorno-Karabakh.[165] Furthermore, the harm against the environment in the Azerbaijani-occupied regions by the Armenian occupation forces impacted negatively on the biodiversity and the ecosystem of the whole occupied

161 ICJ, '*DRC v. Uganda*', para 248.

162 Administrative Department of the President of the Republic of Azerbaijan: Presidential Library.

163 Bakhshiyeva, 'Threats and Provocations Originating from The Republic of Armenia', 113-116, 131.

164 Aynur Azimzade, 'Armenia Plundering Natural Resources in Occupied Azerbaijani Territories', 56. Available online at: < https://irs-az.com/new/files/2019/247/2954.pdf>. Accessed date: 20/Sep/2020; Bakhshiyeva, 'Threats and Provocations Originating from The Republic of Armenia', 115, 120, 123, 127–129.

165 Ibid.

region.[166] The damaged resources, along with the cutting of forests, damage caused to the soil by heavy military techniques, and the loss of rare species of plants and animals in the occupied regions, are all considered the property of Azerbaijan.[167]

It could be argued that Armenia as an occupying power violated its obligation under Article 55 of the Hague Regulations by disrespecting property rights in Nagorno-Karabakh and causing environmental damage, in particular by excessive exploitation and by intentionally damaging natural resources located in the territory.[168]

Another example is that of the Indonesian occupation of East-Timor (Timor-Leste), where it is evident that the forests in the occupied territory were greatly exploited beyond the limits set by the rule of usufruct mentioned above.[169] After the end of occupation in 1999, most of those forests were in an extremely bad state, unable to supply the basic needs of the domestic people, and leaving them deprived of an environment that was "essential for gathering food, medicinal plants, firewood and fodder".[170] Additionally, the erosion of the soil threatened to have grave consequences for agricultural production and water resources.[171]

It should be noted that there is a critical issue that might have an impact on the interpretation of Article 55 of the Hague Regulations and the use of the occupied state's public immovable property by an occupying power: the concept of the principle of permanent sovereignty over natural resources and its applicability in times of occupation. This principle means that all peoples and states have the right to freely use and dispose of their natural resources within their national jurisdiction.[172]

Applying this principle to situations of occupation tends to support a restrictive interpretation of the occupant's rights in relation to the use, exploitation, and disposal of public immovable property, such as natural resources. Notably, the law of occupation has given some support to the principle of permanent sovereignty over natural resources, which, in turn, can reinforce the right of local people in the occupied territory to enjoy the wealth of its natural resources. Therefore, protection of the environment, especially those components that are natural resources, must be provided from any potential harm in the occupied territory that might be the

166 Administrative Department of the President of the Republic of Azerbaijan: Presidential Library, at:15, 24, 34.

167 Ibid, 15–23.

168 Azimzade, 'Armenia Plundering Natural Resources in Occupied Azerbaijani Territories', 56; Bakhshiyeva, 'Threats and Provocations Originating from The Republic of Armenia', 115, 120, 123, 127–129; Administrative Department of the President of the Republic of Azerbaijan: Presidential Library.

169 Sylvain Vité, 'The Interrelation of the Law of Occupation and Economic, Social and Cultural Rights', 647; Commission for Reception, Truth and Reconciliation in East-Timor, Final Report, January 2006, paras 48–49.

170 Ibid.

171 Ibid.

172 Yolanda Chekera and Vincent Nmehielle, 'The International Law Principle of Permanent Sovereignty over Natural Resources as an Instrument for Development: The Case of Zimbabwean Diamonds', (2013) 6 *African Journal of Legal Studies* 69, 83–84.

result of any violations of the principle.[173] In addition to this, "the occupying power is under an obligation not to interfere with the exercise of permanent sovereignty by the local population".[174]

Some scholars have considered the issue of natural resources in occupied territory as a part of immovable property.[175] Dinstein argued against the applicability of the principle of permanent sovereignty over natural resources in times of occupation by holding that the principle is clearly binding as custom in peacetime, but in the case of occupation, the applicability of the principle is still a controversial issue.[176] Some other scholars, like Longobardo, have argued for the applicability of the principle of permanent sovereignty over natural resources in times of occupation and consider it as granted.[177] The ICJ has adopted a controversial position regarding the applicability of the principle in such situations. For example, in the *DRC v. Uganda* case, it confirmed the customary nature of the principle.[178] Yet in the same case, it stressed that the principle is not applicable to "the specific situation of looting, pillage and exploitation of certain natural resources by members of the army of a State militarily intervening in another State".[179] The ICJ's statement in the *DRC v. Uganda* case regarding the dismissal of the applicability of the principle of permanent sovereignty over natural resources to situations of armed conflict and occupation is a controversial statement, since the Court did not specify whether the principle is not applicable only to the specific circumstances of the case itself or to situations of armed conflict and occupations in general. Moreover, the claim that the principle of permanent sovereignty over natural resources is not applicable to situations of occupation might be contradictory to the legal status of occupation as a temporary situation, with only a provisional administration authority, which is not supposed to impact upon the sovereignty of the occupied territory.[180]

Arguably, by considering the interpretation of Article 55 of the Hague Regulations in light of the applicability of the principle of permanent sovereignty over natural resources in situations of occupation, the chance of harming the environment, including biodiversity and the ecosystem functions, would be much less, especially by preventing the occupying power from abuse or overutilisation of the natural resources in the occupied state, where most probably, natural resources may be classified as a public immovable property.

173 Sloan, The United Nations: General Assembly: Economic and Social Council, 'Implications, under International Law', para 52.

174 Ibid, para 51(c).

175 Dinstein, *The International Law of Belligerent Occupation*, 236.

176 Ibid.

177 Marco Longobardo, 'State Responsibility for International Humanitarian Law Violations by Private Actors in Occupied Territories and the Exploitation of Natural Resources', (2016) 63 NILR 251, 255–256.

178 ICJ, '*DRC v. Uganda*', para 244.

179 Ibid.

180 ILC, 'First Report', para 34.

To sum up, Article 55 of the Hague Regulations has a central and significant role in protecting the environment under the rules of the law of occupation through the protection provided to the public property in the occupied territory. Consequently, the present author is convinced that the duty of the occupying power under Article 55 of the Hague Regulations, namely under "safeguard the capital", must include the environmental considerations as an element of such duty.[181] Moreover, the duty of the occupying power includes the sustainable use of natural resources and environmental conservation.[182]

2.2.2.2 Prohibition of Unjustified Destruction and Confiscation of Private Property in the Occupied Territory

Private property under the law of occupation enjoys stronger protection since it is protected under several provisions of the law that prohibit the pillage, confiscation, seizure, and destruction of such property.[183] According to Article 46(2) of the Hague Regulations, private property is protected and cannot be confiscated,[184] and it shall be protected from permanent confiscation during times of occupation.[185] Notably, the protection under the Hague Regulations covers all kinds of private property, both movable and immovable.[186]

It is interesting that the protection of private property in times of occupation is a long-standing norm under customary international humanitarian law and was already acknowledged by non-binding codifications adopted before the Hague Regulations. For example, the Oxford Manual in 1880 provided that "If the powers of the occupant are limited with respect to the property of the enemy state, with greater reason are they limited with respect to the property of individuals".[187] Article 54 of the same Manual confirmed the point that private property in occupied territory must be respected.[188]

The protection provided to private property in times of occupation can play a vital role in protecting the occupied territory's environment, especially by preventing the occupying power from any overexploitation or utilisation of the natural resources in an unsustainable manner, which may have a negative impact on the biodiversity and the ecosystem function of the occupied territory.[189] Some local natural resources could be considered as private property depending on how they

181 Ibid, para 32.

182 Ibid.

183 The Hague Regulations 1907, Article 46. See also Benvenisti, *The International Law of Occupation*, 82.

184 The Hague Regulations 1907, Article 46, para 2.

185 Hans-Peter Gasser, 'Protection of the Civilian Population: Belligerent Occupation', 279.

186 Ibid.

187 *The Laws of War on Land*. Oxford, 9 September 1880, Part II: Application of General Principles: Occupied Territory: C. Rules of Conduct with regard to Property: (B) Private Property.

188 Ibid, Article: 54. See also, 'Project of an International Declaration concerning the Laws and Customs of War', Brussels, 27 August 1874. Article 38.

189 ILC, 'First Report', para 39.

are classified in the national legislation of the occupied territory.[190] For instance, some water resources, such as wells or any other natural springs, might constitute private assets that belong to individuals of the occupied territory, and the same logic can be applied to privately owned lands,[191] which might include some rare species of plants and animals or other natural resources.

The provisions protecting private property also protect the environment, and most of these have been considered as part of customary IHL.[192] For example, Article 53 of the GCIV,[193] which applies exclusively to situations of occupation, provides protection to private property in the occupied territory and, at the same time, it provides minimum protection to the environment.[194]

Furthermore, Article 53 of the GCIV was originally formulated to solely protect private property and it provides protection to the environment in times of occupation by prohibiting the destruction of private property in occupied territory.[195] Moreover, the term "destruction" should be interpreted broadly to cover the damage against the environment,[196] for instance, in the case of environmental damage caused by the extraction of natural resources.[197]

In addition to this, Article 23(g) of the Hague Regulations also provides protection to private property and, as has been argued above, provides indirect protection to the environment in such situations.[198] Furthermore, Article 53(2) of the Hague Regulations provided that "all kinds of ammunition of war, may be seized, even if they belong to private individuals".[199] However, the seizure of private property in times of occupation must be for military purposes, and the occupying power is only allowed to requisition private movable property for the needs of its armed forces.[200]

Since IHL allows the occupying power to seize private immovable property in certain circumstances, such as agricultural lands, this could have environmental consequences. In particular, if the purpose of the seizure is military exercises or other types of military activities, such as the quartering of troops, most probably, such acts will leave an environmental footprint and impact on the biodiversity of the seized area.[201]

190 Cassese, 'Powers and Duties of an Occupant in Relation to Land and Natural Resources', 431.
191 Ibid, 431.
192 Antoine Bouvier, 'Protecting the Natural Environment in a Period of Armed Conflict', 195.
193 The Fourth Geneva Convention 1949, Article (53): "Any destruction by the Occupying Power of real or personal property belonging individually or collectively to private persons, or to the State, or to other public authorities, or to social or co-operative organizations, is prohibited, except where such destruction is rendered absolutely necessary by military operations".
194 Antoine Bouvier, 'Protecting the Natural Environment in a Period of Armed Conflict', at: 195–196.
195 Dam-de Jong, 'International Law and Resource Plunder', 45–47.
196 Ibid, 47.
197 Ibid.
198 Bouvier, 'Protecting the Natural Environment in a Period of Armed Conflict', 195; Daniella Dam-de Jong, 'International Law and Resource Plunder', 45–48.
199 The Hague Regulations 1907, Article 53(2).
200 Ibid, Article 52, Article 53(2).
201 ILC, 'First Report', para 39.

Acknowledging that, in the case of confiscating land that it is agricultural, including crops and/or fruit and trees, the occupying power is allowed to requisite such entities only for the needs of its army.[202] Thus, the protection provided under the law of occupation to private property has an essential protective role regarding the prevention of the occupying power from abusing its status as an administrator over the occupied state and causing extensive destruction or excessive utilisation to such property, which might have environmental consequences, including adverse impacts on the ecosystem functions and the biodiversity of the occupied territory.[203]

Notably, all private assets must be protected from permanent seizure; in the case of seizing real estate, such as land, this must be restored, and where there is damage to these properties, compensation must be paid.[204] Moreover, when an occupying power confiscates a portion of private land, it cannot conduct any fundamental change to that land or cause any extensive destruction, unless there is a justified military need. Moreover, the obligation to protect private property from confiscation without an imperative military necessity is a part of customary IHL, which specifically applies to the occupied state.[205]

The prohibition against the confiscation of private property without an imperative military necessity in an occupied territory was confirmed by national case law from some occupied territories too. For example, the issue of requisitioning private lands in the occupied West Bank in the OPT for establishing civilian settlements has appeared several times before the Israeli Supreme Court. The Israeli High Court, in the 1979 *Beth-El* case, confirmed the prohibition of the confiscation of private property, such as private agricultural land, without absolute military necessity.[206] Yet, the Court's decision in the *Beth-El* case allowed the confiscation of private land, since the Court was satisfied that there were substantial military needs that justified the confiscation.[207] However, some scholars have argued against the Court's decision in the *Beth-El* case by stressing that, "such an overstretched concept of a security based exception to the protection of private property rights clearly contradicts international law" and that "it destroys the guarantee of individual property rights in occupied territories".[208] However, a few months later, the same Court confirmed that the confiscation of private property in occupied territory is a prohibited act unless there is a military necessity for such confiscation.[209] The Court found that there were no clear security aims behind the establishment of the Elon Moreh' settlement near Nablus, and there was no absolute need for the

202 The Hague Regulation 1907, Article 52.

203 ILC, 'First Report', para 39.

204 Hans-Peter Gasser, 'Protection of the Civilian Population: Belligerent Occupation', 292–293.

205 Jean-Marie Henckaerts and Louise Doswald-Beck, *Customary International Humanitarian Law*, Rule 51.

206 *Ayub et al. v. Minister of Defense et al.* (H.C.J 606/78) and (H.C.J 610/78), (March 15, 1979).

207 Ibid.

208 Hans-Peter Gasser, 'Protection of the Civilian Population: Belligerent Occupation', 293.

209 *Dweikat et al. v. Government of Israel et al.*, (H.C.J 390/79), (Judgment of the Israeli Supreme Court, October 22, 1979), known as: *(Elon Moreh case)*. At: 9,18–19.

confiscation of private lands for that purpose.[210] Accordingly, it declared that the *Elon* Moreh settlement was illegal,[211] and it was ruled that this establishment was unlawful.[212] The decision in the *Elon Moreh* case was different to that of *Beth-El* since the Court relied on the Hague Regulations in its decision, namely on Article 52, which deals with the requisition of property in times of occupation.[213]

Considering the issue of the settlements in the OPT from the environmental point of view, the confiscation of Palestinians' private lands in favour of establishing civilian settlements and bypass roads to link the settlements together simultaneously damaged the environment by cutting down thousands of trees and caused degradation of the land, which in turn contributed to the disruption of natural ecosystems in the occupied West Bank and caused an adverse impact on the Palestinians' environment.[214] Moreover, some of the settlements need troops for their protection[215] and, as argued above, the occupying power troops could leave an environmental footprint and have an impact on the biodiversity of the confiscated area.[216] The dramatic increase in the number of settlements and bypass roads in the OPT has had clear environmental consequences, which, in turn, have impacted negatively on the local people, thereby preventing them from living a normal life.[217] Consequently, it is safe to say that such acts constitute a grave breach of the rules of the law of occupation that protect private property in occupied territory, such as in Articles 46 and 53 of the Hague Regulations and Article 53 of the GCIV.

Accordingly, and by applying this logic, the environment can be protected through the prohibition of any kind of acts that result in causing unjustified destruction or confiscation of private property in occupied territory without justified military necessities.[218] Therefore, private property is under strong protection, either by the rules of the law of occupation itself or by other customary IHL norms applicable to situations of occupation, as noted above.[219]

Consequently, and by assuming that the occupying power will respect and apply those rules, the occupying power must, in turn, prevent causing any serious injuries against the occupied territory's environment In particular, it must prevent any

210 Ibid, 18–19.

211 Ibid, 1819, 33.

212 Ibid, 33. For more information about *Elon Moreh case* see: Mazen Qupty, 'The Application of International Law in the Occupied Territories as Reflected in the Judgments of the High Court of Justice in Israel', 3,12–13,16.

213 *Dweikat et al. v. Government of Israel et al.*, at: 19.

214 Z. Brophy and J. Isaac, 'The Environmental Impact of Israeli Military Activities', 8–9; Jean Jaquet, Akiko Harayama, Kaeser D., 'Desk Study on the Environment in the Occupied Palestinian Territories', (The United Nations Environmental Programme 2003) 81-82, 95, 100, 113, 117–118.

215 Hans-Peter Gasser, 'Protection of the Civilian Population: Belligerent Occupation', 293.

216 ILC, 'First Report', para 39.

217 Eyal Hareuveni, 'By Hook and by Crook: Israeli Settlement Policy in the West Bank', (B'Tselem 2010) 52; Eyal Hareuveni, 'Foul Play: Neglect of Wastewater Treatment in the West Bank', (B'Tselem 2009) 11–12.

218 See The Hague Regulations 1907, Article 52 and 53(2); The GCIV 1949, Article 53 and 147.

219 Ibid.; Dinstein, *The International Law of Belligerent Occupation,* 4.

abusive exploitation of private natural resources located in the occupied territory. Otherwise, the occupying power will be considered as violating of international law regarding its obligation under the rules of the law of occupation that protect private property rights in the occupied state, such as Articles 46, 52, and 53/2 of the Hague Regulations and Articles 53 and 147 of the GCIV.

It could be argued that private property is well protected under the rules of the law of occupation in relation to preventing the occupying power from looting or the abusive exploitation of such property. Hence, it strengthens the protection provided to the environment in occupied territory through property-rights provisions under the law of occupation. These rules play a fundamental role in preventing any intensive or deliberate harm to the environment that might impact on the biodiversity and ecosystem functions of the occupied territory.

In light of these arguments, it would seem reasonable to contend that the prohibition of unjustified destruction or confiscation of private property in times of occupation under the rules of the law of occupation applies equally to the environment in the occupied territory, insofar as those components of the environment constitute private property under the domestic law of the occupied territory.

2.2.3 The Supplementary Role of the Additional Protocol 1 in Relation to Protecting the Environment in Times of Occupation through Property Rights Provisions

This subsection examines the role of Additional Protocol 1 (1977) of the Fourth Geneva Conventions 1949 in ensuring extra protection of the environment in the occupied territory through the protection provided for property rights.

2.2.3.1 Protection of Objects Indispensable to the Survival of Civilians in the Occupied Territory under the Additional Protocol 1 (1977) of the Fourth Geneva Conventions of (1949)

The Additional Protocol 1 (AP1) is applicable to situations of occupation for as long as the states parties to it are concerned,[220] or as long as its provisions reflect customary international law. Unlike the Geneva Conventions themselves, the AP1 is not universally ratified. That is, a large number of states have ratified it, whereas a few have not yet, such as Israel and the United States.[221] The AP1 includes several

220 Protocol Additional to the Geneva Conventions of 12 August 1949, and relating to the Protection of Victims of International Armed Conflicts (Protocol I), 8 June 1977. Article 1(3): "This Protocol, which supplements the Geneva Conventions of 12 August 1949 for the protection of war victims, shall apply in the situations referred to in Article 2 common to those Conventions". Article 1(4): "The situations referred to in the preceding paragraph include armed conflicts in which peoples are fighting against colonial domination and alien occupation and against racist régimes in the exercise of their right of self-determination". Article 2 common to the Geneva Conventions of 12 August 1949, "The Convention shall also apply to all cases of partial or total occupation of the territory of a High Contracting Party, even if the said occupation meets with no armed resistance".

221 Dinstein, *The International Law of Belligerent Occupation*, 7–8.

provisions dealing directly with situations of occupation,[222] which at the same time provide protection to property rights in an occupied territory.

The AP1 provides additional protection to the environment in times of occupation by ensuring the occupying power is respecting property rights, and it prohibits any destruction of civilian objects that are indispensable to the survival of the population.[223] Article 54(2) prohibits to

> attack, destroy, remove or render useless objects indispensable to the survival of the civilian population, such as foodstuffs, agricultural areas for the production of foodstuffs, crops, livestock, drinking water installations and supplies and irrigation works, for the specific purpose of denying them for their sustenance value to the civilian population or to the adverse Party, whether in order to starve out civilians, to cause them to move away, or for any other motive.[224]

This rule corresponds to customary international law.[225]

The ICRC has elaborated upon the relationship between Article 54 of the AP 1 and the law of occupation. According to the ICRC,

> As regards Occupying Powers, Article 53 of the Fourth Geneva Convention of 1949 prohibits the destruction of real or personal property, except where such destruction is rendered absolutely necessary by military operations. This is a general rule which is now supplemented by the provisions of Article 54 of the Protocol as regards objects indispensable to the survival of the civilian population.[226]

Furthermore, "An Occupying Power may not destroy objects located in occupied territory which are indispensable to the survival of the civilian population".[227]

Palestinian entities and organisations have argued for the applicability of Article 54 to situations of occupation. For example, in a paper presented to the Conference of the High Contracting Parties to the Fourth Geneva Convention by the Permanent Observer Mission of Palestine to the United Nations, the PLO raised the applicability of Article 54 to the OPT and its important role of providing protection

222 Ibid.

223 The Additional Protocol I (1997), Article 54(2).

224 Ibid.

225 ICRC, 'Customary IHL', 'Rule 54, Attacks against Objects Indispensable to the Survival of the Civilian Population'.

226 ICRC, 'Treaties, States Parties and Commentaries': Protocol Additional to the Geneva Conventions of 12 August 1949, and relating to the Protection of Victims of International Armed Conflicts (Protocol I), (8 June 1977). 'Commentary of 1987': Article 54: 'Protection of Objects Indispensable to the Survival of the Civilian Population'.

227 ICRC, 'Commentary of 1987': Article 54: 'Protection of Objects Indispensable to the Survival of the Civilian Population'.

to natural resources in them.[228] A similar position was expressed by the Al-Haq Human Rights Organisation in 2015.[229]

In addition to this, the report of the Special Rapporteur of the ILC for the protection of the environment in armed conflict clearly considered the applicability of Article 54(2) to situations of occupation and linked the content of the Article to the protection of the environment in times of occupation through the prohibition of the destruction of the civilian indispensable objects.[230] Consequently, it is possible to assume that Article 54 of the AP1 is also applicable to situations of occupation and it provides an important supplementary role providing additional protection to the environment through property rights in the occupied territory, along with other rules under the law of occupation, as has been argued above.

Article 54(2) of the AP1 clearly considers the destruction of foodstuffs, agricultural areas for the production of foodstuffs, crops, livestock, drinking-water installations, and supplies as well as irrigation works to be prohibited acts. Hence, it could enhance the protection provided to the environment in the occupied territory through property rights.[231] The following paragraphs set out this argument.

Arguably, Article 54(2) of the AP1 recognises the relationship between the protection of the environment and civilians' lives and their existence in the occupied territory, in particular, where it prohibits any destruction of agricultural areas, crops, animals, and drinking-water installations. Notably, this list of objects under Article 54(2) is not an exhaustive one.[232] Moreover, it considers protection of these objects as imperative to the survival of the local population.[233]

Therefore, indirect protection of the environment and biodiversity in occupied territory could be provided under the prohibition of the destruction, removal, or disablement of local peoples' objects, indispensable to their survival under Article 54(2) of the AP1. In particular, it provides protection to certain natural resources that the local population depends on to get its foodstuffs and drinking water, such as lakes and rivers that provide drinking water, or that could be used as a source of food, such as fish.[234] In addition, it also provides for the conservation of the forests that the local population of the occupied territory relies on for their food, timber, firewood, and medicinal plants.[235] Hence, these natural resources should also fall within the scope of the protection provided under Article 54(2) of the AP1 as indis-

228 PLO/Palestine, 'Israel's Belligerent Occupation of the Palestinian Territory, including Jerusalem and International Humanitarian Law': 'Paper presented to the Conference of the High Contracting Parties to the Fourth Geneva Convention on Measures to Enforce the Convention in the Occupied Palestinian Territory, including Jerusalem' (15 July 1999).

229 Benjamin Pontin, Vito De Lucia, and Jesus Gamero Rus, 'Environmental Injustice in Occupied Palestinian Territory: Problems and Prospects', 37–39.

230 ILC, 'First Report', para 42.

231 The Additional Protocol I (1977), Article 54(2).

232 Henckaerts and Doswald-Beck, *Customary International Humanitarian Law*, Rule 54, 193.

233 The Additional Protocol I (1977), Article 54.

234 Dam-de Jong, 'International Law and Resource Plunder', 39. Note that Dam-de Jong has mentioned another author but in French language in her article, see footnote: (No. 50) in the article.

235 Ibid.

pensable objects to the survival of the population. Accordingly, they should not be destroyed or removed.

Moreover, such natural resources could be the only sources available to provide civilians with their food, water, or even medicine. Thus, these resources should also be protected under Article 54 of the AP1, since without this, local people in the occupied territory might starve or be obliged to move away. Furthermore, it could be complex to provide a clean sufficient amount of drinking water and foodstuffs without protecting such resources from overexploitation. Consequently, this article also provides protection to the environment in times of occupation by protecting vital natural resources for the survival of local populations. Therefore, the occupying power must administer such resources in a sustainable manner and avoid any pillage or overexploitation, thereby ensuring that it continues to supply the local populations and meet their basic needs, as well as avoiding harm to the environment, biodiversity, and ecosystem functions of the occupied territory.

Furthermore, even non-military activities by the occupying power that could lead to serious degradation of water resources might be considered as meaning to "remove or render useless objects indispensable to the survival of the civilian population",[236] which is prohibited under Article 54(2) of the AP1, and which is also confirmed by the Berlin Rules on Water Resources under Article 54(2).[237] According to these Rules, an occupying power has a responsibility to "administer water resources in an occupied territory in a way that ensures the sustainable use of the water resources and that minimizes environmental harm".[238] Despite the Berlin Rules on Water Resources not being legally binding, they still provide interesting guidelines regarding the protection of the environment in situations of occupation, and they support the argument that the occupying power must administer the resources of the occupied territory in a sustainable manner that avoids harming the environment.

This argument is supported by the object and purpose of Article 54(2), that is, the protection of civilians and the prevention of such policies that might force them to move away.[239] Moreover, this interpretation is supported by both the ICRC[240] and the ILC, which have argued that Article 54(2) of the AP1 can be interpreted in terms of protecting the environment,[241] including water, soil, and air, to the extent that the civilian population rely upon them.[242]

Moreover, Article 69(1) of the AP1 reinforces the occupying power's duty under Article 55 of the GCIV to ensure the provision of food and medical supplies that are

236 ILC, 'First Report', para 42. See also Berlin Rules on Water Resources: International Law Association: Berlin Conference 2004: Water Recourses Law. Article 54(2).

237 Berlin Rules on Water Resources. Article 54(2).

238 Ibid, Article 54(1).

239 ILC, 'First Report', para 42.

240 ICRC Commentary to Additional Protocol I, Article 54(2). Para 2102.

241 ILC, 'First Report', para 42.

242 The United Nations, Environment Assembly of the United Nations Environment Programme: Resolution on Environment and Health, (UNEP/EA.3/Res.4), (30 January 2018), para 5.

considered essential to the survival of the civilian population of the occupied territory and to see them as basic needs of the population in times of occupation. As argued above, forests could be protected objects under Article 54(2) of the AP1, provided there are some plants and other creatures growing and living in the forests that are essential for producing chemical medicines or that can be used as natural ones. Article 69(1) of the AP1 declares objects such as food and medicine as being essential to the survival of the local population in an occupied territory. It emphasises the occupying power's responsibility in terms of providing such objects to the occupied people.[243]

It could, therefore, be argued that Article 69(1) of the AP1 also provides indirect protection to the environment by emphasising the occupying power's responsibility towards ensuring food and medical supplies for the local population in the occupied territory.[244] That is, it provides a kind of indirect protection to the natural sources of such supplies, such as forests, which are an important source of both food and medicinal plants.[245]

Consequently, any intentional harm against forests or other natural resources that provide the occupied territory with basic needs, such as food and medical supplies, by an occupying power (as Russian occupation did in Georgia when it purposely burned and destroyed hundreds of hectares of forests),[246] might constitute a breach of the occupying power's responsibilities under the AP1, namely, under Articles 54(2) and 69(1) of the Protocol.

2.3 The Protection of the Environment under Article 43 of the Hague Regulations and 64 of the Fourth Geneva Convention

In this section, it will be argued that the occupying power accepting its duty to respect the environmental domestic laws and regulations of the occupied territory could provide more protection to the environment in situations of occupation.[247] Notably, the extent to which protection can be provided to the environment in an occupied territory relies on how effectively it is already protected by national laws and environmental regulations.[248] Most states in the world, if not all, have already adopted domestic laws and regulations in relation to the protection of the environment.[249]

243 Additional Protocol I (1977), Article 69 (1): "In addition to the duties specified in Article 55 of the Fourth Convention concerning food and medical supplies, the Occupying Power shall, to the fullest extent of the means available to it and without any adverse distinction, also ensure the provision of clothing, bedding, means of shelter, other supplies essential to the survival of the civilian population of the occupied territory and objects necessary for religious worship".

244 Ibid.

245 Dam-de Jong, 'International Law and Resource Plunder', 39.

246 Hulme, 'Enhancing Environmental Protection', 238; International Law and Policy Institute, Protection of the Natural Environment in Armed Conflict: An Empirical Study (2014), 29–30.

247 ILC, 'First Report', para 49.

248 Ibid.

249 ILC, 'First Report', para 49. For more information and examples about the states that have environmental legislation, see The United Nations Environmental Programmes (UNEP) at:<www.ecolex.org>.

Moreover, many states have ratified Multilateral Environmental Agreements (MEAs), and it is likely that the occupying power or the occupied territory are parties to such agreements. For example, the Basel Convention on the Control of Transboundary Movements of Hazardous Wastes and their Disposal has been ratified by approximately 200 states.[250] Such agreements can be incorporated into the national environmental laws of state parties and, therefore, provide more precise protection of the environment. Thus, the occupying power will have an obligation under the provisions of the law of occupation to respect such national laws. The protection provided by environmental domestic laws of the occupied territory and the extent of these laws regarding the protection of the environment as well as the relationship between these laws and the occupying power's obligations under Article 43 of the Hague Regulations and Article 64 of the GCIV will be demonstrated, in detail, in the following paragraphs.

As argued in the previous sections, the principles governing the situation of occupation and their relationship with the 'conservationist principle' may also provide protection to the environment in occupied territory. This section will demonstrate this relation and the possible environmental protection that could be provided along with other rules of the law of occupation, such as Article 43 of the Hague Regulations and Article 64 of the GCIV.

According to the norms of the law of occupation, the occupying power has an obligation to restore and maintain public order and civil life in the occupied territory. Article 43 of the Hague Regulations provides that "The authority of the legitimate power having in fact passed into the hands of the occupant, the latter shall take all the measures in his power to restore, and ensure, as far as possible, public order and civil life,[251] while respecting, unless absolutely prevented, the laws in force in the country".[252] Furthermore, Article 64 of the GCIV adds certain specifications to the expression "unless absolutely prevented" of the Hague Regulations regarding the domestic laws of the occupied territory. Article 64 allows the occupying power to make changes in the domestic laws and the regulations of the occupied territory in order to enable the occupying power to fulfil its obligations under the Convention, to maintain the orderly government of the occupied territory, and to secure the safety of the occupant's forces and its administration.[253]

250 ILC, 'First Report', para 49. For more information see, The Basel Convention on the Control of Transboundary Movements of Hazardous Wastes and their Disposal: Parties to the Basel Convention on the Control of Transboundary Movements of Hazardous Wastes and their Disposal. (Adopted 22 March 1989, entered in force 5 May 1992). Available online at: < http://www.basel.int/Countries/StatusofRatifications/PartiesSignatories/tabid/4499/Default.aspx>. Accessed date: 22 October 2020.

251 Note: the Hague Regulations, Article.43: "The authority of the legitimate power having actually passed into the hands of the occupant, the latter shall take all steps in his power to re-establish and insure, as far as possible, public order and safety, while respecting, unless absolutely prevented, the laws in force in the country". The authentic French text of Article 43 uses the expression "*l'ordre et la vie publics*", and the provision has been accordingly interpreted to refer not only to physical safety but also to the "social functions and ordinary transactions which constitute daily life".

252 The Hague Regulations 1907, Article 43.

253 The Fourth Geneva Convention 1949, Article 64.

Both Article 43 of the Hague Regulations and Article 64 of the GCIV embody the so-called "conservationist principle".[254] As explained earlier, this means keeping the status of the occupied territory as it was before the occupation. However, the occupying power is required under Article 43 of the Hague Regulations 1907 to ensure the public order and civil life of the occupied state, as noted above. To this end, it must take all possible measures to consider such a duty and to prevent the situation of the occupied state of getting worse.[255] Otherwise, if the situation is worsening in the territory under its occupation, and the occupying power is doing nothing to maintain public order and civil life, it can be considered as a violation of its legal obligations under Article 43 of the Hague Regulations 1907. Therefore, in this scenario, the occupying power has to consider its positive and negative obligations to protect and to prevent the situation in the occupied territory from getting worse in relation to complying with its obligations under the law of occupation. Hence, both articles of the law of occupation allow the occupying power to legislate in very specific situations and when it is essential to maintain public order and civil life in the occupied territory.[256]

Notably, the authentic French text of Article 43 of the Hague Regulations uses the expression "*l'ordre et la vie publics*", which has been interpreted in a wider way. That is, it refers not only to physical safety, as the English translation provides, but also includes the entire social and economic life of the occupied territory. This means that the occupying power has a duty under Article 43 of the Hague Regulations to ensure the protection of all ordinary transactions and social functions that constitute the daily life of the local people in the occupied territory.[257]

To further explain the potential environmental protection under Article 43 of the Hague Regulations, it is deemed appropriate to, first, divide the Article into two main parts that could provide protection to the environment in times of occupation.

The first part concerns the occupant's responsibility to take all possible measures in its power to restore and ensure, as far as possible, the public order, civil life, welfare, and well-being of the occupied territory. Furthermore, by taking into account the above interpretation of the authentic French text of the expression "*l'ordre et la vie publics*", the occupant must ensure the normality of the daily life of the local people living in the occupied territory. This means the occupant needs to comply with its duty under Article 43 of the Hague Regulations in ensuring public order, civil life, and welfare in the occupied territory. Accordingly, to warrant that this duty is complied with, environmental considerations must be taken into account.[258]

The second part relates to respecting the domestic laws and regulations of the occupied territory. Most states have adopted domestic environmental laws and

254 ILC, 'First Report', para 44.

255 See e.g. Marco Longobardo, 'The Relevance of the Concept of Due Diligence for International Humanitarian Law', (2019) 37 *Wisconsin International Law Journal* 44, 73–75.

256 ILC, 'First Report', para 44.

257 Ibid, paras 43, 50.

258 Ibid.

regulations.[259] Therefore, there is an obligation upon the occupying power under Article 43 to respect and apply these laws, unless absolutely prevented.[260] This argument has been supported by the ILC Draft Principles on Protection of the Environment in relation to Armed Conflicts.[261] For instance, Draft Principle 19(3) provides that "An Occupying Power shall respect the law and institutions of the occupied territory concerning the protection of the environment and may only introduce changes within the limits provided by the law of armed conflict".[262] Draft Principle 19(3) became closer to the issue than previously when it specifically mentioned the duty of the occupying power to respect the environmental laws and regulations of the occupied territory.[263] Furthermore, Draft Principle 19(3) reflects the crux of the conservationist principle under the law of occupation, namely, conserving the law and the institutions of the occupied territory, which includes any existing environmental laws and regulations adopted by the occupied territory.[264]

By taking into account the first part of Article 43 and applying it to the environmental issues that were mentioned in the introductory chapter, a practical example can be given from the Iraqi occupation of Kuwait in 1991 and the environmental harm done to that country's environment. The Iraqi occupation's acts against Kuwait's environment have been described as one of humankind's worst environmental disasters.[265] The environmental damage represented mainly damage to its ecological components, including consequences for vegetation cover and wildlife due to the Iraqi occupation.[266] Furthermore, the Iraqi occupation caused grave damage to the Kuwaiti soil.[267] As argued by several researchers, severely disturbed soils are very slow to recover, which has substantial long-term effects on ecosystem recovery and functioning.[268]

Additionally, the Iraqi occupation destroyed a significant number of oil wells[269] and, as a result of this destruction, so-called oil lakes and oil network rivers were

259 Ibid, para 49.

260 The Hague Regulations 1907, Article 43.

261 The ILC Draft Principles on Protection of the Environment in relation to Armed Conflicts, with Commentaries (2022).

262 ILC Draft Principles, Principle 19(3).

263 Ibid.

264 Ibid, Hulme, 'Enhancing Environmental Protection', 213, 215; ILC, 'First Report', paras 44, 46.

265 Samira A. S. Omar, N. R. Bhat, and Adel Asem, 'Critical Assessment of the Environmental Consequences of the Invasion of Kuwait, the Gulf War, and the Aftermath' in Tarek Kassim, Damià Barceló (eds), *Environmental Consequences of War and Aftermath* (Springer-Verlag Berlin Heidelberg 2009) 145.

266 Ibid, 151.

267 Ibid.

268 Ibid, 152.

269 Due to the damage caused to Kuwait's territory by Iraq, several UNSC and UNGA resolutions have been adopted; for example, the UNSC Resolution No. 687 (1991) required Iraq to pay compensation for losses and damage that happened as a direct result of Iraq's unlawful invasion and occupation of Kuwait. It should be noted that the UNSC resolutions are binding. Further details about Iraq's responsibility under international law because of the damage caused to the Kuwaiti environment are illustrated in the following pages.

created.[270] This had grave consequences for Kuwait's vegetation cover, wildlife, soils, and water resources.[271] Moreover, the impact on wildlife was significant since animals were found trapped within the oil lakes, along with a radical impact on plant and faunal communities in areas near those lakes.[272] Further, the "oil sludge killed the upper life forms by its toxicity and killed the deep life forms by suffocation".[273] Moreover, the Iraqi occupation caused severe damage to the water resources of Kuwait.[274] The deliberate harm to the Kuwaiti environment by the Iraqi occupation caused a radical change in habitat quality, with implications for the whole ecosystem of that country.[275]

The resolutions adopted by the UN bodies, particularly by the UNSC and UNGA, can be used as evidence that the severe environmental injuries to Kuwait's territory by Iraqi occupation impacted on the whole life of its population at that time, including its social and economic life.[276] Notably, the UNSC under Resolution No. 687 (1991) created a special subsidiary organ, the UN Compensation Commission, with the specific task to "process claims and pay compensation for losses and damage suffered as a direct result of Iraq's unlawful invasion and occupation of Kuwait in 1990–91".[277]

Acknowledging that when the occupying power is causing severe damage to the local environment of the occupied territory in terms of burning and damaging the natural resources, such as soil and water sources, the full application of Article 43 of the Hague Regulations becomes impossible. Arguably, the deliberate harm against Kuwait's environment by the Iraqi occupation constitutes a grave breach of the occupant's obligation under Article 43 of the Hague Regulations, which demands that the occupying power take all possible measures to restore and to ensure public order, civil life and welfare to the occupied state's population as well as to ensure they will continue to live as a normal life as possible. However, the Iraqi occupation caused damage to all aspects of life in Kuwait during the time of occupation there.

270 Olof Lindén, Arne Jernelöv, Johanna Egerup, 'The Environmental Impacts of the Gulf War 1991', IIASA Interim Report, April 2004, 36–38.

271 Samira A. S. Omar, N. R. Bhat, and Adel Asem, 'Critical Assessment of the Environmental Consequences', 152–155.

272 Ibid.

273 Ibid, 151.

274 Ibid, 155.

275 Ibid.

276 The United Nations: Security Council, Resolution (687) Iraq Kuwait (1991), Section E para 16. See also The United Nations: General Assembly, Resolution (46/216) (1991). See also The United Nations: General Assembly, Resolution (47/151) (A/RES/47/151) (1992). See also The United Nations: Economic and Social Council, 'Situation of Human Rights in Occupied Kuwait: Report on the situation of human rights in Kuwait under Iraqi occupation, prepared by Mr. Walter Kalin. Special Rapporteur of the Commission on Human Rights, in accordance with Commission Resolution 1991/67', (E/CN.4/1992/26), (16 January 1992). Paras 201–209.

277 The United Nations: The United Nations Compensation Commission (UNCC), < https://uncc.ch/home>.

It could be argued that the occupying power has an indirect obligation to protect the environment under the first part of Article 43 of the Hague Regulations. The author assumed this obligation of the occupying power in relation to the environment based on the facts shown from several occupied territories and how damage to the environment has had negative consequences on the lives of civilians, hence preventing them from living a normal life. It is noted that the preparatory work of the Hague Regulations regarding Article 43 did not explicitly address any environmental concerns in times of occupation;[278] regarding this, during the Hague Peace Conferences of 1899 and 1907, the discussion between the participating states relating to Article 43 was mainly about the way the occupying power should administer the occupied territory and the treatment of civilians. The drafters of the Hague Regulations and, namely, the negotiations regarding Article 43, were focused on delineating the occupant's powers and responsibilities to ensure and maintain the public order and the safety of the local population living in occupied territory.

Another similar example to the one above can be seen in the US and the UK occupation of Iraq in 2003. According to what has been argued above, the occupying power under Article 43 has an obligation to ensure public order, civil life, and welfare in the occupied territory.[279] This obligation has a clear link to the protection of the environment as well. That is, the occupying power has an obligation to prevent and to suppress any act that may cause environmental damage.[280]

Between 2003 and 2004, several acts of sabotage against water networks and sanitation systems were recorded in Iraq, which resulted in millions of the local population being deprived of their basic services and needs.[281] Thus, the US and the UK, as occupying powers in Iraq at that time, had a responsibility under the first part of Article 43 of the Hague Regulations to ensure public order, civil life, and the welfare of the local people of Iraq. Without providing protection for water resources and other facilities, such as the sanitation system, maintaining the public order and civil life and ensuring that the occupied population continued to live as normal as possible became impossible. Moreover, the destruction of the water sources and the damage to the sanitation systems increased the risk of spreading epidemics and polluting the water resources, as happened in Iraq in 2003, in particular in terms of an increased pollution burden on the Tigris River. [282]

278 For the preparatory work about Article 43, see The Proceedings of the Hague Peace Conferences. Translation of the official texts, prepared in the Division of International Law of the Carnegie Endowment for International Peace, under the supervision of J. B. Scott. The Conference of 1907. (Vol. i–iii. v.3). The Conference of 1907, Meetings of the Second, Third and Fourth Commissions. (OUP 1921). At:19, 113–114, 237, 1050. Available online at: < https://babel.hathitrust.org/cgi/pt?id=hvd.hnyamj&seq=9>. Accessed date: 1 December 2023.

279 The Hague Regulations 1907, Article 43.

280 ILC, 'First Report', para 47.

281 The United Nations Environment Programme, 'Desk Study on the Environment in Iraq', (2003) 71.

282 Ibid.

Notably, the UNSC raised a special call to the occupying powers of Iraq in relation to promoting the welfare of the Iraqi population, in particular, through the effective administration of the country.[283] As Lehto argued, the obligation to respect the environment in the occupied territory is linked to the occupying power's duty under Article 43 of the Hague Regulations to ensure the welfare of the occupied population.[284] Without providing protection to the environment and its natural resources, promoting welfare will be more complex and sometimes even impossible.

Accordingly, it is possible to suggest that there is a reciprocal relationship between the occupant's responsibility under the first part of Article 43 of the Hague Regulations to maintain the public order, civil life, and welfare in the occupied state and the protection of the environment, including the stable functioning of the ecosystem and also the biodiversity in the occupied state during the period of occupation. The more the environment is protected, the more stable, normal, and civil life the occupied people can have. Consequently, the more environmental issues are addressed by the occupying power, the more it can comply with its responsibility under Article 43 of the Hague Regulations.

By considering the second part of Article 43 of the Hague Regulations and applying the same abovementioned situation of occupation to the occupying power's responsibility under Article 43, as in the example of the US and the UK occupation of Iraq in 2003, it can be seen that, on various occasions, the occupying powers violated the Iraqi national environmental laws and regulations. The environmental violations in Iraq were increased due to the lack of acceptance of/disrespect for the Iraqi environmental laws and regulations, whether by the occupied forces themselves or by different groups aiming to cause damage to the environment for a range of reasons.[285]

According to Article (1) of the Iraqi Law of Protection and Improvement of the Environment No. (3) of the year 1997, "This law aims to protect and improve the environment, including regional waters, from pollution and limit its effects on health, the environment and natural resources".[286] Both occupying powers, the US and the UK, violated the Iraqi Environmental Law when oil pipelines were regularly targeted, resulting in serious spills.[287] Furthermore, "industrial facilities have also been targeted during conflicts by both state and non-state actors".[288]

283 The United Nations: Security Council, (S/RES/1483), (2003), para 4; Hanne Cuyckens, *Revisiting the Law of Occupation* (Brill Nijhoff 2018) 217.

284 ILC, 'First Report', para 50.

285 Hesham Bashir and Alaa Sbeita, *The Occupation of Iraq and Violations of the Environment and Cultural Property* (Al Manhal/The National Centre for Legal Issues 2013) 7–8; ILC, 'First Report', para 47; the UNEP, *Desk Study on the Environment in Iraq*, (2003), 71.

286 The Iraqi Law of Protection and Improvement of the Environment No. (3) of (1997). Article (1). (Iraqi Law of Protection and Improvement of the Environment, No. 27 of 2009, repeals Law No. 3 of 1997 on the protection and improvement of the environment).

287 Conflict and Environment Observatory: Country Brief: Iraq (Published: March 16, 2018). Available online at: < https://ceobs.org/country-brief-iraq/> Accessed date: 8 October 2020.

288 Ibid.

Moreover, a number of authors provided evidence that the US occupation troops dumped chemical, medical, weapons, and devices waste, which contained lead, cadmium, mercury, and some radioactive substances and toxic substances, near to groundwater sources, thus leading to their contamination.[289] Given that the groundwater moved from one place to another, pollution was transmitted with it, which in turn, led to the emergence of different diseases and infections, even in the animals that depended on the groundwater for their drinking. This contamination of such sources was especially acute in the western desert regions of Iraq.[290]

Moreover, the occupying powers of Iraq also polluted the Tigris and Euphrates rivers,[291] in particular, by attacking oil wells, which caused oil to leak into the rivers.[292] This resulted in widespread pollution, the killing of a wealth of fish, and the deaths of waterfowl that lived in their surroundings, such as wild ducks. Moreover, the pollution was transferred to humans, which impacted on their health.[293] That is, through the food-chain process and by infecting drinking water, this led to diseases such as cholera and dysentery.[294]

According to Article 19 of The Iraqi Law of Protection and Improvement of the Environment No. (3) of the year 1997, the following is prohibited: "Draining any industrial, agricultural, household, or service waste into rivers, water bodies, groundwater, air or land".[295] The same Article prohibits any act meant to "Drain any waste containing toxic materials such as pesticides, heavy metals and other toxic compounds into sewage networks and surfaces and make them in line with environmental controls and determinants".[296] Such acts not only constitute a violation of Articles (1) and (19) of the Iraqi Law of Protection and Improvement of the Environment, but also are a violation of Article 43 of the Hague Regulation and Article 64 of the GCIV, in accordance with the occupant's obligation to respect the domestic laws and regulations of the occupied territory.

Notably, the Iraqi Law of Protection and Improvement of the Environment No. (3) of 1997 was in force at the time of the US and the UK occupation of Iraq in 2003 and therefore, they were required to respect and not to violate the Iraqi national laws unless there was an absolute necessity.[297] The UNEP, in its pro-

289 Hesham Bashir and Alaa Sbeita, *The Occupation of Iraq and Violations of the Environment and Cultural Property* (Al Manhal/The National Centre for Legal Issues 2013) 70.
290 Ibid.
291 Ibid, 56.
292 Ibid, 69.
293 Ibid, 69-71.
294 Ibid, 71-72.
295 The Iraqi Law of Protection and Improvement of the Environment No. (3) of (1997). Article (19) Paragraph (1).
296 Ibid, Article (19) Paragraph (5).
297 Note that "This law has been repealed according to the Environmental Protection and Improvement Law No. (27) of (2009), and the regulations and instructions issued under Law No. 3 of 1997 remain in force in a manner that does not contradict the provisions of Law No. 27 of 2009 until the issuance of what replaces or repeals them". For more information about the Environmental Protection and Improvement Law No. (27) of (2009), see Republic of Iraq: Supreme Judicial

gress report about the environmental situation in Iraq in 2003, demanded that the Iraqi institutions for environmental governance at domestic and national levels be rebuilt, in relation to proper handling of the environmental issues.[298] The occupying powers in Iraq had created the so-called 'Coalition Provisional Authority' (CPA) to administer the territory of Iraq, and the CPA had established an interim Governing Council that assigned a new cabinet, including a Minster of the Environment.[299] However, the environmental problems continued during the whole period of the occupation, and experts claimed that the impacts on the Iraqi environment and the contamination of water sources would continue for a long time after the occupation ended.[300] It could be argued that the lack of acceptance of and/or disrespect for the environmental laws and regulations of an occupied state by the occupying power can lead to further environmental consequences, hence impacting upon the public order, civil life, and welfare of the local people living in the occupied territory.

A similar example to that above is Russia occupying and deliberately damaging areas of Georgia with large-scale fires in the occupied forests, which in turn, had grave consequences for Georgia's wildlife.[301] Such acts by the Russian occupation constituted a violation of Georgian environmental law. For example, Article 45(1) of the Georgian environmental law No. (519) of the year 1996 provides that "Natural ecosystems, landscapes and areas shall be protected from pollution, disturbance, damage, degradation, depletion and decomposition".[302] Furthermore, Article 45(2)(e) and (d) clearly includes the forests as a subject of the protection provided under Article 45.[303] Moreover, Article 46(2) of the same law provides protection to wildlife when its states that: "Any action that may cause damage to wildlife, habitats, breeding areas and migration routes shall be prohibited".[304]

Consequently, it is safe to say that the Russian occupying forces violated Georgian domestic environmental law when they deliberately destroyed by fire, on a large scale, green forests, with grave consequences for wildlife. Hence, Russia, as an occupying power in Georgia, also breached its obligations under Article 43 of the Hague Regulations, both the first and the second parts: the first concerns the duty of the occupant to restore and ensure the public order, civil life, and welfare of the occupied people, and the second pertains to the obligation of the occupying power to respect the domestic laws of the occupied state, which obviously Russia did not.

Council: Iraqi Legislation Database at: < http://iraqld.hjc.iq:8080/LoadLawBook.aspx?page=3&SC=220220063754564&BookID=21796>.

298 The United Nations Environment Programme (UNEP), 'Environment in Iraq: UNEP Progress Report', (2003), 29.

299 Ibid.

300 Hesham Bashir and Alaa Sbeita, *The Occupation of Iraq and Violations of the Environment and Cultural Property*, 71.

301 Hulme, 'Enhancing Environmental Protection', 238; International Law and Policy Institute, Protection of the Natural Environment in Armed Conflict: An Empirical Study (2014), 29–30.

302 Law of Georgia on Environmental Protection, (No. 519), of (1996). Article 45(1).

303 Ibid, Article 45 (2)(e) and (d).

304 Ibid, Article 46 (2).

As mentioned above, the Armenian occupation of the Azerbaijani territory of Nagorno-Karabakh involved deliberate environmental harm, such as intentionally destroying natural resources, polluting water sources, and blocking water canals, which impacted on agricultural lands and crops, along with the extreme utilisation of other natural resources in an unsustainable manner in the occupied region.[305]

According to a recent report published by the Presidential Library of the Republic of Azerbaijan, the Armenian occupation caused severe injuries to the environment and its elements, such as the cutting down and destruction of forests, which caused the termination of rare plants and animals exclusively living there,[306] as well as the destruction of water canals and water sources, which impacted on the productivity of crops in the occupied regions.[307] In addition to this, approximately 1,098,000 livestock have been lost because of the Armenian occupation, since 1989.[308]

The deliberate harm to the Azerbaijani occupied region's environment caused by the Armenian occupation has impacted on the biodiversity and the ecosystem.[309] Taking into account the applicability of Article 43 of the Hague Regulations and Article 64 of the GCIV in a time of occupation, Armenia, as an occupying power, has an obligation to respect the Azerbaijani domestic laws and regulations, along with the Armenian obligations under property rights norms in the time of occupation, the extent to which it may provide protection to the environment in the Azerbaijani occupied territory Nagorno-Karabakh. Further, this relies on how effectively the environment is protected under the environmental national laws and regulations of Azerbaijan.

According to the Law of the Republic of Azerbaijan about Environmental Protection of 1999 No. 678-IQ, and as amended in 2020, Article 3 provides that the basic principle of environmental protection includes "ensuring protection of biological diversity of the environment".[310] In addition to this, Article 62 of the same law states that "Natural complexes and sites of special environmental, scientific, cultural, and aesthetic interest inhabited by endangered species and land or water areas wholly or partially and temporarily or permanently off-limits to human activity shall be considered protected areas".[311] Moreover, the abovementioned report indicates that the occupied areas of Azerbaijan have several natural reserves and rare species of plants and animals,[312] and therefore these areas are protected

305 Bakhshiyeva, 'Threats and Provocations Originating from The Republic of Armenia', 113–116, 131; Administrative Department of the President of the Republic of Azerbaijan: Presidential Library, 21–24.

306 Administrative Department of the President of the Republic of Azerbaijan: Presidential Library, 13,15.

307 Ibid, 23–24.

308 Ibid, 34.

309 Bakhshiyeva, 'Threats and Provocations Originating from The Republic of Armenia', 113-116, 131; Administrative Department of the President of the Republic of Azerbaijan: Presidential Library, 15, 24.

310 Republic of Azerbaijan: Environmental Protection Law of (1999), (No. 678–IQ), Article 3.

311 Ibid, Article 62.

312 Administrative Department of the President of the Republic of Azerbaijan: Presidential Library, 15–34.

under Article 62 of the Environmental Protection Law 1999 of the Republic of Azerbaijan. Arguably, the acts conducted by the Armenian occupation constitute a breach of the domestic Environmental Protection Law 1999 of the Republic of Azerbaijan.

Armenia has been held legally accountable for respecting Azerbaijani environmental domestic law, in accordance with the caused damage to the Azerbaijani environment in the occupied areas of Azerbaijan. For instance, Article 78 of the same abovementioned law states that "Individuals and legal entities guilty of environmental safety violations shall be held accountable".[313] Moreover, as argued above, since the destruction of property in the occupied territory can have environmental dimensions, Armenia has been accused of destroying natural resources (property) along with causing other environmental injuries in the occupied parts of Azerbaijan.

Moreover, Article 79 (1) of the same law provides that "Legal entities and individuals responsible for damage to the environment, public health, and property of citizens, organizations, and the state shall make restitution as provided by law".[314] Furthermore, paragraph (5) of the same Article adds that "Full restitution shall be made for damage to the life and property of citizens caused by environmental safety violations".[315] It could be argued that the Armenian breach of the Azerbaijani environmental domestic law constitutes a violation of the former's obligations under the law of occupation as an occupying power, namely, to Article 43 of the Hague Regulations and Article 64 of the GCIV.

Furthermore, the domestic law of the occupying power may be considered as another source of obligations towards occupying forces, particularly when that power is a state party to one of the MEAs ratified by the parties of the conflict and implemented in the domestic laws, whether of the occupying power or the occupied one. For instance, since Palestine and Israel are both state parties to the Basel Convention,[316] they both have legal obligations under the convention. However, when Israel, as an occupying power, moved and dumped hazardous waste in the occupied West Bank in a way that conflicted with the Convention's obligations, it was not only violating its own obligation under the Basel Convention but was also breaching Palestinian environmental law, since according to Article (76) of this Law, "any natural or juridical person who causes environmental harm as a result of action or omission in contradiction with the provisions of this law or any international convention of which Palestine is part of, shall be compelled to the payment of convenient compensations in addition to the penal liability explicated in this law".[317] Notably, every international environmental treaty ratified by Palestine has

313 Republic of Azerbaijan: Environmental Protection Law of (1999), (No. 678–IQ), Article 78.
314 Ibid, Article 79 (1).
315 Ibid, Article 79 (5).
316 The Basel Convention on the Control of Transboundary Movements of Hazardous Wastes and their Disposal: Parties to the Basel Convention on the Control of Transboundary Movements of Hazardous Wastes and their Disposal.
317 'Palestinian Environmental Law' (1999), Article 76.

become a part of the domestic law,[318] and Israel, as an occupying power, as argued above, has obligations to respect the domestic environmental laws applicable in the occupied territory, according to what Article 43 of the Hague Regulations provides.

Moreover, according to the Basel Convention's Secretariat, Israel's acts are considered illegal and a violation of its obligations under the Convention, specifically, under Article 2(3) and 2(9).[319] The Secretariat added that these industrial zones are under Israeli jurisdiction and thus waste must be brought to Israel for disposal and not to the Palenstinian Auto's territory.[320] Consequently, Israel has violated the main aim of the Basel Convention and additionally, contravened Article 4(3) of the Basel Convention, which states that the illegal trafficking of hazardous waste is a criminal act under international law.[321]

However, it should be noted that the case of the Israeli occupation of Palestine can be more controversial and complex compared to the other mentioned examples of situations of occupation, in particular regarding the occupying power's duty to respect the domestic laws of the occupied territory. By way of explanation, the current domestic laws applicable in Palestine have been adopted by the Palestinian Authority (PA) during the time of the Israeli occupation there, including the environmental domestic laws and regulations. However, the law of occupation demands that the occupying power respect the national laws of the occupied territory that are in force at the time of occupation, and the application of the law in force in Palestine before the Israeli occupation is problematic. Hence, it is important to mention the other legal regimes that were applicable in Palestine before and at the time when Israel took over the OPT in 1967.

Multiple legal systems have an impact on the legal structures in the OPT. The division of Palestine also led to the emergence of complicated and varying legal systems in the West Bank, Gaza Strip, and Jerusalem in particular after 1948.[322] Regarding which, in 1948, Jordan took over the West Bank, including East Jerusalem. The West Bank submitted to the Jordanian legal system, which is influenced by the Latin legal system, and Egypt had administration over the Gaza Strip.[323] In 1967, when Israel took over and occupied the West Bank, Gaza Strip, and East Jerusalem, Jordanian law was still the main legal regime applicable to the West Bank and East Jerusalem, while British Mandate Law (Common Law) was still applicable and effective in the Gaza Strip.[324]

318 Ibid, Article 77.
319 The Basel Convention, Article 2(3), and 2(9).
320 Al-Haq Organization, 'Environmental Rights Case Succeeds in Holding Israel Accountable for Illegal Hazardous Waste Dumping in Palestine', (25 August 2016).
321 The Basel Convention, Article 4(3).
322 Birzeit University, Institute of Law, 'Legal Status in Palestine: Palestinian Judicial system: Historical Evolution of the Palestinian Legal System'; Gamal Abouali, 'Natural Resources under Occupation: The Status of Palestinian Water under International Law', (1998) 10 Peace International Law Review, 443–461.
323 Ibid.
324 Birzeit University, Institute of Law, *Legal Status in Palestine*.

Regarding the applicability of Jordanian law in the West Bank and East Jerusalem, it included some environmental and water laws and regulations that organised the use of the natural resources and the ownership of such resources, along with other related issues regarding such matters on both banks of the Jordan river.[325] However, after 1967, Israel had imposed military law (military orders).[326] Moreover, Israel had extended its internal water legal system to some areas in the OPT, while in some other areas, it had kept the operation of some aspects of Jordanian water laws and regulations. However, the occupying power used these provisions not as means of serving the needs of the local population in the OPT, but rather as means of strictly controlling Palestinian consumption of water.[327]

Consequently, there is no clear answer about the application of the law in force in Palestine before the Israeli occupation, and the issue is still problematic. This is especially so since the OPT has a variety of legal systems that were applicable before the Israeli occupation.[328]

In all the abovementioned instances, the occupying power breached its obligations under Article 43 of the Hague Regulations 1907 and Article 64 of the GCIV. These provisions demanded that the occupying power respect the domestic laws in force at the time of occupation for an occupied state. Unless there is an obvious threat caused by keeping these laws in force, it might impact on the security situation of the occupied state or constitute an obstacle to the application of IHL norms.[329] In addition to this, the occupying power may establish its own bodies to maintain the public order in the occupied state, if this is deemed necessary.[330]

Notably, the obligation of an occupying power to respect the environment in occupied territory is mainly derived from Article 43 of the Hague Regulations, as has been argued above.[331] Furthermore, this argument has been supported by the ILC Draft Principles Commentary Report. In particular, when the Report confirmed the general obligations of an occupying power under Draft Principle 20(1) in relation to the obligation to "respect and protect the environment of the occupied territory … and take environmental considerations into account in the administration of such territory", it drew upon Article 43 of the Hague Regulations, which requires the occupying power to consider the welfare of the occupied people and to restore and maintain public order and civil life in the occupied territory.[332] Noting that, the ILC, emphasises the idea that the protection of the environment and the

325 Abouali, 'Natural Resources under Occupation', 447–456.

326 Birzeit University, Institute of Law, *Legal Status in Palestine*.

327 Abouali, 'Natural Resources under Occupation', 456.

328 For more information about the legal system in Palestine, see Glenn Robinson, 'The Politics of Legal Reform in Palestine', (1997) 27 *Journal of Palestine Studies* 51.

329 The Hague Regulations 1907, Article 43.; the Fourth Geneva Convention 1949, Article 64.

330 The Fourth Geneva Convention 1949, Article 64 (2).

331 ILC, 'First Report', para 50.

332 The United Nations: General Assembly, 'Report of the International Law Commission', Seventy-first session, (29 April–7 June and 8 July–9 August 2019) (A/74/10) (20 August 2019). 'ILC Draft Commentary', 267–268.

welfare of the occupied population are linked to each other, especially, when it mentioned that, "the authentic French text of article 43 uses the expression '*l'ordre et la vie publics*', and the provision has been accordingly interpreted to refer not only to physical safety but also to the 'social functions and ordinary transactions which constitute daily life', in other words, to the entire social and economic life of the occupied region". The ILC added that, "this interpretation is also supported by the *travaux préparatoires*: in the Brussels Conference of 1874, where the term '*vie publique*' was interpreted as referring to '*des fonctions sociales, des transactions ordinaires, qui constituent la vie de tous les jours*'".[333] Therefore, it could be argued that the preparatory work of Article 43 of the Hague Regulations as mentioned in the Brussels Conference of 1874 can also be used to support the argument that the occupying power's obligation under Article 43 to consider the welfare of the occupied population and to ensure that it lives as normal a life as possible entails an environmental dimension.

Neither article includes the word "environment", as such; however, their extent must cover the issues of the environment in an occupied territory, as argued above, whether by ensuring that life in occupied territory continues as normally as possible under the occupant's temporary authority, and particularly, when the occupying power is asked to maintain the public order, civil life, and welfare of the local population during the time of occupation. Such an obligation needs to take into account the social and economic aspects of the ordinary life of the occupied territory. Hence, the perfect implementation of this duty would be impossible without taking into account the environmental considerations, along with respecting the domestic environmental laws and regulations of the occupied state.[334]

Against this background, it could be argued that there is sufficient evidence to support the claim that the occupying power's responsibility towards the protection of the environment in the occupied territory has a clear connection with its principle and duty of ensuring that the occupied people can continue to live as normal a life as possible. This can be achieved by maintaining and restoring public order, civil life, security, welfare, and well-being in the occupied territory, in accordance with its obligation under Article 43 of The Hague Regulations.[335] Arguably, the level of this responsibility can differ depending on the length of occupation, for

333 Ibid, under footnote No. 1290; see 'Actes de la Conférence de Bruxelles de 1874 sur le projet d'une convention internationale concernant la guerre' (1874), p. 23. Available online at: <https://babel.hathitrust.org/cgi/pt?id=mdp.35112104530417&seq=5&q1=vie+publique>. Accessed Date:02/Dec/2023. Please note, it was the Belgian delegate who suggested that "*la vie publique*" meant "*des fonctions sociales, des transactions ordinaires, qui constituent la vie de tous les jours*". For the English Language translation of the Brussels Conference of 1874 and other related information, see ICRC: IHL Databases: Project of an International Declaration concerning the Laws and Customs of War. Brussels, 27 August 1874. < https://ihl-databases.icrc.org/en/ihl-treaties/brussels-decl-1874?activeTab=undefined> ; ILC, 'First Report', para 43, footnote No. 175.

334 The Hague Regulations 1907, Article 43; The Fourth Geneva Convention 1949, Article 64.

335 The Hague Regulations 1907, Article 43; The ILC Draft Principles on Protection of the Environment in relation to Armed Conflicts, with Commentaries (2022), Draft Principle 19(2); Tristan Ferraro, 'The Law of Occupation and Human Rights Law: Some Selected Issues', in Robert Kolb,

as Lehto argued, the more protracted the occupation is, the more responsibility the occupant has to address the environmental issues.[336] Therefore, it would seem reasonable to conclude that both Articles 43 of the Hague Regulations and 64 of the GCIV can be used as effective instruments under the law of occupation to provide more active protection to the environment in situations of occupation.

2.4 The Protection of the Environment in Times of Occupation by Protecting Public Health and Hygiene in the Occupied Territory

This section starts by giving attention to the approach taken by the ILC special rapporteur (Marja Lehto) in 2018, when she linked public health and hygiene in the occupied territory under Article 56 of the GCIV to the occupying power's responsibility in regard to the protection of the environment.[337] The occupying power, under Article 56 of GCIV, has a duty to ensure and maintain public health and hygiene in the occupied state.[338] Thus, any impact on human health caused by contamination of the environment or environmental degradation by an occupying power in occupied territory (whether by intentionally polluting the environment or by disrespecting the national environmental laws and regulations of the occupied state) must be prohibited, according to Article 56 of the GCIV.[339] It is noteworthy that such acts against the environment, especially the contamination of the soil and water sources, might affect human health through the food-chain process, especially through contaminated grazing animals and marine life[340] upon which human populations may depend for nutrition.[341]

This argument has been supported by the ILC Draft Principles on Protection of the Environment in relation to Armed Conflicts. Draft Principle 19(2) confirmed that the occupying power shall take all possible measures to prevent significant environmental harm that might prejudice the health and well-being of the local population of the occupied territory.[342] Accordingly, there is a clear existence of a due diligence obligation upon the occupying power to take proactive measures to address urgent environmental problems in order to prevent any significant harm to the environment.[343] According to the ILC, "the obligation of due diligence can be

Gloria Gaggioli, *Research Handbook on Human Rights and Humanitarian Law* (Edward Elgar 2013) 279; ILC, 'First Report', paras 45, 47.

336 ILC, 'First Report', para 47.

337 Ibid, para 65–66.

338 The Fourth Geneva Convention, Article 56.

339 Hulme, 'Enhancing Environmental Protection', 210–211.

340 Omar, Bhat, and Asem, 'Critical Assessment of the Environmental Consequences of the Invasion of Kuwait, the Gulf War, and the Aftermath', 155.

341 Ibid.

342 The ILC Draft Principles on Protection of the Environment in relation to Armed Conflicts, with Commentaries (2022), Draft Principle 19(2).

343 The United Nations: General Assembly, 'Report of the International Law Commission', Seventy-first session, (29 April–7 June and 8 July–9 August 2019) (A/74/10) (20 August 2019). 'ILC Draft Commentary', 267–275; Draft Principle (21) of the ILC Draft Principles regarding the 'Protection

deduced from a number of international conventions as the standard basis for the protection of the environment from harm".[344] Therefore, it is safe to say that the due diligence obligation is also related to the protection of the environment in times of occupation, and that the occupant has a duty to consider such obligation in relation to preventing any significant harm to the environment in the occupied territory.

Interestingly, as the report of the ILC Draft Commentary provides, the crux of the Draft Principle 20(2)[345] relies on Article 55(1) of the AP1, which links the protection of the environment to the health or survival of the population.[346] The adoption of Article 55(1) of the AP1 reflects subsequent developments and increased awareness under IHL of the environmental harm in armed conflict situations to human health. More details about the AP1 1977 and the preparatory work of the AP1 will be provided in the following paragraphs. Furthermore, the report indicates the main purpose of the Draft Principle 20(2) is to confirm that significant harm to the environment could have grave consequences for the local people of the occupied territory and to emphasise the close link between the protection of the quality of the environment and biodiversity, as well as to ensure a viable and healthy ecosystem.[347]

The present author agrees that, considering the broad interpretation of Article 56 of the GCIV, any act against the environment that can affect public health and hygiene in an occupied territory must be a prohibited act in accordance with the Article, and that must include all kind of acts executed purposefully against the environment, since, as argued above, it might have direct and indirect consequences for public health and hygiene for the occupied territory's population.[348] Notably, the preparatory work of Article 56 of the GCIV did not address environmental issues and/or any other environmental-related considerations in occupied territory. The preparatory work discussed the duty of the occupying power to ensure and maintain the public health and hygiene of the occupied population, as well as to

---

of the Environment in relation to Armed Conflicts'; Longobardo, 'The Relevance of the Concept of Due Diligence for International Humanitarian Law', 73–75.

344 The United Nations: General Assembly, 'Report of the International Law Commission', Seventy-first session, (2019). 'ILC Draft Commentary', 279.

345 Please note, Draft Principle 20(2) mentioned in the text on this page now becomes with the 2022 edition Draft Principle 19(2).

346 The Additional Protocol I (1977), Article 55(1): "Care shall be taken in warfare to protect the natural environment against widespread, long-term and severe damage. This protection includes a prohibition of the use of methods or means of warfare which are intended or may be expected to cause such damage to the natural environment and thereby to prejudice the health or survival of the population". The United Nations: General Assembly, 'Report of the International Law Commission', Seventy-first session., (2019). 'ILC Draft Commentary', 272. (Please note that the present author is using the new Draft Principles order as has been adopted by the ILC in 2022, in which the Draft Principles are still the same but the numbering of them is different).

347 The United Nations: General Assembly, 'Report of the International Law Commission', Seventy-first session, (2019). 'ILC Draft Commentary', 270–271.

348 ILC, 'First Report', paras 65–66; Hulme, 'Enhancing Environmental Protection', 210–211.

take into consideration the occupied population's needs.[349] The analysis of Article 56 of the GCIV provided by the ILC Draft Commentary Report and the ILC's "First Report" constitute a cornerstone of considering Article 56 of the GCIV in relation to the protection of the environment in occupied territory. In particular, this can be seen when the ILC adopted similar language under Draft Principle 20(2) to that enshrined under Article 56 of the GCIV, linking the occupant's duty to protect the health of the occupied population to the occupant's duty to protect and to prevent any environmental harm and to take environmental considerations into account. Therefore, Article 56 of the GCIV can provide some protection to the environment in an occupied territory within the law of occupation itself.

2.5 The Protection of the Environment in Times of Occupation when there Are Active Hostilities or Attacks in the Occupied Territory

In addition to what has been discussed above, it is worth mentioning that Article 1(4) of the AP1 provides that "armed conflicts in which people are fighting against colonial domination, alien occupation or racist regimes are to be considered international conflicts".[350] Hence, there is always an opportunity for a potential military confrontation during times of occupation, and in this regard, Articles 35 and 55 of the AP1 provide a fundamental standard in relation to respecting and protecting the natural environment during any military attacks in times of occupation. Thus, it can apply in cases when the occupying power is intentionally attacking the occupied state's environment, such as with examples that have been mentioned previously in the chapter. Both Articles 35(3) and 55(1) are considered by the ICRC to be part of customary international humanitarian law.[351]

According to Article 35 (3) of the AP1, "It is prohibited to employ methods or means of warfare that are intended, or may be expected, to cause widespread, long-term and severe damage to the natural environment".[352] Furthermore, Article 55 of the same protocol states that "care shall be taken in warfare to protect the natural environment against widespread, long-term and severe damage. This protection includes a prohibition of the use of methods or means of warfare which are intended or may be expected to cause such damage to the natural environment and thereby to prejudice the health or survival of the population". [353]

349 For the origin of Article 56 of the GCIV 1949, see the preparatory work of the GCIV 1949: Final Record of the Diplomatic Conference of Geneva of 1949, Vol. I, at 122; Final Record of the Diplomatic Conference of Geneva of 1949, Vol. II-A, at: 666–668, 747–748, 830–831, 856–858; Final Record of the Diplomatic Conference of Geneva of 1949, Vol. II-B, at: 194, 418–421; Final Record of the Diplomatic Conference of Geneva of 1949, Vol. III, at: 135–136. All Volumes are available online at: < https://www.loc.gov/item/2011525350/>. Accessed date: 2 December 2023.

350 The Additional Protocol I (1977), Article 1(4).

351 Henckaerts and Doswald-Beck, *Customary International Humanitarian Law*, Rule 45.

352 The Additional Protocol I (1977), Article 35 (3).

353 Ibid, Article 55 (1).

Here, it is relevant to mention that there are some differences between these Articles, even though they share the same threshold: "widespread, long-term, and severe damage". Article 55(1) repeats the same prohibition on the use of methods and means provided under Article 35(3). However, Article 35(3) relates to all methods or means of warfare, whether on land, at sea, or in the air, while Article 55(1) pertains to the part dealing with the protection of the civilian population and their objects on land against the impact of hostilities.[354] Article 55(1) extends to a state's territorial waters, whereas Article 35(3) extends to the damage on the high seas.[355] Thus, it might be argued that Article 35(3) has a wider scope compared to that under Article 55(1). However, it must be said that both provisions are still important to provide protection to the environment in times of armed conflict and occupation.

Arguably, after significant endeavours by the international community to prohibit attacks against the environment, as mentioned under Article 35(3) and Article 55(1) of the AP1, this prohibition has been considered as a customary international law rule. Accordingly, all nations are bound by those two articles, even if they are not state parties to the AP1.[356] In addition, the ICRC has already considered both Articles 35(3) and 55(1) as customary law norms, such that the occupying power must be legally bound under these two provisions regarding any violation by attacks against the occupied state's environment during an occupation.[357]

The issue of the customary status regarding the prohibition of attacks against the environment under Article 35(3) and 55(1) of the AP1 requires more clarification since there are a few states, such as the US, UK and France, that do not agree upon the customary status of such a rule. As noted above, there are significant states practices around the world that support the emergence of such a prohibition to become a customary rule. Furthermore, this prohibition has been set in many states' military manuals.[358] In addition to this, causing widespread, long-term and severe damage to the environment is an offence under the local laws of a significant number of states, regardless of whether they are state parties or not to the AP1.[359] Widespread practice by the international community in terms of the methods of armed conflict and use of conventional weapons shows a widespread acceptance of the customary law nature of such a rule under Articles 35(3) and 55(1) of the AP1. However, the contrary practice of some states, such as the United States, the United

354 The Additional Protocol I (1997), Article 49(2). For further analysis of the differences between Article 35(3) and Article 55(1) of the Additional Protocol I, see A. P. V. Rogers, *Law on the Battlefield* (2nd edn, Manchester University Press 2004), 166–169.

355 See footnote No. 55, in Rogers, *Law on the Battlefield*, 168.

356 Henckaerts and Doswald-Beck, *Customary International Humanitarian Law* , Rule 45.

357 Ibid.

358 See, for example, the military manuals of the United Kingdom (page 316, para 12.24); Canada (page 4–13, para 446).

359 To see examples of states that adopted such prohibition in their legislation, see the list of states included in footnote No. 53 of Henckaerts and Doswald-Beck, *Customary International Humanitarian Law*, page 152, Rule 45.

Kingdom, and France, in this regard is not totally consistent.[360] For example, their statements in some contexts that the rule embodied under Articles 35(3) and 55(1) is not customary contradict those made in other contexts, particularly in their military manuals, in which such a rule is indicated as binding as long as it is not applied to nuclear weapons.[361] It could be argued that the contrary practice by those three states is not sufficient to consider such a rule as not a customary one.[362] Therefore, the author believes that this rule does reflect a customary IHL norm. However, the United States, the United Kingdom, and France should also be bound by this rule except as far as any use of nuclear weapons is concerned.[363]

The ILC Draft Principles on Protection of the Environment in relation to Armed Conflicts, namely Draft Principles 13(2) and 15, reflect the ICRC rules that relate directly to environmental protection in times of armed conflict, that is, Rules 43–45.[364] The ICRC Rules, especially Rules 43 and 44, as well as Draft Principles 13(2), 14, and 15 provisionally adopted by the ILC, reflect the general rules of protection of the environment under customary IHL during times of armed conflict.[365] The ICRC Rules mainly consider situations where the outbreak of hostilities takes place, and they might apply to situations of occupation where only active hostilities occur.[366]

As an example, the case of the Iraqi occupation of Kuwait in 1991 can be used, where grave environmental consequences resulted from deliberate harm to Kuwaiti territory. It has been argued that, even if Iraq had not ratified the AP1, it was still bound by Article 35/3 and 55/1, as these two Articles had become customary international law norms that must be respected by all states world-wide.[367]

It could be argued that, by considering the crux of Articles 35(3) and 55(1) of the AP1 away from the literal context of both articles, and by taking into account the broad interpretation and considering the concept of systematic destruction and the cumulative effects of the environmental degradation by an occupying power (in particular, in prolonged occupation), the environmental harm might cross the thresholds of widespread, long-term, and severe damage. For example, hazardous waste and dumping or moving of solid waste resulting from the occupying power's

360 Henckaerts and Doswald-Beck, *Customary International Humanitarian Law*, page 152, Rule 45.

361 See, for example, the military manuals of the United Kingdom (page 316, para 12.24); the United States of America (pages 378–379, 417–418).

362 Henckaerts and Doswald-Beck, *Customary International Humanitarian Law*, page 154, Rule 45.

363 For further discussion about the customary status of Article 35(3) and 55(1) of the API, see Karen Hulme, 'Natural Environment', in in Elizabeth Wilmshurst and Susan Breau (eds), *Perspectives on the ICRC Study on Customary International Humanitarian Law* (Cambridge University Press 2007) 228–233.

364 The ILC, Draft Principles on Protection of the Environment in relation to Armed Conflicts (2022). Principles 13(2) and 15.

365 Sjöstedt, *The Role of Multilateral Environmental Agreements*, 70–73.

366 Henckaerts and Doswald-Beck, *Customary International Humanitarian Law*, Rules 43–45.

367 Shilpi Gupta, 'Iraq's Environmental Warfare in the Persian Gulf', (1993) 6 *GEO INT'L ENVTL L REV* 251, 260. Cited in: Dieter Fleck (ed), *The Handbook of International Humanitarian Law* (2nd edn, Oxford University Press 2008) 251, 260.

activities, or any other kinds of detrimental activities by the occupying power's administration in an occupied state, may fall under the thresholds of Article 35(3) and Article 55(1) of the AP1. For instance, dumping and moving hazardous waste has been proven to have consequences for the environment, in particular by polluting soil, drinking-water sources, and agricultural areas as well as damaging crops.[368] Consequently, the thresholds of widespread, long-term, and severe damage could be met in such situations.

2.6 The Protection of the Environment in Times of Occupation under Other Provisions of the Law of Occupation

In this section, it will be argued how the protection of the environment in occupied territory is linked to the full implementation of other articles under the law of occupation. In particular, the articles that are keen to keep the occupied people living as normal life as possible and consider their welfare in the occupied territory are salient.

For example, there is possible environmental protection that could be provided under Article 55 of the GCIV. As already discussed above, Article 43 of the Hague Regulations demands that the occupying power ensures the maintenance of public order, civil life, and welfare of the occupied territory. Additionally, Article 55 of the GCIV has gone further and is more specific when it imposes on the occupying power the duty to ensure that the local people of an occupied territory have all the fundamental supplies to meet their basic needs.[369] It could, however, be argued that without environmental conservation, the full implementation of Article 55 of the GCIV would be impossible. Hence, providing fundamental supplies to the population of the occupied state would be impacted upon as well, and the lack of essential supplies would have an impact on the welfare of the population. Thus, it is a violation to the occupying power's duty under Article 43 to ensure welfare and public order in the occupied territory, since welfare and public order highly rely on the ability of the occupying power to provide as normal a life as possible for the local people living under occupation.

Arguably, the occupying power's responsibility to ensure that the local people of an occupied state have all their fundamental needs met might have environmental dimensions. In the first place, under Article 55 of the GCIV, for these needs to be met, the occupying power shall first depend on the resources of the occupied state itself, as the Article clearly requires the provision of food and medical supplies to the local people. As argued earlier, some food and some kinds of medicines are provided from the natural resources of the occupied territory, and without protecting the environment, such resources might be harmed, whether by the occupying

368 Jad Isaac, Khaldoun Rishmawi, 'Status of the Environment in the State of Palestine – 2015', (The Applied Research Institute (ARIJ) – Jerusalem 2015), 105.

369 The Fourth Geneva Convention IV. Article 55; Hans-Peter Gasser, 'Protection of the Civilian Population: Belligerent Occupation', 272.

power or by groups from the occupied territory itself. This will affect the occupant's ability to provide all fundamental supplies to the local populations in the occupied territory.

Furthermore, it could be reasonably argued that respecting and applying the national environmental laws and regulations of the occupied territory would help to protect such resources from getting harmed, since most states have adopted environmental laws that include specific provisions protecting natural resources and organising the legal use of such resources. Therefore, respecting the national environmental laws of the occupied territory could help in effectively implementing Article 55 of the GCIV and, in turn, provide some protection to the environment.

In cases where the occupying power has exploited the natural resources located in an occupied territory in an unsustainable manner that would definitely have an impact on the ability of occupied people to obtain their basic needs, the productivity of these resources would be decreased. That is, the basic needs of the occupied people could not be met in this case.

Additionally, the occupying power may intentionally damage the environment, as happened in Kuwait under the Iraqi occupation in 1991 and in Iraq under the US and UK occupation in 2003, where local people in both examples suffered from a lack of their basic and essential needs that they critically needed for their survival especially food and medical supplies, and one of the main reasons was the fact that the occupying power had intentionally destroyed their environment.

Therefore, the relationship between the occupying power's responsibility to ensure that local people continue to live as normally as possible during the time of occupation can be linked to the protection of the environment and keeping it as safe and protected as possible. In particular, Article 55 of the GCIV directly states that the occupying power should ensure that basic needs, including food and medical supplies, are provided from the resources of the occupied territory itself. Consequently, by ensuring the effective implementation of Article 43 of the Hague Regulations in terms of maintaining the civil life, public order, and welfare of the occupied people and giving them all their fundamental needs under Article 55 of the GCIV, some protection to the environment can be provided as well. Otherwise, the occupant will violate its obligations under both articles.

Furthermore, it is worth mentioning that the occupying power has a responsibility towards the occupied territory and its inhabitants under the law of occupation. For example, Article 29 of GCIV provides that "The Party to the conflict in whose hands protected persons may be, is responsible for the treatment accorded to them by its agents, irrespective of any individual responsibility which may be incurred".[370] The concept of the protected person under Article 4 of the GCIV is that "Persons protected by the Convention are those who, at a given moment and in any manner whatsoever, find themselves, in case of a conflict or occupation, in the hands

370 The Fourth Geneva Convention 1949, Article 29.

of a Party to the conflict or Occupying Power of which they are not nationals".[371] In the context of occupation, protected persons are the local people living in the occupied territory and living under the provisional and temporary authority of the occupant.[372] It could be argued that "as soon an adversary has control over a person or group of persons in accordance with Article 4 of the Fourth Geneva Convention the provisions relative to occupied territories are applicable".[373] Consequently, it is in this sense that the occupying power assumes responsibility for the local people and their occupied territory.[374]

By considering the relationship between the general responsibility of the occupying state under Article 29 of GCIV towards the occupied people and their territory to its responsibility under Article 43 of the Hague Regulations, involving the responsibility to ensure and maintain public order, civil life, and welfare in the occupied territory, the indirect protection of the environment can be provided as well. In particular, respecting the environment of the occupied territory should be considered the general occupying power's duty as well as maintaining the public order, civil life, and welfare of the occupied people under Article 43 of the Hague Regulations, as argued above.

Therefore, it could be argued that the occupying power's duty under Article 29 of the GCIV shall include environmental responsibilities as well, such as respect and prevention of any environmental harm against the occupied people or their territory. Otherwise, the effective implementation of both Articles 29 of the GCIV and 43 of the Hague Regulations would be impossible, since the occupying power is expected to administer the occupied territory for the benefit of the local people and fulfil the obligation to ensure that they can continue to live as normal a life as possible; both have a clear connection to the protection of the environment.[375]

Moreover, it is widely recognised that environmental protection is one of the public functions of the modern state.[376] Consequently, it is possible to assume that the occupying power, as an administration power over the occupied territory, has a responsibility under Article 29 of the GCIV to take the environmental considerations into account while it is still administering the occupied territory.

371 Ibid, Article 4.

372 Hans-Peter Gasser, 'Protection of the Civilian Population: Belligerent Occupation', 273; Dikker Hupkes, *What Constitutes Occupation? Israel as the Occupying Power in the Gaza Strip after the Disengagement* (E.M. Meijers Instituu 2008), 29–30; Kalandarishvili-Mueller, *Occupation and Control in International Humanitarian Law*, 147–148; International Committee of the Red Cross, Treaties, States Parties and Commentaries, Convention (IV) relative to the Protection of Civilian Persons in Time of War. Geneva, 12 August 1949. Commentary of 1958, Article 29.

373 Michael Siegrist, *The Functional Beginning of Belligerent Occupation* (Geneva Graduate Institute 2011). Available online at: < https://books.openedition.org/iheid/94#bodyftn24>. Accessed date: 3 December 2023.

374 Hans-Peter Gasser, 'Protection of the Civilian Population: Belligerent Occupation', 273.

375 ILC, 'First Report', para 50.

376 Ibid.

2.7 Conclusion

This chapter has set out an analytical framework of the law of occupation in relation to the protection of the environment during times of occupation. It has been argued that the Hague Regulations, the GCIV, and the AP1 constitute the main parts of the law of occupation. Moreover, it is held that they can all provide protection to the environment, even if most of the time, the provided protection is indirect. However, they still set limitations and obligations that the occupying power must consider while it administers the occupied territory, and by taking into account these obligations and responsibilities, the protection of the environment can be provided as well.[377]

The first part of the chapter discussed the main principles governing the situation of occupation by linking the conservationist principle to the occupying power's obligation to keep the status of the occupied territory as it was before the occupation occurred. This includes respecting the domestic laws and regulations while emphasising the occupant's temporary position there, and this can include the environmental dimension.

In the second part of the chapter, it was argued that possible protection could be provided by the effective implementation of the property rights provisions under the law of occupation, such as Article 55 of the Hague Regulations 1907. Furthermore, the occupying power's obligation to protect, respect, and consider the public order, civil life, welfare, and well-being of the occupied people along with respecting the domestic laws and regulations of the occupied territory has been advocated in the third section of the chapter. Article 43 of the Hague Regulations was drawn upon in order to provide protection to the environment in occupied territory by considering the perfect implementation of Article 43 of the Hague Regulations along with the duty of the occupant under Article 64 of the GCIV, namely the part asking the occupying power to respect the applicable national laws of the occupied territory. Examples have been given from the experience of Iraq, Azerbaijan, Georgia, and Palestine, with consideration of the occupying power's responsibilities in accordance with those nations' environmental laws.

Consequently, it is possible to conclude that, if an occupying power disregards the occupied territory's property rights, public order, civil life, welfare, and national environmental laws and regulations, the occupants' activities will continue to cause harm and depletion of the environment, which could lead to degradation of the ecosystem and thus have negative consequences for the long-term biodiversity of the occupied territory.[378] Accordingly, this author is convinced that the occupying power has an obligation under the law of occupation to consider, respect, and protect the environment in the occupied territory and to take environmental considerations into account while it is administering the occupied territory.[379]

377 Ibid, para 40.
378 The UNEP, *Environmental Assessment of the Gaza Strip*, (2009), 38.
379 ILC, 'First Report', para 50.

In short, and according to what has been illustrated so far, even though IHL rules provide protection to the environment in occupied territories, this is not always explicit or sufficiently adequate to ensure that the protection of the environment in times of occupation is completely effective. Therefore, the following chapter examines environmental protection under IHRL and argues that this can be linked to the extent that the population of the occupied territory can enjoy their fundamental rights, such as the right to life and the right to health.

3 The Role of International Human Rights Law in the Protection of the Environment in Times of Occupation

This chapter will focus on how damage to the environment in times of occupation has a tangible impact on the enjoyment of human rights by individuals living in occupied territory. It analyses the protection of the environment in times of occupation through International Human Rights Law (IHRL), with the aim of ascertaining whether it fills the gaps where the law of occupation is silent – as has been already argued in the previous chapter. Additionally, it examines how environmental protection in times of occupation can contribute to the enjoyment of a number of human rights for the occupied people.

In a contemporary world, more than ever, environmental damage and degradation clearly have an adverse impact on the quality of human life and the full enjoyment of human rights.[1] Environmental damage can lead to the violation of specific human rights, including the right to life, health, housing, self-determination, and property, as well as to the right to a clean and healthy environment. This chapter explores the role of IHRL in relation to the protection of the environment in occupied territory. The question as to how IHRL obligations can contribute to the protection of the environment in occupied territory is addressed.

It should be stressed not only that environmental harm raises issues of human rights, but also that the failure to protect such rights can lead to further environmental degradation as well as prevent any progress towards environmental protection.[2] Bearing that in mind, the legal impact of occupation extends only to territories over which the occupant exercises effective control. This point is of crucial importance for the application of IHRL in occupied territory, since "the relationship between the Occupying Power as the temporary holder of authority and the population under its control seems an invitation for human rights law given that it is crafted for precisely such a relationship".[3] Thus, it is normal that international law imposes a

1 David Hunter, James Salzman, and Durwood Zaelke, *International Environmental Law and Policy* (5th edn, Foundation Press 2015) 1323.

2 Ibid, 1324.

3 Gerd Oberleitner, *Human Rights in Armed Conflict: Law, Practice, Policy* (Cambridge University Press 2015) 222.

DOI: 10.4324/9781003518068-3

set of strict responsibilities upon the occupying power, aiming to protect the rights of the civilian populations living in the occupied territory.[4]

Before considering the role of IHRL in the protection of the environment in occupied territory, it is necessary to establish that such law applies in situations of occupation and is not entirely displaced by IHL. Subsequently, the complementary role between the law of occupation and human rights law is examined, with the objective of determining the occupying power's responsibilities towards the environment in the occupied territory. Finally, some of the contemporary and debatable issues regarding environmental human rights and the right to a healthy environment in situations of occupation are addressed. An analytical framework for IHRL and environmental protection in situations of occupation is provided throughout the chapter.

In the words of Lynda Collins, environmental rights are "arguably the most universal form of human rights, since they derive from the basic biological needs of all humans, transcending national borders and legal traditions".[5] Accordingly, it is necessary to bring environmental rights and the protection of the environment in times of occupation under IHRL into the spotlight, with the aim being to provide a more comprehensive analysis of the issue.

Examples from different occupied territories around the world, such as the Russian occupation of Crimea in Ukraine, the Moroccan occupation of Western Sahara, the Israeli occupation of the OPT, and some other examples, are discussed in detail to demonstrate how environmental harm by the occupying power can affect the enjoyment of several human rights in such situations. The harm inflicted includes the right to life, health, self-determination, property, and privacy under both covenants of human rights, as well as under the European Convention on Human Rights (ECHR) and other international and regional human rights declarations and conventions.

3.1 The Application of International Human Rights Law in Times of Occupation

3.1.1 Continuing Application of IHRL in Armed Conflict and Occupation

The applicability of IHRL in times of occupation and its relationship with IHL have been a subject of debate for a long time, and have been discussed extensively by international law scholars.[6] Today, it is widely recognised that IHRL applies in

4 Ilias Bantekas and Lutz Oette, *International Human Rights Law and Practice* (3rd edn, Cambridge University Press 2020) 731.

5 Lynda Collins, 'The United Nations, Human Tights and the Environment', in Anna Grear and Louis Kotzé (eds), *Research Handbook on Human Rights and the Environment* (Edward Elgar 2015) 222.

6 See e.g. Arai-Takahashi, *The Law of Occupation*, 401–407; Longobardo, *The Use of Armed Force in Occupied Territory*, 62; Benvenisti, *The International Law of Occupation*, 12–15; Sylvain Vité, 'Occupation' in Ben Saul and Dapo Akande (eds), *The Oxford Guide to International Humanitarian Law* (OUP 2020) 300–303, 314.

times of occupation.[7] However, there are still some issues that raise the question of its practical applicability in such circumstances.[8] This section briefly explores some of these issues before examining the potential applicability of IHRL in the protection of the environment in an occupied territory.

In 1996, in the Nuclear Weapons Advisory Opinion, the International Court of Justice (ICJ) held that IHRL applies to situations of armed conflict.[9] However, whether the Court's opinion was the basis for a broader application of IHRL extraterritorially to situations of armed conflict and occupation remains unclear.[10]

The International Law Commission (ILC) in the draft articles on the effects of armed conflicts on treaties provides that IHRL treaties continue to be in operation in times of armed conflict.[11] Moreover, some IHRL conventions allow for derogations in times of war; thus they implicitly recognise that these conventions are applicable in armed conflict.[12]

In addition to this, during an occupation, the occupying power must govern a territory in a way similar to what it used to be in peacetime, where the relationship between the government of the occupied territory and its people is regulated by human rights.[13] To explain the issue in more detail, first, one has to assess whether IHRL obligations are set aside in favour of IHL, and only the latter regulates the situation of occupation; or whether IHRL is *per se* applicable in such situations, along with IHL. There are two possible scenarios for applying IHRL to the situations of occupation.

The first scenario is the extraterritorial application of IHRL and how the occupying power may carry out its human rights obligations while it is exercising effective control outside its own sovereign territory. As the previous chapter explained, occupation means exercising authority beyond one's borders, and in relation to applying IHRL obligations extraterritorially, a state must exercise effective control over another territory and/or persons.[14] The second scenario is when the occupying

7 See e.g. René Provost, *International Human Rights and Humanitarian Law* (Cambridge University Press 2002) 19. Contra, see Michael Dennis, 'Application of Human Rights Treaties Extraterritorially in Times of Armed Conflict and Military Occupation' (2005) 99 *American Journal of International Law* 119–141, 119.

8 Noam Lubell, 'Human Rights Obligations in Military Occupation' (2012) 94 *International Review of the Red Cross*, 318.

9 Legality of the Threat or Use of Nuclear Weapons, Advisory Opinion, I. C.J. Reports 1996, para 25.

10 Michael Dennis, 'Application of Human Rights Treaties Extraterritorially in Times of Armed Conflict and Military Occupation' (2005) 99 *American Journal of International Law* 119, 119.

11 'Draft Articles on the Effects of Armed Conflicts on Treaties', with commentaries. Adopted by the International Law Commission at its 63rd session in 2011, and submitted to the General Assembly as a part of the Commission's report covering the work of that session, UN Doc (A/66/10), draft Article 7.

12 See e.g. Article 4 of the International Covenant on Civil and Political Rights, 1966; Article 15 of the European Convention on Human Rights, 1950; Article 27 of the American Convention on Human Rights, 1969.

13 Longobardo, *The Use of Armed Force in Occupied Territory*, 69–71.

14 Oberleitner, *Human Rights in Armed Conflict: Law, Practice, Policy*, 224.

power is deemed to have taken over the ousted government's IHRL obligations, without any necessity to consider the extraterritorial application of IHRL.[15]

A detailed analysis of all cases and views on the application of IHRL in times of armed conflict and occupation will not be feasible in these pages; however, the following paragraphs will serve to point out some of the key concerns and approaches to this issue in such situations.

3.1.2 Extraterritorial Application of IHRL to Situations of Occupation

The argument that IHRL does apply extraterritorially to situations of armed conflict and occupation has been widely asserted, in particular, by the jurisprudence of the International Court of Justice (ICJ) and the European Court of Human Rights (ECtHR), Human Rights Committee (HRC), and different UN human rights bodies. The idea that IHRL applies extraterritorially when an occupation is established has been confirmed by the ICJ on a number of occasions. For example, in its advisory opinion on the *Legal Consequences of the Construction of a Wall in the Occupied Palestinian Territory*, it stated that

> the Court considers that the protection offered by human rights conventions does not cease in case of armed conflict … As regards to the relationship between international humanitarian law and human rights law, there are three possible situations: some rights may be exclusively matters of international humanitarian law; others may be exclusively matters of human rights law; yet others may be of both these branches. In order to answer the question, the Court will have to take into consideration both these branches of international law, namely human rights law and, as *lex specialis*, international humanitarian law.[16]

Specifically, the ICJ has provided the extraterritorial application of the International Covenant on Civil and Political Rights (ICCPR), the International Covenant on Economic, Social and Cultural Rights (ICESCR), and the United Nations Convention on the Rights of the Child (UNCRC) in the context of outside of the State Parties' borders (extraterritorially) and under what circumstances.[17] For instance, in the Wall Advisory Opinion, the Court examined the scope of application of the ICCPR when it discussed the issue as it has been defined under Article 2 (1) of the ICCPR, which provides the following:

> Each State Party to the present Covenant undertakes to respect and to ensure all individuals within its territory and subject to its jurisdiction the rights recognized in the present Covenant, without distinction of any kind, such as

15 Ibid.

16 ICJ, Wall Advisory Opinion, para 106.

17 Ibid, para 107.

> race, colour, sex, language, religion, political or other opinion, national or social origin, property, birth or other status.[18]

Additionally, the Court argued that

> this provision can be interpreted as covering only individuals who are both present within a state's territory and subject to that state's jurisdiction. It can also be construed as covering both individuals present within a state's territory and those outside that territory but subject to that state's jurisdiction.[19]

Moreover, in the same Advisory Opinion, the Court stated that

> while the jurisdiction of States is primarily territorial, it may sometimes be exercised outside the national territory. Considering the object and purpose of the *International Covenant on Civil and Political Rights*, it would seem natural that, even when such is the case, state parties to the Covenant should be bound to comply with its provisions.[20]

Hence, the ICJ confirmed that the ICCPR is "applicable in respect of acts done by a state in the exercise of its jurisdiction outside its own territory".[21] Furthermore, in the same Advisory Opinion, some states argued in favour of the extraterritorial application of the ICCPR and other human rights treaties.[22]

The ICJ, in the same Advisory Opinion, also addressed the issue of the ICESCR in particular, when it held that it "contains no provision on its scope of application. This may be explicable by the fact that this Covenant guarantees rights which are essentially territorial. However, it is not to be excluded that it applies both to territories over which a state party has sovereignty and to those over which that state exercises territorial jurisdiction".[23]

Furthermore, the Court mentioned the Committee's own Economic, Social and Cultural Rights perspective, which confirmed that "the State party's obligations under the Covenant apply to all territories and populations under its effective control".[24] Additionally, the ICJ affirmed that

> the territories occupied by Israel … have been subject to its territorial jurisdiction as the occupying power. In the exercise of the powers available to it

18 Ibid, para 108.

19 Ibid.

20 Ibid, para109.

21 Ibid, para 111.

22 For more detail about States' 'Written proceedings' in the Wall ADvistory Opinion, see: <https://www.icj-cij.org/en/case/131/written-proceedings>. See also Oberleitner, *Human Rights in Armed Conflict: Law, Practice, Policy*, 151.

23 ICJ, Wall Advisory Opinion, para 112.

24 Ibid; the United Nations, Economic and Social Council, Committee on Economic, Social and Cultural Rights, 'CONSIDERATION OF REPORTS SUBMITTED BY STATE PARTIES UNDER ARTICLES 16 AND 17 OF THE COVENANT: Concluding Observations of the Committee on Economic, Social and Cultural Rights (Israel)', (E/C.12/1/Add.90), (26 June 2003), para 31.

> on this basis, Israel is bound by the provisions of the International Covenant on Economic, Social and Cultural Rights. Furthermore, it is under an obligation not to raise any obstacle to the exercise of such rights in those fields where competence has been transferred to Palestinian authorities.[25]

As regard to the UNCRC, the Court applied the same logic as the ICCPR and ICESCR, arguing that Article 2 of the UNCRC provides that "State Parties shall respect and ensure the rights set forth in the … Convention to each child within their jurisdiction". Thus, the UNCRC is also applicable within the OPT.[26] Accordingly, the ICJ confirmed the applicability of both UN Covenants, as well as other human rights conventions, such as the UNCRC, to the situation in the OPT.[27]

It could be argued that the logic of the ICJ behind considering the abovementioned IHRL documents applicable extraterritorially to the OPT is because Israel as an occupying power is exercising effective control over such territories, and therefore, the ICJ considered the extraterritorial jurisdiction to be arising based on such control.[28] Thus, Israel was bound by those documents based on such logic.[29]

Another example where the ICJ has considered the extraterritorial application of IHRL instruments in times of occupation can be found in the *DRC v. Uganda* case.[30] The Court considered the extraterritorial application of several human rights treaties, such as the ICCPR, UNCRC, UNCRC Optional Protocol, and African Charter of Human Rights.[31] Notably, the ICJ in the same case clearly affirmed the application of IHRL, along with IHL, in the occupied territory.[32] For example, the Court stressed that the occupying power's obligation to ensure public order under Article 43 of the Hague Regulations comprises its "duty to secure respect for the applicable rules of international human rights law and international humanitarian law, to protect the inhabitants of the occupied territory".[33]

Arguably, the ICJ's logic in the *DRC v. Uganda* case of considering the extraterritorial application of IHRL to the DRC was also based on the fact that Uganda was an occupying power, and it was exercising effective control over the territory

25 ICJ, Wall Advisory Opinion, para 112.

26 Ibid, para 113; UNCRC, Article 2.

27 Ibid, paras 107–113. Under Paragraph 109 of the same case, the Court stated that "while the jurisdiction of States is primarily territorial, it may sometimes be exercised outside the national territory". For more detail and similar cases about the applicability of International Human Rights Law where the State exercises its jurisdiction on foreign territory, see: It has ruled on the legality of acts by Uruguay in cases of arrests carried out by Uruguayan agents in Brazil or Argentina (*López Burgos v. Uruguay* case), (No. 52/79).

28 ICJ, Wall Advisory Opinion, paras 109, 112.

29 Ibid, paras 109, 112–113.

30 ICJ, *DRC v. Uganda*, paras 216, 345.

31 Ibid, paras 217, 219; Ralph Wilde, 'Human Rights Beyond Borders at the World Court: The Significance of the International Court of Justice's Jurisprudence on the Extraterritorial Application of International Human Rights Law Treaties', (2013) 12 *Chinese Journal of International Law* 639, 660–661.

32 ICJ, *DRC v. Uganda*, para 178.

33 Ibid.

of the DRC.[34] As Kalandarishvili-Mueller pointed out, when a state exercises effective control over another state's territory, that gives rise to IHRL obligations.[35]

Additional evidence that the IHRL applies in situations of occupation extraterritorially is the ICJ judgment in the *Georgia v. Russian Federation* case of 2011.[36] Here, Russia had effective control represented by "exercising governmental authority" over Abkhazia and South Ossetia.[37] It meant that the standard for determining jurisdiction under human rights treaties was applied over those territories. In 2008, both Georgia and Russia were parties to the Convention on the Elimination of All Forms of Racism (CERD).[38] After holding public hearings and Russia's preliminary objections, the Court declared that Russia's obligations under the Convention extended to acts and omissions attributable to it, which had their locus within Georgia's territory and in particular, in Abkhazia and South Ossetia.[39]

Nonetheless, it is still important to argue for and demonstrate in more detail the issue of the applicability of IHRL conventions and how they could bind states' actions that are undertaken extraterritorially, in this case, in occupied territory.[40] Thus, it is necessary to first investigate the approach of the UN human rights conventions regarding the jurisdiction clauses. However, before doing so, it should briefly be explained what jurisdiction means, thus facilitating understanding of the logic behind the extraterritorial application of IHRL to situations of occupation. State jurisdiction means "the capacity of governmental conduct to affect the individual enjoyment of a right", and it is related to the relationship between the persons and the state in regard to any violation of their rights, as protected by IHRL conventions.[41] In this regard, Kalandarishvili-Mueller stated that the extraterritorial application of IHRL depends on one key element, which is "exercise of jurisdiction", and that means "a state exercising control over an individual (personal connection) and over territory (spatial connection)".[42] If this is the case, IHRL treaties will apply.[43] Therefore, the notion of jurisdiction is linked also to the extraterritorial control exercised by a state over an individual or a territory, and not limited to a state's national territory and borders.[44]

34 Ibid, 180, 216.

35 Kalandarishvili-Mueller, *Occupation and Control in International Humanitarian Law*, 151.

36 Application of the International Convention on the Elimination of All Forms of Racial Discrimination (*Georgia v. Russian Federation*), Preliminary Objections, Judgment, I.C.J. Reports 2011, p. 70.

37 Ibid, paras 16, 17(1), and 111.

38 Ibid.

39 Ibid, See also, similar to the *Georgia v. Russian Federation* case, a pending case before the ICJ between *Ukraine v. Russian Federation* regarding the application of the International Convention on the Elimination of All Forms of Racial Discrimination in such circumstances. This can reinforce the argument that the occupying power has a duty to respect and apply human rights norms to the occupied territory.

40 For more information about the extraterritorial application of human rights conventions, see Marko Milanovic, *Extraterritorial Application of Human Rights Treaties: Law, Principles, and Policy* (Oxford University Press 2011).

41 Longobardo, *The Use of Armed Force in Occupied Territory*, 68.

42 Kalandarishvili-Mueller, *Occupation and Control in International Humanitarian Law*, 142–143.

43 Ibid.

44 Longobardo, *The Use of Armed Force in Occupied Territory*, 68.

The ICCPR is the only human rights treaty with such a dual requirement, specifically, by the strict language and using the word "and" as a cumulative demand the duality of "territory" and "jurisdiction", so that only persons who are in the territory and fall under the jurisdiction of a state party are covered and protected by Covenant.[45] However, there is another possible and alternative interpretation to the meaning of Article 2(1) of the ICCPR: the obligation of the State Party to the Covenant covers all individuals within the territory and also within its jurisdiction, even if they are not within its territory, for they are still subject to its jurisdiction.[46]

The first interpretation is more literal, and the reading is more specific, with the cumulative requirement of Article 2(1) of the ICCPR. However, the ICJ in the Wall Advisory Opinion argued that the Covenant also covers "both individuals present within a state's territory and those outside that territory but subject to that state's jurisdiction".[47] Moreover, the HRC in its General Comment (No. 31) on the Nature of the General Legal Obligation Imposed on State Parties to the ICCPR held that "a State party must respect and ensure the rights laid down in the Covenant to anyone within the power or effective control of that State Party, even if not situated within the territory of the State Party".[48] In addition, "this principle also applies to those within the power or effective control of the forces of a State Party acting outside its territory, regardless of the circumstances in which such power or effective control was obtained, etc.".[49] In addition to this, the Committee added that "the Covenant applies also in situations of armed conflict to which the rules of international humanitarian law are applicable. While, in respect of certain Covenant rights, more specific rules of international humanitarian law may be especially relevant for the purposes of the interpretation of Covenant rights, both spheres of law are complementary, and not mutually exclusive".[50]

Furthermore, the HRC on a different occasion argued that "it would be unconscionable to interpret the responsibility under Article 2 of the Covenant as to permit a state party to perpetrate violations of the Covenant on the territory of another state, whose violations it could not perpetrate on its own territory".[51] Moreover, the Second Optional Protocol to the ICCPR only contains jurisdiction clauses without

45 See Article 2 (1) of the ICCPR, "Each State Party to the present Covenant undertakes to respect and to ensure to all individuals within its territory and subject to its jurisdiction the rights recognized in the present Covenant". See Dominic McGoldrick, 'The Extraterritorial Application of the International Covenant on Civil and Political Rights' in Fons Coomans and Menno Kamminga (eds), *Extraterritorial Application of Human Rights Treaties* (Intersentia-Antwerp 2004) 47–48.

46 McGoldrick, 'The Extraterritorial Application', 47–48.

47 ICJ, Wall Advisory Opinion, para 108.

48 UN Human Rights Committee (HRC), General Comment No. 31 [80], The nature of the general legal obligation imposed on State Parties to the Covenant, (26 May 2004), (CCPR/C/21/Rev.1/Add.13), para 10.

49 Ibid.

50 Ibid, para 11.

51 The Human Rights Committee, *Sergio Euben Lopez Burgos v. Uruguay*, Communication No. R.12/52, U.N. Doc. Supp. No. 40 (A/36/40) at: 176 (1981), para 12.3.

any reference to the word "territory".[52] Thus, it is rejecting the cumulative demand and the duality of "territory" and "jurisdiction" under Article 2 (1) of the ICCPR.

Similarly, the UNCRC refers only to the word "jurisdiction", without mentioning the word "territory" at all. For example, Article 2(1) of the Convention provides that "State Parties shall respect and ensure the rights set forth in the present Convention to each child within their jurisdiction without discrimination of any kind".[53] In addition to this, the Committee on the Rights of the Child in its General Comment No. 6 on Articles 38 of the Convention and Articles 3 and 4 of the Optional Protocol to the Convention on the Rights of the Child on the involvement of children in armed conflict held that these provisions "entail extraterritorial effects".[54]

Furthermore, the Convention on the Protection of the Rights of All Migrant Workers (CMW) replaces the word "and" used in the ICCPR by the word "or", so it is "within their territory or subject to their jurisdiction".[55] Hence, the abovementioned human rights treaties are denying the specific cumulative demand of both "territory and jurisdiction", as provided in the ICCPR.

All the abovementioned treaties – ICESCR, CEDAW, and the Convention on the Rights of Persons with Disabilities (CRPD) – do not include a general jurisdiction clause. In fact, the ICESCR contains no provision on its scope of application at all. The ICJ in the Wall Advisory Opinion, as mentioned above, considered that the ICESCR "applies both to territories over which a State party has sovereignty and to those over which that State exercises territorial jurisdiction".[56] Furthermore, the Committee on Economic, Social and Cultural Rights clearly affirmed that State Parties to the Covenant must apply and respect the provisions of the Covenant to all territories and populations under its effective control.[57] Along with the ICJ's

52 For example, the Second Optional Protocol to the International Covenant on Civil and Political Rights, aiming at the abolition of the death penalty, (adopted and proclaimed by General Assembly Resolution (44/128) of (15 December 1989). Article (1) Para (1): "No one within the jurisdiction of a State Party to the present Protocol shall be executed". And Para (2): "Each State Party shall take all necessary measures to abolish the death penalty within its jurisdiction".

53 Convention on the Rights of the Child (adopted and opened for signature, ratification, and accession by General Assembly Resolution (44/25) of (20 November 1989), (entry into force 2 September 1990). Article 2(1).

54 UN Committee on the Rights of the Child (CRC), General comment No. 6 (2005): Treatment of Unaccompanied and Separated Children Outside their Country of Origin, (1 September 2005), (CRC/GC/2005/6), para 28.

55 International Convention on the Protection of the Rights of All Migrant Workers and Members of Their Families (adopted by General Assembly Resolution (45/158) of (18 December 1990). Article (7) provides that "State Parties undertake, in accordance with the international instruments concerning human rights, to respect and to ensure to all migrant workers and members of their families within their territory or subject to their jurisdiction etc.".

56 ICJ, Wall Advisory Opinion, para 112.

57 The United Nations, Economic and Social Council, Committee on Economic, Social and Cultural Rights, 'CONSIDERATION OF REPORTS SUBMITTED BY STATE PARTIES UNDER ARTICLES 16 AND 17 OF THE COVENANT: Concluding Observations of the Committee on Economic, Social and Cultural Rights (Israel)', (E/C.12/1/Add.90), (26 June 2003), para 31.

interpretations and the comments from the Committee of the ICESCR on the scope of the application, it is safe to assume that the ICESCR extends to include all territories and populations under the effective control of one of the State Parties to the Convention that is exercising jurisdiction outside of its own borders.[58] Accordingly, the ICESCR applies to the situations of occupation as well. It seems reasonable to argue that human rights conventions, generally and the ICCPR, specifically, are applicable in the situations of occupation, and they are allowing for the extraterritorial application of their obligations under such terms.[59]

Moving on to regional treaties, the ECHR does not mention the word "territory" in relation to the scope of its application, but it obliges State Parties to the Convention to "secure to everyone within their jurisdiction" the rights and freedoms under the Convention.[60] Nowadays, jurisdiction under the ECHR is understood as covering extraterritorial activities outside the borders of state parties to the Convention.[61] In particular, the scope of extraterritorial jurisdiction under the Convention has been progressively clarified in several cases on Article 1 over the last decade. It was especially relevant in cases considering the extraterritorial application of the ECHR in the situation of occupation for a range of territories, such as Cyprus, Georgia, and Iraq.[62] For example, the ECtHR in the *Loizidou v. Turkey* case provided that "the obligation to secure, in such an area, the rights and freedoms set out in the Convention derives from the fact of such control whether it be exercised directly, through its armed forces, or through a subordinate local administration".[63] Another similar judgment was given in accordance with the Turkish occupation of Northern Cyprus, when the ECtHR declared that Turkey was obliged by the ECHR provisions in the territory of the occupied Northern Cyprus.[64]

Similarly, in the *Al-Skeini v. the United Kingdom,* and *Al-Jedda v. the United Kingdom* cases,[65] the ECtHR considered the extraterritorial application of the ECHR outside of the State Parties' jurisdiction, namely, during the occupation

58 Ibid.

59 Andreas Zimmermann, 'Extraterritorial Application of Human Rights Treaties – The Case of Israel and the Palestinian Territories Revisited', in Isabelle Buffard, James Crawford, Alain Pellet, and Stephan Wittich (eds), *International Law between Universalism and Fragmentation* (Martinus Nijhoff 2008) 763–764; Murray, *Practitioners' Guide to Human Rights Law in Armed Conflict*, 66, para 3.30 (a).

60 See the ECHR, (1950), Article (1).

61 Oberleitner, *Human Rights in Armed Conflict: Law, Practice, Policy*, 154. For example, see *Loizidou v. Turkey*, ECtHR, (Appl. No 40/1993), (435/514), Preliminary Objection of 23 February 1995; *Al-Jedda v. the United Kingdom*, Grand Chamber, Judgment (2011) ECtHR (App No 27021/08); *Al-Skeini and Others v. the United Kingdom* (Appl. No. 55721/07), (ECtHR, 7 July 2011).

62 Murray, *Practitioners' Guide to Human Rights Law in Armed Conflict*, 59, para 3.11.

63 *Loizidou v. Turkey* (1995), para 62.

64 For example, see the ECtHR's judgments in these cases when it considered the extraterritorial application of the ECHR in Northern Cyprus, which occupies by Turkey; *Loizidou v. Turkey*, (merits), Reports of Judgments and Decisions 1996-VI, (18 December 1996), para 16; *Cyprus v. Turkey*, ECtHR, (Appl. No. 25781/94), Judgment of (10 May 2001), paras 71, 77, 101.

65 *Al-Jedda v. the United Kingdom*, Grand Chamber, Judgment ECtHR (App No 27021/08), (2011).

of Iraq in 2003.[66] The ECtHR determined that the ECHR was fully applicable to the actions committed by the United Kingdom as an occupying power in Iraq.[67] Furthermore, in the *Al-Skeini* case, the ECtHR stressed that there was an obvious jurisdictional link between the United Kingdom and the Iraqi victims, in accordance with the purposes of Article 1 of the ECHR.[68] However, the UK argument in the *Al-Skeini* case differentiated between being an occupant and having such control as required to apply human rights obligations, and that was clear from what Brooke stated in the UK Court of Appeal: "it is quite impossible to hold that the UK, although an occupying power for the purposes of the Hague Regulations and Geneva IV, was in effective control of Basrah City for the purposes of ECHR jurisprudence at the material time".[69] However, the ECtHR disagreed with the UK submission and emphasised that the circumstances in the *Al-Skeini* case did entail a jurisdictional link that created human rights obligations under the ECHR upon the United Kingdom.[70] The ECtHR confirmed that the jurisdictional link of the UK troops engaged in such security operations, exercised some of the public powers normally, and the UK military forces had authority and control over the area and the individuals there.[71] Accordingly, the UK had obligations to respect and to ensure human rights obligations under the ECHR.[72] Lubell, for example, argued that, the essence of the extension of IHRL obligations to occupied territory is based on the fact that the "occupied territory is in effect under the authority and control of the occupying State".[73]

Furthermore, it is quite clear that when a state party to the ECHR is exercising effective control over a territory outside its borders, as in the *Hassan v. the United Kingdom* case, the United Kingdom had obligations under the Convention to ensure and secure the rights and freedoms in the area under its control.[74] Moreover, the ECtHR directly addressed the co-application of the IHL and IHRL for the first time in this particular case.[75] In light of this, the ECtHR, in the same case, also referred to the ICJ's decision in the Wall Advisory Opinion, especially given that the latter recognised the applicability of IHRL along with IHL in such situations.[76] The *Chiragov and Others v. Armenia* case can be seen as another example, when

66 *Al-Skeini and Others v. the United Kingdom*, ECtHR (Appl. No. 55721/07), (7 July 2011).

67 Ibid, paras 194–150.

68 Ibid, para 150.

69 *The Queen (on the Application of Mazin Mumaa Galteh Al-Skeini and Others) v. The Secretary of State for Defence*, [2005] EWCA Civ 1609, United Kingdom: Court of Appeal (England and Wales), 21 December 2005.

70 *Al-Skeini and Others v. the United Kingdom*, ECtHR (2011), para 149.

71 Ibid.

72 Ibid, para 137.

73 Noam Lubell, 'Challenges in Applying Human Rights Law to Armed Conflict', (2005) 87 *International Review of the Red Cross* 737, 740.

74 *Hassan v. the United Kingdom*, Judgment, ECtHR (App. No. 29750/09), (16 September 2014), paras 75–80.

75 Ibid, para 102.

76 Ibid.

the ECtHR emphasised the application of the ECHR in the territories of Azerbaijan that were occupied by Armenia.[77]

In all the above instances, in statements either by the ICJ or by the ECtHR, the responsibility of an occupying power to respect both IHRL and IHL in an occupied territory has been confirmed. Therefore, it could be argued that the duty of an occupying power to respect and secure human rights during situations of occupation is not a disputed issue anymore and that the occupying power is bound by IHRL conventions.[78] However, there are some human rights that might be derogated from during times of armed conflict and occupation, such as labour rights, whilst there are some other human rights called the inalienable rights that remain applicable at all times to all individuals, and derogation is not possible. For example, there are certain rights that can never be infringed on or amended – that are "non-derogable" even during times of armed conflict and occupation, states-of-emergency situations, or other exceptional circumstances – such as the right to life.[79]

Furthermore, the Human Rights Committee (HRC) argued that the protection of the rights under the ICCPR, once accorded, devolves with territory and continues to belong to the people, notwithstanding any changes in the administration of that territory.[80] Moreover, a number of scholars have supported this position and have taken the application of IHRL in times of occupation as granted. They have considered this application as a complement to the overall regulatory framework in such situations, and there is no doubt that IHRL is fully applicable in times of occupation and that occupying powers must respect and consider the applicability of both IHRL and IHL during such situations.[81] Fraenkel stated that "the international bill of rights should apply to situations of occupations at least after the purely military phase of the occupation has ended".[82] As Lubell argued, the basis for this view is that the occupying power is only an administrator of the occupied territory, and therefore must abide by human rights law obligations when it is dealing with individuals in the territory under its control.[83]

77 *Chiragov and Others v. Armenia*, ECtHR, (Judgment (Merits), (Appl. No.13216/05), Judgment of (16 June 2015), paras 32, 63, 67, 96, 100, 128, 168, 220.

78 Murray, *Practitioners' Guide to Human Rights Law in Armed Conflict*, 99, paras 10.02; Longobardo, *The Use of Armed Force in Occupied Territory*, 70.

79 ICCPR, Article 4, paras (1) and (2); Walter Kalin (ed), *Human Rights in Times of Occupation: The Case of Kuwait* (Law Books in Europe LBE 1994) 25; The ICJ, the Nuclear Advisory Opinion (1996), para 25; Médecins Sans Frontières, 'The Practical Guide to Humanitarian Law: Fundamental Guarantees'. Available online at: <https://guide-humanitarian-law.org/content/article/3/fundamental-guarantees/>. Accessed date: 3 December 2023.

80 UN Human Rights Committee (HRC), CCPR General Comment No. 26: Continuity of Obligations, (8 December 1997), (CCPR/C/21/Rev.1/Add.8/Rev.1), para 4.

81 Murray, *Practitioners' Guide to Human Rights Law in Armed Conflict*, 99, paras 4.56 and 4.58; Longobardo, *The Use of Armed Force in Occupied Territory*, 71.

82 Ernest Fraenkel, *Military Occupation and the Rule of Law* (Oxford University Press 1944), 205–206.

83 Lubell, 'Human Rights Obligations in Military Occupation', 319.

However, some scholars reject the idea of the extraterritorial application of IHRL to situations of armed conflict and occupation. For example, Modirzadeh adopted a completely different approach compared to the ICJ, ECtHR, HRC, and numerous international law scholars, arguing against the extraterritorial application of IHRL to such situations. For instance, she contended that the ICJ Wall Advisory Opinion is an unsatisfying and confusing way to approach the actual application of IHRL during such situations. She added that the ICJ has not given any example of how IHRL should actually be applied in such scenarios.[84]

It was pointed out that "human rights law was not originally drafted to apply in extraterritorial exertions of military force and occupation … precisely because the relationship necessary for the spirit and letter of human rights law to hold does not exist between the invaders and the invaded – nor should it".[85] Moreover, she argued that applying IHRL in such situations could run the risk of confusing all actors, for example, how commanders will embed human rights interpretation in their orders and many other issues that have never been cleared by those that support the extraterritorial application of IHRL to situations of armed conflict and occupation, adding that such application could raise expectations that can never be met. For example, people under occupation cannot possibly enjoy the same human rights as those living in peacetime in another country, which in turn, creates false expectations among civilians regarding the application of IHRL in occupied territory.[86] Therefore, claiming that IHRL applies extraterritorially in times of armed conflict and occupation along with IHL ones is disconnected from reality as it is has been experienced by populations living in such countries.[87]

In the view of the present author, it would be better to apply IHRL extraterritorially in situations of armed conflict and occupation for different reasons. First, more human rights law obligations in such situations will mean more human rights enjoyment by civilians and, in turn, more protection to the environment can be provided – as will be discussed in detail later in the chapter. Second, as explained above, the ICJ, ECtHR, several UN bodies, and numerous scholars support the extraterritorial application of IHRL to such situations, and the opposite position finds very limited support. Accordingly, it could be argued that IHRL is not only a mirror opposite to IHL and applies only in times of peace, but rather that it always applies in peace and in war, including in situations of occupation.[88]

It is quite clear from the above reasoning that there is considerable support from international law bodies for holding that occupying powers must abide by IHRL, especially through the extraterritorial application of the human rights obligations.

84 Naz Modirzadeh, 'The Dark Sides of Convergence: A Pro-Civilian Critique of the Extraterritorial Application of Human Rights Law in Armed Conflict', (2010) 86 *U.S. Naval War College International Law Studies* (Blue Book) Series 349, 360–368.

85 Ibid, 367.

86 Ibid, 364, 370, 373.

87 Ibid, 370–373.

88 Dinstein, *The International Law of Belligerent Occupation*, 79–81, 84–85; Lubell, 'Human Rights Obligations in Military Occupation', 318–319.

That is, it is quite clear that the occupying power is obliged to apply its human rights obligations where it is exercising extraterritorial jurisdiction over an occupied territory. In particular, those obligations are derived from the IHRL treaties, which the occupying power has already ratified.[89] It should be noted that in some cases, both the occupying power and the occupied territory could be party to the same conventions, in which case the issue might be less of a difficulty to resolve. For example, in *DRC v. Uganda*, the ICJ determined the applicability of several legal instruments, such as the ICCPR and the UNCRC, where the Court noted that both states were party to such Conventions.[90] However, it is not always the case that both states can be party to the same conventions and equally bound by same human rights treaties. For example, in the *Al-Skeini* case, the United Kingdom holds obligations under the ECHR, while clearly Iraq is not a state party to it.[91] Thus, the United Kingdom had to keep its own human rights obligations under the ECHR extraterritorially.

3.1.3 Other Issues Regarding the Application of IHRL to Situations of Occupation

The second scenario/source is that the occupying power has must respect the human rights obligations ratified by the ousted government of the occupied territory, particularly if those obligations have been already considered and integrated into the occupied state's domestic law.[92] Thus, IHRL obligations that derive from the treaties ratified by the occupied state could also remain of relevance to situations of occupation. Therefore, the law of occupation may necessitate the adherence, by the occupier, to certain human rights obligations to which the occupied territory is a party.[93] In particular, if the local law of the occupied territory includes the incorporation of IHRL standards.

Moreover, it is important to point out that there are some fundamental human rights, such as the right to life and the prohibition of torture, that will bind all states under customary international law (CIL).[94] Thus, regardless of the treaties to which the occupying power and the occupied territory are a party, the former will be bound and have to respect all human rights obligations that are considered as a part of CIL.[95] Accordingly, it could be argued that customary human rights may be

89 Longobardo, *The Use of Armed Force in Occupied Territory*, 70.

90 ICJ, *DRC v. Uganda*, para 219.

91 See *Al-Skeini v. United Kingdom*.

92 Lubell, 'Human Rights Obligations in Military Occupation', 334–335.

93 Ibid, 334–337.

94 See, for example, Bertrand Ramcharan, 'The Concept and Dimensions of the Right to Life', in Bertrand Ramcharan (ed), *The Right to Life in International Law* (Martinus Nijhoff 1985) 28. See also William Schabas, *The Customary International Law of Human Rights* (Oxford University Press 2021), 109–114. For the "prohibition of torture", see the ECtHR, *Al-Adsani v. The United Kingdom*, (Application No. 35763/97), Judgment of (21 November 2001), paras 60–61.

95 Lubell, 'Human Rights Obligations in Military Occupation', 334–335.

considered as the third source of human rights obligations applicable to situations of occupation.

The Vienna Declaration and Programme of Action declared the following:

> Effective international measures to guarantee and monitor the implementation of human rights standards should be taken in respect of people under foreign occupation, and effective legal protection against the violation of their human rights should be provided, in accordance with human rights norms and international law, particularly the Geneva Convention relative to the protection of Civilian Persons in Time of war … and other applicable norms of humanitarian law.[96]

Ultimately, it could be argued that, to provide more sufficient protection to human rights in times of occupation, the best solution is a straightforward reliance not solely on one of these scenarios, but rather on a combination of them all. Accordingly, and as has been argued above, the occupying power is obligated to respect and ensure respect of IHRL obligations in situations of occupation,[97] since there is nothing in its conventions' texts indicating that they are not applicable to such situations.[98]

Proceeding from this position that human rights obligations can coexist and apply in situations of occupation alongside IHL, the occupying power is resposnibile under IHRL to promote, respect, and protect individuals' rights living under its effective control. This conclusion places the focus not on the question of whether IHRL can apply in times of occupation, but rather on how its applicability could be fundamental to strengthening the protection of the environment in situations of occupation.

3.2 The Relationship between IHRL and IHL

In this section, the relationship between IHRL and IHL in times of occupation is examined. IHRL, for example, may provide more specificity for the interpretation of some notions under the provisions of the law of occupation, such as the notion of "civil life" under the aforementioned Article 43 of the Hague Regulations 1907. In some cases, both branches of international law regulate the same issue, whilst sharing the same aim to enrich and deepen the rules of each other. This could include environmental questions, and, by considering the concurrent application of IHRL in situations of occupation, environmental protection might be strengthened. The following paragraphs will examine how the complementary relation between both laws could provide more protection to the environment, especially by providing a

96 World Conference on Human Rights, Vienna Deceleration and Programme of Action, (A/CONF.157/23), (12 July 1993), para 3.

97 Longobardo, *The Use of Armed Force in Occupied Territory*, 69.

98 Ibid, 66; Oberleitner, *Human Rights in Armed Conflict: Law, Practice, Policy*, 222–227; Arai-Takahashi, *The Law of Occupation*, 401–407.

more exact interpretation and formulation of the obligations of the occupying power that the law of occupation was silent about or has not given enough thought to.

The relationship between IHRL and IHL in situations of occupation started to become clearer after the Second World War.[99] The international concern about the connection between the two had increased after the disregard and neglect of human rights in several occupied territories during the Second World War, particularly the countries that were under German occupation.[100] For example, William Bishop pointed out that "The greatest impetus for UN action for international protection of human rights grew out of the almost universal reaction against the German Nazi oppression of persons in Germany and in the territories occupied by Germany during World War II".[101] Hence, more attention was paid to demonstrating the relation between IHRL and IHL after the end of the Second World War, specifically to the IHL conventions and by the work of scholars. For instance, the AP1 of the Fourth Geneva Conventions 1949 in 1977 provided under Article 72 that "the provisions of this section are additional to the rules concerning humanitarian protection of civilians and civilian objects in the power of a Party to the conflict contained in the Fourth Convention … as well as to other applicable rules of international law relating to the protection of fundamental human rights during international armed conflict".[102] Furthermore, Article 75 of the 1977 API on "fundamental guarantees" is directly derived from the 1966 United Nations Covenant on Civil and Political Rights.[103]

Despite IHRL instruments not being mentioned explicitly in 1977 API, "their presence is there nonetheless".[104] The complementarity charter of the relationship between IHRL and IHL in times of armed conflict has been clearly corroborated under the API of the Fourth Geneva Conventions 1949. Dietrich Schindler, for example, linked IHRL to the Geneva Conventions of 1949 when he stated that the provisions of the Geneva Conventions of 1949 may be considered not only as obligations that have to be met by the State Parties to the Conventions, but also

99 Adam Roberts, 'The Applicability of Human Rights Law during Military Occupations', (1987) 13 *Review of International Studies* JSTOR 39, 42.

100 Ibid.

101 William Bishop, *International Law: Cases and Materials* (3rd edn, Little, Brown & Co., 1971) 470.

102 The Additional Protocol I (1977), Article 72.

103 During the preparatory work for the API, Committee III examined and discussed Article 75 of the API, which was officially adopted in the last session of the Diplomatic Conference in 1977. Article 65, which has become Article 75, was examined by the delegates and it was stated that the 1966 International Covenant on Civil and Political Rights and Article 65 (which has become Article 75) of draft Protocol I in fact dealt with the same legal situation and set out the fundamental guarantees. Furthermore, it was stated that the amendment made to Article 65 of draft Protocol I was chiefly based on the 1966 ICCPR. For further information, see Official Records of the Diplomatic Conference on the Reaffirmation and Development of International Humanitarian Law Applicable in Armed Conflicts, Geneva, 1974–1977; Vol. 15: Summary Records of Committee III: Third and Fourth Sessions; Reports of Committee III), at: 28, 31, 34, 45, 52, 190–191, 489–490. Available online at: <https://library.icrc.org/library/docs/CD/CD_1977_ACTES_ENG_15.pdf>/ <https://library.icrc.org/library/search/Notice/2374> . Accessed date: 4 December 2023.

104 Roberts, 'The Applicability of Human Rights Law during Military Occupations', 43.

as individual rights of the protected persons.[105] Furthermore, other scholars have indicated in their works the essential nexus between IHRL and IHL, with particular reference to situations of occupation. For example, Adam Roberts stated that some IHRL instruments may contain provisions that fill gaps in IHL at such times. In particular, in examples of prolonged occupations, it may present problems different from those addressed under IHL.[106]

Other landmark evidence of the connection between the two branches of international law was the UN Conference on Human Rights held in 1968 in Tehran. The Conference has been marked as the first occasion when the UN showed real interest in a more advanced development of IHL, with specific reference to the human rights situation in times of occupation, particularly when it asked occupying powers to respect freedoms and human rights in the occupied territories.[107]

The ICJ has addressed the relationship between IHRL and IHL in two Advisory Opinions and one Judgment.[108] The relationship between these two branches of international law in situations of armed conflict and occupation has also been addressed by the regional courts, such as the ECtHR,[109] IACtHR,[110] as well as by the HRC.[111] In the case of human rights courts and other human rights bodies, it is important to note that their authority only allows them to investigate international human rights law violations in specific scenarios. This distinguishes these legal bodies from the ICJ, which has general subject-matter jurisdiction. Subsequently, the question is: if these bodies take into consideration IHL in determining whether IHRL has been violated or not, to what extent and in which circumstances would that be done?

To answer these questions, it is important first to explain the meaning of complementarity and *lex specialis* in dealing with the relation between IHL and IHRL. There are, in fact, two main views on their relationship, one based on the complementarity of the two branches, the other on the prevalence of IHL.

*3.2.1 The Concepts of "Complementarity" and "***Lex Specialis***" in International Law, with Specific Reference to IHRL and IHL in Times of Armed Conflict and Occupation*

Many authors consider that the relationship between IHRL and IHL is governed by complementarity.[112] Such a relation has been recognised in several soft law

105 Dietrich Schindler, 'The International Committee of the Red Cross and Human Rights', (1979) *International Review of the Red Cross*, Issue 208.

106 Roberts, 'The Applicability of Human Rights Law during Military Occupations', 40.

107 The United Nations, Final Act of the International Conference on Human Rights, (Tehran 1968), 5; Roberts, 'The Applicability of Human Rights Law during Military Occupations', 43.

108 See ICJ, Nuclear Weapons Advisory Opinion, para 25; Wall Advisory Opinion, para 106; *DRC v. Uganda*, para 216.

109 See *Hassan v. the United Kingdom*, paras 96–107.

110 See *Serrano Cruz v. El-Salvador*, Preliminary Objections, IACtHR, 23 November 2004, paras 112–113.

111 See the HRC General Comment No.31, para 11.

112 See, for example, Hans-Peter Gasser, 'International Humanitarian Law and Human Rights Law in Non-International Armed Conflict: Joint Venture or Mutual Exclusion', (2002) *German YB Int'l L*, Vol. 45, 149–162.

documents of the UN, such as Resolution XXIII adopted by the International Conference on Human Rights in 1968.[113] Some scholars have argued that the separation of IHRL and IHL in times of armed conflict and occupation is "artificial and hinders efforts to maximize the effective protection of the human person".[114] However, others have expressed opposing views regarding the convergence and the complementary relationship between the two branches of international law and disagree with such relation, even adopting a strict point of view and arguing for the importance of their separation in situations of armed conflict and occupation.[115]

The complementarity relationship between IHRL and IHL means that these two branches should not be interpreted as contradicting each other, but rather they should support, influence, and reinforce each other by sharing common values, subjects, and principles.[116] In this context, it is important to mention that complementarity reflects a means of interpretation enshrined under Article 31(3)(c) of the Vienna Convention on the Law of Treaties (VCLT) that demands, in interpreting a treaty, that "relevant rules of international law applicable in the relations between the parties"[117] be taken into account. Therefore, Article 31(3)(c) of the VCLT indicates that international treaties must be interpreted in consideration to one another. This rule embodies the idea that international law can be understood as a coherent system in which different sets of legal rules coexist in harmony. Hence, it could be argued that IHRL can be interpreted in the light of IHL and *vice versa*.[118]

An opposite view holds that the relation between IHRL and IHL can be described as one between general and specialised law, in which IHL is the *lex specialis*.[119] The principle of *lex specialis* is derived from the "legal maxim in the interpretation of laws, both in domestic and international law" – *"lex specialis derogat legi generali"*. This essentially means that, in the case of a normative conflict, more specific rules will prevail over more general ones.[120] The principle of *lex specialis*

113 Human Rights in Armed Conflicts. Resolution XXIII adopted by the International Conference on Human Rights, Teheran, (12 May 1968) <http://hrlibrary.umn.edu/instree/1968a.htm>. Accessed date 20 March 2022.

114 Theodor Meron, *Human Rights in Internal Strife: Their International Protection* (Cambridge University Press 1987), 28.

115 Naz Modirzadeh, 'The Dark Sides of Convergence: A Pro-Civilian Critique of the Extraterritorial Application of Human Rights Law in Armed Conflict', (2010) 86 *International Law Studies* 349–410.

116 Cordula Droege, 'The Interplay Between International Humanitarian Law and International Human Rights Law in Situations of Armed Conflict', (2007) 40 *Israel Law Review* 310, 337.

117 VCLT, Article 31 (3) (c); United Nations: General Assembly, 'Fragmentation of International Law: Difficulties Arising from the Diversification and Expansion of International Law: Report of the Study Group of the International Law Commission'. (A/CN.4/L.702), (18 July 2006), para 14.

118 See, for example, *Serrano Cruz v. El-Salvador*, Preliminary Objections, IACtHR, (23 November 2004), paragraph 112; Case of the *Afro-descendant Communities displaced from the Cacarica River Basin (Operation Genesis) v. Colombia*, Judgment, IACtHR, (20 November 2013), para 221; Droege, 'The Interplay', 337.

119 ICJ, Nuclear Weapons Advisory Opinion, para 25; Wall Advisory Opinion, para 106; Droege, 'The Interplay', 337.

120 Nancie Prud'homme, 'Lex Specialis: Oversimplifying a More Complex and Multifaceted Relationship', (2007) 40 *Israel Law Review* 356, 366–370.

is an accepted principle of interpretation in international law.[121] The ICJ has used the principle to describe the relationship between IHRL and IHL in situations of armed conflict and occupation on different occasions.[122] The relationship between the two in times of armed conflict situations was discussed for the first time by the ICJ in the Advisory Opinion on the *Legality of the Threat or Use of Nuclear Weapons* in 1996, when it was held that:

> The Court observes that the protection of the International Covenant of Civil and Political Rights does not cease in times of war, except by operation of Article 4 of the Covenant whereby certain provisions may be derogated from in a time of national emergency. Respect for the right to life is not, however, such a provision. In principle, the right not arbitrarily to be deprived of one's life applies also in hostilities. The test of what is an arbitrary deprivation of life, however, then falls to be determined by the applicable *lex specialis*, namely, the law applicable in armed conflict which is designed to regulate the conduct of hostilities. Thus, whether a particular loss of life, through the use of a certain weapon in warfare, is to be considered an arbitrary deprivation of life contrary to Article 6 of the Covenant, can only be decided by reference to the law applicable in armed conflict and not deduced from the terms of the Covenant itself.[123]

Along those lines, Doswald-Beck commented on the ICJ's conclusion on the relationship between IHL and IHRL in the Advisory Opinion on Nuclear Weapons, pointing out that "this is a very significant statement, for it means that humanitarian law is to be used to actually interpret a human rights rule. Conversely, it also means that, at least in the context of the conduct of hostilities, human rights law cannot be interpreted differently from humanitarian law".[124]

In the Wall Advisory Opinion, which, as abovementioned, was the first time that the ICJ addressed the relationship between IHL and IHRL in situations of occupation, the Court supported the applicability of the latter to situations of occupation, but it stressed that, in cases of normative conflicts, the law of occupation is the *lex specialis* because it is specifically designed for such situations.[125] The ICJ characterisation of IHL as *lex specialis* in the abovementioned situations can be understood as meaning that in a case where there is a direct conflict with a rule of IHRL in times of armed conflict or in times of occupation, IHL takes precedence.[126] Accordingly, the ICJ under both Advisory Opinions proposed a new model of the parallel and continued application of the two fields of international law in times of

121 Droege, 'The Interplay', 338.
122 ICJ, Nuclear Weapons Advisory Opinion, para 25; Wall Advisory Opinion, para 106.
123 ICJ, Nuclear Weapons Advisory Opinion, para 25.
124 Louise Doswald-Beck, 'International Humanitarian Law and the International Court of Justice on the Legality of the Threat or Use of Nuclear Weapons', (1997) 37 *International Review of the Red Cross* 35, 51.
125 ICJ, Wall Advisory Opinion, para 106.
126 Bantekas and Oette, *International Human Rights Law and Practice*, 726–728.

armed conflict and occupation, but with some form of primacy and prevalence to IHL over IHRL in such situations.

In this vein, some scholars support the ICJ approach. For example, Michael Dennis argued that the obligations assumed under IHRL were never intended to replace the *lex specialis* of IHL. Extending the protection provided under IHRL instruments to armed conflict and occupation situations is likely to produce more confusion and a dubious route, rather than offering more clarity or problem solving, and thus increase the gap between legal theory and state compliance with international norms.[127]

In contrast, others have downplayed the relevance of the principle of *lex specialis* in this debate. While it is accepted by the ICJ that in some situations IHL can be *lex specialis* or the prevailing norm over IHRL during armed conflict and occupation, the prevailing norm could change in other situations, depending on each case itself and its specific circumstances. Simply put, IHL and IHRL could both be either the *lex specialis* or *lex generalis*, depending on the situation at hand.[128]

In any case, displacing IHRL in favour of IHL would be only an exceptional result that can be invoked when a normative conflict cannot be solved through interpretation. Pursuant to the Advisory Opinion on Nuclear Weapons, both IHL and IHRL serve as an interpretative tool for each other, and thus they should be interpreted in light of each other to avoid a normative conflict before dismissing one of the two because it lacks special character.[129] In the Nuclear Weapons Advisory Opinion, the ICJ used the *lex specialis* principle as a device of interpretation, where IHL interpreted the right to life without dismissing the application of IHRL. In other words, there are clear instances where the *lex specialis* principle has been used by the ICJ to interpret the terms of another more general norm.[130] Therefore, whilst both laws could apply side by side, IHL plays the greater role of the two. Accordingly, it can be understood from the ICJ in the Nuclear Weapons Advisory Opinion that the Court has clearly applied Article 31(3)(c) VCLT to the situation at hand, even though the Court mentioned *lex specialis* as an interpretive tool.

On the other hand, the ICJ in the Wall Advisory Opinion proposed a slightly different approach to the articulation of the relationship between IHRL and IHL. In particular, it suggested that there are three different options when considering the parallel application of IHRL and IHL in situations of armed conflict and occupation, as has been discussed earlier.[131] However, it is not clear from the Wall Advisory Opinion if the ICJ, when mentioning the *lex specialis* between IHL and IHRL as a way to solve a normative conflict, could be considered as taking a conservative position in favour of IHL over IHRL or seeing it as an interpretive tool, which could be considered as a progressive position in favour of IHRL. The Court,

127 Dennis, 'Application of Human Rights Treaties Extraterritorially', 141.

128 Prud'homme, 'Lex Specialis', 373.

129 Ibid, 374.

130 Joost Pauwelyn, *Conflict of Norms in Public International Law: How WTO Law Relates to other Rules of International Law* (Cambridge University Press 2003), 410.

131 See ICJ, Wall Advisory Opinion, para 106.

on the one hand, appeared to be promoting the complementarity of IHL and IHRL, proposing that in some situations, only one of them would apply exclusively, and in others, both branches would apply concurrently. On the other hand, the ICJ fell back on the *lex specialis* rule to shape its reasoning and assert that both laws apply to the situation at hand, but IHL is the *lex specialis* over IHRL.[132]

In this author's mind, both the Advisory Opinions on the Wall and on Nuclear Weapons create confusion and infuse doubts on how to tackle and articulate the issue of the parallel and the co-existent application of IHL and IHRL in situations of armed conflict and occupation. However, both Advisory Opinions are valuable and important since they provide the most authoritative legal determination that IHRL continues to apply in times of armed conflict and occupation, that is, not only in times of peace.

One scholar argued that the *lex specialis* principle is more appropriate for addressing the conflict between norms at the domestic level or within a single treaty or between treaties that are part of the same legal system.[133] As has been argued above, uncertainties might arise when attempts are made to apply the *lex specialis* principle as a device to resolve the norms conflict between two different international legal frameworks without a pre-determined or defined relationship between them.[134]

In light of the above statement, it could be argued that domestic legal systems provide the best environment for the application of the *lex specialis* principle. In a hierarchical system with an organised structure, institutions, and legal frameworks, the *lex specialis* principle proves to be a valuable conflict-solving tool in national legal orders, and the norms conflict can be resolved by depending on the hierarchical system and by giving priority to the higher norm over the lower one.[135]

Conversely, the international legal system seems to be a less conducive environment for the application of the *lex specialis* principle, in particular when there is a norms conflict between two different and independent subjects of international law, such as IHL and IHRL. The fact is that international law as a system lacks a legal hierarchy, with no logical relations existing between its legal frameworks and norms. Hence, it is difficult to identify what is general and specific and to decide whether one law should have primacy over another.[136] In other words, the international legal system is, indeed, very different from the domestic one.[137] For example,

> there is no centralised legislator in the international legal system. Norms are created by the subjects of international law themselves in a variety of fora, many of which are disconnected and independent from each other, creating

132 Ibid.

133 Anja Lindroos, 'Addressing Norm Conflicts in a Fragmented Legal System: The Doctrine of Lex Specialis', (2005) 74 *Nordic Journal of International Law* 27, 39–41.

134 Ibid.

135 Ibid, 39.

136 Prud'homme, 'Lex Specialis', 380–381.

137 Lindroos, 'Addressing Norm Conflicts in a Fragmented Legal System', 28.

> a system different from the more coherent domestic legal order. Where national law is strongly based on hierarchy and institutional structures, the international normative order may be viewed from the perspective of bilateral state relations, something that does not easily lend itself to the establishment of systemic relations between norms. This lack of systemic relations and a centralised law-making process are essential differences between the domestic and the international legal order.[138]

According to those differences between the domestic legal system and the international one, the *lex specialis* principle is a suitable tool to solve the norms conflict at the national level; however, it fails to play the same role and to be efficient at the international level.[139]

Eventually, the vagueness and uncertainty of applying the *lex specialis* principle means that using it as a norms-conflict-solving tool or even as an interpretative tool proves its inability to tackle the issue of the parallel application and the co-existence of IHL and IHRL in times of armed conflict and occupation. Therefore, using the *lex specialis* principle as a norms-conflict-solving device in such scenarios might lead to decisions being made based on political or other motivations rather than on sound legal grounds. Thus, sound legal policy requires, in the first place, the harmonisation and co-application between overlapping international norms.[140]

In the context of jurisprudential development, the ICJ, in the case of *DRC v. Uganda*, undoubtedly made a step toward the harmonisation between IHL and IHRL. It addressed the relationship between the two[141] when the Court quoted what it had previously said in the Wall Advisory Opinion, but this time omitted the reference to the principle of *lex specialis*.[142] The ICJ found Uganda responsible for violations of both IHL and IHRL in the occupied region of Ituri. Furthermore, since the ICJ considered that acts conducted by Uganda's occupying forces in the occupied region of the DRC represented a violation of both IHL and IHRL at the same time, it did not provide any specific guidance as to when a situation should primarily be analysed through the perspective of IHL or through that of IHRL.[143] In this context, it is important to note that the ICJ has recently released its decision on reparations in *DRC v. Uganda* (2022). The Court, in its decision, adopted the

138 Ibid.

139 Prud'homme, 'Lex Specialis', 380–381. This paragraph is not related to IHL as such. The aim of this paragraph is to argue that the *lex specialis* principle is more appropriate for addressing the issue of norms conflict at the domestic level rather than the international one. In other words, using the *lex specialis* principle as a device to solve the norms conflict between two different and independent international legal frameworks, such as IHRL and IHL, may create confusion, and uncertainties might arise. However, the *lex specialis* principle is a perfect device to resolve norm conflicts at the domestic level, because of the norms hierarchy.

140 Orna Ben-Naftali and Yuval Shany, 'Living in Denial: The Application of Human Rights in the Occupied Territories', (2003) 37 *Israel Law Review* 17, 56.

141 ICJ, *DRC v. Uganda* (2005), para 216.

142 Ibid, para 216.

143 Ibid, para 219.

same approach as its previous one in 2005 regarding the parallel application of both IHRL and IHL in the occupied regions of the DRC by Uganda.[144] It confirmed that Uganda had violated its obligations as an occupying power under both IHRL and IHL laws in the occupied regions of the DRC.

In addition to this, and as mentioned earlier, the HRC has itself pronounced on the relationship between IHRL and IHL. It avoided the use of the *lex specialis* formulation as such and instead found that "both spheres of law are complementary, not mutually exclusive".[145]

Among other international human rights bodies, the Inter-American Commission of Human Rights (IACHR) has followed the jurisprudence of the ICJ in both the abovementioned advisory opinions. For instance, the IACHR in a case between Ecuador and Colombia has clearly expressed the synergy and complementarity between IHRL and IHL, expressing how both laws are based on the same principles and values.[146] However, the IACHR has stated that the *lex specialis* law is IHL, particularly when it held that

> although the *lex specialis* with respect to acts taking place in the context of an armed conflict is IHL, this does not mean that international human rights law is inapplicable. On the contrary, it means that when applying the law of human rights, in this case the American Convention, International Humanitarian Law, as the specific rule governing armed conflict, is resorted for interpretation.[147]

The ECtHR, in *Hassan v. the United Kingdom*, also considered the connection between IHL and IHRL in such situations.[148] In this case, it considered the application of both branches of international law, but it determined that IHL is considered as the primary framework since it includes explicit rules designed for such situations.[149]

There is a range of different questions that shall be taken into consideration concerning this issue. One is whether it is correct to think that the IHL is the only *lex specialis* that applies to such situations, or rather to consider both IHL and IHRL as

144 The ICJ, *Armed Activities on the Territory of the Congo* (*DRC v. Uganda*) Judgment (9 February 2022), paras, 5, 52, 54, 55, 65, 69, 78, 125, 133, 145, 188, 241.

145 UN Human Rights Committee (HRC), General comment No. 31 [80], The Nature of the General Legal Obligation imposed on State Parties to the Covenant, (26 May 2004), (CCPR/C/21/Rev.1/Add.13), para 11.

146 Report No.112/10 Inter-state Petition IP-02 Admissibility Franklin Guillermo Aisalla Molina (Ecuador-Colombia), Report No. 112/10, Inter-American Commission on Human Rights (IACHR), (21 October 2011), paras 117–121.

147 Franklin Guillermo Aisalla Molina (Ecuador-Colombia), Report No. 112/10, (IACHR), para 122. See also a similar case where the IACHR previously adopted a similar approach regarding the principle of *lex specialis* in situations of armed conflict: *Coard et al. v. United States*, Report N. 109/99 – Case 10.951, Inter-American Commission on Human Rights (IACHR), 29 September 1999, para 42.

148 *Hassan v. the United Kingdom,* paras 102–107.

149 Ibid, paras 105–106.

special bodies of law that properly apply to such situations in which human rights issues of persons are engaged.[150] While the Wall and Nuclear Advisory Opinions proceeded on the basis that IHL was the *lex specialis* law, it is not clear from subsequent jurisprudence of the ICJ, especially from the case law of the *DRC v. Uganda*, that this logic still applies. If one understands the principle of *lex specialis* not as a principle to solve conflicts of norms between IHRL and IHL as such, but rather as one that provides more specific interpretation in such scenarios, it would itself embody the meaning of complementarity between the two laws, as provided above. This comes very close to the interoperative method enshrined under Article 31(3)(c) of the VCLT, where international treaties must be interpreted in light of one another.[151] For example, the IACHR, in the decision in the *Santo Domingo Massacre v. Colombia*, noted that it was able to use and to refer to the rules and principles of IHL "as a supplementary norm of interpretation" of the relevant provisions contained in the Inter-American Convention on Human Rights with regard to the alleged violation of rights.[152]

The rules of interpretation found in the VCLT give legitimacy to the theory of harmonisation.[153] The Convention affirms that: "There shall be taken into account, together with the context … any relevant rules of international law applicable in the relations between the parties".[154] Therefore, in contrast to the *lex specialis* principle, the harmonisation approach not only provides an ideal theoretical legal model for the parallel application of IHL and IHRL, but also finds support in the VCLT and its general rule of treaty interpretation.[155]

The theory of harmonisation supports an approach that brings IHL and IHRL closer to each other, while acknowledging the specificities and differences between each of them. It also accepts that, the two branches of international law are distinct from each other, yet they are mutually complementary.[156] Therefore, such a legal theoretical model would provide a solid basis to articulate the co-existence and the relationship between IHL and IHRL in times of armed conflict and occupation. Note that "harmonisation" will be used in this book as a synonym for "complementarity", since the harmonisation approach to tackling the relationship between IHRL and IHL is not a novel or a new concept, for it has also been referred to as the complementarity between both branches of law.[157]

150 Daniel Bethlehem, 'The Relationship between International Humanitarian Law and International Human Rights Law in Situations of Armed Conflict', (2013) 2 *Cambridge Journal of International and Comparative Law* 180, 194; Malcolm N. Shaw, *International Law* (9th edn, Cambridge University Press 2021), 1045.

151 Droege, 'The Interplay', 340.

152 Inter-American Court of Human Rights, Case of the *Santo Domingo Massacre v. Colombia*, (Judgment of November 30, 2012), paras 23–25.

153 Prud'homme, 'Lex Specialis', 392.

154 VCLT: Article 31(3)(c).

155 Ibid; Prud'homme, 'Lex Specialis', 392–393.

156 Prud'homme, 'Lex Specialis', 387–388.

157 Ibid, 388.

Finally, it should be noted that IHL may not always be considered the primary framework; it depends on the situation and on each case itself. For example, where IHL is less explicit or less developed, IHRL may be considered the *lex specialis* law or the primary framework since it has more explicit rules that are designed for a given situation. Hence, in some situations, the *lex specialis* law could be IHL, while in others, it could be IHRL.[158] Both laws remain applicable to the situations of armed conflict and occupation, and they may contribute to, and inform, the overall legal framework and regulation of the given situation.[159] However, this does not necessarily mean that both laws would always point in the same direction. For instance, there are some cases where both laws are pertaining to the same subject matter but they produce different outcomes, such as the issue of property rights in times of occupation. Private property rights enjoy strong protection under the law of occupation, as has been argued in the previous chapter, whereas IHRL may allow some limitations of these rights depending on balancing and proportionality, with fewer strict restrictions when compared to the law of occupation.[160] For example, the ECtHR, in relation to property rights in Northern Cyprus, has balanced the property rights of Greek-Cypriots, where theirs were violated, against the rights of Turkish settlers, and it partly legitimised dispossession of Greek-Cypriots' property by the settlers in *Demopoulos and others v. Turkey* decision,[161] which in turn, undermined the protection of property rights under the law of occupation. Yet both laws share the same objectives and regulate the same subject matter more than they could ever potentially conflict. For instance, the ICESCR rights seem to be especially relevant in times of occupation since, in both international and regional courts' decisions, the ICESCR rights have been linked and tied to territorial control situations, which include situations of occupation.

Against this background, it could be argued that it should not be a question of which law IHL or IHRL prevails, but rather which gives the best possible protection to achieve the common purpose in such a situation. Therefore, the harmonisation approach would be the ideal solution to consider the application and the co-existence of IHL and IHRL to situations of armed conflict and occupation.[162] For these reasons, the author will adopt such an approach in relation to articulating the relationship between IHL and IHRL regarding environmental protection in times of occupation.

It is thus reasonable to conclude that the issue of determining the primary framework or which law is the *lex specialis* – whether it is IHL or IHRL, in times of armed conflict and occupation – is still an inconsistent and controversial matter

158 Murray, *Practitioners' Guide to Human Rights Law in Armed Conflict*, 81–88.

159 Ibid.

160 Gross, *The Writing on the Wall*, 280–381, 389.

161 *Demopoulos and others v. Turkey*, (App. No. 46113/99), Eur. Ct. H.R (2010).

162 For further information about the harmonisation of laws and the concept of harmonisation, see generally, Antonios Platsas, *The Harmonisation of National Legal System: Strategic Models and Factors* (Edward Elgar 2017), 6–9.

among the international bodies, as discussed above. It is acknowledged here that some different branches of international law are relevant and applicable during situations of occupation. Even when they do not specifically address the question of occupations *per se*, and therefore cannot be viewed as core parts of the law on occupations, they may still have considerable importance in such situations.[163] Hence, the relationship between IHRL and IHL, specifically the provisions of the law of occupation, in most cases can be described as a symbiotic and complementary relation.

The following section will assess the role of IHRL and its institutions that operate to protect human rights at the international, regional, and national levels, with particular focus on the protection of the environment in the occupied territory through these institutions. How IHRL provisions can strengthen the protection of the environment in such situations will also be examined.

3.3 The Role of International Human Rights Law for the Protection of the Environment in Times of Occupation

The majority of IHRL conventions were drafted and adopted before environmental issues became a matter of concern for the international community.[164] For that reason, there is no explicit reference to a binding right to a clean and healthy environment under IHRL conventions. However, there are some human rights, such as the right to life and the right to health, which have included some formulations and references to environmental issues. Therefore, comprehensive analysis and clarification of the application of IHRL regarding environmental protection, in times of occupation, is required.

3.3.1 Recognition of Environmental Human Rights

The United Nations is the central organisation in the field of human rights at the global level, which has gradually developed a comprehensive and extensive international human rights system. It is a multitiered and sophisticated system that fulfils a leadership role in the setting of new human rights standards. As showed in the Preamble of the UN Charter, "fundamental human rights" are one of the UN's main concerns.[165] Only 3 years after the UN was established, the UNGA adopted the Universal Declaration of Human Rights (UDHR).[166] A few years after the adoption of the UDHR, the UNGA adopted the two core human rights Covenants,[167]

163 Roberts, 'The Applicability of Human Rights', 40.

164 For the full list of the preparatory works of the (ICCPR) and (ICESCR), see UN Human Rights Treaties: *Travaux Préparatoires* (ICCPR) and *Travaux Préparatoires* (ICESCR).

165 The United Nations Charter.

166 UNGA, Universal Declaration of Human Rights, G.A. res. 217A (III), U.N. Doc A/810 at 71 (1948).

167 UNGA, Res. 2200A (XXI). International Covenant on Economic, Social and Cultural Rights, International Covenant on Civil and Political Rights and Optional Protocol to the International

which came into force in 1976. Along with these two human rights Covenants, the UDHR constitutes the so-called International Bill of Human Rights. The UN adopted additional important human rights treaties, such as the Convention on the Elimination of all Forms of Racial Discrimination (CERD),[168] the Convention on the Rights of the Child (UNCRC),[169] and the Convention on the Elimination of all Forms of Discrimination against Women (CEDAW),[170] among others.

A close examination of the progression of environmental human rights during the last decades indicates that the UN has played a significant role in the recognition of environmental human rights.[171] The following paragraphs will examine such protection, with a specific focus on the situations of occupation. They will address in more detail the co-ordination and the co-application between those rights and IHL as well as the obstacles that face the application of such rights in situations of occupation, with practical examples from several occupied territories around the world.

There are three different types of environmental human rights that have been identified when considering the systems of the UN.[172] The first pertains to the "Existing Rights" approach, acknowledging that environmental degradation, contamination, and deprivations have an impact on the enjoyment of existing human rights, such as the right to life and health.[173] For example, the ICESCR under Article 12 clearly asks States to take actions for "the improvement of all aspects of environmental and industrial hygiene",[174] thereby allowing everyone to enjoy the right to the highest attainable standard of physical and mental health.[175] The UN Committee on Economic, Social and Cultural Rights interprets this Article as requiring States to "prevent and reduce the population's exposure to harmful substances such as radiation and harmful chemicals or other detrimental environmental conditions that directly or indirectly have an impact upon human health"[176] and to "to take all necessary measures to safeguard persons within their jurisdiction from infringements of the right to health by third parties" as well as to "enact

Covenant on Civil and Political Rights. (A/RES/21/2200), (16 December 1966). Available online at: <http://www.un-documents.net/a21r2200.htm>. Accessed date: 12 April 2021.

168 UNGA, Res. 2106 A (XX). International Convention on the Elimination of All Forms of Racial Discrimination (A/RES/20/2106) (21 December 1965).

169 UNGA, Res. 44/25. Convention on the Rights of the Child. (A/RES/44/25), (5 December 1989).

170 UNGA, Res. 34/180. Convention on the Elimination of All Forms of Discrimination against Women (A/RES/34/180) (18 December 1979) (entry into force 3 September 1981).

171 Collins, 'The United Nations, Human Rights and the Environment', 220.

172 Ibid, 223.

173 Ibid; see also UNGA, Res. 2398 (XXIII) (3 December 1968).

174 The ICESCR, Article 12(2)(b).

175 Ibid.

176 The UN Committee on Economic, Social and Cultural Rights, General Comment No. 14: The Right to the Highest Attainable Standard of Health (Art. 12). Adopted at the 22nd Session of the Committee on Economic, Social and Cultural Rights on 11 August 2000 (Contained in Document E/C.12/2000/4), para 15.

and enforce laws to prevent the pollution of water, air and soil by extractive and manufacturing industries".[177]

Environmental harm may also violate other existing human rights, such as the right to privacy and family life, property rights, housing, an adequate standard of living, food, self-determination, and development.[178] Therefore, most of the human rights – if not all of them – are vulnerable to environmental degradation, and the full enjoyment of all human rights strongly relies on a sound environment.[179] As Judge Weeramantry argued in his separate opinion in the *Gabcikovo-Nagymaros Project Case*, "The protection of the environment is likewise a vital part of contemporary human rights doctrine, for it is a *sine qua non* for numerous human rights such as the right to health and the right to life itself ... as damage to the environment can impair and undermine all the human rights spoken of in the Universal Declaration and other human rights instruments".[180]

In addition to this, the ICJ, in the Wall Opinion, has indirectly applied environmental human rights to the situation of occupation through the existing rights approach and, specifically, under the right to property. For example, the Court argued that the occupying power acts against the environment in the OPT, such as through the destruction of agricultural lands, the cutting and destruction of olive and fruit trees, and the destruction of water wells and other water sources, which is affecting the enjoyment of human rights of the Palestinian people and thus constitutes a clear violation of human rights obligations. Furthermore, the ICJ has stated that such acts against the environment by the occupying power in the OPT are a violation of the right to food, along with other human rights.[181]

Moreover, several reports by UNHRC Special Rapporteurs have linked some of the environmental problems in the OPT, especially the environmental problems that followed the establishment of the Israeli Wall, to violations of basic human rights, such as the right to self-determination and to food along with other human rights.[182] Whilst such reports are not legally binding to Israel, they are still quite

177 The UN Committee on Economic, Social and Cultural Rights, General Comment No. 14: The Right to the Highest Attainable Standard of Health (Art. 12). Adopted at the 22nd Session of the Committee on Economic, Social and Cultural Rights on 11 August 2000 (Contained in Document E/C.12/2000/4), para 51.

178 UNGA, 'Human Rights Obligations Relating to the Enjoyment of a Safe, Clean, Healthy and Sustainable Environment', (A/73/188) (19 July 2018), para 13; Collins, 'The United Nations, Human rights and the Environment', 226.

179 Collins, 'The United Nations, Human Rights and the Environment', 226.

180 Gabčíkovo-Nagymaros Project (Hungary/Slovakia), Judgment, I.C.J. Reports 1997, 7. Separate Opinion of Vice-President Weeramantry, 91–92.

181 ICJ, Wall Advisory Opinion, paras 133–134.

182 The United Nations, Economic and Social Council, 'The Right to Food', Report by the Special Rapporteur, Jean Ziegler: Mission to the Occupied Palestinian Territories. (E/CN.4/2004/10/Add.2) (31 October 2003), paras 35, 44, 46, 49. See also UNGA, 'Report of the Special Committee to Investigate Israeli Practices Affecting the Human Rights of the Palestinian People and Other Arabs of the Occupied Territories', (A/58/311) (22 August 2003), para 26. See also the United Nations: Economic and Social Council, 'Report of the Special Rapporteur of the Commission on Human Rights, John Dugard, on the situation of human rights in the Palestinian territories occu-

important since they document the environmental violations in the OPT and show the consequences of such violations for the enjoyment of human rights.

It is now well accepted by UN bodies and international tribunals, such as the ICJ, that environmental harm could violate a variety of human rights in addition to the right to life and health.[183] This type of environmental human rights has been applied at the regional level, as in the European System, for example.[184] The ECHR and the ECtHR have had a profound impact on the development of international and national human rights law.[185] The ECtHR has made a major and influential contribution to the development of IHRL, with its jurisprudence having been referred to by national, regional, and international courts and bodies.[186]

This contribution includes important jurisprudence on the right to life, right to privacy, right to property, and several others. It also comprises some leading judgments that consider environmental interests.[187] Regarding the situations of occupation, as argued earlier, the ECtHR has made some prominent judicial decisions at such times. In particular, it decided that, in some situations where armed forces of a state party to the convention engage in operations extraterritorially, such as occupations, the state party should continue to be obliged by the convention's provisions even if one state is a party to the ECHR and the other is not – for example, in the case of the United Kingdom and Iraq.[188] On the other hand, there are situations of occupation where a state party to the convention occupies another region/territory of another state party to the same convention (both states are parties to the ECHR) – as in the case of Russia and Ukraine.

However, the question is to what extent the ECtHR has considered the environmental interests in such situations and applied the existing human rights approach to such scenarios. The environment, as such, is not mentioned in the human rights guaranteed by the ECHR and its protocols. The reason behind this could be that at the time that the ECHR was adopted and through the process of its adoption (preparatory work), the drafters had not given interest to environmental issues as such.[189] Nevertheless, the Court has confirmed that the effective enjoyment of the

---

pied by Israel since 1967, submitted in accordance with Commission resolution 1993/2 A', (E/CN.4/2004/6), (8 September 2003), para 9.

183 Collins, 'The United Nations, Human Rights and the Environment', 226.

184 For more information about the other human rights systems and environmental protection, see David Hunter, James Salzman, and Durwood Zaelke, *International Environmental Law and Policy* (5th edn, Foundation Press 2015) 1339–1356.

185 Bantekas and Oette, *International Human Rights*, 253.

186 Ibid.

187 See, for example, the ECtHR: *Budayeva and Others v. Russia*, Judgment (22 March 2008), (Applications nos. 15339/02, 21166/02, 20058/02, 11673/02 and 15343/02), paras 172–182. For more recent case, see *National Movement Ekoglasnost v. Bulgaria* (ECtHR), Judgment (15 December 2020), (Application no. 31678/17); *Ilias Bantekas and Lutz Oette*, 248–249, 253.

188 See, for example, *Al-Jedda v. the United Kingdom*; *Al-Skeini and Others v. the United Kingdom*.

189 Council of Europe, The European Convention on Human Rights, 'Preparatory work'. Available online at: <https://www.coe.int/en/web/human-rights-convention/preparatory-works>. Accessed date: 6 December 2023.

rights that are encompassed in the Convention relies, notably on a sound, healthy, quiet, and decent environment conducive to the well-being of individuals, and that situations when individuals are directly impacted upon by environmental harm may cause human rights to arise under the Convention. Furthermore, several decisions of the ECtHR have shown how there is a clear link between the protection of the environment and the enjoyment of human rights under the ECHR, such as the right to life, to health, and to property.[190]

The Court's judgments have also shown that states are not only obliged to refrain from arbitrary interference (negative obligation), but they also have obligations to implement adequate measures to protect human rights under the convention from the environmental hazards that might impact upon peoples' ability to enjoy and to exercise their rights under the Convention.[191] For example, Article 8 under the ECHR (the right to private and family life) has been interpreted by the ECtHR on various occasions as having a close link with the environment. For instance, severe environmental damage and pollution may affect individuals' well-being and might prevent them from enjoying their homes[192] in such a way as to affect their private and family life adversely, which has been made clear from several examples of case law before the ECtHR.[193] There are other human rights under the ECHR that have been interpreted by the ECtHR to have a close link with the environment, such as the right to life and the right to property. Thus, it has been established under ECHR that environmental impacts can give rise to the violation of Convention obligations. However, the question is whether or not these rights have been implemented by the Court in situations of occupation and to the environmental interests there.

There has been no specific case before the ECtHR regarding a situation of occupation, human rights, and the environment taken together. Most of the cases pertaining to situations of occupation before the Court have been associated with a clear violation of one of the rights protected under the Convention, but there has been no specific case regarding situations of occupation where environmental harm prevents individuals from enjoying their rights under the ECHR. The possible scenarios where a violation of the ECHR provisions by one of the state parties might take place in situations of occupation and where the state party (occupying power) harms the environment of the other state (occupied state), thereby causing a

190 The ECtHR, *Öneryıldız v. Turkey*, (Application no. 48939/99), Judgment (30 November 2004); *Manual on Human Rights and the Environment* (Council of Europe Publishing, 2nd edn, 2012) 30–31; European Court of Human Rights, 'Environment and the European Convention on Human Rights' (Press Unit 2022).

191 See generally, Council of Europe, Department for the Execution of Judgments of the European Court of Human Rights, Environment: Thematic Factsheet (October 2020), 2.

192 A "home", according to the ECtHR, is the place, for example a physically defined area, where private and family life develops; 45 at: <https://www.echr.coe.int/LibraryDocs/DH_DEV_Manual_Environment_Eng.pdf>.

193 David Hunter, James Salzman, and Durwood Zaelke, 1350–1351. See also, the ECtHR decision (*Lopez Ostra v. Spain*, ECtHR/COURT (CHAMBER) (App.No.16798/90) (09 December 1994), when the Court found a violation to Article 8 by Spain because of a waste-treatment plant that prevented the applicant from enjoying her right to private and family life under the Convention.

violation to the individuals' rights under the Convention, are discussed below, with a particular focus on the right to life, privacy, and property under the Convention.

The second type of environmental human rights is "procedural environmental rights",[194] which will be discussed more in Chapter 4. These mainly include the right of individuals to access environmental information, with a corresponding state duty to inform; the right to participate in environmental decision-making; and the right to have access to competent administrative and judicial organs regarding environmental matters.[195]

It should be noted that the UN has played an important role in the recognition of procedural environmental rights through adopting some binding and non-binding international instruments.[196] The Rio Declaration on Environment and Development is an example of the non-binding-instruments (soft law), in which the declaration has articulated procedural environmental rights, namely under Principle 10 of the Declaration, which states that:[197]

> Environmental issues are best handled with participation of all concerned citizens … each individual shall have appropriate access to information concerning the environment that is held by public authorities … and the opportunity to participate in decision-making processes. States shall facilitate and encourage public awareness and participation by making information widely available, effective access to judicial and administrative proceedings etc.[198]

In addition to the soft-law instruments regarding procedural environmental rights, there are also some international binding instruments in this area. For example, the Espoo Convention on Environmental Impact Assessment in a Transboundary Context requires the State Parties to the convention to "ensure that the public of the affected Party in the areas likely to be affected be informed of, and be provided with possibilities for making comments or objections on, the proposed activity, and for the transmittal of these comments or objections to the competent authority of the Party of origin, either directly to this authority or, where appropriate, through the Party of origin".[199] Accordingly, it is clear that the UN has played a significant role in the recognition of this type of environmental human rights too.

The third type of environmental human rights is "the free-standing right to the environment" or the independent right to a healthy and balanced environment.

194 Collins, 'The United Nations, Human Rights and the Environment', 223, 227.

195 Dinah Shelton, 'Human Rights, Environmental Rights, and the Right to Environment', (1991) 28 *Stan J Int'l L* 103, 117.

196 Collins, 'The United Nations, Human Rights and the Environment', 223, 227–228.

197 'Rio Declaration' (1992).

198 Ibid, Principle 10.

199 The United Nations: Convention on Environmental Impact Assessment in a Transboundary Context – the 'Espoo (EIA) Convention' (adopted in 1991 and entered into force on 10 September 1997), Article 3, para 8. See also the United Nations Economic Commission for Europe (UNECE), Convention on Access to Information, Public Participation in Decision-making and Access to Justice in Environmental Matters (Aarhus Convention) (25 June 1998).

Arguably, the UN gets credit for taking the first step of launching the idea/concept of the independent right to a healthy and balanced environment,[200] particularly after the adoption of the Stockholm Declaration on the Human Environment in 1972.[201] Principle 1 of the declaration provides that:

> Man has the fundamental right to freedom, equality and adequate conditions of life, in an environment of a quality that permits a life of dignity and well-being, and he bears a solemn responsibility to protect and improve the environment for present and future generations.[202]

The Preparatory Committee for the UN Conference on the Human Environment stated that the draft of the Stockholm Declaration was "based on the recognition of the rights of individuals to an adequate environment".[203] Some authors have argued that the Stockholm Declaration was the main starting point for recognising, codifying, and constitutionalising the right to the environment as an independent and fundamental right in domestic laws between States worldwide.[204] However, there are others who have contended that this Declaration has acknowledged only the relationship between existing human rights and the environment and has not really recognised an individual right to a healthy environment as such.[205]

Twenty years after the adoption of the Stockholm Declaration, the UN adopted the Rio Declaration and stated in Principle 1 of the declaration that "human beings are at the centre of concerns for sustainable development. They are entitled to a healthy and productive life in harmony with nature".[206] John Lee argued that Rio's Declaration Principle 1 captures the ideals of the human right to a healthy environment, if not explicitly recognising such a right.[207] This perspective has been criticised by other commentators. For example, it has been argued that Principle

200 Marc Pallemaerts, 'Introduction: Human Rights and Environmental Protection' in Maguelonne Dejeant-Pons, Marc Pallemaerts, Sara Fioravanti, *Human Rights and the Environment: Compendium of Instruments and Other International Texts on Individual and Collective Rights Relating to the Environment in the International and European Framework* (Council of Europe Publishing 2002), 11–12.

201 Collins, 'The United Nations, Human Rights and the Environment', 229.

202 'Stockholm Declaration' (1972). Principle (1).

203 The United Nations: General Assembly, Preparatory Committee for the United Nations Conference on the Human Environment (A/CONF.48/PC/17) (15 March 1972), para 77.

204 David Boyd, *The Environmental Rights Revolution: A Global Study of Constitutions, Human Rights, and the Environment* (UBC Press 2012), 112–113. See also Marc Pallemaerts, 'Introduction: Human Rights and Environmental Protection' in Maguelonne Dejeant-Pons, Marc Pallemaerts, Sara Fioravanti, *Human Rights and the Environment: Compendium of Instruments and Other International Texts on Individual and Collective Rights Relating to the Environment in the International and European Framework* (Council of Europe Publishing 2002) 11–12.

205 Sumudu Atapattu, 'The Right to a Healthy Life or the Right to Die Polluted? The Emergence of a Human Right to a Healthy Environment Under International Law' (2002) 16 *Tulane Environmental Law Journal* 65, 81.

206 'Rio Declaration' (1992), Principle (1).

207 John Lee, 'The Underlying Legal Theory to Support a Well-Defined Human Right to a Healthy Environment as a Principle of Customary International Law' (2000) 25 *Colum J Envtl L* 283, 308.

1 of the Rio Declaration has even less specific legal rights language compared to Principle 1 of the Stockholm Declaration and does not include any single "rights" word. It merely provides that human beings are *entitled to* rather than having *a right to*.[208] However, Lee disagreed with that interpretation, using reference to Black's Law Dictionary, which specifies that "one definition of being entitled to something is to be granted a legal right to it".[209] Furthermore, Ksentini, as Special Rapporteur on Human Rights and the Environment, argued that the self-standing right to the environment itself had already been acknowledged at national, regional, and international levels.[210]

Likewise, the Bizkaia Declaration on the Right to the Environment confirmed the existence of a self-standing right to a healthy environment, when Article 1 stated: "Everyone has the right, individually or in association with others, to enjoy a healthy and ecologically balanced environment".[211]

In a more recent move by the UNGA, it officially recognised the right to a clean, healthy, and sustainable environment as a human right.[212] This resolution confirms a 2021 resolution adopted by the Human Rights Council.[213] Neither of the resolutions adopted by the UNGA and UNHRC are binding. However, they are still extremely important, since they come at a moment where environmental degradation, biodiversity loss, climate change, and pollution all represent a serious threat to humans and their development. Moreover, and more recently, the UN Committee on the Rights of the Child has recognised children's right to a clean, healthy, and sustainable environment.[214]

It should be noted that all the abovementioned documents are strongly suggestive of customary law status to the right to a healthy environment. In particular, after the adoption of both the Stockholm and Rio Declarations, most states recognised this right in their domestic constitutions, and that is strong evidence for the existence of the right to a healthy environment in customary international law.[215] The UN, undoubtedly, has facilitated and significantly supported the codification of an individual right to a healthy environment in most national constitutions of the

208 Atapattu, 'The Right to a Healthy Life', 82.
209 Lee, 'The Underlying Legal Theory', 308, footnote 121.
210 Ksentini Final Report, Annexes: Annex I: Draft Principles on Human Rights and the Environment, Principle (2), 75. See also Ksentini Final Report, para 31. See also Collins, 'The United Nations, Human Rights and the Environment', 230.
211 The United Nations Educational, Social, and Cultural Organisation (UNESCO): General Conference; 30th Session, The Declaration of Bizkaia on the Right to the Environment (30C/INF.11) (24 September 1999), Article (1).
212 United Nations General Assembly, 'The Human Right to a Clean, Healthy and Sustainable Environment' (A/76/L.75) (26 July 2022), 76th session, agenda item 74 (b).
213 United Nations General Assembly, Human Rights Council, 'The Human Right to a Safe, Clean, Healthy and Sustainable Environment' (A/HRC/48/L.23/Rev.1) (5 October 2021).
214 The UN Committee on the Rights of the Child, 'General Comment No. 26 (2023) on Children's Rights and the Environment with a Special Focus on Climate Change' (22 August 2023) (CRC/C/GC/26).
215 Collins, 'The United Nations, Human Rights and the Environment', 231–232.

states.[216] Hence, it has been contributing to the eventual emergence of such a right as an independent and self-standing one.[217]

The increasing constitutional recognition of environmental rights and environmental obligations globally reflects a growing awareness of the importance of environmental protection, as well as environmental values. This has led to a greater acceptance of a right to a healthy environment.[218] The widespread state practice in this area supports the view that the right to a healthy environment reflects customary international law.[219]

In sum, the UN has applied environmental human rights to situations of occupation through its different bodies and, in particular, the existing rights approach. However, the issue of applying a self-standing independent right approach to the environment as such is still a controversial issue. In particular, there is currently no official recognition of the right to a healthy environment under the global IHRL conventions.

3.4 Human Rights that Promote Environmental Protection and the Applicability to the Situations of Occupation: "The Existing Rights Approach"

This section will address the question as to how IHRL can provide protection to the environment in times of occupation through the guaranteed upholding of different human rights, such as the right to life, to health, to self-determination, and to property. IHRL treaties do not include such a right to the environment. However, there are provisions under several IHRL treaties that could be linked to the protection of the environment. Along with treaties, this section will take into account the UDHR,[220] which is not a treaty[221] but an instrument that codifies customary international law in the field of human rights.[222]

However, before engaging in a discussion about the relationship between human rights and the protection of the environment in times of occupation and the possible

216 Human Rights Council, 'Report of the Special Rapporteur on the Issue of Human Rights Obligations Relating to the Enjoyment of a Safe, Clean, Healthy and Sustainable Environment' (A/HRC/37/59) (24 January 2018), paras 11–16.

217 UNGA, 'The human Right to a Clean, Healthy and Sustainable Environment' (A/76/L.75) (26 July 2022), 76th session, agenda item 74 (b).

218 David Boyd, 'The Constitutional Right to a Healthy Environment', (2012) 54 *Environment: Science and Policy for Sustainable Development* 3, 4.

219 'Analytical Study on the Relationship between Human Rights and the Environment: Report of the United Nations High Commissioner for Human Rights' (A/HRC/19/34) (16 December 2011), para 31.

220 United Nations, 'Universal Declaration of Human Rights', <https://www.un.org/en/about-us/universal-declaration-of-human-rights>.

221 The UDHR was adopted as a resolution by the UNGA on 10 December 1948. The UNGA resolutions are non-binding. In other words, resolutions adopted by the GA on agenda items are considered to be recommendations and are not legally binding on the Member States.

222 The European Parliament, 'The Universal Declaration of Human Rights and its relevance for the European Union'.

environmental protection provided under the existing rights approach, it is worth first considering briefly some related issues, such as the progressive realisation and the derogation of the ICESCR. This will help in ascertaining to what extent states could derogate from the rights under the ICESCR in times of armed conflict and occupation or limit them in accordance with Article 4 of the covenant. It should be noted that the ICESCR does not have a derogation clause;[223] however, states' practice and other international bodies have accepted the derogations from specific rights in times of armed conflict and other emergency situations that might be considered a threat to the life of the nation, such as labour rights.[224]

Even if, in exceptional scenarios, Article 4 of the ICESCR applies and the occupying power claims a public emergency, and there is a need to ensure and maintain public order and welfare of the local population in the occupied territory, that does not mean that it has the authority or the ability to derogate from all its obligations under the ICESCR. It might be able to derogate only from some and specific rights, as mentioned above, which are labelled as "labour rights" and represented mainly by the right to work and rights related to trade unions, but not all other rights under the ICESCR.

The non-derogability character of all other rights under the ICESCR, in particular, the so-called survival or subsistence rights, such as the right to health, to food, and to water, is justified by the fact that it looks inherently unnecessary to derogate from these rights to promote the general welfare and/or to ensure or restore the public order.[225] This logic should also apply to the occupied territory. However, the non-derogability charter of the right to health, for example, does not deprive the occupying power of reacting in a flexible manner to situations where there is instability or tensions in the occupied territory in the implementation of their legal duties under the right to health. In particular, the principle of progressive realisation under the ICESCR, along with the general limitation clause under Article 4 of the same Covenant, can both offer some kind of flexibility for states to adapt their implementation strategies for ESCR in unstable or difficult situations.[226] For states to do that and to be able to react in a more flexible manner regarding the full realisation of human rights under the ICESCR, they have to show that the limitations of some rights under the Covenant are important for the aim of promoting the welfare of the local population, or at least that the implementation of their obligations preserves the general welfare of the people to the greatest extent pos-

223 "The term derogation is used to refer, generally, to the suspension or suppression of a law under particular circumstances. In International Human Rights Law, certain major treaties contain derogation clauses, which allow a State to suspend or restrict the exercise of certain treaty rights in emergency situations". For more see: <https://casebook.icrc.org/a_to_z/glossary/derogations>.

224 The ICESCR, Articles 6–8(1). See also Amrei Muller, 'Limitations to and Derogations from Economic, Social and Cultural Rights', (2009) 9 *Human Rights Law Review* 557, 592, 596–597.

225 Ibid, 571–572, 599.

226 Amrei Müller, 'The Right to Health and International Humanitarian Law: Parallel Application for Building Peaceful Societies and the Prevention of Armed Conflict', (2015) 32 *Wisconsin International Law Journal* 416, 422–424.

sible.[227] Accordingly, the occupying power should consider progressive realisation when applying the right to health in such situations. The occupying power cannot completely restrict or derogate such right or argue that, because of the situation of occupation, there is a need to derogate such a right. Yet, it could still limit it in particular and specific circumstances and conditions, as noted above.

There are also some other conditions for allowing states to react in a flexible manner or applying some limitations towards the implementation of their legal obligations under the ICESCR in situations of armed conflict and occupation. However, limitations must respect the principle of proportionality, which means that states have a duty to show that the scope and severity of a limitation are proportionate to the goal that seeks to achieve – ultimately, to promote, or at least preserve, the general welfare of the population.[228] There must be a delicate balance between the required limitations in unstable situations, such as situations of armed conflict and occupation, that promote or preserve the "general welfare" of the population. Otherwise, such limitations might be considered illegal and void.

It should also be kept in mind that the power to impose limitations on human rights is essentially about regulating the exercise of these rights, rather than eliminating or extinguishing them completely.[229] Further, states do not have the freedom to impose limitations on the rights under the covenant arbitrarily or in any manner they might choose.[230] Instead, limitations of human rights under the ICESCR would be permitted only in certain circumstances and under certain conditions, as discussed above.[231] However, some states, rather than invoking Article 4 of the ICESCR, "would simply rely on the notion of progressive realization (to the maximum of their available resources) to justify any limitations on a *de facto* rather than a *de jure* basis".[232] However, the provisions of Article 2 (progressive realisation) "should relate only to the general level of attainment of rights and should not be invoked by states as grounds for imposing numerous limitations on them".[233] The argument about the progressive realisation and the limitation clause under the ICESCR is an unresolved debate between scholars and even between states themselves.

Moreover, it is important to mention that Article 4 (1) of the ICCPR allows for derogations from the guarantees of the ICCPR "in times of public emergency

227 Muller, 'Limitations to and Derogations from Economic, Social and Cultural Rights', 570-575, 585-588.

228 Philip Alston and Gerard Quinn, 'The Nature and Scope of State Parties' Obligations under the International Covenant on Economic, Social and Cultural Rights', (1987) 9 *Human Rights Quarterly* 156, 205–206.

229 Nihal Jayawickrama, *The Judicial Application of Human Rights Law: National, Regional, and International Jurisprudence* (Cambridge University Press 2002), 184–185.

230 UNGA, Official Records, 'Annotations on the Text of the Draft International Covenants on Human Rights' (Prepared by the Secretary-General), agenda item 28 (Part II), Document: A/2929, (New York 1955), para 50.

231 Ibid.

232 Alston and Quinn, 'The Nature and Scope of State Parties' Obligations', 205.

233 UNGA, 'Annotations on the Text of the Draft International Covenants on Human Rights', para 50.

which threatens the life of the nation". Even if, in exceptional scenarios, Article 4 (1) applies and the occupying power claims a public emergency, it does not exclude the significance of the Covenant. For example, it lists several rights that cannot be derogated, even in times of emergency or any other situation, including times of armed conflict. Among those rights is the right to life.[234] Moreover, Article 4 (1) forbids state parties to the ICCPR to apply derogations that are "inconsistent with their other obligations under international law".[235] To conclude, as far as rights of the ICCPR have their equivalents in the provisions of the law of occupation or other sources of IHL that apply to situations of occupation, whilst at the same time an occupying power has obligations under such provisions, no derogation is allowed or even possible.[236]

The following paragraphs will examine in detail how some provisions under several human rights conventions, such as the ICCPR, ICESCR, CEDAW, and UNCRC, can be related to the enjoyment of a safe and healthy environment and at the same time applicable to the situations of occupation. Taking into account the complementarity relation between the law of occupation (IHL) and IHRL, it can be helpful in relation to providing as sufficient and sound protection to the environment as is possible in such situations.

3.4.1 The Protection of the Environment through the Protection of the Right to Life under IHRL in Times of Occupation

According to Article 6 (1) of the ICCPR, "Every human being has the inherent right to life. This right shall be protected by law. No one shall be arbitrarily deprived of his life".[237] It is clear that the right to life prohibits the state from taking life intentionally or negligently.[238] However, the question is whether the right goes beyond the prohibition of taking life and could also include positive obligations on the occupying power to promote life expectancy for the occupied people, such as the provision of providing a better quality of drinking water or taking steps that would prevent polluted water sources or any other natural resources while it is administrating the occupied territory.

The Human Rights Committee has acknowledged the relationship between the right to life under Article 6 of the ICCPR and environmental protection.[239]

234 ICCPR, Article 4 paras (1) and (2); Kalin, *Human Rights in Times of Occupation: The Case of Kuwait*, 25; The ICJ, the Nuclear Advisory Opinion (1996), para 25.

235 ICCPR, Article 4(1).

236 Kalin (ed), *Human Rights in Times of Occupation: The Case of Kuwait*, 25.

237 ICCPR: Article (6) para (1).

238 Robin Churchill, 'Environmental Rights In Existing Human Rights Treaties', in Alan Boyle and Michael Anderson (eds), *Human Rights Approaches to Environmental Protection* (Oxford University Press 1996) 90.

239 Human Rights Committee, 'General Comment No. 36 on Article 6 of the International Covenant on Civil and Political Rights, on the Right to Life', (CCPR/C/GC/36), (3 September 2019), paras 26, 62; The United Nations: Office of the United Nations High Commissioner for Human Rights: Special Procedures of the United Nations Human Rights Council. 'Mapping Human Rights Obli-

The Committee has identified pollution to the environment, specifically to water sources and agricultural lands, as implicating the right to life. The Committee has referred to a specific example from a situation of occupation in its Concluding Observations regarding Israel's third periodic report, when it affirmed that "The Committee is concerned about water shortages disproportionately affecting the Palestinian population of the West Bank, due to prevention of construction and maintenance of water and sanitation infrastructure, as well as the prohibition of construction of wells. The Committee is further concerned about allegations of pollution by sewage water of Palestinian land, including from settlements".[240]

The Human Rights Committee has adopted the view that the right to life under the ICCPR involves states' obligations to take all positive measures to raise life expectancy. Furthermore, the Committee under the reporting process has always sought information about states' specific measures regarding public health and the environment.[241] Moreover, the Human Rights Committee, in its general comment No. 36 on Article 6 of the ICCPR, has clearly stated the following: "environmental degradation ... constitutes some of the most pressing and serious threats to the ability of present and future generations to enjoy the right to life".[242] The Committee also added: "Implementation of the obligation to respect and ensure the right to life, and in particular life with dignity, depends, inter alia, on measures taken by State parties to preserve the environment and protect it against harm and pollution".[243] The Human Rights Committee under its general comment No. 36 on Article 6 of the ICCPR has confirmed the occupying power's responsibility to protect civilians' lives while it continues to occupy the territory, for which is assumed it has a legal obligation to apply the Covenant along with its obligations under IHL.[244]

Under IHL, the right to life is protected by several provisions that are applicable to the situations of occupation, and the occupying power has obligations to respect and not to violate, such provisions. For example, regarding Article 27(1) of the GCIV and Article 75(2)(a) of the API, which is a customary international humanitarian law,[245] both provisions under IHL prohibit acts that might violate the right to life or any kind of acts that endanger the lives of individuals.[246] Some

gations Relating to the Enjoyment of a Safe, Clean, Healthy and Sustainable Environment: Individual Report on the International Covenant on Civil and Political Rights' (Report No.2) (December 2013), para 39.

240 The United Nations: International Covenant on Civil and Political Rights, 'Consideration of Reports Submitted by State parties under Article 40 of the Covenant: Concluding Observations of the Human Rights Committee (Israel)' (CCPR/C/ISR/CO/3) (3 September 2010), para 18.

241 Dominic McGoldrick, *The Human Rights Committee: Its Role in the Development of the International Covenant on Civil and Political Rights* (Clarendon Press 1991) 329–330. See also, Human Rights Committee, General comment No. 36 on Article 6, para 62.

242 Human Rights Committee, General Comment No. 36 on Article 6, para 62.

243 Ibid.

244 Ibid, para 63.

245 See Henckaerts and Doswald-Beck, *Customary International Humanitarian Law.*

246 See Fourth Geneva Convention 1949, Article 27(1), "Protected persons are entitled, in all circumstances, to respect for their persons, their honour, their family rights, their religious convictions and

acts against the environment might put the right to life in danger, such as what happened in Kuwait under the Iraqi occupation with the burning of oilwells heavily polluting the water and the coastline, which had long-term consequences for the ecosystem functions of the whole region. Knowing that the environment was intentionally attacked by the Iraqi forces in Kuwait, such deliberate and premeditated acts against the environment by the occupying power contradicted its duty to respect and not to violate the right to life of civilians by any kind of acts embodied under Articles 27(1) of the GCIV and Article 75(2)(a) of the API.[247] Therefore, the occupying power has a legal duty to respect the corresponding guarantees under IHL regarding the protection of the right to life while it has effective control over occupied territory, along with its obligations under IHRL, namely the guarantees of the ICCPR regarding the right to life.[248] The cumulative application of IHL and IHRL, in this case, is meaningful as it is reinforcing the protection of the right to life of individuals in times of occupation.

Accordingly, any practice by an occupying power that contradicts and is inconsistent with its duty under IHL, which includes potential risk to the lives of civilians in occupied territory and other persons protected under IHL, including the targeting of civilians, their objects and properties, and objects indispensable to the survival of the occupied population; indiscriminating attacks against the environment; and the failure to apply the principles of precaution and proportionality, could also lead to the violation of the occupying power's obligation under Article 6 of the ICCPR.[249]

As has been explained in the previous chapter, various civilian objects cover private property, including farms, domestic gardens, domestic animals, and livestock. At the same time, some of these properties might also consider objects indispensable to the survival of the civilian population. For example, the population depends on livestock and farming for their survival. By attacking or destroying such objects, the occupying power could put the lives of civilians in the occupied territory in danger. These objects are protected by IHL. For example, the API to the Fourth Geneva Conventions 1949 provides protection to civilians' lives and their objects, as well as to the objects indispensable to the survival of the civilian population.[250] Another example, Article 54(2) prohibits the occupying power to "attack, destroy, remove or render useless objects indispensable to the survival of

practices, and their manners and customs. They shall at all times be humanely treated, and shall be protected especially against all acts of violence or threats thereof and against insults and public curiosity". See also the Additional Protocol I 1977 to the Fourth Geneva Conventions 1949: "The following acts are and shall remain prohibited at any time and in any place whatsoever, whether committed by civilian or by military agents: (a) violence to the life, health, or physical or mental well-being of persons".

247 Kalin (ed), *Human Rights in Times of Occupation: The Case of Kuwait*, 106, 118–120.

248 Ibid, 26–27.

249 For more about the relationship between Article 6 of the ICCPR and IHL, see generally, ICJ, Nuclear Weapons Advisory Opinion, paras 24–25.

250 The Additional Protocol I (1977). Articles 48, 54(2), and 57(2)(a)(ii).

the civilian population, such as foodstuffs, agricultural areas for the production of foodstuffs, crops, livestock, drinking water installations and supplies and irrigation works".[251] According to the Committee, such acts against those objects constitute a violation to the right to life of civilians since they have been considered under the API as indispensable objects to the survival of the civilians, and by attacking or destroying them, the civilians' lives would be endangered.[252] Furthermore, Article 48 of the API provides that "the Parties to the conflict shall at all times distinguish between the civilian population and combatants and between civilian objects and military objectives".[253] This Article is crucial for the protection of the right to life in the conduct of hostilities since it embodies the principle of distinction between the civilians and their objects and combatants and their military objectives. Additionally, Article 57(2)(a)(ii) of the same protocol emphasises the States' duty to take all feasible precautions regarding minimising and avoiding any incidental loss of civilian life or injury to civilians and also to avoid any unnecessary damage to their objects.[254]

It could be argued that Articles 48, 54(2), and 57(2)(a)(ii) of the API clearly consider the destruction of civilian objects, including such as foodstuffs, agricultural areas for the production of these, crops, livestock, drinking-water installations, and supplies and irrigation works, a prohibited act. Hence, this could enhance the protection provided to the environment in the occupied territory through the protection provided to the right to life under the API in general and IHL in particular. [255]

Acknowledging that such acts can also have grave consequences for the environment in occupied territory and that numerous objects are also part of that environment, attacking or destroying them would mean not only that the lives of civilians would be endangered, but also might have an impact on the biodiversity and on the ecosystem of the occupied area. Arguably, Article 54(2) of the API recognises the relationship between protecting the environment and civilians' lives and their existence in occupied territory, in particular when it prohibits any destruction against agricultural areas, crops, animals, and drinking-water installations. Notably, this list of objects under Article 54(2) is not exhaustive.[256] Besides, it considers these objects imperative to the survival of the population.[257] Bearing that in mind, Articles 48, 57(2)(a)(ii), and the crux of Article 54 of the API have been considered customary international humanitarian law norms.[258] Accordingly, such acts constitute a violation of the occupying power's obligations regarding the right to life under both IHRL and IHL.

251 Ibid, Article 54(2).
252 Human Rights Committee, General Comment No. 36 on Article 6, para 64.
253 Additional Protocol I, Article 48.
254 Ibid, Article 57(2)(a)(ii).
255 Ibid, Article 48 and Article 54(2).
256 Henckaerts and Doswald-Beck, *Customary International Humanitarian Law*, Rule 54.
257 Additional Protocol I (1977), Article 54.
258 ICRC, 'Customary IHL', Rules 1, 54, 89.

The abovementioned articles under IHL can be of crucial importance in areas where there may be an outbreak of hostilities, since in times of occupation, the situation on the ground can vary considerably, not only in time but also in different regions of the occupied territory. The situation in some regions could be relatively calm and similar to a peace situation, whilst in others, there could be hostilities and a situation similar to a wartime scenario.[259]

Such provisions under the API could provide important protection to civilians' lives and their objects, whilst at the same time indirectly providing additional protection to the environment, as has been explained above. Therefore, it could be argued that the abovementioned Articles under the API that are relevant and provide direct and indirect protection to the right to life in times of armed conflict and occupation could also indirectly provide protection to the environment and biodiversity in the occupied territory.

Against this background, the occupying power under Article 6 of the ICCPR also has an indirect duty to take all possible measures to protect the environment and its natural resources from all kinds of pollution and other activities that might impact negatively on the enjoyment of the right to life of civilians in occupied territory and in regard to providing a healthy and safe environment to the occupied people through its obligation to promote life expectancy under its general responsibility to protect the right to life under the ICCPR. Moreover, by taking positive measures that will protect the environment and the natural resources from pollution, which will reflect favourably on the whole ecosystem situation in the occupied territory, it will also help to protect biodiversity, which in turn will contribute to reducing infant mortality and raising life expectancy among the population. Numerous studies have shown that where regions are highly environmentally polluted by toxic and chemical residues, there is a degradation of natural resources, which might threaten the right to life.[260] The right to life is contingent upon the realisation of several other human rights, including the rights to food, water, and to a healthy environment.[261] For example, in Iraq during and after the armed conflict and occupation, there was a dramatic increase in birth defects and congenital malformations among new-born babies and young children due to environmental contamination, which was mostly caused by toxic and hazardous chemicals (toxic remnants of the armed conflict and occupation).[262] Considering the fact that toxins and hazardous

259 Louise Doswald-Beck, 'The Right to Life in Armed Conflict: Does International Humanitarian Law Provide All the Answers?' (2006) 88 *International Review of the Red Cross* 881, 892.

260 Dinah Shelton, 'Environmental Rights' in Philip Alston (ed), *Peoples' Rights* (OUP 2005), 226.

261 Human Rights Council, 'Report of the Special Rapporteur on the Implications for Human rRghts of the Environmentally Sound Management and disposal of Hazardous Substances and Wastes' (A/HRC/33/41) (2 August 2016), para 27.

262 Ibid, paras 1–2, 16; Samira Alaani, Mozhgan Savabieasfahani, Mohammad Tafash, and Paola Manduca, 'Four Polygamous Families with Congenital Birth Defects from Fallujah, Iraq', (2011) 8 Int. J. Environ. Res. Public Health 89, 90–91, 95; UN Human Rights Council: 'Iraq: Grave Human Rights Violations during the War and Occupation in Iraq', 22nd Regular Session (25 February–22 March 2013).

chemicals contaminate air, water, food, and other sources of exposure, this could have deadly or lifelong impacts on mental and physical health.[263] Furthermore, exposure to toxic chemicals during crucial periods of a child's development can have an impact on the way in which genes are expressed, leading to deadly or adverse developmental outcomes for some children.[264] According to an independent study, "these defects could be due to environmental contaminants which are known components of modern weaponry".[265] Furthermore, during the occupation of Iraq, the occupying powers caused severe injuries to the environment, especially by using prohibited weapons under international law, such as depleted uranium and white phosphorus, which caused air and soil pollution and contamination of the environment. This had grave consequences for children and human health in Iraq at the time of occupation.[266]

Bearing in mind that, in the case where children's life and health are in danger due to the occupant's acts and activities in the occupied territory, it must be legally responsible under the UNCRC for such violations, particularly if it is a state party to the UNCRC. On some occasions, the occupied state could be also a state party to the same convention, and sometimes the convention could integrate it as a part of its domestic laws and regulations. Therefore, the occupying power has an additional obligation to respect such provisions while it administers the occupied territory. Furthermore, the ICJ confirmed the applicability of the UNCRC to situations of occupation.[267]

The UNCRC is one of the few IHRL instruments that requires State Parties to take action to prevent any environmental harm that might affect or violate children's rights under the Convention.[268] Environmental harm is a pressing human rights challenge, particularly the impact it has on children's rights and the violations of those resulting from environmental harm, which may have permanent, lifelong, and even transgenerational consequences.[269] According to the Committee on the Rights of the Child, "Children everywhere suffer violations of their rights to life, development, health, food, water, education, culture, play and other rights because governments fail to protect the natural environment".[270] According to Article 6 of the UNCRC, "State Parties recognize that every child has the inherent

263 'Report of the Special Rapporteur on the Implications for Human Rights of the Environmentally Sound Management and Disposal of Hazardous Substances and Wastes' (2016), para 7.

264 Ibid, para 28.

265 Samira Alaani, Mozhgan Savabieasfahani, Mohammad Tafash, and Paola Manduca, 'Four Polygamous Families with Congenital Birth Defects from Fallujah, Iraq', 95.

266 UN Human Rights Council: 'Iraq: Grave Human Rights Violations during the War and Occupation in Iraq', 22nd Regular Session (25 February - 22 March 2013). See also
مركز الامارات للدراسات و البحوث الاستراتيجية، " الحروب والبيئة: حالة العراق والخليج العربي"
(2004 مايو UAE 31).

267 ICJ, Wall Advisory Opinion, paras 107–113.

268 The UN Committee on the Rights of the Child: Report of the 2016 day of General Discussion: Children's Rights and the Environment, (2016), 6–7.

269 Ibid, 4.

270 Ibid.

right to life" and "State Parties shall ensure to the maximum extent possible the survival and development of the child".[271]

Accordingly, the occupying power has legal obligations under IHRL and IHL during the time of the occupation to protect children's right to life and survival along with everyone else's right to life from environmental hazards, including any dangerous toxic and hazardous chemicals that cause pollution to air, water, and soil, which in turn have grave consequences that might eventually lead to death. Therefore, to comply with this duty and protect the right to life, the occupant has to take environmental considerations into account while it administers the occupied territory.

3.4.2 The Protection of the Environment through the Protection of the Right to Health under IHRL in Times of Occupation

A healthy environment and the right to health are mutually reinforcing. This subsection addresses the following questions: to what extent do IHRL and IHL recognise the relationship between the right to health and the protection of the environment in times of occupation? To what extent does it obligate the occupying power to respect this mutual relationship? In other words, what are the obligations under the right to health and IHL that could mitigate or help prevent adverse environmental consequences in times of occupation? Finally, how could the parallel application of the right to health and IHL during times of occupation help to protect the environment?

The ICESCR, under Article 12, asks State Parties to the Covenant to take all available, accessible, reasonable, and appropriate measures in order to improve all aspects of environmental and industrial hygiene, thereby allowing everyone to enjoy the right to the highest attainable standard of physical and mental health.[272] The way in which this standard is realised is seen as progressive, rather than instant.[273] The progressive realisation of the right to health means that state parties to the Covenant "have a specific and continuing obligation to move as expeditiously and effectively as possible towards the full realization of Article 12".[274] Therefore, the right to health is subject to progressive realisation, as well as to resource availability.[275] In simple words, "a state is required to be doing better in two years time than it is doing today, while resource availability means that

271 The UNCRC, Article (6).

272 The ICESCR, Article 12(2)(b); The UN Committee on Economic, Social and Cultural Rights, General Comment (No. 14): The Right to the Highest Attainable Standard of Health (Art. 12). Adopted at the 22nd Session of the Committee on Economic, Social and Cultural Rights on (11 August 2000), (Contained in Document E/C.12/2000/4), para 12.

273 The UN Committee on Economic, Social and Cultural Rights, General Comment (No. 14): The Right to the Highest Attainable Standard of Health (Art. 12), paras 30–31.

274 Ibid, para 31.

275 Paul Hunt and Rajat Khosla, 'Climate Change and the Right to the Highest Attainable Standard of Health' in Stephen Humphreys (ed), *Human Rights and Climate Change* (Cambridge University Press 2009), 248.

what is required of a developed state is of a higher standard than what is required of a developing state".[276] Translating this into situations of occupation, the occupying power must employ all means available and accessible to it to reach the desired result of allowing the local population of the occupied territory to enjoy the highest attainable standard of health, while respecting the law of occupation.[277] Consequently, "the assessment of what is attainable is relative and dependent on the availability of resources within a state".[278] In the case of occupation, this means within the occupied territory.

The Committee on Economic, Social, and Cultural Rights holds that "States are under the obligation to respect the right to health by, *inter alia*, refraining from unlawfully polluting air, water and soil".[279] Accordingly, states have the obligation to develop and implement policies, taking measures and actions to reduce and eliminate pollution of air, water and soil.[280] Thus, the ICESCR clearly confers explicit environmental obligation upon states due to the reference to environmental hygiene in Article 12(2)(b), as well as because of the Committee's interpretation of the article. Therefore, it could be argued that the ICESCR includes an environmental component, especially when it is linked to the full enjoyment of the right to physical and mental health. It promotes a sound and supportive environment and places emphasis on states' responsibility to take all possible measures to protect and safeguard the population within their jurisdiction. Accordingly, it could be argued that a similar obligation is applicable to situations of occupation if the occupying power and/or the occupied state are state parties to the ICESCR. An example of this can be seen in the *DRC v. Uganda* case, where both states were parties to the ICESCR. [281] In this case, the occupying power had an obligation under Article 12(2)(b) of the ICESCR to ensure the protection of the environment in the occupied territory, in accordance with its duty to guarantee that everyone was enjoying their right to the highest attainable standard of physical and mental health in the occupied territory.

The Committee on the Rights of the Child has recurrently stated that environmental challenges could threaten the implementation of the UNCRC, particularly regarding the health, development, and basic well-being of children.[282] For example, in its General Comment on the right of the child to the enjoyment of the highest

276 Ibid, 248.

277 See Marco Longobardo, 'The Duties of Occupying Powers in Relation to the Prevention and Control of Contagious Diseases Through the Interplay between International Humanitarian Law and the Right to Health' (2022), 55 *Vanderbilt Journal of Transnational Law* 757, See also John Tobin, *The Right to Health in International Law* (Oxford University Press 2011), 121.

278 Tobin, *The Right to Health in International Law*, 124.

279 UN Committee on Economic, Social and Cultural Rights, General Comment (No. 14), para 34. See also a similar point held by the committee under its General Comment (No. 15), para 21, when the committee confirmed again that States should refrain from "unlawfully diminishing or polluting water".

280 UN Committee on Economic, Social and Cultural Rights, General Comment (No. 14), para 36.

281 For example, *DRC v. Uganda*, with both states being parties to the ICESCR.

282 Collins, 'The United Nations, Human Rights and the Environment', 237.

attainable standard of health, the UNCRC Committee demands that "States should take measures to address the dangers and risks that local environmental pollution poses to children's health in all settings".[283] Furthermore, the UNCRC Committee also stated that "environmental degradation and contamination arising from business activities can compromise children's rights to health, food security and access to safe drinking water and sanitation".[284]

As provided in the Article 24 of the UNCRC, State Parties to the Convention shall "pursue full implementation" of the child's right to the highest attainable standard of health, especially "through the provision of adequate nutritious foods and clean drinking water, taking into consideration the dangers and risks of environmental pollution".[285] In addition to this, the UNCRC, under the same article, asked State Parties to the Convention to ensure environmental hygiene and sanitation. Moreover, it linked this to children's health and nutrition under their right to the enjoyment of the highest attainable standard of health under the Convention.[286] Knowing that, the UNCRC continues to apply to situations of occupation, as with all other IHRL conventions, along with IHL, as discussed at the beginning of the chapter.

The ICJ in the Wall Advisory Opinion has specifically mentioned and confirmed the applicability of the UNCRC to situations of occupation.[287] Therefore, the protection offered to the right to health and to the environment under it does not cease during such times.[288] On the contrary, it could play a vital role in relation to strengthening the protection provided to the environment in such situations, in particular, after the Committee on the Rights of the Child emphasised the states' responsibility to consider the protection of the environment in relation to allowing children to enjoy their right to health. This means that there is a close link between the enjoyment of the right to health under the UNCRC and a safe, clean, healthy environment.[289]

283 UN Committee on the Rights of the Child (CRC), General Comment (No. 15) (2013) on the Right of the Child to the Enjoyment of the Highest Attainable Standard of Health (art. 24) (17 April 2013) (CRC/C/GC/15), para 49.

284 UN Committee on the Rights of the Child (CRC), General Comment (No. 16) (2013) on State Obligations Regarding the Impact of the Business sector on Children's Rights (17 April 2013) (CRC/C/GC/16), para 19.

285 The United Nations Convention on the Rights of the Child (adopted and opened for signature, ratification, and accession by General Assembly Resolution (44/25) of 20 November 1989), (entry into force 2 September 1990). Article 24(2)(c).

286 Ibid, Article 24(2)(e).

287 See ICJ, Wall Advisory Opinion, paras 107–113.

288 ILC, 'First Report', para 67.

289 UN Committee on the Rights of the Child (CRC), General Comment (No. 15) (2013) on the Right of the Child to the Enjoyment of the Highest Attainable Standard of Health (art. 24) (17 April 2013) (CRC/C/GC/15), para 49; UN Committee on the Rights of the Child (CRC), General Comment (No. 16) (2013) on State Obligations Regarding the Impact of the Business Sector on Children's rights (17 April 2013) (CRC/C/GC/16), para 19.

The occupying power has obligations under IHRL to keep the population in the occupied territory safe and healthy, and in doing so, it needs to ensure that they are protected from the spread of any kind of epidemics and diseases. Concerns regarding public health in occupied territories emerged quite early and a long time before any official adoption of IHRL documents, in particular through some state practice pertaining to IHL. For example, in 1895, the Japanese occupation of some parts of China adopted some important rules regarding public health of the population in the occupied regions in relation to preventing the spread of epidemics and diseases.[290] Likewise, in the Second World War, during the Allies' occupation of Italy, some measures were taken by the occupying power to protect the occupied population from the spread of diseases.[291] The public health challenge posed by environmental degradation and contamination, particularly in situations of armed conflict and occupation, represents a grave risk to the health and well-being of the local population, especially for those living in poverty in occupied territories. The occupying power has an obligation, arising from the right to the highest attainable standard of health, to take all reasonable and accessible steps to protect the environment throughout the duration of the occupation.[292] That is, in addition to protecting public health and preventing the spread of epidemics and diseases among the population of the occupied territory, the occupying power has to take environmental interests into account while it administers the occupied territory. Hence, there is a strong close link between clean and healthy environmental conditions and public health and hygiene on the one hand, and the ability of the occupied people to exercise and to enjoy their right to health in the occupied territory under IHRL, on the other. For example, environmental contamination and derogation may be linked directly to the violation of the right to health under the ICESCR.[293]

In general, environmental contamination can be linked to a vast variety of associated health problems. These could be even worse in situations of armed conflict and occupation, facilitating the spread of infectious diseases among the local population as well as giving the upper hand to the fast spread of microbial pathogens, which seize opportunities created by such extraordinary situations, in particular the weakness of the of public health infrastructure during times of armed conflict and occupation.[294] For example, if the occupying power has resorted to "the aerial and naval bombardment of terrain, which often destroys vital infrastructure such as water treatment plants", and denies civilians clean water, this will promote waterborne illness among the population.[295] Furthermore, "the deliberate and collateral

290 Longobardo, 'The Duties of Occupying Powers in Relation to the Prevention and Control of Contagious Diseases', 766.

291 Ibid.

292 About the topic generally, see ILC, 'First Report', paras 63–76.

293 Ibid, para 64.

294 Jessica Jacoby, 'Public Health Impacts: Introduction' in Jay Austin and Carl Bruch (eds), *The Environmental Consequences of War: Legal, Economic, and Scientific Perspectives* (Cambridge University Press 2000), 380.

295 Ibid, 379–380.

effects of environmental destruction and contamination through the use or storage of military defoliants, toxins, and waste" could have grave and long-term health consequences for the local population of the occupied territory.[296]

3.4.2.1 The Concurrent Application of IHRL and IHL and the Protection to the Environment through the Considerations of the Right to Health

The provisions of IHL on the protection of civilians' health cover the same subject matter as the right to health set out under Article 12 of the ICESCR.[297] In this case, the right to health can be interpreted in light of states' health-related obligations under IHL, such as their obligations under Article 43 of the Hague Regulations and Article 56 of the GCIV. Such a use of IHL would be supported by an interpretation and application of states' obligations under the right to health that are influenced by the so-called principle of systemic integration,[298] as provided under Article 31(3)(c) of the VCLT, as well as the complementary interpretation and implementation of the right to health under Article 12 of the ICESCR and states' health-related obligations under the provisions of IHL (the corresponding guarantees under IHL) based on Article 31(3)(c) of the VCLT.[299] The following paragraphs will examine the complementarity relation between Article 12 of the ICESCR and some provisions of IHL, such as Article 43 of the Hague Regulations 1907 and Article 56 of the GCIV, in an attempt to strengthen the protection provided to the environment in situations of occupation.

The occupying power, under Article 56 of the GCIV, has a duty to ensure and maintain public health and hygiene in the occupied territory, as has been demonstrated in the previous chapter. Therefore, any impact on human health that could at the same time lead to contagious diseases among the population caused by contamination of the environment by an occupying power in an occupied territory (whether by deliberately polluting the environment or by disrespecting the domestic environmental laws of the occupied territory) must be a prohibited act, according to Article 56 of the GCIV.[300] Acts against the environment, such as the contamination of the soil and water sources (whether coastline or groundwater) by the occupying power forces or any other types of acts by the occupier's administration power, might affect human health through the food-chain process, in particular through contaminated grazing animals and marine life upon which human populations depend. These sources are crucial for their survival and daily nutrition habits.

296 Ibid, 380–381.
297 Müller, 'The Right to Health and International Humanitarian Law', 434–435.
298 The United Nations: General Assembly, International Law Commission, 'Report of the Study Group of the International Law Commission: Finalized by Martti Koskenniemi', 'Fragmentation of International Law: Difficulties Arising from the Diversification and Expansion of International Law' (A/CN.4/L.682) (13 April 2006), para 430.
299 Müller, 'The Right to Health and International Humanitarian Law', 435.
300 Hulme, 'Enhancing Environmental Protection', 210–211.

[301] The contamination of the environment, in particular water sources, could cause several infectious diseases among the population of the occupied territory, such as cholera, typhoid, and polio, and consequently could affect the public health situation.[302] Therefore, the acts conducted by the occupying power against the environment that at the same time affect public health and hygiene in the occupied territory could constitute a violation of its obligation under Article 56 of the GCIV.

Moreover, large-scale environmental damage can severely impact upon occupied peoples' ability to enjoy and fully exercise their right to health under Article 12 of the ICESCR, in particular when such damage to the environment causes serious and long-term health consequences for the local population living in the occupied territory. For example, when Iraq occupied Kuwait in 1991, the Iraqi occupying forces intentionally, and systematically, burned and damaged hundreds of oil wells, and the occupying forces used explosive weapons to do that. The result of such unlawful acts led to large quantities of crude oil spilling into the Gulf and severely polluting the seawater and the coastline.[303] The environmental pollution that was caused by burning and damaging oil wells in Kuwait by the Iraqi occupying forces at that time caused several health problems among the local population. According to doctors' reports in Kuwait after the war and occupation, there was a dramatic increase in health problems, particularly among vulnerable groups, such as children, the elderly, and already sick persons. Such health problems can be attributed to environmental pollution caused by the Iraqi occupying forces.[304] Some of the serious health consequences resulting from such environmental pollution were cancers, which remained in the long term after the end of the occupation and might even have health consequences for future generations.[305]

The environmental damage in the case of the Iraqi occupation of Kuwait can be seen as a clear example of where the occupying power not only violated its obligations under Article 12 of the ICESCR but also under IHL, namely Article 56 of the GCIV and its duty to ensure and maintain public health and hygiene in the occupied territory. Furthermore, in cases such as the abovementioned, the occupying power also violated its obligations under Article 35(3) and Article 55 of the API of the Fourth Geneva Conventions, where both articles have been considered customary international humanitarian law. Thus, the occupying power has a legal obligation to consider these articles and not abnegate its duty under such provisions. Both have clearly prohibited any methods or means intended or may be expected to cause "damage to the natural environment, which is widespread, long-term-and severe".[306] Therefore, such acts against the environment, particularly the contamination of the soil and water sources by the occupying power, undoubtedly

301 Samira A. S. Omar, N. R. Bhat, and Adel Asem, 'Critical Assessment of the Environmental Consequences of the Invasion of Kuwait', 155.
302 See generally, WHO: <https://www.who.int/news-room/fact-sheets/detail/drinking-water>.
303 Kalin (ed), *Human Rights in Times of Occupation: The Case of Kuwait*, 115–119.
304 Ibid.
305 Ibid,118–119.
306 The API (1977), Article 35(3) and 55.

constitute a serious violation of the occupier's obligations under both IHRL and IHL. [307]

This right could be argued from the broader perspective of Article 43 of the Hague Regulations 1907 and in particular, under the notion of *civil life*, which encompasses public health in occupied territory.[308] The indirect protection of the environment can be provided for too. Despite Article 43 of the Hague Regulations not addressing health issues in occupied territory directly, it does embody a general rule regarding the administration of such territory, which is broad enough to cover the protection of public health in such situations.[309] It could be argued that Article 43 of the Hague Regulations is central in relation to the occupier's responsibilities regarding public health in the occupied territory, in particular the notion of civil life.

According to case law from Israel regarding the situation of the occupation in the OPT, the High Court of Justice explained that the notion of civil life includes several aspects, such as welfare, hygiene, and health.[310] The contamination of the environment, including water, air, and soil pollution, is itself a serious threat to civil life in the occupied territory. Such pollution might have several serious health consequences with a long-term impact on the local population of the occupied territory, which could fall within the scope of Article 43 of the Hague Regulations. The ILC's report in 2018 also provided that the occupying power's duty under Article 43 of the Hague Regulations in relation to restoring and maintaining public order and civil life in the occupied territory includes health components.[311] The occupying power has an obligation, in this regard, to consider and to give more attention to public health issues, in particular in the "aftermath of hostilities and urgent risks to health arising".[312] Accordingly, the occupying power's duty to restore and to ensure civil life under Article 43 of the Hague Regulations should also include protection of the environment in relation to providing the highest attainable standard of health.

It is clear that a healthy, safe, and clean environment, including clean water, is one of the main determinants of health.[313] The occupying power needs to guarantee that it is in compliance with its duty under Article 43 of the Hague Regulations, which requires it to restore and ensure civil life whilst also providing the highest attainable standard of health during the time of occupation. It could be argued that the grounds for this conclusion are based on the preparatory work of the Hague Regulations and the previous codification on the law of occupation, namely Brussels Conference 1874, where the French text of the term "*vie publique*" was interpreted as referring to "*des fonctions sociales, des transactions ordinaires, qui*

307 Kalin (ed), *Human Rights in Times of Occupation: The Case of Kuwait*, 119.

308 Longobardo, 'The Duties of Occupying Powers in Relation to the Prevention and Control of Contagious Diseases', 767.

309 Ibid.

310 CA 393/82 *Society Lawfully Registered v. Commander of the IDF* 37(4) PD 785, 18 (1983) (Isr.).

311 ILC, 'First Report', para 65.

312 Ibid.

313 The Committee on Economic, Social and Cultural Rights, General Comment (No.14), para 4.

constituent la vie de tous les jours". The provision has been interpreted to refer not only to physical safety but also to the "social functions and ordinary transactions which constitute daily life", in other words, to the entire social and economic life of the occupied region.[314] Accordingly, the occupant's duty to restore and ensure civil life in occupied territory includes also health components, such as the healthcare of the occupied population, which is part of the occupant's obligation under Article 43 to ensure that the occupied population continue to live as normal a life as possible, which falls in line with the interpretation of the term "*vie publique*" under Brussels Conference 1874 that considers and covers the "*la vie de tous les jours*" daily life in the occupied territory. Therefore, to avoid harming and polluting the environment is defined as a must, especially after the Committee on ESCR recognised the interrelationship between the enjoyment of the right to health under Article 12 of the ICESCR, on the one hand, and environmental degradation and contamination, on the other.[315]

It is important to mention that environmental contamination could have negative consequences for animals and plants as well, and, through the food-chain process, might lead to human infections. By adopting all possible measures to protect the environment from all types of contamination, in accordance with the duty to provide the highest attainable standard of health and the protection of the health structure in the occupied territory under Article 12 of the ICESCR, this would not only protect human health against diseases resulting from the environmental contamination, but also provide indirect conservation and protection to the biodiversity and ecosystem functions in the occupied territory.[316]

Moreover, the spread of environmental pollution in an occupied territory may impair civil life, as recognised under Article 43 of the Hague Regulations, if such contamination impacts on the normal daily life of the local population, including their social and economic lives. Further, marine, coastal, groundwater, air, and soil environmental contamination might have grave consequences for all living creatures in the occupied territory, including humans, animals, and plants, which not only affects the public health and hygiene situation under Article 43 of the Hague Regulation and Article 56 of the GCIV of the occupied territory, but also could further lead to a violation of the occupied people's right to enjoy the highest attainable standard of health under Article 12 of the ICESCR.[317]

314 The United Nations: General Assembly, 'Report of the International Law Commission', 71st session (29 April–7 June and 8 July–9 August 2019) (A/74/10) (20 August 2019). 'ILC Draft Commentary', 267–268, under footnote no. 1290.

315 The Committee on Economic, Social and Cultural Rights, General Comment (No.14), paras 4, 15; ILC, 'First Report', para 66.

316 Ibid, paras 70–71.

317 The notion of "civil life" under Article 43 does include social and economic life in the occupied territory, as has been demonstrated by relevant case law. See generally, CA 393/82 *Society Lawfully Registered v. Commander of the IDF* 37(4) PD 785, 18 (1983) (Isr.); Marco Sassòli, 'Article 43 of the Hague Regulations and Peace Operations in the Twenty-First Century' (International Humanitarian Law Research Initiative) (2004), 3, 15. See also Longobardo, 'The Duties of Occupying Powers in Relation to the Prevention and Control of Contagious Diseases', 767–768, 771–773,

Furthermore, the public health duties of the occupying power under the above-mentioned provisions should also include protection of the local population from adverse health consequences of all types of contamination or any other health risks that could be related to environmental degradation resulting from the occupant's acts and activities, including industrial and administrative activities. If this conclusion is correct, the law of occupation can play a crucial role along with IHRL in relation to providing protection to the environment through the protection provided to public health and hygiene and to the healthcare structure of the occupied territory. Hence, the occupying power's duty to protect the environment is also part of its obligation to progressively realise the right to the highest attainable standard of physical and mental health during the time of occupation.

The health of populations requires more than providing them with medical care. A state should also take into account the environmental, social, economic, and political conditions that could threaten the health of people and render them in need of medical care in the first place.[318] The same logic is applicable to the occupying power that has effective control over the occupied territory. For this reason, the right to health is quite an inclusive right, extending not only to timely and appropriate medical healthcare but also to the underlying determinants of health, such as access to safe and clean water and adequate sanitation, an acceptable supply of safe clean food, and healthy environmental conditions.[319]

As President Roosevelt affirmed in 1939, "[t]he ill health of the people is a public concern; ill health is a major cause of suffering, economic loss and dependency; good health is essential to the security and progress of the Nation".[320] This statement can be read in conjunction with Article 43 of the Hague Regulation, such that the occupying power has a duty to ensure and maintain public order and civil life in the occupied territory. The notion of civil life covers the social and economic life of the community too, as has been explained above.[321] All of these aspects of civil life are connected and very closely linked to each other, since if one of them is impacted upon, such as health, all of the others might be too, as President Roosevelt's declaration provided a long time ago.

Similarly to the aspects of civil life under Article 43 of the Hague Regulations, the right to health under Article 12 of the ICESCR also demands that consideration

---

778–780. See also ILC, 'First Report', paras 65, 70; Philippe Sands and others, *Principles of International Environmental Law* (4th edn, Cambridge University Press 2018), 818.

318 Paul Hunt and Rajat Khosla, 'Climate Change and the Right to the Highest Attainable Standard of Health' in Stephen Humphreys (ed), *Human Rights and Climate Change* (Cambridge University Press 2009), 238.

319 The UN Committee on Economic, Social and Cultural Rights, General Comment (No. 14): The Right to the Highest Attainable Standard of Health (Art. 12), para 11.

320 As cited in WHO, Official Records of the World Health Organization No. 2: Proceedings and Final Acts of the International Health Conference Held in New York from 19 June to 22 July 1946 (UN WHO Interim Commission June 1948) 31.

321 See generally: CA 393/82 *Society Lawfully Registered v. Commander of the IDF* 37(4) PD 785, 18 (1983) (Isr.); Longobardo, 'The Duties of Occupying Powers in Relation to the Prevention and Control of Contagious Diseases', 766–770, 781–783.

must be given to "both the individual's biological and socio-economic preconditions and a State's available resources in determining the highest level of health which is attainable by an individual".[322] The highest attainable standard of health is different from one state to another, depending on the availability of resources within the state itself and other specific conditions, such as the existence of an armed conflict.[323]

The occupying power's duty under Article 43 of the Hague Regulations (to ensure and maintain) and its duty under Article 12 of the ICESCR (to progressively realise) are complementary and support the interpretation, application, and implementation of each other based on the logic of Article 31(3)(c) of the VCLT. This is especially relevant regarding the protection of the right to health, while still considering all the other aspects of civilian life in an occupied territory, such as their social and economic well-being. Translating this reasoning into the field of environmental contamination, both provisions are seeking to protect the health and hygiene of civilians; however, under both, the occupying power only has a duty to protect the right to health in light of the means available. Nevertheless, if it fails to do so while it has effective control and continues to administer the occupied territory, including all underlying determinants of health, such as healthy environmental conditions during the whole period of occupation, it could incur a legal responsibility.

It could also be argued that the occupying power has the same obligations as under Article 12(2)(b) of the ICESCR under the domestic laws and regulations of the occupied state. For example, in the case where the occupied state has already adopted health laws and regulations, the occupying power has a legal obligation under the law of occupation to respect and not violate them. Accordingly, and as has been argued above, there is extra protection to the environment in times of occupation that can be provided through the right to health, not only by the occupying power's obligation under Article 12 of the ICESCR, Article 24 of the UNCRC, Article 43 of the Hague Regulations (civil life), and Article 56 of the GCIV (public health and hygiene) but also through its duty to respect the laws in force (domestic laws and regulations) in the occupied territory under the provisions of the law of occupation.

Therefore, the occupying power has a duty under IHRL and IHL to take all possible measures to prevent significant environmental harm that might prejudice the health of the local population of the occupied territory.[324] Consequently, it could be argued that the occupier should also have a due diligence obligation in relation

322 The UN Committee on Economic, Social and Cultural Rights, General Comment (No. 14): The Right to the Highest Attainable Standard of Health (Art. 12), para 9; Tobin, *The Right to Health in International Law*, 124.

323 Tobin, *The Right to Health in International Law*, 124.

324 The United Nations: General Assembly, International Law Commission: 'Protection of the Environment in Relation to Armed Conflicts: Text and Titles of the Draft Principles Provisionally Adopted by the Drafting Committee on First Reading' (A/CN.4/L.937) (6 June 2019), Principle 20 (2).

to the protection of the environment in times of occupation and thus has a duty to consider such an obligation in relation to preventing any significant harm to the environment in the occupied territory that might have an impact on the local population's ability to enjoy their right to health under Article 12 of the ICESCR.[325]

Accordingly, Article 43 of the Hague Regulations and Article 56 of the GCIV should be interpreted taking into consideration the right to health embodied in Article 12 of the ICESCR, which requires states to take "steps" to guarantee the highest attainable standard of health. Thus, using both Articles 43 of the Hague Regulations, namely the notion of "civil life" and Article 56 of the GCIV, "ensuring and maintaining public health and hygiene" in occupied territory, as the interpretive context of Article 12 of the ICESCR pursuant with the interpretation tool embodied under Article 31(3)(c) of the VCLT can strengthen and enhance the protection provided to the environment in times of occupation through the occupant's duty to ensure that everyone is enjoying the highest attainable standard of physical and mental health. Consequently, there is a complementarity relationship between the provisions under IHL, namely, Article 43 of the Hague Regulations, Article 56 of the GCIV, and Article 12 of the ICESCR under IHRL, as has been argued above. Such provisions provide protection to the right to health in times of occupation, and hence it is reasonable to argue that it is important to provide protection to the environment and to ensure it is protected from all types of contamination in relation to allowing the occupied people to enjoy and safely exercise their right to health in such situations. Accordingly, such a complementary relation between these rules, and particularly the dynamic approach of IHRL to the progressive realisation of the right to health, strengthens the occupying power's obligations regarding the protection of civilians' health in the occupied territory, which in turn, would reflect positively on general protection provided to the environment in times of occupation.

3.4.2.2 The Second Part of Article 43 of Hague Regulations, the Conservationist Principle and the Protection of the Environment under the Right to Health

The requirement under Article 12 of the ICESCR and under Article 24 of the UNCRC is to reach the highest attainable standard of health. The question is whether the concurrent application between IHRL and IHL regarding the law of occupation may stand at some point against such a requirement in relation to reaching the highest attainable standard of health under both provisions and therefore, limit the protection provided to the environment under those provisions. The law of occupation, specifically Article 43 of the Hague Regulations and the conservationist principle, may be in conflict with the health and well-being of the local population since they limit the circumstances in which the occupying power can lawfully alter the law in force in the occupied territory to enhance the right to health.

One of the obstacles to the application of the right to health under Article 12 of the ICESCR and Article 24 of the UNCRC in times of occupation is the

325 Ibid, Principle 22.

conservationist principle under Article 43 of the Hague Regulations. If the occupying power has the duty to protect the environment through the protection provided to health within the boundaries of the national law of the occupied territory, it may be difficult to adapt old legislation to new environmental threats to public health. The occupying power will need to plan long-term actions to protect the health of individuals in the occupied territory from new diseases or health outbreaks caused by environmental hazards and/or contamination that was not considered by the ousted sovereignty in its domestic laws and regulations or did not even exist before the beginning of the occupation.

These issues are seen as especially problematic when an occupation lasts for a long time, such as in the case of the OPT. The health and well-being of the local population could be served better outside the constraints of the provisions of the law of occupation, such as that under Article 43 of the Hague Regulations regarding altering the law in force in the occupied territory. Indeed, it states that it "is preoccupied with the maintenance of the status quo in light of the temporary character of the occupying power's administration".[326] It does not create privileges for the occupying powers, but it does allow them to alter the law in force in the occupied territory rather than impose restraints on them to guarantee that the civil life of the local population can continue as normally as possible.[327]

The conservative language of Article 43 of the Hague Regulations has been criticised for its strictness towards the occupying power's authorities in times of occupation.[328] However, even with its strict language, "unless absolutely prevented", it still allows a considerable amount of flexibility in relation to altering the law in force in the occupied territory for very specific purposes. However, even with this exception allowing the law in force of the occupied territory to be altered in very particular circumstances, Article 43 of the Hague Regulations does not give the occupying power any sovereignty over the occupied territory.[329] It could be argued that Article 43 of the Hague Regulations tries to create a balance between stability and change, that is, between the interests of the occupying power and those of the local population of the occupied territory.[330]

According to Article 43 of the Hague Regulations 1907, the occupying power has a legal obligation to respect the laws in force in the occupied territory unless absolutely prevented from doing so.[331] That means these laws might be subject to some modifications, if the occupying power is absolutely prevented from maintaining or respecting the laws in force of the occupied territory.[332] However, Article 43 of the Hague Regulations has not explained or provided any clear statement

326 Longobardo, 'The Duties of Occupying Powers in Relation to the Prevention and Control of Contagious Diseases', 770–771.
327 Sassòli, 'Article 43 of the Hague Regulations and Peace Operations', 5–6.
328 Ibid.
329 Ibid.
330 Benvenisti, *The International Law of Occupation*, 89–90.
331 The Hague Regulations 1907. Article 43.
332 Ibid.

regarding what it means by "absolutely prevented" or when the occupying power has the right to enact legislative measures or when to alter the laws in force of the occupied territory.[333] Some have argued that a literal interpretation of Article 43 seems to suggest that the occupying power is authorised to alter the law in force in the occupied territory or to enact new legislative measures only insofar as they restore and ensure public order and civil life,[334] and thus it is forbidden from enacting legislation in other fields.[335]

It could be important to alter the law in force in the occupied territory or to enact new legislative measures by an occupying power, such as provisions that consider public health and hygiene, food security and the welfare of the occupied people, in particular, the children.[336] For instance, upon occupying Palestine in 1917, the British promulgated norms/notices concerning "prices of food, public health and sanitation, cruelty to animals, cutting down trees,... all of which have been enforced

333 To understand how the concept of "unless absolutely prevented" was embodied in Article 43 of the Hague Regulations, it is important first to look at their origin in Articles 2 and 3 of the Brussels Declaration/Conference of 1874. Article 2 states that "the authority of the legitimate Power being suspended and having in fact passed into the hands of the occupants, the latter shall take all the measures in his power to restore and ensure, as far as possible, public order and safety". Article 3 states that "with this object he shall maintain the laws which were in force in the country in time of peace, and shall not modify, suspend or replace them unless necessary". When Articles 2 and 3 of the Brussels Declaration are read in combination, it becomes clear that both the power to "modify, suspend, or replace" under Article 3 and the legislative authority under Article 2 can be exercised only in case of necessity. https://ihl-databases.icrc.org/en/ihl-treaties/brussels-decl-1874?activeTab=undefined. The content of both Articles of the Brussels Declaration of 1874 was enshrined a few years later under Articles 43 and 44 of the Oxford Manual 1880. https://ihl-databases.icrc.org/en/ihl-treaties/oxford-manual-1880. Later on, both Articles were eventually integrated into one single Article in the 1899 Hague Regulations. At the 1899 Hague Conference, Mr. Beernaert, the Belgian delegate, opposed the inclusion of Article 3 of the Brussels Declaration because it used the more permissive term "unless necessary". However, Mr. Bihourd, the representative of France, suggested a proposal to omit Article 3 of the Brussels Declaration of 1874 but to preserve its spirit by adding the following phrase to Article 2 of the same Declaration: "while respecting unless absolutely prevented the laws in force in the country". The amendment suggested by Mr. Bihourd at the Hague Conference 1899 was adopted by 23 votes in favour and 1 against (Japan). Therefore, thanks to Mr. Bihourd's proposal, the phrase "unless absolutely prevented" was introduced in Article 43 of the Hague Regulations. For further information about the issue, see *The Proceedings of the Hague Peace Conferences. Translation of the Official Texts*, prepared in the Division of International Law of the Carnegie Endowment for International Peace under the supervision of James Brown Scott. The Conference of 1899. At: 52, 427–428, 520. Available online at: <https://ogc.osd.mil/Portals/99/proceedings_of_the_hague_peace_conferences_the_conference_of_1899%20%281%29.pdf>. Accessed date: 7 December 2023.

334 Edmund H. Schwenk, 'Legislative Power of the Military Occupant under Article 43 Hague Regulations' (1945), 54 Yale LJ 393, 395.

335 Ibid.

336 See *Final Record of the Diplomatic Conference of Geneva of 1949* (Berne, 1950), (Vol. II-A), 672, 747, 830–831, 856. For example, during the 37th meeting (Committee III), it was suggested that 'in adopting health and hygiene measures and their implementation, the Occupying Power shall take into consideration the moral and ethical susceptibilities of the population of the occupied territory'; 747.

by the military magistrate".[337] Moreover, the British occupation slightly amended the law in force in Palestine and slightly modified the judicial system there in relation to making it more in accordance with international law. For example, it made the punishment system more humane by increasing the discretion of judges.[338] The British occupation administration, at that time, aimed to protect the interests of the occupied population, and to achieve that aim, it had to amend the domestic laws in relation to improving and safeguarding welfare, thus ensuring normal life for the local population in Palestine.[339] It argued that, of course, any concern expressed by the occupant for the well-being of the local people in the occupied territory was not above suspicion.[340]

However, Edmund Schwenk argued that such a limitation under the second part of Article 43 of the Hague Regulations regarding the occupant's ability to adopt new legislative measures or even to alter the law in force in the occupied territory might be inconsistent with the first part of Article 43 of the Hague Regulations, which states that the entire "authority of the legitimate power having in fact passed into the hands of the occupant".[341]

It could be argued that the meaning of "unless absolutely prevented" is controversial even more than 100 years after the date of the adoption of the provision – the meaning of such an exception is still contested amongst scholars and different international law bodies. For example, some suggest such an exception could mean "absolute necessity",[342] whilst others contend it means just "necessity",[343] and still others have argued that it refers to "sufficient justification" to change the law in force, and so on.[344] Some other authors have said it means "reasonableness".[345] Hence, there are several approaches to how the exception under Article 43 of the Hague Regulations has been interpreted.

In more general terms, it is unfortunate that Article 43 of the Hague Regulations does not offer a set criterion to decide which adjustments are lawful and which are not. It is evident that, in recent decades, courts have indeed accepted a great variety

337 Norman Bentwich, 'The Legal Administration of Palestine under the British Military Occupation' (1920–1921) ,1 *Brit YB Int'l L* 139, 145.

338 Ibid, 144–146.

339 Benvenisti, *The International Law of Occupation*, 91; Bentwich, 'The Legal Administration of Palestine under the British Military Occupation', 145; Yoram Dinstein, 'Legislation Under Article 43 of the Hague Regulations: Belligerent Occupation and Peacebuilding', (Occasional Paper Series, No.1), (Program on Humanitarian Policy and Conflict Research (HPCR)/ Harvard University), (2004), 8.

340 Dinstein, 'Legislation Under Article 43 of the Hague Regulations', 8.

341 Schwenk, 'Legislative Power of the Military Occupant', 395.

342 Ibid, 401.

343 Yoram Dinstein, 'The International Law of Belligerent Occupation and Human Rights', (1978) 8 IYHR 104, 112.

344 Ernst Feilchenfeld, *The International Economic Law of Belligerent Occupation*, (Monograph Series of the Carnegie Endowment for International Peace, Division of International Law, No. 6. Washington 1942), 89.

345 Myres McDougal and Florentino Feliciano, *Law and Minimum World Public Order: The Legal Regulation and International Coercion* (Yale University Press 1961) 767.

of legislation by occupying powers as legitimate alterations to the laws in force in the occupied territory. For example, the exercise of the Israeli Supreme Court regarding legislation in the OPT is very relaxed and quite permissive.[346] This recognition of broader powers for altering the laws in force of the occupied territory, in particular the obligation to alter local laws that are in conflict with IHRL standards, has "implied more discretion for the occupant, and less formal constraints on its measures".[347]

The negative formulation of Article 43 of the Hague Regulations, namely "unless absolutely prevented", has been replaced under Article 64 of the GCIV, with more precise, albeit less restrictive,[348] provisions that the occupying power can alter the law in force of the occupied territory in relation "to fulfil its obligations under the present Convention".[349] The obligations, in this case, would be to protect the public health and hygiene of the local population embodied under the GCIV.[350] Complying with its duty under Article 43 of the Hague Regulations to restore and to ensure civil life in the occupied territory,[351] this in turn would help to reach the highest attainable standard of health under Article 12 of the ICESCR and under Article 24 of the UNCRC.

The reference in Article 64(2) of the GCIV to legislate or to alter the laws in force of the occupied territory "which are essential to enable the Occupying Power to fulfil its obligations", embodied under the GCIV, "must be extended to all applicable IHL, since IHL cannot possibly require specific conduct from an occupying power and also prohibit it to legislate for that purpose".[352] Moreover, the occupying power has the right to alter the law in force or to legislate to implement its IHRL obligations.[353] The second paragraph of Article 64 of the GCIV should be interpreted in as broad a sense as possible to allow the occupant to legislate and to subject the occupied population to all laws that are essential for the protection of their civil life and welfare, as well as to help the occupying power in the case where the national laws of the occupied territory are in conflict with its obligations under international law and modify them for such purposes.[354] For example, if the local legislation contravenes IHRL standards and contradicts the occupying power's obligations under IHRL, it has a legal duty not only to alter such legislation but also to make a new law to introduce as many changes as necessary to abolish those

346 David Kretzmer and Yaël Ronen, *The Occupation of Justice: The Supreme Court of Israel and the Occupied Territories* (Oxford University Press 2021) 133–134, 140–143.

347 Benvenisti, *The International Law of Occupation*, 91.

348 Sassòli, 'Article 43 of the Hague Regulations and Peace Operations', 7–8.

349 The GCIV, Article 64 (2)

350 Ibid, Article 56 (1)

351 Sassòli, 'Article 43 of the Hague Regulations and Peace Operations', 14–15.

352 Ibid, 12.

353 Benvenisti, *The International Law of Occupation*, 102–104; Sassòli, 'Article 43 of the Hague Regulations and Peace Operations', 12–14.

354 Benvenisti, *The International Law of Occupation*, 100–102; Sassòli, 'Article 43 of the Hague Regulations and Peace Operations', 7.

parts to IHRL standards, as well as in relation to complying with its human rights obligations, if the existing legislation prevents it from doing so.[355]

As can be seen, human rights law obligations enlarge the scope of law-making by the occupying power. Nonetheless, the risk of abuse of a broader interpretation by the occupant must not be ignored, as it is the occupying power's discretion that decides whether a legislative act is needful or not.[356] Indeed, occupants have, in some cases, utilised contentions based on the application of IHRL to restrain the protection provided by the provisions of the law of occupation to the ousted government and the occupied population. Since "the most important contribution of an occupying power to civil life in an occupied territory is to maintain the orderly government of the territory, Article 64 (2) of Convention IV explicitly allows it to legislate for that purpose".[357] However, the occupying power might use the discretionary authority to alter the law in force in the occupied territory, the argument being based on the application of IHRL in relation to limit the protection offered by the law of occupation, namely Article 43 of the Hague Regulations, to the ousted government as well as to the local population of the occupied territory.

As Dinstein simply put it: one should always be doubtful when an occupying power states that it needs to amend the domestic laws in the occupied territory for the benefit of the local population.[358] Additionally, he stated that "a professed humanitarian concern may camouflage a hidden political agenda, and it may be prudent to guard the inhabitants from the bear's hug of the occupying power".[359] For that reason, there must be a genuine necessity for each new enacted legislation by an occupying power or for any modification to the local laws of the occupied territory. Otherwise, it might be considered as an abuse of the power that has been given originally to the occupant by the law of occupation and that it has misused to achieve hidden unknown agendas and not the allowed exception under the law of occupation to ensure and restore the civil life and welfare of the local population in the occupied territory.

Bearing that in mind, Article 154 of the GCIV provides that the provisions of the GCIV complement those of the Hague Regulations. Hence, the meaning of Article 43 of the Hague Regulations can be safely interpreted by Article 64(2) of the GCIV.[360] Accordingly, the duty not to alter the domestic laws and regulations

355 Benvenisti, *The International Law of Occupation*, 102–104. Sassòli, 'Article 43 of the Hague Regulations and Peace Operations', 13.

356 Gerhard Von Glahn, *The Occupation of Enemy Territory: A Commentary on the Law and Practice of Belligerent Occupation* (Minneapolis, University of Minnesota Press 1957), 100.

357 Sassòli, 'Article 43 of the Hague Regulations and Peace Operations', 14–15.

358 Dinstein, *The International Law of Belligerent Occupation*, 132.

359 Ibid.

360 The GCIV, Article 154: "In the relations between the Powers who are bound by the Hague Conventions respecting the Laws and Customs of War on Land, whether that of July 29, 1899, or that of October 18, 1907, and who are parties to the present Convention, this last Convention shall be supplementary to Sections II and III of the Regulations annexed to the above-mentioned Conventions of The Hague".

of the occupied territory is not absolute, and the occupying power could do so in very specific circumstances to comply with its obligations under IHL and IHRL.

However, since the exact meaning of Article 43 of the Hague Regulations is vague, occupying powers have sometimes invoked its ambiguity to justify broad legislative powers. They have sometimes relied on the obligation to respect domestic laws "unless absolutely prevented" in order to escape from their responsibility to ensure the welfare and normal life of the occupied population.[361] Therefore, "unless absolutely prevented" must be interpreted by the occupant in light of Article 64(2) and in light of other IHRL obligations, in good faith, and in relation to ensuring the well-being of the local population of the occupied territory and not for any other reason. Accordingly, Article 64 may be understood as interpreting the expression "unless absolutely prevented" contained in the Hague Regulations and clarifies that only changes "essential" for legitimate purposes are allowed.[362]

To conclude, Article 64 can surely be considered to provide cases where the occupying power is absolutely prevented from respecting the laws in force in the occupied territory, and when it could and could not alter the laws in force and/or enact new legislation measures in that territory. In this regard, it is worth mentioning that, in some cases, the relationship between the protection of the environment and ensuring the highest attainable standard of health may require the occupying power to adopt some new measures to prevent the outbreak of diseases caused by environmental contamination. In doing so, it might need to adopt some interventions with respect to the environment and the right to health at the same time. Therefore, it may also need to alter the domestic laws of the occupied territory in order to prevent and control new health issues or disease outbreaks and/or pandemic caused by such contamination or because of poor environmental hygiene conditions in the occupied territory. Those necessarily limited alterations by an occupying power should also aim to enhance the protection provided to the environment against contamination and to the right to health, as well as to ensure the occupant is complying with its obligation under both IHRL and IHL to protect the public health and hygiene of the local population in times of occupation.[363] For example, this would be the case if there were new medicines or vaccines created after the beginning of the occupation that have been provided by health companies to fight against some diseases caused by environmental hazards or contamination, such as water, soil, or air contamination, that were not known before the beginning of the occupation of the ousted government. At the same time, those new medical scientific developments could help to prevent or to reduce the effect of the new health problems/outbreaks resulting from environmental hazards/environmental contamination/poor environmental health conditions and so on. In such a scenario,

361 Benvenisti, *The International Law of Occupation*, 89–95; Sassòli, 'Article 43 of the Hague Regulations and Peace Operations', 2.

362 Sassòli, 'Article 43 of the Hague Regulations and Peace Operations', 7.

363 See generally, Longobardo, 'The Duties of Occupying Powers in Relation to the Prevention and Control of Contagious Diseases', 769–772.

that might justify some modifications of the local law of the occupied territory by the occupying power in relation to tackling the issue.

This is just a simple example, but it is enough to show that health problems caused by environmental contamination and the need to control such health issues may be seen as one of the fields in which Article 43 of the Hague Regulations and the conservationist principle (in particular) and the law of occupation (in general) may be in conflict with the health and well-being of the occupied population, on the one hand, and with the protection of the environment, on the other. However, if the occupying power absolutely needed to take action, finding it essential to alter the law in force of the occupied territory to fight against such diseases and/or health outbreaks, and at the same time, did not take action because of its obligation under Article 43 of the Hague Regulations and the role of the conservationist principle, that might appear to be a way to escape its responsibility to ensure the highest attainable standard of health under Article 12 of the ICESCR and Article 24 of the UNCRC. Moreover, it could be used to deny its responsibility to ensure the highest attainable standard of health under the notion of civil life in Article 43 of the Hague Regulations and under Article 56 of the GCIV. However, Article 43 of the Hague Regulations must always be interpreted in light of additional applicable rules to such situations, such as Article 64(2) of the GCIV, as well as IHRL provisions, which are also applicable to situations of occupation, as has been argued above. Therefore, Article 43 of the Hague Regulations must be interpreted taking into consideration all other applicable international law rules.

Consequently, it could be argued that healthy environmental conditions in occupied territory could even be considered a *sine qua non* for the effective implementation of the right to health under both IHRL and IHL. Thus, the occupying power has a duty to apply such environmental rights to ensure the health of the local population while it continues administrating and having effective control over the occupied territory.

To summarise, such acts by the occupying powers against the environment, including all types of environmental pollution, depletion of resources, and destruction of vital health-related infrastructure and other vital infrastructure such as water treatment plants, denying civilians access to clean water sources, would appear to violate its trustee obligations as an administrator of the occupied territory and to breach its IHRL and IHL obligations to ensure the highest attainable standard of health under Article 12 of the ICESCR and Article 24 of the UNCRC. It also allows it to eschew the provisions of quality public health and hygiene under Article 43 of the Hague Regulations for restoring civil life and under Article 56 of the GCIV for the protected population.

However, it is possible also to conclude that the protection provided by IHRL to the environment through the right to health in times of occupation is lower than that offered by the same provision in peacetime due to its concurrent application with IHL. In other words, the law of occupation sometimes could limit the protection provided to the environment under IHRL because of its constraints, which mainly seek to keep the *status quo* in light of the temporary character of the occupant's administration, as has been demonstrated above. This is the case in particular regarding the second part of Article 43 of the Hague Regulations and its strong link with the conservationist principle.

3.4.3 The Right to Self-Determination and the Right of a People to Natural Wealth and Resources under IHRL and the Protection of the Environment in Occupied Territory

Self-determination as a rule of international law was recognised by the United Nations in 1945, namely under Article 1(2) of the Charter of the United Nations.[364] A few years later, it was recognised as a human right in both Covenants of human rights of the UN.[365] According to Article 1 of both Covenants, "All peoples have the right of self-determination",[366] and "All peoples may, for their own ends, freely dispose of their natural wealth and resources without prejudice to any obligations arising out of international economic co-operation, based upon the principle of mutual benefit, and international law. In no case may a people be deprived of its own means of subsistence".[367] How this right can provide protection to the environment in the context of occupation is of particular relevance for this research.

The Committee of the ICCPR has stressed that environmental harm can impact on the enjoyment of the right to self-determination and the right of people to freely dispose of their natural wealth and resources under Article 1 of the ICCPR.[368] The Committee has also provided that environmental degradation and exploitation can implicate those rights.[369] To better understand the relationship between the right to self-determination and the right to freely dispose of natural wealth and resources, on the one hand, and the protection of the environment in times of occupation, on the other, we need to first assess and analyse what the terms of "freely dispose", "deprived of" and "means of subsistence" mean and what they imply.

The meaning of "freely dispose" can be understood and interpreted in light of the context of Article 47 of the ICCPR, which confirms that all people have the right to fully and freely enjoy and utilise their natural wealth and resources.[370] However, that does not mean that there can be no limitations or restrictions upon

364 Charter of the United Nations: (signed on 26 June 1945), (entry into force 24 October 1945). Chapter I – Purposes and Principles: Article 1 (2).

365 Thomas Musgrave, *Self-Determination and National Minorities* (Oxford University Press 1997) 62.

366 The ICCPR and the ICESCR, Article (1) para 1.

367 Ibid, para 2.

368 The United Nations: Office of the United Nations High Commissioner for Human Rights: Special Procedures of the United Nations Human Rights Council. 'Mapping Human Rights Obligations Relating to the Enjoyment of a Safe, Clean, Healthy and Sustainable Environment: Individual Report on the International Covenant on Civil and Political Rights' (Report No.2) (December 2013), para 33, 19.

369 Ibid, paras 36 and 37, 20.

370 The ICCPR, Article 47. See also Paul Taylor, *A Commentary on the International Covenant on Civil and Political Rights: The UN Human Rights Committee's Monitoring of ICCPR Rights* (Cambridge University Press 2020), 130–132.

the use of natural resources. For example, ecological concerns must be taken into consideration.[371] This logic can be applied to instances of occupation and to the administration responsibilities of the occupying power in occupied territory. It has been argued that the context of Article 1(2) is meant to warn against foreign illegal exploitation which might violate peoples' right under the covenants, particularly when such exploitation by a foreign power can lead to deprivation of the local population's means of subsistence.[372] Furthermore, the enjoyment of the right to freely dispose of natural wealth and resources can, to some extent, rely on the protection of these resources from environmental pollution.[373]

The notion "deprived of" relates to a situation in which forces outside of control of the community undermine the resource base.[374] It is argued that this phrase is the most relevant in relation to assessing the right of people to self-determination, as when natural resources being exploited by a foreign power against the will of the local population, preventing them from using and enjoying such resources.[375] Therefore, foreign powers, including the occupant, in exercising an effective control over another state's territory, have a legal obligation under Article 1(2) to avoid and to prevent deprivation of the local population from their means of subsistence, including their own lands.[376]

Lastly, the phrase "means of subsistence" includes everything that is essential for upholding the lives of the people in question. It is further worth raising the question as to whether there are any specific criteria to classify between resources that represent "means of subsistence" and those that do not.

To answer this question, it should first be argued that means of subsistence cannot just include the resources that are directly linked to human intake, for it must also include all means that are crucial for upholding and supporting human life. For example, mineral resources that compromise an important element of the surface environment of the earth and, at the same time, are finite and non-renewable,[377] such as gold, silver, zinc, phosphate, and sand, can be sold and can generate valuable financial resources (income). Moreover, they have the potential to create good job opportunities for the local population, which can represent means of subsistence as well.[378] Thus, there can be no doubt that these resources constitute an important economic source/asset for any country that has them.[379]

371 Hans Haugen, 'The Right to Self-Determination and Natural Resources: The Case of Western Sahara', (2007) 3 Law Environmental Development Journal (LEAD) 70, 73.

372 Taylor, *A Commentary on the International Covenant on Civil and Political Rights*, 130–132; Haugen, 'The Right to Self-Determination and Natural Resources', 72–73.

373 Taylor, *A Commentary on the International Covenant on Civil and Political Rights*, 131–132.

374 Haugen, 'The Right to Self-Determination and Natural Resources', 73.

375 Ibid.

376 Ibid.

377 Gordon Brown and Georges Calas, 'Environmental Mineralogy – Understanding Element Behavior in Ecosystems' (2011) 343 *Comptes Rendus Geoscience* 90, 91–92.

378 Haugen, 'The Right to Self-Determination and Natural Resources', 77.

379 Ibid.

Several instances from different countries represent a clear example of how these resources attract foreign greed, and might end up with the country becoming an occupied territory, such as Morocco in Western Sahara. However, the occupying power must always administer the natural and mineral resources of the occupied territory in a way that ensures their sustainable use,[380] as has been demonstrated in the previous chapter.

It is believed that the resources that represent "means of subsistence" might enjoy stronger protection during times of occupation, and the occupant has to protect and save them, specifically from environmental hazards and pollution. This will ensure that the local population can continue to have their own means of subsistence and be able to exercise their right to self-determination. It could be argued that this logic has corresponding guarantees under IHL, namely, under Article 54(2) of API to the Fourth Geneva Conventions, since the provision prohibits any destruction of civilian objects that are indispensable to the survival of the population, such as "foodstuffs, agricultural areas for the production of foodstuffs, crops, livestock, drinking water installations etc.".[381] The occupying power has a legal obligation to respect this provision, as has been discussed in the previous chapter.

Due to the fact that the availability of "means of subsistence" can represent a strong reason for any community to stay or to move forward, environmental factors such as keeping a healthy ecosystem, including unpolluted natural resources, can play a critical role in this regard. It should be borne in mind that the occupying power has a duty to take environmental considerations into account while it continues administering and exercising effective control over the occupied territory.[382] Therefore, it could be argued that there is a strong link between the occupying power's responsibility to protect the environment and the right of the occupied people to fully and freely dispose of their own natural wealth and resources, together with the availability of means of subsistence, on the one hand, and their ability to enjoy and to exercise their right to self-determination, on the other. Accordingly, the occupying power has an obligation under IHRL to protect these resources from any environmental harm and contamination that might impact on the ability of occupied people to exercise and enjoy their right to self-determination and the right of a people to natural wealth and resources under Article 1 of the Covenants.

In accordance with IHL, this puts limits on the authority of the occupying power and balances between its interests and the occupied population. This supports and complements the meaning and interpretation of the three abovementioned terms of "freely dispose", "deprived of" and "means of subsistence" under Article 1(2) of both Covenants of human rights. For example, under Article 55 of the Hague Regulations 1907, the occupying power cannot exploit or use the natural resources

380 The Hague Regulations 1907, Article 55; Michael Bothe, 'Protection of the Environment in Relation to Armed Conflict' in Dieter Fleck (ed), *The Handbook of International Humanitarian Law* (4th edn, Oxford University Press 2021), 350.

381 The Additional Protocol I (1977), Article 54(2).

382 Bothe, 'Protection of the Environment in Relation to Armed Conflict', 350.

of the occupied territory in an unsustainable manner, and it has the limited right of usufruct to exploit natural wealth and resources.[383] Furthermore, Article 55 of the GCIV imposes on the occupying power the duty to ensure that the population of an occupied territory has all fundamental supplies to meet their basic needs.[384]

It could, however, be argued that without environmental conservation, the effective implementation of Article 55 of the GCIV would be impossible, and therefore providing fundamental supplies to the population of the occupied territory may be impacted upon as well. Arguably, the occupying power's responsibility of ensuring that the population of an occupied territory has all their fundamental needs met under Article 55 of the GCIV might have some environmental dimensions. In the first place, under it, for these needs to be met, the occupying power shall first depend on the resources of the occupied territory itself, as the Article clearly asks it to provide food and medical supplies to the local population. As argued earlier, some food and some medicines are provided from the natural resources of the occupied territory itself and, without protecting the environment, such natural resources might be harmed, whether by the occupying power or by third parties on the occupied territory. Thus, it directly affects the occupant's ability to provide all fundamental and basic needs to the populations of the occupied territory. Hence, the requirements of the occupying power under Article 55 of the GCIV might not be fully met.

In cases where the occupying power has overexploited the natural wealth and resources of an occupied territory in an unsustainable manner, that might lead to decreased productivity of those resources, and that could have some environmental consequences, such as desertification and drought. This, in turn, could prevent the occupied population from freely enjoying and disposing of their natural wealth and resources, which might have an impact on their ability to meet their basic and fundamental needs. According to Longobardo, "the international community has realised that the availability of natural resources is one pivotal component of the principle of self-determination – people can actually gain independence, determine its constitutional architecture, and choose an international policy only if it has full control over its resources".[385] Therefore, such acts by the occupying power may effect the occupied populations' ability to exercise their right to self-determination under Article 1 of both Covenants of human rights.

Furthermore, the occupying power's obligation under Article 1 of both ICCPR and ICESCR not to violate the occupied people's right to self-determination and their right to freely dispose of and enjoy their natural wealth and resources can be linked to its obligation under Article 43 of the Hague Regulations 1907 to consider public order, civil life, and welfare and to provide as normal a life as possible for

383 The Hague Regulations 1907, Article 55.

384 The GCIV, Article 55. See also Hans-Peter Gasser, 'Protection of the Civilian Population: Belligerent Occupation', 272.

385 Marco Longobardo, 'The Palestinian Right to Exploit the Dead Sea Coastline for Tourism', (2015) 58 *German YB Int'l L* 317, 339.

the occupied population. It can also be linked to the conservationist principle under the same provision. The occupying power does not acquire any sovereignty of the ousted occupied state.[386] That is, it has no authority to introduce any permanent or fundamental change in the occupied territory that might prevent the occupied population from exercising their right to permanent sovereignty over their natural wealth and resources, as well as their right to self-determination.[387]

Bearing that in mind, the duty under Article 43 of the Hague Regulations, as has been argued in the previous chapter, has economic and social dimensions since numerous natural resources have economic values, and populations depend on them for both their income and their survival. Such obligations under both provisions can support and complement each other in relation to providing extra protection to the environment in the occupied territory. Accordingly, under the provisions of the law of occupation, the occupying power might use the natural wealth and resources of the occupied territory. However, the right of usufruct is limited regarding the exploitation of such resources for the benefits of the civilians living in the occupied territory or in order to cover the expenses of the occupation, as has been explained in the previous chapter. Therefore, it could be argued that there is convergence and complementarity between the provisions of the law of occupation, such as Article 43 and Article 55 of the Hague Regulations 1907, Article 55 GCIV, and Article 1 of both Covenants of human rights – all addressing the right to self-determination and the right to permanent sovereignty of natural wealth and resources in a time of occupation.

When the occupying power is illegally overexploiting the natural wealth and resources in an occupied territory, such as oil and water, this would not only be considered a violation of the right to self-determination and the right to freely dispose of the natural wealth and resources under Article 1 of both ICCPR and ICESCR, but would also violate the occupying power's obligations under Articles 43 and 55 of the Hague Regulations, as well as Article 55 of the GCIV. Bearing that in mind, as demonstrated in the previous chapter, the overexploiting of the natural wealth and resources can have grave and long-term consequences for ecosystem functions and cause enormous biodiversity loss along with other potential injuries to the local environment of the occupied territory.

Consequently, the protection that can be provided to the environment through the occupying power's obligation to respect and not violate the occupied people's right to self-determination and to freely dispose of natural wealth and resources not only protects the ecosystem from the negative consequences resulting from overexploiting of the natural wealth and resources, but also can ensure that the occupying power is complying with its obligations under the provisions of the law

386 Yutaka Arai-Takahashi, 'Preoccupied with Occupation: Critical Examinations of the Historical Development of the Law of Occupation', (2012) 94 *International Review of the Red Cross* 51, 53–54; Nico Schrijver, *Sovereignty over Natural Resources: Balancing Rights and Duties* (Cambridge University Press 2008), 267.

387 Arai-Takahashi, 'Preoccupied with Occupation: Critical Examinations', 53–54; Longobardo, 'The Palestinian Right to Exploit the Dead Sea Coastline', 338–343; ILC, 'First Report', paras 44, 46.

of occupation. That is, it can promote the civil life and welfare of the occupied population while ensuring that they continue to have their basic and fundamental needs met during the whole period of occupation. To ensure this duty under Article 1 of both Covenants of human rights is implemented, environmental considerations must be taken into account by the occupying power during the time of occupation. Thus, it is safe to assume that there is a reciprocal complementarity relationship between the occupant's obligations under Article 1 of both Covenants of human rights, Articles 43 and 55 of the Hague Regulations, and Article 55 of the GCIV, with the protection of the environment including the stable functioning of the ecosystem and biodiversity in the occupied territory.

Therefore, the more the environment is protected, the more freedom the occupied population can enjoy to exercise their right to self-determination and to freely dispose of their natural wealth and resources, as well as to live a more stable, normal, and civil life. Accordingly, the more environmental issues are addressed by the occupying power, the more it can comply with its responsibility under Article 1 of both ICCPR and ICESCR as well as its obligations under Articles 43 and 55 of the Hague Regulations and Article 55 of the GCIV. Otherwise, the occupant will violate its obligations under both IHRL and IHL. However, in case the occupant is not a state party to both covenants of human rights, the Martens Clause, and the API 1977 to the Fourth Geneva Conventions 1949, then it can be invoked as providing general principles of international law in relation to protecting civilians living in the occupied territory. For example, this is so in cases not covered by IHRL and IHL treaties or when dealing with a non-state party to such treaties. In this case, the occupied population are still under the protection of the principles of international law derived from established custom, from the principles of humanity, and from the dictates of public conscience.[388] According to Article 1(2) of the API 1977, "in cases not covered by this Protocol or by other international agreements, civilians and combatants remain under the protection and authority of the principles of international law derived from established custom, from the principles of humanity and from the dictates of public conscience".[389] According to the ICRC Commentaries on Article 1(2) of the API 1977, "this paragraph is taken from the famous clause, known as the 'Martens clause'".[390] Therefore, the Martens Clause and the API 1977 both provide authority that goes beyond treaty law and custom; they consider the principles of international law, such as those of humanity. It should be noted that, the Martens Clause can be found in the preamble of the

388 See, ICRC, International Humanitarian Law Databases, 'Protocol Additional to the Geneva Conventions of 12 August 1949, and relating to the Protection of Victims of International Armed Conflicts (Protocol I), 8 June 1977: Commentary of 1987, Article 1 – General Principles and Scope of Application: Paragraph 2'. Available online at: <https://ihl-databases.icrc.org/en/ihl-treaties/api-1977/article-1/commentary/1987?activeTab=undefined>. Accessed date: 8 December 2023.

389 Ibid.

390 Ibid.

1899 and 1907 Hague Regulations.[391] In relation to the protection of the environment, and even if the occupying power is not a state party to any of the covenants of human rights, it may still hold some environmental responsibilities towards the occupied territory and its population under the logic of the Martens Clause and the Article 1(2) of the API. For example, in an attempt by the ILC to environmentalise the Martens Clause, it states that "in cases not covered by international agreements, the environment remains under the protection and authority of the principles of international law derived from established custom, from the principles of humanity and from the dictates of public conscience".[392] One scholar has argued that, whilst the Martens Clause's main aim is to ensure respect for humanity, environmental protection *per se* could be taken into consideration as well.[393] Accordingly, it may be claimed that by greening the Martens Clause, the environment can enjoy protection even in situations where an occupying power is not a state party to any of IHRL, IHL, or IEL treaties or when a treaty itself does not provide protection to the environment as such. Hence, the occupied population can continue to enjoy exercising their right to self-determination and to freely dispose of their natural wealth and resources, with this logic also being applicable to the enjoyment of all other human rights that are related to a clean and healthy environment.

It should be noted that, as argued in the previous chapter, the author does not agree with the ICJ's dictum in the *DRC v. Uganda* (2005) case[394] regarding the inapplicability of the principle of permanent sovereignty over natural resources in times of armed conflict and occupation.[395] By applying the principle to the situations of occupation, this will tend to support a restrictive interpretation of the occupant's rights in relation to the use, exploitation, and disposal of natural wealth and resources in occupied territory. In addition to this, the occupying power is under a legal obligation not to interfere with the exercise of permanent sovereignty by the local population.[396] Moreover, the claim that the principle of permanent sover-

391 See the Preamble of the Hague Convention of 1899 <https://ihl-databases.icrc.org/en/ihl-treaties/hague-conv-ii-1899/preamble>; the Preamble of the Hague Conventions of 1907 <https://ihl-databases.icrc.org/en/ihl-treaties/hague-conv-iv-1907/preamble>. For further information about the Martens Clause, see Rupert Ticehurst, 'The Martens Clause and the Laws of Armed Conflict', available online at: <https://www.onlinelibrary.iihl.org/wp-content/uploads/2021/07/Martens-Clause-LOAC.pdf>. Accessed date: 8 December 2023.

392 ILC, Draft principles on Protection of the Environment in Relation to Armed Conflicts 2022, Draft Principle 12.

393 Sjöstedt, *The Role of Multilateral Environmental Agreements*, 117, 120.

394 The ICJ, *DRC v. Uganda* (2005), para 244. The ICJ has stressed that the principle is not applicable to "the specific situation of looting, pillage and exploitation of certain natural resources by members of the army of a State militarily intervening in another State".

395 See for example the General Assembly Resolution 1803 (XVII) of (14 December 1962). The Resolution has clearly confirmed the rights of peoples to permanent sovereignty over their natural wealth and resources. See also, in favour of the application of the principle of permanent sovereignty over natural resources in times of armed conflict and occupation, Longobardo, 'State Responsibility for International Humanitarian Law', 255–256.

396 Sloan, The United Nations: General Assembly: Economic and Social Council, 'Implications, under International Law', para 51 (C).

eignty over natural resources is not applicable to situations of occupation might be contradictory to the legal status of occupation as a temporary situation, with only a provisional administration authority that is not supposed to impact upon the sovereignty of the occupied territory.[397]

It should, however, be noted that, the Court's conclusion in *DRC v. Uganda* seems to be inconsistent with the practice of the Human Rights Council as well as UNGA and UNSC resolutions. These all emphasise the application of the principle of permanent sovereignty over natural resources in times of occupation. For example, the Human Rights Council affirmed "the applicability of the principle of permanent sovereignty over natural resources to the Palestinian situation as an integral component of the right to self-determination".[398] It could be argued that the ICJ in *DRC v. Uganda* did not consider the fact that the principle of permanent sovereignty over natural resources emerged as a natural result of the principle of self-determination.[399] The ICJ has already confirmed the applicability of the principle of self-determination in times of occupation in the Wall Advisory Opinion.[400]

The UNGA has also confirmed the application of the principle in the OPT and other occupied Arab territories, such as Syrian Golan.[401] Moreover, the Court's position is against some of the UNSC binding resolutions, such as when considering the situation of Iraq under the occupation. The UNSC affirmed the right of Iraq to permanent sovereignty over its natural resources,[402] not to mention the fact that the principle of permanent sovereignty over natural resources is mentioned under Article 1 of both ICCPR and ICESCR, where the ICJ confirmed their applicability to the situation of the OPT as binding upon Israel.[403] Therefore, the ICJ's position on the application of the principle of permanent sovereignty over natural resources in *DRC v. Uganda* appears to be inconsistent with the Human Rights Council, UNGA, and UNSC practice, as well as with the Court's own jurisprudence.

Hence, it could be argued that Article 1 (2) of both ICCPR and ICESCR reinforces the right of occupied people to enjoy their natural wealth and resources, and, at the same time, it is precisely related to the right to self-determination. Thus, it would be irrational to consider only the right to self-determination as being applicable to situations of occupation and that the permanent sovereignty over the natural resources is not, since both principles share a common origin.[404]

397 ILC, 'First Report', para 34.

398 Human Rights Council, Human Rights Situation in Palestine and other Occupied Arab Territories, 'Right of the Palestinian People to self-determination', (A/HRC/RES/49/28), (11 April 2022).

399 Longobardo, 'The Palestinian Right to Exploit the Dead Sea Coastline', 344.

400 ICJ, Wall Advisory Opinion, paras 88, 122, 149.

401 United Nations: General Assembly, 'Permanent Sovereignty of the Palestinian People in the Occupied Palestinian Territory, including East Jerusalem, and of the Arab Population in the Occupied Syrian Golan over their Natural Resources' (A/RES/70/225) (23 February 2016).

402 United Nations: Security Council, Resolution 1483 (2003), adopted by the Security Council at its 4761st meeting on (22 May 2003); UNSC, (SC Res. 1546). Adopted by the Security Council at its 4987th meeting on (8 June 2004).

403 ICJ, Wall Advisory Opinion, paras 88, 111, 112.

404 Longobardo, 'The Palestinian Right to Exploit the Dead Sea Coastline', 345.

Therefore, the occupying power has a legal obligation under IHRL to protect the environment and its natural resources from any harm that might result from an act or violation of such a right. By respecting and not violating people's rights to self-determination and the right to freely dispose of their natural wealth and resources in situations of occupation, the chance of harming the environment, including the biodiversity and ecosystem functions, would be much lower, in particular by preventing the occupying power and limiting its authority from abuse or overutilisation of the natural resources in the occupied territory. Finally, it can be safely said that Article 1 of both Covenants of human rights can play a notable role in providing protection to the environment in situations of occupation, as has been demonstrated above. Hence, the occupying power has an obligation to take all possible measures to protect the occupied peoples' collective rights to enjoy and to exercise their right to self-determination, and in order to fulfil this obligation, it must take environmental considerations into account.

3.5 The Protection of the Environment through Property Rights under IHRL in Times of Occupation

As discussed in Chapter 2, property rights under the law of occupation can play an important role in providing protection to the environment in times of occupation, especially through the protection provided to private property and how this type of property can enjoy stronger protection than public property. This section will examine how property rights under IHRL can extend this protection and impose more restrictions on the occupying power regarding the use of private property in occupied territory and how that, in turn, can help to protect the environment. The focus is on the need to examine how IHRL can strengthen the protection provided to the environment through property rights provisions.

First and foremost, it is important to mention that there is no such right to property under the global human rights system.[405] Looking at the Article 17 of the UDHR, which is not binding formally speaking, this concerns the right to property.[406] However, the right to property is recognised under regional and national human rights systems, such as the European,[407] American,[408] African,[409] and Arab[410] ones, along with states' national laws,[411] as well as under several treaties that prohibit discrimination, such as CEDAW and CERD. In addition, Article 17 of the ICCPR could also provide a kind of protection to private property through that in relation to the family and home life. The following paragraphs will explain the

405 John Sprankling, 'The Global Right to Property', (2014) 52 *Colum. J. Transnet's L.* 464, 1–2.
406 The UDHR, Article 17.
407 The Protocol 1 of the ECHR, Article 1.
408 The IACHR, Article 21.
409 The African Charter, Article 14.
410 The Arab Charter, Article 25.
411 Sprankling, 'The Global Right to Property', 9–10.

right to property under those different legal instruments and how they could help save the environment in times of occupation.

Protocol 1 of the ECHR, for example, includes the right to property. The right itself does not include any environmental elements or any guarantee to enjoy the right to a healthy and balanced environment. However, the ECtHR has linked the right to property under the Convention to environmental interests and how individuals' right to safely enjoy their properties and possessions can, on some occasions, depend on how effectively the environment is protected and what environmental standards and measures have been taken by a state to ensure the protection of individuals' properties from environmental hazards.[412] The ECtHR has confirmed that the effective exercise of the right to property does not only rely on the state's duty not to interfere, but also requires it to take positive and proactive measures to protect this right.[413] Therefore, states have an obligation not only not to interfere but also to take positive measures to protect the right to property from environmental hazards or any dangerous activities, where the right of property might be at risk.[414]

This logic is also applicable to situations of occupation, where a state party to the convention is involved.[415] That is, it will have an obligation under Article 1 of Protocol 1 of the ECHR to take environmental considerations into account while it administers and has effective control over another state's territory.[416] By emphasising the linkage between property rights, both private and public, under Protocol 1 of the ECHR and protection of the environment, this could practically promote animal and plant conservation, At the same time, it could keep a region safe and free from pollution, which would play an important role in encouraging the provision of ecosystem services, which in turn, would promote human health and well-being.[417]

The ECtHR has found that the environment is an important consideration and may require states to ensure certain environmental standards in relation to allowing individuals the full enjoyment of their own properties.[418] There is no case law before the ECtHR on the right to property under Article 1 of Protocol 1 to the ECHR regarding the protection of the environment and situations of occupation

412 The ECtHR, *Öneryıldız v. Turkey* (Application no. 48939/99), Judgment (30 November 2004); paras 134–138.

413 See, for example, the ECtHR: *Budayeva and Others v. Russia*, para 172.

414 See, for example, *Öneryıldız v. Turkey*; Manual on Human Rights and the Environment. (Council of Europe Publishing, 2nd edn, 2012) 62–63, 68, 71–74.

415 See, for example, the case law regarding property rights from occupied Northern Cyprus: *Loizidou v. Turkey*, ECtHR, (Appl. No 40/1993) (435/514), Preliminary Objection of 23 February 1995.

416 For case laws where the ECtHR considered the linkage between the enjoyment and safe exercise of the right to property under the ECHR and environmental interests, see: The ECtHR, *Öneryıldız v. Turkey* (Application no. 48939/99), Judgment (30 November 2004), paras 134–138; See also the ECtHR: *Budayeva and Others v. Russia*, paras 172–182; For a more recent case, see *National Movement Ekoglasnost v. Bulgaria* (ECtHR), Judgment (15 December 2020) (Application no. 31678/17).

417 See Megan McArdle, 'How Property Rights Could Help Save the Environment' (May 29, 2012).

418 Manual on Human Rights and the Environment (Council of Europe Publishing, 2nd edn, 2012) 62–71.

immediately. Arguably, when private property, such as trees, parks, and gardens, are compromised, the right to property under Article 1 of Protocol 1 to the ECHR provides protection to it as well.[419] Applying the property rights approach to ecological issues in occupied territory might help address several environmental problems and be an effective way to benefit not only people, but also land, animal, plant, soil, and other resources. Indeed, the ECtHR on different occasions has considered environmental harm and pollution as an obstacle that can lead to a breach of several human rights under the Convention and its Protocol 1.[420]

Article 21 of the IACHR provides that "Everyone has the right to the use and enjoyment of his property".[421] Furthermore, Article 25 of the Arab Charter of Human Rights (ACHR) regarding the right to private property sees that "The right to private ownership is guaranteed to every citizen. Under no circumstances shall a citizen be arbitrarily or illegally deprived of all or part of his property".[422] While the above discussion concerning IACHR and ACHR conventions does not apply specifically to occupation as such, it would seem reasonable to argue that the commitment to respect and protect property rights under those conventions and charters also extends to any state party that has jurisdiction and effective control over another state's territory.

Globally, nonetheless, the right to property itself is not a binding right under the UDHR, and it is not officially recognised under either of the Covenants of human rights. It has been adopted by some global human rights conventions and ratified by a vast number of states world-wide. However, 97 percent of states are parties to CEDAW, and the convention has clearly stated that states have obligations regarding property. For example, Article 16 of the Convention provides that "State Parties shall take all appropriate measures to eliminate discrimination against women in all matters" and "in particular shall ensure the same rights for both spouses in respect of the ownership, acquisition, management, administration, enjoyment and disposition of property etc.".[423] CEDAW's Committee has stressed that "in conflict and post-conflict situations, State parties are bound to apply the Convention and other international human rights and humanitarian law when they exercise territorial or extraterritorial jurisdiction. The Convention applies to a wide range of situations, including wherever a State exercises jurisdiction, such as occupation and other forms of administration of foreign territory".[424] The Committee gave recommendations to state parties to the Convention to respect, protect, and

419 Dienelt, *Armed Conflicts and the Environment*, 186.

420 See generally, the European Court of Human Rights, 'Guide to the Case-law of the European Court of Human Rights – Environment' (Council of Europe 2022).

421 IACHR, Article 21.

422 League of Arab States, Arab Charter on Human Rights, 15 September 1994. Article 25.

423 CEDAW, Article 16(1)(h).

424 The United Nations, Convention on the Elimination of All Forms of Discrimination against Women, Committee on the Elimination of Discrimination against Women, General Recommendation No. 30 on Women in Conflict Prevention, Conflict and Post-conflict Situations (CEDAW/C/GC/30) (18 October 2013), para 9. See also, from the same reference, paras 4 and 21.

fulfil all the rights guaranteed by the Convention, which applies extraterritorially for occupying powers in situations of foreign occupation.[425]

Environmental human rights have been taken up by various UN bodies charged with the implementation of specific human rights treaties, with CEDAW being just one of those. For example, the Committee of the Convention has recognised the procedural environmental rights of women, while also addressing the possibility of environmental violations of rights protected under CEDAW.[426] Notwithstanding this, the Convention has not formally adopted or recognised an independent right to the environment as such. However, the Committee of the Convention in its annual report has reported to the UNGA that it has asked all State Parties to the Convention to take measures and to introduce policies and programmes to "improve the environmental and living conditions of women and children, and of girls in particular".[427] Moreover, the Committee has recognised that environmental harm could undermine all human rights protected under CEDAW. In addition to this, the Committee has on different occasions linked the quality of the environment to the enjoyment and exercise of women's fundamental rights, such as the right to health the right to an adequate standard of living, including the right to safe and clean drinking water and sanitation,[428] the right to freedom of movement; the right to development; and the right to property.[429] In addition to this, CERD,[430] CPRMW,[431] and CRPD[432] have all included a right to property.

As enshrined in Article 17 of the UDHR, this was reaffirmed by CEDAW, CERD, CPRMW, and CRPD. This language seemingly recognises that the non-binding right to property under the UDHR was incorporated into CEDAW, CERD,

425 The United Nations, Convention on the Elimination of All Forms of Discrimination against Women, Committee on the Elimination of Discrimination against Women, General Recommendation No. 30 on Women in Conflict Prevention, Conflict and Post-conflict situations (CEDAW/C/GC/30) (18 October 2013), para 12 (C).

426 See The United Nations: Office of the United Nations High Commissioner for Human Rights, Special Procedures of the United Nations Human Rights Council, 'Mapping Human Rights Obligations Relating to the Enjoyment of a Safe, Clean, Healthy and Sustainable Environment: Individual Report on the United Nations Convention on the Elimination of All Forms of Discrimination against Women' (Report No.4) (December 2013).

427 Report of the Committee on the Elimination of Discrimination against Women for the Twenty-fourth & Twenty-fifth Sessions, Implementation of Article 21 of the Convention: Gender and Sustainable Development (1 January 2001), U.N. Doc. (A/56/38), 385.

428 For example, Article 14(2)(h) of the CEDAW Convention provided that State Parties to the Convention shall ensure to women in rural areas the right to "enjoy adequate living conditions, particularly in relation to … sanitation … and … water supply".

429 See The United Nations: Office of the United Nations High Commissioner for Human Rights, Special Procedures of the United Nations Human Rights Council, 'Mapping Human Rights Obligations Relating to the Enjoyment of a Safe, Clean, Healthy and Sustainable Environment: Individual Report on the United Nations Convention on the Elimination of All Forms of Discrimination against Women' (Report No. 4) (December 2013), paras 15–17, 22, 26, 30, 32–33, 37, 43; See also footnote no. 50 of the same Report.

430 CERD, Article 5(V).

431 CPRMW, Article 15.

432 CRPD, Article 12(5).

CPRMW, and CRPD's binding treaties. Accordingly, it imposes an obligation on all state parties to respect that right.[433] However, it is clear that the right to property under those treaties is only to protect specific groups and their proprieties against discrimination. Thus, it cannot be said that it is applicable to everyone since there is no such provision in those treaties expressly recognising a general right to property.

The UNGA Resolution 41/132 states that there is "the right of everyone to own property alone as well as in association with others".[434] The Resolution emphasises the importance of the content of Article 17 of the UDHR and Article 16 of CEDAW and confirms the right of everyone to enjoy their own property. Moreover, it has linked this right to the widespread enjoyment of other basic human rights.[435] However, this Resolution is a non-binding one.

All of the IHL provisions on the protection of civilians' private property in times of occupation cover the same subject matter as the right to property set out under CEDAW,[436] CERD,[437] CPRMW,[438] and CRPD.[439] These laws can be interpreted in light of each other in accordance with Article 31(3)(c) of the VCLT. In this case, the right to property under the abovementioned IHRL treaties can be interpreted in light of the occupying power's property-related obligations under IHL, such as its obligations under Article 46 of the Hague Regulations and Article 53 of the GCIV.

In this respect, the provisions under IHL complement and correspond to property rights articles under IHRL treaties in the sense that they address in detail the occupying power's duties towards private property in times of occupation. In particular, Article 46 of the Hague Regulations covers both types of private property (movable and immovable), and Article 53 of the GCIV prohibits any destruction of it. Furthermore, the parallel application of IHL and the abovementioned treaties under IHRL is important, since the ICCPR and ICESCR do not include such a right to property. Accordingly, applying the harmonisation approach between IHL and IHRL treaties to the protection of private property may strengthen the protection provided to the environment in such situations. For example, anti-discrimination treatises of property-related provisions can indirectly provide protection to the environment in the same way that some articles under IHL can do, since they forbid any acts against property that might prevent the protected people under those treaties from enjoying their right to that which is privately owned.

It is worth mentioning that there is a strong trend among international law scholars to support the claim that the right to property is already a part of customary international law.[440] In particular, there has been widespread adoption of such a right in states' national laws, as well as the almost universal ratification of anti-

433 Sprankling, 'The Global Right to Property', 13–14.
434 UN General Assembly (41st sess.: 1986–1987), (A/RES/41/132).
435 Ibid.
436 CEDAW, Article 16.
437 CERD, Article 5(V).
438 CPRMW, Article 15.
439 CRPD, Article 12(5).
440 See generally, Sprankling, 'The Global Right to Property', 21–24; see also Ursula Kriebaum, August Reinisch, 'Property, Right to, International Protection', (*Max Planck Encyclopedias of International Law* (MPIL) (2019).

discrimination treaties that clearly include a right to property along with the UNGA Resolution, which has been adopted without any opposition from states. However, the global right to property is still neither officially recognised as a customary law nor as a general principle and is still a subject of extensive debate.[441]

Consequently, the questions that can be asked are the following: how could property rights provide protection to the environment in scenarios of occupation? To what extent does the occupant have an obligation to respect such rights while it administers the occupied territory?

To address these questions, a practical example from a scenario of occupation where environmental harm led to violations of property rights is given. That is, the environmental harm and contamination caused by the Titan Plant in Russian-occupied Crimea can be considered as a violation to the right to property under Article 1 of the Protocol 1 of the ECHR, as well as of the occupying power's obligations under Article 46 of the Hague Regulations. The pollution to the atmosphere has impacted negatively on the way that local residents are living and enjoying their own private property along with harm being done to the plants and domestic animals that are located either in private gardens and/or private lands in the areas near to the Titan factory.[442] Furthermore, the pollution has prevented people from safely enjoying and exercising their right to property, as well as the plants and animals living inside those properties as a part of it and which must be conserved from any environmental disaster and contamination.[443] Russia, as an occupying power in Crimea, has a legal obligation under Article 1 of Protocol 1 of the ECHR, which it is party to, as well as under Article 46 of the Hague Regulations regarding the protection of property rights from any environmental harm and contamination in Russian-occupied Crimea.[444]

441 For more information about the argument regarding the global right to property under Customary International Law and the General Principles of Law, see Sprankling, 'The Global Right to Property', 16–25.

442 There is no specific case law before the ECtHR against Russia in regard to such violation of the right to property under Article 1 of the Protocol 1 to the ECHR regarding the environmental damage inflicted in Crimea. However, there have been similar events where the ECtHR in imilar scenarios to that of Russia and Crimea has found a violation of the right to property because of environmental hazards and industrial activities. See for example, the ECtHR, *Öneryıldız v. Turkey* (Application no. 48939/99), Judgment (30 November 2004), paras 134–138; see also a more recent case held before the ECtHR, for which the Court found a violation of the right to property under Article 1 of the Optional Protocol to the Convention and linked the violation to the right to property to environmental hazards similar to what happened in Russian-occupied Crimea; European Court of Human Rights, *Dimitar Yordanov v. Bulgaria* (Application no. 3401/09), Final Judgment (6 December 2018), paras 57–66.

443 Ukraine Crisis Media Centre, 'Environmental Disaster in Crimea: Key Things to Know', (8 September 2018); Sergio Caliva, 'Chernobyl 2.0 – The Crimean Ecological Disaster', (30 September 2018). Available online at: <https://www.vocaleurope.eu/chernobyl-2-0-the-crimean-ecological-disaster/> Accessed date: 28 June 2021.

444 Russia ratified the Protocol No.1 of the ECHR in (5 May1998). See Council of Europe: Chart of Signatures and Ratifications of Treaty 009, Protocol to the Convention for the Protection of Human Rights and Fundamental Freedoms (ETS No. 009).

Arguably, the right to property could provide protection for the environment and at the same time protect the population's property from environmental hazards and pollution. Accordingly, it could be argued that there is a mutual interrelationship between protecting the environment and protecting private property in times of occupation. For example, when the occupying power provides protection for the environment, this could contribute to ensuring the right to property is safely exercised by the local population. If the occupying power adopts specific measures and takes particular actions in relation to protecting the environment, this will, in turn, reflect positively on and provide indirect protection to individuals' property and allow them to enjoy and exercise their right to property without any major obstacles resulting from environmental injuries, hazards, and pollution.

On the other hand, by ensuring, respecting, and protecting the right to property itself and considering the legal responsibility not to violate such a right, the protection of the environment can be indirectly strengthened and enhanced. For example, domestic gardens, agricultural lands, farms, parks, domestic animals, and livestock could be considered private property. The occupying power should provide protection to such proprieties from any danger, hazards, activities, and detrimental actions caused by its forces and/or third parties, including commercial and industrial companies. That could in turn help to ensure, firstly, people being able to continue safely exercising and enjoying their right to property without any non-consensual interference, such as imposed dangerous waste and/or emissions from an occupant's armed forces and/or third parties, such as industrial companies.

Secondly, at the same time, it ensures that the ecosystem services can continue functioning normally and the safety of the biodiversity, including the quality of air, soil, and water, as well as enhancing species conservation, in such private property and in the occupied territory as a whole. Noting that many rare species, including various types of plants, animals, and insects, rely on private lands, farms, and other similar privately owned areas for their habitat, if these species are not conserved on such private property, they may not be conserved at all.[445] Accordingly, the protection of the environment in times of occupation can be strengthened and enhanced through the occupying power's obligation to ensure, protect, and respect private property in areas where it administers and continues to exercise effective control. Therefore, the right to property can provide protection for the environment and at the same time to property from environmental contamination.

Finally, this author believes that a property rights–based solution can strengthen the protection of the environment and solve several environmental problems in occupied territories, if not most of them. In turn, this will reflect positively on filling the gaps regarding the protection of the environment in situations of occupation. For example, and as noted above, protection and consideration of property rights by the occupying power in the occupied territory will ensure better conservation of

445 McArdle, 'How Property Rights Could Help Save the Environment'.

the ecosystem and biodiversity. It will provide stronger protection of the environment from hazardous waste, emissions, and other types of pollution, such as air, soil, and water pollution, as well as enhancing species conservation.

Notwithstanding, there is no such binding right to private property under the global human rights system. The right to a home and family under Article 17 of the ICCPR and Article 8 of the ECHR could be interpreted to provide protection to peoples' privately owned property through the general protection provided to home and family life under the provisions. Thus, in the following paragraphs, it will be argued that it is possible to provide protection to private property through Article 17 of the ICCPR and Article 8 of the ECHR and their corresponding guarantees under IHL.

3.5.1 Right to a Home and Family and Environmental Protection in Situations of Occupation

The right to a home and family life has been enshrined under Article 17 of the ICCPR,[446] which can be interpreted as prohibiting environmental damage that might affect it.[447] For example, any act by the occupying power that causes harm to the environment, which at the same time has a negative impact on family and home life, could be considered a violation of Article 17 of the ICCPR.[448] Whilst the ICCPR does not include any single right to property as such, it does contain a right to freedom from arbitrary or unlawful interference with the home.[449] Thus, this provision could be invoked by an individual whose home and/or property, such as farms, yards, and/or crops, is impacted upon by different forms of contamination or other environmental hazards and degradation.[450] The UN Human Rights Committee has found that the State's failure to protect the fruit trees, farm animals, fish, crops, and water resources that people depend on for their livelihood constitutes a violation of Article 17 of the ICCPR, since all of them constitute components of their privacy, family life, and homes.[451]

The same logic is also applicable to situations of occupation. Since Article 17 of the ICCPR has corresponding guarantees under IHL, it requires the occupying power to consider family life, privacy, home, and all other privately owned

446 ICCPR, Article 17: "No one shall be subjected to arbitrary or unlawful interference with his privacy, family, home".

447 The United Nations: United Nations Environment Programme (UNEP): 'Protecting the Environment During Armed Conflict: An Inventory and Analysis of International Law', (United Nations 2009), 48.

448 Ibid, 48–49.

449 The ICCPR, Article 17.

450 Robin Churchill, 'Environmental Rights in Existing Human Rights Treaties', in Alan Boyle and Michael Anderson (eds), *Human Rights Approaches to Environmental Protection* (Oxford University Press 1996), 92.

451 The United Nations, International Covenant on Civil and Political Rights, Human Rights Committee, 'Views Adopted by the Committee under Article 5 (4) of the Optional Protocol, Concerning Communication No. 2751/2016' (CCPR/C/126/D/2751/2016) (20 September 2019), para 7.7.

property. For example, private property under the law of occupation enjoys strong protection, because, as discussed in Chapter 2, it is protected under several provisions of the law of occupation that forbid the pillage, confiscation, and destruction of such property.[452] The rules governing the treatment of private property in times of occupation are contained mainly in Articles 46–54 of the Hague Regulations and under the GCIV, such as Article 53.

According to Article 46(2) of the Hague Regulations, private property is protected and cannot be confiscated,[453] and all of it shall be protected from permanent confiscation during times of occupation.[454] Notably, protection under the Hague Regulations covers all kinds of private property, both movable and immovable.[455] Moreover, the protection of private property in occupied territory is a long-standing norm under customary IHL. However, the protection provided under Article 46 of the Hague Regulations to private property in occupied territory is not absolute, since Article 53 mentions some exceptions as to when and where private property in some cases could be seized.

However, the seized property must be returned and compensation paid when the occupation ends.[456] Such rules under the law of occupation can play a vital role in protecting the environment by preventing the occupying power from over-exploitation of the natural resources in an unsustainable manner that may have a negative impact on the biodiversity and ecosystem functioning of the occupied territory.[457]

If the properties and homes of occupied people are impacted upon by various forms of pollution or environmental degradation resulting from occupants' activities, those people have the right to invoke Article 17 of the ICCPR against the occupying power's activities that were detrimental to their homes and/or proprieties, along with the protection provided under Article 46 of the Hague Regulation, as discussed above and in detail in the previous chapter.

On the regional level, only the European human rights system includes the right to private property, a home, and family life. The other regional human rights systems, such as the Arab, African, and American ones, do not embody such a right. Applicants under the European human rights system often depend on the right to

452 The Hague Regulations 1907, Article 46. See also Benvenisti, *The International Law of Occupation*, 82.

453 The Hague Regulations 1907, Article 46 (2).

454 Gasser, 'Protection of the Civilian Population: Belligerent Occupation', 279.

455 Ibid.

456 The Hague Regulations 1907, Article 53: "All appliances, whether on land, at sea, or in the air, adapted for the transmission of news, or for the transport of persons or things, exclusive of cases governed by naval law, depots of arms, and, generally, all kinds of munitions of war, may be seized, even if they belong to private individuals, but must be restored and compensation fixed when peace is made."

457 ILC, 'First Report', para 39.

private property and family life enshrined in Article 8 of the ECHR,[458] rather than on the right to property, to deal with environmental matters.[459]

Recently, as mentioned above, Crimea experienced an environmental disaster involving toxic emissions, including sulphuric acid, that were released into the air from the Titan plant near Armyansk city and affected animal, plant, and human life in the occupied region.[460] Due to this catastrophe, Ukraine informed the United Nations, namely the director of the UN Environmental Programme Regional Office for Europe, about the ecological disaster in occupied Crimea.[461] It was known that the factory needed a huge amount of water to operate and the water that used to feed the factory coming from the Dnieper/Dnipro River had been cut by the Ukrainian authorities after the Russian occupation of Crimea. The water shortage caused a serious problem for the Crimean Titan factory, since the factory relied on the old technology of production that entailed the storage of waste containing sulphur compounds, along with other chemical substances, in a large lake within the factory's territory. However, due to water shortages and dry weather, the lake was almost dry and started emitting harmful chemicals into the atmosphere. These chemicals started poisoning the environment, and as a result, birds along with other animals were found dead. This was due to air and water contamination.[462]

After the ecological catastrophe that happened due to the release of sulphur compounds from the Crimean Titan plant,[463] the city, its inhabitants, the proprieties, and the surrounding agricultural areas were exposed to serious danger.[464] Chemical substances that leaked from the Titan plant caused an environmental disaster by polluting the air of the city and nearby towns, and the consequence of that pollution was the evacuation of thousands of children from Armyansk to different areas.[465] These chemical substances that leaked into the air of occupied Crimea settled on

458 The ECHR, Article 8: "(1) Everyone has the right to respect for his private and family life, his home and his correspondence. (2) There shall be no interference by a public authority with the exercise of this right except such as is in accordance with the law and is necessary in a democratic society in the interests of national security, public safety or the economic well-being of the country, for the prevention of disorder or crime, for the protection of health or morals, or for the protection of the rights and freedoms of others".

459 Dienelt, *Armed Conflicts and the Environment*, 187–189. See also *Hatton and Others v. the United Kingdom*, the ECtHR, Judgment (Application no. 36022/97) (8 July 2003), para 96, where the ECtHR confirmed that "There is no explicit right in the Convention to a clean and quiet environment, but where an individual is directly and seriously affected by noise or other pollution, an issue may arise under Article 8".

460 Caliva, 'Chernobyl 2.0 – The Crimean Ecological Disaster', (30 September 2018).

461 Ukraine Crisis Media Centre, 'Environmental Disaster in Crimea: Key Things to Know', (8 September 2018).

462 Ibid; Warsaw Institute, 'Ecological Disaster in the Crimea' (7 September 2018). Available online at: <https://warsawinstitute.org/ecological-disaster-crimea/>. Accessed date: 21 June 2021.

463 Caliva, 'Chernobyl 2.0'; Yuri Zoria, 'What Caused the Environmental Disaster in Occupied Crimea? A Chemist Explains', (21 September 2018); Power and Weir, 'Stress-testing the ILC's Draft Principles on Environmental Protection during Occupation'.

464 Ibid.

465 Zoria, 'What Caused the Environmental Disaster in Occupied Crimea?'

buildings, houses, plants, cars, trees, yards, and crops. Furthermore, several individuals from that territory were diagnosed in hospitals with allergic conjunctivitis, pharyngitis, and bronchitis, whilst others experienced eye, throat, and skin irritations.[466] Despite it being unsure whether the environmental disaster was deliberate or an accident, Russia, as the occupying power, has the responsibility and the duty to protect the environment and to ensure the safety and the health of the occupied people and their properties, as well as to respect and protect human rights from any violation in the occupied territory. Furthermore, under IHL, Russia, as an occupying power, has a due diligence obligation. As noted above, this argument has been supported by the ILC when it confirmed under Draft Principle 19(2) that the occupying power shall take all possible measures to prevent significant environmental harm that might prejudice the health and well-being of the local population of the occupied territory.[467] This duty, in particular, is a specification of the obligation to restore and ensure "civil life" under Article 43 of the Hague Regulations.[468] Furthermore, one scholar argued that the duty to restore and ensure "public order" under Article 43 of the Hague Regulations includes several due diligence obligations related to the administration of occupied territory.[469] Due diligence is also relevant for the occupant's duty to provide healthcare for the local population of the occupied territory.[470] Thus, the occupying power, which is in this case Russia, should have taken proactive measures to address urgent environmental problems so as to prevent any significant harm to it and to the local population.[471] Accordingly, the occupying power has positive and negative obligations to respect, protect, and prevent environmental harm in occupied territory.

The criteria applied by the UN Human Rights Committee in the *Portillo Caceres v. Paraguay* case,[472] as well as by the ECtHR in *Hatton and Others v. the United Kingdom*,[473] were, first, the environmental pollution having directly impacted upon the occupied people, their homes and their private and family life; and second, the impact having been serious. These two criteria have been met in Crimea's situation

466 Ibid; Warsaw Institute, 'Ecological Disaster in the Crimea' (7 September 2018).

467 The ILC Draft Principles on Protection of the Environment in relation to Armed Conflicts, with Commentaries (2022), Draft Principle 19(2).

468 Longobardo, 'The Relevance of the Concept of Due Diligence for International Humanitarian Law', 75.

469 Ibid, 74.

470 GCIV 1949, Article 56.

471 UNGA, 'Report of the International Law Commission', 71st session (29 April–7 June and 8 July–9 August 2019) (A/74/10) (20 August 2019). 'ILC Draft Commentary', 267–275; Draft Principle (21) of the ILC Draft Principles regarding the 'Protection of the Environment in Relation to Armed Conflicts'; Longobardo, 'The Relevance of the Concept of Due Diligence for International Humanitarian Law', 73–75; ILC, 'Third Report', 86.

472 Greta Reeh, 'Human Rights and the Environment: The UN Human Rights Committee Affirms the Duty to Protect', Blog of the European Journal of International Law (2019).

473 *Hatton and Others v. the United Kingdom*, ECtHR, Judgment (Application no. 36022/97), (8 July 2003), para 96.

too,[474] since the unidentified substance directly and seriously impacted upon people, their families, houses, farms, yards, and animals. Therefore, it can be argued that Russia, as an occupying power in Crimea, has an obligation under Article 8 of the ECHR and Article 17 of the ICCPR[475] to protect the local population from any environmental degradation and from any consequences of environmental pollution, such as happened in Armyansk city, which constitutes a violation of the right to private and family life and having a home. Russia's failure to protect occupied people from the environmental disaster and the consequences of the environmental pollution for the individuals and their property constitutes a violation of Article 8 of the ECHR and Article 17 of the ICCPR, as well as Article 46 of the Hague Regulations.

Accordingly, it could be argued that the consequences of environmental pollution and environmental degradation in situations of occupation can result in a violation of the right to private and family life and to having a home. Therefore, by considering the aforementioned argument, such a right could add extra protection to the environment under IHRL in situations of occupation.

To summarise, the right to a home and family life under Article 17 of the ICCPR and Article 8 of the ECHR protect these from environmental pollution, such as toxic emissions and any other forms of environmental pollution that can interrupt the right to a home, and, as argued above, they could represent forms of protection for the environment as well. Therefore, it seems quite reasonable to ground obligations upon states regarding environmental protection in times of occupation on the basis of property rights, including the right to a home and family life.

3.6 Conclusion

The chapter has demonstrated through the examination of the variety of human rights – with a specific concentration on situations of occupation and the occupant's responsibility to provide protection to the environment – that a safe, healthy, and clean environment in situations of occupation plays a critical role in protecting and promoting human rights, such as the right to life and the right to health, in such situations. The relationship between the enjoyment of human rights by occupied people and the occupying power's obligations under IHRL to protect the environment is an explicitly and implicitly interrelated one.

Certain aspects of the linkage are, though, in need of strengthening and further clarity, in order to more effectively promote the protection of the environment,

474 For more information about the criteria adopted by the UN Human Rights Committee regarding the State's duty to protect individuals, their families, and their homes from environmental degradation and pollution under article 17 of the ICCPR, see: The United Nations, International Covenant on Civil and Political Rights, Human Rights Committee, 'Views Adopted by the Committee under Article 5 (4) of the Optional Protocol, Concerning Communication No. 2751/2016' (CCPR/C/126/D/2751/2016) (20 September 2019), paras 7.7 and 7.8.

475 Russia is a state party to the ICCPR, see: United Nations: Human Rights Office of the High Commissioner: International Covenant on Civil and Political Rights.

including the ecosystem and biodiversity in an occupied territory, particularly through IHRL instruments. For example, greater elucidation is needed as to how to apply legal mechanisms to bring the occupying power before international tribunals about its acts against the environment in the occupied state, particularly through the violations of its obligations under IHRL. Moreover, the adoption of a binding right to a clean and healthy environment by the UN is needed. Whilst the UNGA has recently adopted such a right, the resolutions adopted are non-binding.[476]

The analytical framework of IHRL set out in this chapter in relation to the protection of the environment in times of occupation has also argued that IHRL treaties, such as ICCPR, ICESCR, UNCRC, and CEDAW, have not formally recognised such an independent right to the environment. However, they have all recognised that environmental harm and environmental degradation can undermine all human rights protected under those treaties. The chapter further discussed the role of different human rights Committees, such as those of UNCRC and CEDAW, and how their interpretation is so important in regard to providing protection to the environment through respecting, protecting, and fulfilling the obligations under the conventions. For example, the Committee on CEDAW has, on several occasions, emphasised the relationship between women's enjoyment of their rights under the Convention and the protection of the environment.

The chapter further explained that, by applying IHRL along with IHL, they can complement and harmonise with each other, such as the implementation of the right to health under Article 12 of the ICESCR and states' health-related obligations under the provisions of IHL (the corresponding guarantees under IHL). That is, they can enrich each other and provide better and enhanced protection to the environment in times of occupation.

According to what has been demonstrated so far, the protection of the environment in times of occupation under IHRL could be considered a very important addition to the protection provided under the law of occupation in relation to providing more sufficient and efficient protection to the environment in situations of occupation. However, the protection of the environment in occupied territory still needs further, more specific, and extra-legal protection. Therefore, the following chapter will examine the possible environmental protection under International Environmental Law (IEL) in times of occupation in relation to helping to fill the existing major gaps under public international law regarding the protection of the environment in such situations.

476 The United Nations General Assembly, 'The Human Right to a Clean, Healthy and Sustainable Environment', 76th session, agenda item 74 (b) (A/76/L.75) (26 July 2022).

4 The Role of International Environmental Law in the Protection of the Environment in Times of Occupation

This chapter examines the protection that can be provided under International Environmental Law (IEL) to the environment in times of occupation. The role of IEL is demonstrated, both customary and conventional, and how its implementation can add an extra layer of protection to the environment in times of occupation.

IEL, which emerged mainly in the early 1970s,[1] is the legal and regulatory framework devised by the international community to address global environmental challenges. It is a dynamic and rapidly growing field of international law that encompasses a wide range of innovative legal tools to deal with a varied array of multifaceted environmental problems. These problems include some of the most significant environmental challenges facing the global community, including ones that emerge from or are interrelated to armed conflict and occupation situations.[2]

Most scholarly work on the topic has focused on the protection of the environment in times of armed conflict, not including situations of occupation, and only under IHL and IHRL. Hence, the examination of the role of Multilateral Environmental Agreements (MEAs) in particular, and IEL in general, during times of occupation mostly remains an unexplored area. Whilst IHL and IHRL are well-developed bodies of international law, the vagueness of their relevant rules relating to the protection of the environment could be enriched, informed, and clarified by IEL. Furthermore, given that the consequences of environmental damage are difficult to assess and foresee, IEL contains important principles, such as that of prevention and the precautionary approach. Both have been developed to deal with uncertain aspects that are inherent in environmental issues.[3]

The author's stance is mainly based on what has been argued in the previous chapters: that international law is a coherent legal system, and its rules complement and harmonise each other. This means that its rules must be understood as having

1 Ulrich Beyerlin and Jenny Stoutenburg, 'Environment, International Protection', Oxford Public International Law (2013) 2.

2 Lavanya Rajamani and Jacqueline Peel, 'International Environmental Law: Changing Context, Emerging Trends, and Expanding Frontiers' in Lavanya Rajamani and Jacqueline Peel (eds), *The Oxford Handbook of International Environmental Law* (Oxford University Press 2021) 2.

3 Sjöstedt, *The Role of Multilateral Environmental Agreements*, 136.

DOI: 10.4324/9781003518068-4

been drafted and coordinated to complement and function alongside each other.[4] The International Court of Justice (ICJ) on different occasions has supported the integration approach of international law over a fragmented one, in particular when it has considered the application of IEL along with other bodies of international law to resolve some of the environmental issues between states.[5] That is clear also in the language used under Article 31(3)(c) of the VCLT, which states that, in interpreting a norm, "any relevant rules of international law applicable in the relations between the parties" may be considered.[6] Accordingly, IEL may be interpreted in light of IHL and the latter in light of IEL, as required. Thus, the protection provided under IEL should remain valid even when applying other areas of international law, and that should include IHL. The harmonisation between IEL and IHL could contribute to improving the coherency between different rules in the international legal system and, at the same time, strengthen the protection provided to the environment in times of armed conflict and occupation. Furthermore, acknowledging the growing fragmentation of different bodies of international law, the ILC has stressed the view that international law is to be conceptualised as a system and applied in a coherent manner.[7] Additionally, the ILC's Draft Principles on the Protection of the Environment in Relation to Armed Conflict[8] is a call for a more integrated approach between different international law branches in such situations.[9] Therefore, considering the integration approach between public international law branches would enhance and strengthen the protection of the environment in times of armed conflict and occupation.

Non-legally binding or soft law instruments of IEL have addressed directly the issue of the environment and the outbreak of hostilities and occupation. For example, the Stockholm Declaration 1972,[10] the Rio Declaration 1992,[11] the World Charter of Nature 1982,[12] the IUCN Draft Covenant,[13] and many other non-legally binding documents have expressed a position for states to respect and protect the environment in times of armed conflict and occupation. Accordingly, they provide an important indication regarding the application of IEL at all times as well as

4 United Nations: General Assembly, 'Fragmentation of International Law: Difficulties Arising from the Diversification and Expansion of International Law: Report of the Study Group of the International Law Commission'. (A/CN.4/L.702) (18 July 2006), para 14.

5 See for example, the Gabčíkovo-Nagymaros Project (*Hungary v. Slovakia*) Judgment, I. C. J. Reports 1997, p. 7. Paras 112,140; ICJ, Nuclear Weapons Advisory Opinion, para 226.

6 VCLT, Article 31(3)(c).

7 United Nations: General Assembly, 'Fragmentation of International Law', para 14.

8 The ILC Draft Principles on Protection of the Environment in relation to Armed Conflicts, with Commentaries (2022).

9 Carl Bruch, Cymie Payne, and Britta Sjöstedt, 'Armed Conflict and the Environment', in Lavanya Rajamani and Jacqueline Peel (eds), *The Oxford Handbook of International Environmental Law* (Oxford University Press 2021) 882.

10 'Stockholm Declaration' (1972), Principle 26.

11 'Rio Declaration' (1992), Principles 23, 24.

12 'The World Charter for Nature' (1982), Principles 5, 20.

13 IUCN Draft International Covenant on Environment and Development (IUCN Draft Covenant).

much of their content reflecting already customary international law related to the protection of the environment. More discussion about soft law instruments of IEL is provided later in the chapter.

The chapter begins by considering the application of IEL in times of occupation. The application of MEAs to such situations is argued for, and then the important role that these play in enhancing environmental protection in times of occupation is explained. Finally, the main challenges that are facing the continued application of IEL, in particular MEAs, to situations of occupation are discussed.

4.1 The Application of International Environmental Law in Times of Occupation

The application of IEL in times of occupation is still a controversial issue that needs to be analysed in relation to understanding how, and to what extent, its provisions continue to apply in times of occupation and whether they can provide meaningful protection that can help to fill the gaps identified in earlier chapters regarding the protection of the environment in such situations.

4.1.1 The Application of Customary International Environmental Law to Situations of Armed Conflict and Occupation

Customary international environmental law (CIEL) is rapidly developing to encompass a general duty to protect and conserve the environment. Environmental declarations and other soft law documents play a pivotal role in identifying CIEL. Several environmental declarations, including the Stockholm and Rio Declarations, contain many principles that are now considered customary international law related to environmental protection. These principles have become widely accepted and are consistently cited and reiterated in treaties, jurisprudence, and national laws related to environmental protection.[14]

This subsection focuses on the analysis of the content of CIEL along with other various sources, such as the case law of the ICJ, the works of the ILC on various topics, and the interconnection between them, as well as the principles of customary international environmental law. These are examined to identify customary international norms that protect the environment during times of armed conflict and occupation. Additionally, the opinions of scholars on this subject are also evaluated as supplementary means of identifying customary environmental rules. In this regard, the work of the ILC is helpful in identifying customary law because it is tasked with the responsibility of advancing international law under Article 13(1)(a) of the UN Charter.

The ICJ, in the Nuclear Weapons Advisory Opinion, addressed the issue of the continued application of IEL in times of armed conflict when it stated that

14 Alexandre Kiss and Dinah Shelton, *Guide to International Environmental Law* (Martinus Nijhoff Publishers 2007) 89–110.

it "indicates important environmental factors that are properly to be taken into account in the context of the implementation of the principles and rules of the law applicable in armed conflict".[15] In addition, the ICJ affirmed the responsibility of states to protect the environment, citing the Rio Declaration's Principle 24 to support this stance, which demonstrates the ICJ's efforts to implement IEL in situations of armed conflict and occupation. [16] The ICJ also referred to the principle of no harm in IEL, underscoring states' responsibility to respect other states' environments.[17] As a result, the ICJ contributed to the formation of customary international law related to environmental protection during armed conflict and occupation.[18] The ICRC also endorsed the continued application of IEL during armed conflict, referencing the ICJ's Nuclear Weapons Advisory Opinion. [19]

Principle 26 of the Stockholm Declaration 1972 addresses the protection of the environment in times of armed conflict, when it provides that "Man and his environment must be spared the effects of nuclear weapons and all other means of mass destruction".[20] Principle 26 of the Stockholm Declaration was adapted and integrated into Principle 24 of the Rio Declaration 20 years after. However, the context was slightly modified. Principle 24 of the Rio Declaration in the second sentence comes closer to the view that the environment should be protected during times of armed conflict when it provides that "States shall therefore respect international law providing protection for the environment in times of armed conflict and co-operate in its further development, as necessary", and states agreed on environmental protection in such scenarios.[21] Principle 24 is an important one since it was adopted consensually by all participating states at the conference.[22] Furthermore, Principle 24 of the Rio Declaration reflects some of the rules that are already accepted as customary international law related to the protection of the environment in armed conflict, such as Articles 35(3) and 55(1) of the API to the Fourth Geneva Conventions 1949.[23]

Additionally, the 1982 World Charter for Nature adopted by the UNGA states that nature should be safeguarded against deterioration caused by war or other hostile activities and that military operations that harm it should be avoided.[24] These provisions in the World Charter for Nature align with Principle 26 of the Stockholm Declaration and Principle 24 of the Rio Declaration, which assert that the environment should be protected during times of armed conflict. Taken together, the

15 ICJ, Nuclear Weapons Advisory Opinion, para 33.
16 Ibid, para 30.
17 Ibid, para 29.
18 Ibid, paras 29, 30, and 33.
19 Henckaerts and Doswald-Beck, *Customary International Humanitarian Law*, Rule 44.
20 'Stockholm Declaration' (1972), Principle 26.
21 'Rio Declaration' (1992), Principle 24.
22 Marie-Louise Tougas, 'Principle 24: The Environment in Armed Conflict', in Jorge Viñuales (ed), *The Rio Declaration on Environment and Development: A Commentary* (Oxford University Press 2015) 574; Dienelt, *Armed Conflicts and the Environment*, 97–98.
23 Tougas, 'Principle 24', 52–53, 574–579.
24 'The World Charter for Nature', (1982), Principles 5, 20.

Stockholm Declaration, World Charter for Nature, and Rio Declaration demonstrate the shared interests and awareness among states regarding the challenges and threats faced by the environment during armed conflicts. These documents were adopted over the course of several years, indicating the continued relevance of this issue among states and the international community's sustained concern about it for decades.

The ILC's Draft Principles on protecting the environment during occupation are highly significant as they specifically address the environmental conditions in occupied territories. Draft Principles 19–21 impose specific obligations on the occupying power to protect the environment during occupation. The ILC's Draft Principles are discussed in this section because they draw upon various sources in IEL, including soft law instruments, and some of these instruments include principles that have already been accepted as CIEL.

According to Draft Principle 19, "General Environmental Obligations of an Occupying Power", there are three different legal obligations upon the occupying power regarding the environment of the occupied territory. First, "An Occupying Power shall respect and protect the environment of the occupied territory in accordance with applicable international law", including relevant obligations under IHL, IHRL, and IEL,[25] and it must "take environmental considerations into account in the administration of such territory".[26]

Draft Principle 19(1) is clearly in line with the occupying power's obligation under article 43 of the Hague Regulations, in particular the duty to consider the public order, civil life, and welfare of the occupied population as an administrator of the occupied territory. It could be argued that Draft Principle 19 in general, and paragraph one in particular, seem to come in line with the occupying power's obligation under Principle 23 of the Rio Declaration. This Principal states that "the environment and natural resources of people under oppression, domination and occupation shall be protected".[27] In some sense, Principle 23 has two distinct and simultaneously related aspects: the first is giving rights to people, such as those living under occupation, to enjoy the benefits arising from the exploitation of natural resources within their occupied territory, which is called "permanent sovereignty".[28] The second aspect is providing special protection to the environment from any risks that may arise by an occupying power or any foreign domination, which is called "environmental protection".[29] Notably, with Principle 23, the Rio Declaration has become the first universal legal instrument to emphasise

25 The ILC Draft Principles on Protection of the Environment in Relation to Armed Conflicts, with Commentaries (2022). Principle 19(1), 158–161; Daniëlla Dam-de Jong, 'Enhancing Environmental Protection in Relation to Armed Conflict: An Assessment of the ILC Draft Principles', (2021) 44 *Loy. L.A. Int'l & Comp. L. Rev* 129, 148–150.

26 The ILC Draft Principles on Protection of the Environment in relation to Armed Conflicts, Principle 19(1), 158.

27 'Rio Declaration' (1992), Principle 23.

28 Tignino, 'Principle 23', 559.

29 Ibid.

the rights of people living under occupation "in relation to both the use of natural resources and the protection of the environment".[30] The origin of Principle 23 of the Rio Declaration is based on the principle of permanent sovereignty over natural resources, which is itself a principle that reflects customary international law.[31] The interconnection between the two aspects of Principle 23 of the Rio Declaration, namely "permanent sovereignty" and "environmental protection", is acknowledged, and it is difficult to separate them in practice. In some instances, not respecting natural resource rights may result in environmental harm, while in others, harm done to the environment by the occupying power may jeopardise the viability and usefulness of natural resources in the occupied territory.[32]

Second, Draft Principle 19(2) confirms the occupying power's duty to "take appropriate measures to prevent significant harm to the environment of the occupied territory that is likely to prejudice the health and well-being of the population of the occupied territory".[33] In order to understand paragraph 2, it is important to consider the broader obligation upon the occupying power outlined in paragraph 1. The intention of paragraph 2 is to suggest that causing significant harm to the environment in an occupied territory could have adverse consequences on the population living in that territory.[34]

Draft Principle 19(2) should be read in the context of the occupying power's obligation under Article 56 of the GCIV and Article 12 of the ICESCR regarding the legal duty to consider the right to health of the occupied population. Furthermore, Draft Principle 19(2) comes in line with the crux of Principle 1 of the Stockholm Declaration,[35] which confirms the human "fundamental right to freedom, equality and adequate conditions of life, in an environment of a quality that permits a life of dignity and well-being".[36] The ICJ in the Nuclear Weapons Advisory Opinion holds that "the environment is not an abstraction but represents the living space, the quality of life, and the very health of human beings, including generations unborn".[37] The ICJ's words are very similar to the content of Principle 1 of the Stockholm Declaration, in the other words, the ICJ has recalled Principle 1 of the Stockholm Declaration, but in its own words confirming the right of people to a healthy environment. It is argued that Principle 1 of the Stockholm Declaration has already been accepted as customary international law.[38]

30 Ibid, 557.
31 The ICJ, *DRC v. Uganda*, (2005), para 244; Tignino, 'Principle 23', 560–561.
32 Tignino, 'Principle 23', 559–560.
33 The ILC Draft Principles on Protection of the Environment in relation to Armed Conflicts, Draft Principle 19(2).
34 Ibid, 162.
35 Ibid, 161–162.
36 'Stockholm Declaration', Principle 1.
37 ICJ, Nuclear Weapons Advisory Opinion, para 29.
38 Jutta Brunnée, 'The Stockholm Declaration and the Structure and Processes of International Environmental Law' in Aldo Chircop, Theodore McDorman, and Susan Rolston (eds), *The Future of Ocean Regime-Building: Essays in Tribute to Douglas M. Johnston* (Brill Nijhoff 2009), 53.

Third, Draft Principle 19(3) provides that "An Occupying Power shall respect the law and institutions of the occupied territory concerning the protection of the environment and may only introduce changes within the limits provided by the law of armed conflict". This paragraph aligns with the occupant's duty under article 43(2) of the Hague Regulations and Article 64 of the GCIV. The ILC in the commentary on Draft Principle 19(3) has cited Principle 10 of the Rio Declaration, which affirms the right of access to justice in environmental matters as one of the sources that Draft Principle 19(3) is based upon.[39] Furthermore, it could be argued that Principle 10 of the Rio Declaration may reflect CIEL, the reason behind this being that Principle 10 has been confirmed by several international and regional instruments, including the Aarhus Convention and the Johannesburg Declaration on Sustainable Development as well as being widespread and consistent state practice.[40] Additionally, various courts, such as the ECtHR, have upheld the right to information, participation, and justice in environmental matters, making clear reference to Principle 10, even in cases unrelated to occupied territory.[41] This is further evidence that Draft Principle 19 in its three paragraphs is linked to IEL principles, much of the content of which reflects customary international law.

The ILC's Draft Principle 20 pertains to the responsibility of the occupying power to ensure the sustainable use of natural resources in the occupied territory.[42] This principle is closely related to Article 55 of the Hague Regulations and the rules of usufruct, which govern the use of resources in occupied territories. Draft Principle 20 can also be viewed in conjunction with Principle 23 of the Rio Declaration, in particular, with the first aspect, "permanent sovereignty", which affirms the customary international law principle of permanent sovereignty over natural resources, as discussed above. This principle of permanent sovereignty applies to occupied territories, meaning that the occupying power must manage natural resources sustainably and allow the occupied population to benefit from

39 See the ILC Draft Principles on Protection of the Environment in relation to Armed Conflicts, with Commentaries (2022). Draft Principle 19(3), 165, footnote 777. See also Principle 10 of the Rio Declaration: "States shall facilitate and encourage public awareness and participation by making information widely available. Effective access to judicial and administrative proceedings, including redress and remedy, shall be provided".

40 For more information see Jonas Ebbesson, 'Principle 10: Public Participation' in Jorge Viñuales (ed), *The Rio Declaration on Environment and Development: A Commentary* (Oxford University Press 2015), 287–309.

41 See for example, the ECtHR, *Tatar v. Romania*, (67021/01), (27/January/2009). The ECtHR made reference to Principle 10 of the Rio Declaration in order to interpret the right to private and family life under article 8 of the ECHR.

42 Draft Principle 20: "To the extent that an Occupying Power is permitted to administer and use the natural resources in an occupied territory, for the benefit of the protected population of the occupied territory and for other lawful purposes under the law of armed conflict, it shall do so in a way that ensures their sustainable use and minimizes harm to the environment".

the utilisation of those resources.[43] It can be said that the ILC's Draft Principles 19 and 20[44] convey the idea that the occupying power must act in the interests of the occupied population and these interests must compromise - respect for the environment of the occupied territory.[45]

ILC Draft Principle 21 prohibits transboundary environmental harm outside of the occupied state.[46] It also obliges the occupying power to prevent activities inside the occupied territory from causing significant harm to the environment of other States or other areas beyond the territory of the occupied state or national jurisdiction.[47] Accordingly, Draft Principle 21 formulates a due diligence obligation upon the occupying power.[48] Furthermore, this Principle clearly builds on the duty of vigilance identified by the ICJ in the *DRC v. Uganda* case,[49] as well as constituting a reflection of the principle "no harm" and those of "prevention" derived from IEL, namely from Principle 21 of the Stockholm Declaration and Principle 2 of the Rio Declaration.[50] The obligation not to cause harm to other states' environment under both principles is considered CIEL.[51]

The ILC Draft Principles 19–21 can be read as entailing an evolutionary interpretation of the provisions of the law of occupation regarding the protection of the environment. In other words, these Principles suggest an interpretation of the law of occupation that allows for adaptations in relation to better protection of the environment, which can make the law of occupation greener and more considerate of the environmental issues in occupied territory. It implies that the interpretation of the law of occupation is not fixed or static but rather evolves with changing circumstances and perspectives to provide better protection to the environment in such situations.[52]

43 Tignino, 'Principle 23', 559–263.

44 The ILC in its second reading of the Draft Principles decided to slightly change the language of the Draft Principles and to add the word "protected" before the word "persons" under Draft Principle 19(2), as well as the word "population" after the word "protected" under Draft Principle 20, to complement and harmonise the Draft Principles in line with Article 4 of the GCIV. The logic behind this is that the first reading might be used by the occupying power as an excuse to extend such protection provided under those Draft Principles to settlers living illegally in occupied territory.

45 Marco Longobardo, 'Animals in Occupied Territory', in Anne Peters, Jérôme De Hemptinne, and Robert Kolb, *Animals in the International Law of Armed Conflict* (Cambridge University Press 2022), 224–225.

46 Draft Principle 21 is not analysed in detail because it bans environmental harm outside the occupied territory, and the current chapter is focusing on the harm inside the occupied territory by the occupying power.

47 The ILC, Draft Principles on Protection of the Environment in relation to Armed Conflicts (2022), Principle 21.

48 ILC, 'Third Report', 86.

49 ICJ. *DRC v. Uganda*, (2005), para 189.

50 Dam-de Jong, 'Enhancing Environmental Protection in Relation to Armed Conflict', 150; ILC, 'First Report', para 81.

51 ILC, 'First Report', para 81.

52 See generally, Dam-de Jong, 'Enhancing Environmental Protection in Relation to Armed Conflict', 150–151.

The content of the three Draft Principles, to a large extent, reflects developments in state practice and international case law.[53] Thus, one could make the argument that the ILC's Draft Principles 19–21 reflect customary international law related to protection of the environment in times of armed conflict and occupation.[54] As argued above, the content of the Draft Principles 19–21 are based on IEL principles, and some of these already reflect CIEL,[55] such as much of the content of the Stockholm and Rio Declarations.[56] The ILC, in different reports, has suggested that soft law instruments under IEL must be taken into consideration in relation to strengthening the protection provided to the environment in situations of armed conflict and occupation, having also confirmed the customary status of much of the content of these instruments.[57]

It should be noted further that, even if the abovementioned soft law documents under IEL reflect customary international law, they have not provided any clear provision regarding the application of IEL treaties to situations of armed conflict and occupation. None of these documents contains even a single definite rule for or against the application of IEL during such times. The one and only exception is the UNGA Resolution 49/50, which invites all states to disseminate widely the *Guidelines for Military Manuals and Instructions on the Protection of the Environment in Times of Armed Conflict* compiled by the ICRC, the guidelines of which under Article 5 provide that "international environmental agreements and relevant rules of customary law may continue to be applicable in times of armed conflict to the extent that they are not inconsistent with the applicable law of armed conflict".[58] However, the ICRC guidelines are non-binding and they have not been officially approved by the UNGA.[59]

In addition to the IEL declarations mentioned earlier, the UNGA has passed several resolutions focused on protecting the environment during times of armed

53 Ibid.

54 Sjöstedt, *The Role of Multilateral Environmental Agreements*, 73.

55 ILC, 'First Report', para 81 (e.g., the ILC considered the no harm principle, or the due diligence obligation contained in Principle 21 of the Stockholm Declaration and Principle 2 of the Rio Declaration as customary law in the context of environmental protection).

56 Jorge Viñuales, 'The Rio Declaration on Environment and Development: Preliminary Study' in Jorge Viñuales (ed), *The Rio Declaration on Environment and Development: A Commentary* (Oxford University Press 2015), 52–53; Dienelt, *Armed Conflicts and the Environment*, 99; Foo Kim Boon, 'The Rio Declaration and its Influence on International Environmental Law', *Singapore Journal of Legal Studies*, (1992), 347–364, at 350–364; The United Nations: Reports of International Arbitral Awards, 'Eritrea Ethiopia Claims Commission, Final Award – Pensions: Eritrea's Claims 15, 19 & 23' (19 December 2005), Vol. XXXVI, 471.

57 ILC, 'First Report' 'Second Report'; 'Third Report'; See also the United Nations, 'Report of the International Law Commission on the Work of its Seventy-First Session' (2019) UN Doc (A/74/10), Chapter VI.

58 The United Nations: General Assembly, Resolution adopted by the General Assembly [on the report of the Sixth Committee (A/49/737)], (A/RES/49/50) (1995), Paragraph 11; ICRC, 'Guidelines for Military Manuals and Instructions on the Protection of the Environment in Times of Armed Conflict', 30 April 1996, article, *International Review of the Red Cross*, No. 311. Article 5.

59 See Report of the Secretary-General, UN Doc (A/49/323) (19 August 1994).

conflict and occupation.[60] These resolutions, while not being legally binding on states, are significant in raising awareness and reinforcing the notion that the environment should be safeguarded in such situations. However, they do not change existing laws governing environmental protection during armed conflict and occupation but rather emphasise that the environment must be protected in such scenarios. It is important to note that the UNGA resolutions may serve as evidence of *opinio juris* for states that voted in favour of their adoption.[61] When states vote in favour of a UNGA resolution, they may indicate that they consider the principles or norms contained in the resolution to reflect customary international law.[62] UNGA resolutions may also serve as evidence of state practice or expressions of the views and attitudes of the international community on a particular issue, which could contribute to the development of customary international law in future.[63] In fact, the ICJ acknowledged the significance of UNGA resolutions in shaping *opinio juris* in its ruling on the Nicaragua case in 1986, when it asserted that "*opinio juris* may, though with all due caution, be deduced from, *inter alia*, the attitude of the Parties and the attitude of States towards certain General Assembly resolutions … The effect of consent to the text of such resolutions ... may be understood as an acceptance of the validity of the rule or set of rules declared by the resolution by themselves".[64] Accordingly, there is no reason not to consider the UNGA resolutions regarding the protection of the environment in times of armed conflict and occupation as strong evidence of *opinio juris* of the states voted in favour of their adoption as well as strong evidence that those states believe that these rules regarding the protection of the environment in scenarios of armed conflict and occupation should be universally accepted. They should help in codifying existing customary norms or helping to create new norms of customary law in the context of environmental protection in times of armed conflict and occupation.[65]

To sum up, the obligations of the occupying power regarding the protection of the environment in occupied territory under the ILC's Draft Principles 19 to 21, including its positive and negative obligations to respect, protect, and prevent environmental harm in occupied territory; the sustainable use of natural resources of the occupied territory; and respecting the environment of other states (avoiding transboundary environmental harm) have been discussed. The obligations embodied under the three Draft Principles 19–21 have their equivalents under IEL and, as discussed above, they incorporate direct references to IEL Principles to enhance

60 For example, Res. (No: 3175), (XXVIII), (17 December 1973), Res. (No: 3336), (XXIX) (17 December 1974), Res. (No: 3516), (XXX), (15 December 1976), Res. (No. 37/135), (17 December 1982), Res. (No:3092), (XXVIII) B (7 December 1973), Res. (No: 37/88) C, (10 December 1982).

61 Brian Lepard, *Customary International Law: A New Theory with Practical Applications* (Cambridge University Press 2010), 209.

62 Ibid, 208–209.

63 Ibid.

64 Military and Paramilitary Activities in and against Nicaragua (*Nicaragua v. United States of America*). Merits, Judgment. I.C.J. Reports 1986, 14, para 188.

65 See generally, the ICJ, (*Nicaragua v. United States of America*), para 188.

the protection of the environment in times of occupation. Thus, it is possible to conclude that the three Draft Principles 19–21 can be seen as reflecting customary international law in the context of environmental protection in times of occupation. In fact, the ILC's Draft Principles have moved the law of occupation closer to IEL, as many of the terms and references used by the ILC originate from this corpus of law.[66]

4.1.2 The Application of Environmental Treaties to Situations of Armed Conflict and Occupation

Scholars and international courts have focused more on the relationship between IHL and IHRL in situations of armed conflict and occupation rather than exploring how IEL treaties apply to these situations. Before discussing in detail the application of environmental treaties to situations of occupation, it is important, first, to briefly define what such treaties are and their different types.

4.1.2.1 International Environmental Law Treaties (Brief Overview)

An environmental treaty can be adopted bilaterally, regionally, or globally.[67] The definition of treaty provided by the VCLT is "an international agreement concluded between states in written form and governed by international law".[68] Environmental agreements are intended to create international legal rights and obligations between state parties. It is usually evident from the characteristics and context in which the treaty was adopted as to whether it was intended to create binding commitments.[69] This subsection focuses only on the application of regional and international environmental agreements (MEAs) to situations of armed conflict and occupation, such as the 1971 Ramsar Convention, the 1972 World Heritage Convention, the 1979 Berne Convention (Convention on the Conservation of European Wildlife and Natural Habitats), and the 1992 Biodiversity Convention. MEAs are "agreements between three or more states that assist with addressing specific environmental problems at national, regional and global levels".[70]

The following paragraphs discuss the application of MEAs to situations of armed conflict and occupation. Specifically, the role of MEAs in enhancing environmental protection in such situations is addressed, with a particular focus on the treaties mentioned above. The analysis of the MEAs encompasses an assessment of their continued application to situations of armed conflict and occupation, as

66 Sjöstedt, *The Role of Multilateral Environmental Agreements,* 84-85; Hulme, 'Natural Environment', 237.

67 Philippe Sands and others, *Principles of International Environmental Law* (4th edn, Cambridge University Press 2018), 104–106.

68 VCLT (1969), Article 2(1)(a).

69 Sands and others, *Principles of International Environmental Law*, 104–106.

70 The United Nations: Food and Agriculture Organisation of the United Nations, 'What are MEAs?'

provided by the ILC.[71] The author argues that MEAs can apply at all times, in peace and war, and they can strengthen and enhance environmental protection during times of armed conflict and occupation. As noted above, IHL does not prioritise environmental protection as such. Thus, the assessment of the continued application of MEAs may offer new paths to environmental protection in such situations, as well as fill the gap on how MEAs may contribute in such regard, since their potential in this context has not been widely explored. The assessment of MEAs is also important because they are the only treaties under public international law designed to cover specific environmental problems as such. In addition to this, they are usually constructed to protect a certain component of the environment, such as wetlands and biodiversity.[72] To this end, MEA assessment is important and needed to advance environmental protection in times of armed conflict and occupation and to show the possibilities of how they and IHL can support and complement each other in this regard. For example, MEAs can address issues that are not regulated by IHL and inform the application of the latter in matters related to environmental protection. Hence, MEAs harbour the inherent potential to complement and reinforce environmental protection under IHL in times of armed conflict and occupation.

4.1.2.2 The Continued Application of MEAs to Situations of Armed Conflict and Occupation

Most MEAs do not specifically address the issue of their continued application during armed conflicts and occupation.[73] However, it is argued that if an environmental treaty does not explicitly state otherwise, it should be applied at all times.[74] While most MEAs do not provide clear guidance on how armed conflict may impact on their application,[75] there are a few exceptions, such as the World Heritage Convention, which provides indirectly for continued application in times of armed conflict.[76]

71 ILC, "Draft Articles on the Effects of Armed Conflicts on Treaties", with commentaries.

72 Sjöstedt, *The Role of Multilateral Environmental Agreements*, 141.

73 Marco Roscini, 'Protection of Natural Environment in Time of Armed Conflict', in Louise Doswald-Beck, Azizur Chowdhury, Jahid Bhuiyan (eds), International *Humanitarian Law: An Anthology* (LexisNexis Butterworths 2009) Electronic copy, 26. <https://papers.ssrn.com/sol3/papers.cfm?abstract_id=1351888>.

74 Sjöstedt, *The Role of Multilateral Environmental Agreements*, 166, 173–174.

75 The reasons why most MEAs seldom contain any provisions on how armed conflict affects their operation and application could be because, in the first place, they are adopted to address specific environmental issues and to achieve specific environmental goals. MEA drafters may also assume that IHL adequately addresses the environmental protection in armed conflict, for example, under the API 1977, and that therefore there is no need to cover the issue again under the environmental treaties.

76 Convention Concerning the Protection of the World Cultural and Natural Heritage (the World Heritage Convention) (adopted 23 November 1972) (entered into force 15 December 1979), Article 11(4).

A landmark work on the topic of the continued application of MEAs to situations of armed conflict was conducted by the ILC when it adopted in 2011 draft articles on the "Effects of Armed Conflict on Treaties".[77] The ILC's work is an essential starting point since some of the draft articles assume the continued application of IEL treaties to armed conflict situations. In an annex to the draft articles, the ILC included a list of several treaties from different bodies of international law that are generally presumed to apply to situations of armed conflict.[78] The list includes "treaties relating to the international protection of the environment".[79] Furthermore, Draft Article 3 provides that "The existence of an armed conflict does not *ipso facto* terminate or suspend the operation of treaties" between states parties to the armed conflict and between a state that is party to the conflict and a state that is not.[80] The Draft Article 3 clearly supports the view that IEL treaties continue to apply along with other legal regimes during times of armed conflict. However, those treaties still might be suspended in armed conflict because of other factors related to their nature or owing to particular characteristics of the conflict itself.[81]

Draft Article 4 establishes that the first and main stage of the assessment is whether a treaty remains in operation during time of armed conflict or not depends on the treaty itself. If it contains provisions on its operation during times of armed conflict, then those provisions shall apply.[82] However, most MEAs do not expressly regulate the issue of the outbreak of hostilities or the situations of armed conflict and occupation. The ILC, in this case, proposed applying the rules on treaty interpretation to determine the continued applicability to the environmental treaty in question, which is called "the applicability assessment's second stage", as the ILC's 2011 Draft Articles suggested.[83] The second stage, according to Draft Article 5, depends on the broader reference of "international rules on treaty interpretation" that corresponds to Article 31(3)(c) and Article 32 of the Vienna Convention on the Law of Treaties (VCLT).[84] The second stage, according to the ILC, requires a deep examination of the treaty's meaning, object, and purpose; subsequent practice; analysis of preparatory work; and the circumstances of its conclusion in relation

77 "Draft Articles on the Effects of Armed Conflicts on Treaties", with commentaries; Draft Article 7.

78 "Draft Articles on the Effects of Armed Conflicts on Treaties", with commentaries, 108.

79 Ibid; please note that the ILC relies on different primary and secondary sources to affirm the presumption that environmental treaties apply in situations of armed conflict. The main primary source was the ICJ Nuclear Weapons Advisory Opinion, paras 29–33, as discussed in the text above; for secondary sources, see, for example, Dapo Akande, 'Nuclear Weapons, Unclear Law? Deciphering the Nuclear Weapons Advisory Opinion of the International Court' (1998) 68 *BYBIL* 165, 183–184.

80 "Draft Articles on the Effects of Armed Conflicts on Treaties", with commentaries, Draft Article 3, paras (a) and (b).

81 Sjöstedt, *The Role of Multilateral Environmental Agreements*, 150.

82 "Draft Articles on the Effects of Armed Conflicts on Treaties", with commentaries, Draft Article 4.

83 See "Draft Articles on the Effects of Armed Conflicts on Treaties", with commentaries, Draft Article 5.

84 Ibid, Draft Article 5(2).

to establishing whether the treaty continues to apply or not during times of armed conflict and occupation.[85]

The third and last stage of the assessment is the overall assessment depending upon factors related to the nature of the treaty itself and on the characteristics of the armed conflict.[86] The nature of the treaty refers to the treaty's subject matter, object and purpose, content, and the number of state parties to the convention.[87] The characteristics of the armed conflict refer to such as its territorial extent, its scale, intensity, and duration.[88] Both factors, according to Draft Article 6 of the ILC Draft Articles on the effects of armed conflicts on treaties, should be taken into account in case the first and second assessment stages fail to determine the continued application of a peacetime treaty to situations of armed conflict and occupation. Draft Article 6 provides a broader perspective by including factors that go well beyond the rules of treaty interpretation.[89] For example, factors related to the nature of the treaty include the treaty's subject matter, and several MEAs' subject matter or object is to protect a common concern to all state parties to the convention.[90] Sometimes, the common concern is even shared by the whole international community and not only state parties to that convention.[91] For example, protecting both cultural and natural world heritage sites must be seen as a duty not only owed to one state but also to all state parties, and these must be protected and saved for the interest of the whole international community.[92] Hence, to allow derogation from some obligations or remove some of the provisions from the treaty in times of armed conflict and occupation might undermine and could threaten the operation of the entire treaty. That might also affect third states that are not part of the armed conflict.[93] Accordingly, MEAs have to remain in force for all state parties to be effective, and that must include times of armed conflict and occupation in relation to ensuring the continued protection of states' common concern. Therefore, the subject matter of a treaty is an important element in relation to determining its continued application and operation during times of armed conflict and occupation. Since such subject matter could include considerations regarding the kind of interests the treaty protects or how derogations, suspension or termination of the treaty might have negative impacts on the third states or other state parties to the convention, the subject matter of the treaty is important, as it can justify the

85 Ibid.

86 Ibid, Draft Article 6(a) and (b).

87 Ibid.

88 Ibid.

89 Ibid, Draft Article 6(3).

90 The Biodiversity Convention is one MEA the subject matter of which is to protect the common concern of all state parties to the Convention.

91 Jutta Brunnée, 'Common Areas, Common Heritage, and Common Concern', in Daniel Bodansky, Jutta Brunnée, and Ellen Hey (eds), *The Oxford Handbook of International Environmental Law* (Oxford University Press 2008), 553–555.

92 Ibid, 553–555.

93 Rüdiger Wolfrum and Nele Matz, *Conflicts in International Environmental Law* (Springer Verlag 2003), 132–133.

continued application of the treaty in times of armed conflict and occupation.[94] According to some scholars, environmental treaties should remain in force during times of armed conflict based on the common interest that they consider and protect.[95] Another observer argued that peacetime treaties should continue to apply in armed conflict between belligerents themselves and between them and neutral states. However, belligerents could in particular, and in specific cases, be required, by the necessities of war, to suspend the operation of such treaties between them.[96] Such a suspension would not be possible and would reflect negatively on the rights of third/neutral states to the conventions.[97] Suspension of environmental treaties among the belligerents may affect the rights owed to the third states to the convention, particularly in the case where the convention protects a common concern to all state parties. However, the negative impact on the neutral states must be clear, evident, and visible.[98] Furthermore, regarding the environmental treaties, at some point, it could be difficult to demonstrate the negative impact on the rights owed to the third-state parties because of the suspension of the treaty between the belligerent states.[99] Still, the fact remains that most environmental treaties' subject matter is to protect and consider a common concern to all its state parties. Thus, relying on factors such as the nature of the treaty and, in particular, its subject matter is a useful method that would support the continued application of environmental treaties during times of armed conflict and occupation.

According to the second element of the third stage of assessment suggested by the ILC under Draft Article 6, the factors considered are based not on the subject matter of the MEA itself but rather on the characteristics of the relevant armed conflict.[100] This refers to the armed conflict's territorial extent, scale, intensity, duration, and other factors.[101] For example, the territorial extent, the scale of damage, and the intensity of the hostilities can all be factors that affect the application and the operation of an environmental treaty. For example, if the scale of destruction is wide and the intensity of hostilities is strong, this might affect the ability of the state/s to act in accordance with their obligations under an environmental treaty.[102] If the situation is characterised as less hostile, there will be no reason for belligerent states not to comply with their environmental obligations under MEAs.

If this conclusion is correct, in situations of occupation that are generally characterised as closer to peacetime situations without actual active hostilities at all

94 Sjöstedt, *The Role of Multilateral Environmental Agreements*, 154–155.
95 Vöneky, 'A New Shield for the Environment', 27.
96 Wil D. Verwey, 'Protection of the Environment in Times of Armed Conflict: In Search of a New Legal Perspective', (1995) 8 *LJIL* 7, 26–28.
97 Ibid.
98 Ibid.
99 Ibid.
100 "Draft Articles on the Effects of Armed Conflicts on Treaties", with commentaries, Draft Article 6(2).
101 Ibid, Draft Article 6(b).
102 Sjöstedt, *The Role of Multilateral Environmental Agreements*, 154–156.

times, the occupying power should continue complying with its obligations under the ratified environmental treaties. Accordingly, the continuous application in times of occupation of MEAs based on the second element "characteristics of the armed conflict" of the third stage of the assessment provided under Draft Article 6 of the ILC's Draft Articles can be a call for the continued operation of MEAs in situations of occupation.

However, it should be noted that an environmental treaty may still not apply in armed conflict and occupation even after completing the suggested three-stage assessment as provided by the 2011 ILC's Draft Articles. In this respect, it could be argued that the presumption of the continued application provided under Draft Article 7 of MEAs to armed conflict can be reversed, since the other Draft Articles 4, 5, and 6 provide particular factors and criteria to determine the continued application of such treaties to armed conflict. This weakens the presumption of the continued application of treaties in times of armed conflict provided under Draft Articles 3 and 7.[103] Accordingly, it could be argued that the foundation of the Draft Articles is vague and has left the issue regarding the assessment of the application of environmental treaties in times of armed conflict and occupation unresolved.[104] The UNGA simply took note of them,[105] and consequently, no general rule based on the ILC's 2011 Draft Articles can be formulated in this regard.[106] However, the ILC's 2011 Draft Articles are still a very welcome addition and a progressive move towards more formal legal assessment of the continued application of MEAs in the future.

It could, however, be argued that it would be better if the ILC's in the 2011 Draft Articles built the argument on the presumption of the continued application of the MEAs during times of armed conflict on the idea that this was owing to the inability to break them into a multitude of bilateral relations. Some, if not many, of the peacetime treaties, including MEAs, were suspended during armed conflict situations between belligerent states but continued to apply between these and third states, "neutral states", to the conflict.[107] However, for most MEAs, assuming such a dual system is technically not possible, because the obligations contained in them are indivisible,[108] and much of their subject matter is to protect a common concern

103 As provided by Draft Article 3, the ILC presumed that "the existence of an armed conflict does not *ipso facto* terminate or suspend the operation of treaties".

104 Karine Bannelier-Christakis, 'International Law Commission and Protection of the Environment in Times of Armed Conflict: A Possibility for Adjudication?' (2013), 20 *Journal for International Cooperation Studies* 129, 139–141; Carl Bruch, Cymie Payne, and Britta Sjöstedt, 'Armed Conflict and the Environment', in Lavanya Rajamani and Jacqueline Peel (eds), *The Oxford Handbook of International Environmental Law* (Oxford University Press 2021), 866–867.

105 The United Nations: General Assembly, 'Effects of Armed Conflicts on Treaties', (18 December 2017), (A/RES/72/121), paras 2, 3.

106 Sjöstedt, *The Role of Multilateral Environmental Agreements*, 158.

107 Bannelier-Christakis, 'International Law Commission and Protection of the Environment in Times of Armed Conflict', 140–141.

108 NB: very few MEAs do contain "parallel" or distinct obligations – for example, where some states have ratified amendments but others have not (e.g. aspects of the Montreal protocol).

of all states parties. Hence, suspending them between belligerents may affect the rights owed to the third states, as provided under Draft Article 6. Thus, it is hard to imagine how it is possible that some environmental treaties can be inapplicable or suspended between belligerent states and at the same time applicable in all other types of relations between belligerent states and third "neutral" states. Accordingly, it is reasonable to argue that MEAs will still be in effect in times of armed conflict and occupation due to the impracticality of breaking them into a multitude of bilateral relations.

The ILC's approach in the 2011 Draft Articles differs from that adopted by the ICJ in the Nuclear Weapons Advisory Opinion in two main aspects. First, the ICJ focused its attention mainly on whether particular obligations within a treaty could apply, rather than the applicability of the treaty itself.[109] Second, it could be understood from the ICJ statement that the peacetime IEL treaty obligations are suspended during armed conflict unless they are adopted with the intention to apply them during that time.[110] Hulme interpreted the ICJ's statement and stated that "seemingly, if such obligations were not so intended they would be suspended as between belligerent states for the duration of the conflict".[111] However, it is tricky to understand or to discover the intention of states where the treaty is silent.[112] In contrast to the ICJ approach, the ILC's is a more progressive, positive one that supports the possibility of MEAs' continued application in times of armed conflict and occupation. Moreover, the ILC deliberately omitted reference to the states' intentions regarding the treaty's status in relation to determining the continuous application of the treaty to situations of armed conflict and occupation.[113] Arguably, it seems like the ILC's reasoning behind this is to avoid giving weight to the ICJ's statement in order to favour a more progressive approach. The ILC states that "the drafters of treaties rarely provide an indication of their intention regarding the effect of the existence of an armed conflict on the treaty. Wherever such an intention is discernible, it would most likely be through a provision of the treaty".[114] However, the intention of the state parties to any convention is the decisive element in any interpretation process.[115] One could argue that the ILC was not accurate in omitting reference to the parties' intentions.[116] It could have been more precise in its stance by adhering only to the treaty interpretation process outlined in Article 31 of the VCLT, rather than omitting the reference to the parties' intention. Having

109 ICJ, Nuclear Weapons Advisory Opinion, para 30.
110 Ibid.
111 Karen Hulme, *War Torn Environment: Interpreting the Legal Threshold* (Brill Publisher 2004), 141.
112 Ibid.
113 Sjöstedt, *The Role of Multilateral Environmental Agreements*, 153.
114 "Draft Articles on the Effects of Armed Conflicts on Treaties", with commentaries, Draft Article 5(3).
115 Sjöstedt, *The Role of Multilateral Environmental Agreements*, 154.
116 "Draft Articles on the Effects of Armed Conflicts on Treaties", with commentaries, Draft Article 5(3).

established the ordinary or the objective meaning of any treaty through the interpretation process expressed by the VCLT is, in reality, about determining the intention of the state parties to the convention.[117] As Sjöstedt argued, the interpretation process adopted by the VCLT is the primary means of treaty interpretation, and the intention of the negotiators is the supplementary one.[118] Therefore, it is always better to put more emphasis on the rules on treaty interpretation expressed in the VCLT,[119] in particular if the peacetime treaty itself does not expressly regulate or provide any specific provision regarding its application in times of armed conflict and occupation. It should be noted that the VCLT does not provide any clear or direct answer on how treaties are affected in times of armed conflict and occupation. For example, Article 73 of the VCLT, which partly deals with the outbreak of hostilities, does not mention how treaties are affected in such situations.[120]

It could be argued that the fact that the ILC's approach in the 2011 Draft Articles is different from that of the ICJ in the 1996 Nuclear Weapons Advisory Opinion is mainly because of the years' gap between them and the development that happened meanwhile. Therefore, it is possible to say that the matter can be clarified through a chronological analysis. In 1996, there was a lack of agreement regarding the application of human rights treaties in times of armed conflict and occupation. Consequently, the possibility of extending the application of environmental treaties was not considered by the ICJ. However, in 2011, the ILC relied on the 2004 Wall Advisory Opinion and the 2005 *DRC v. Uganda* case, which both provided a framework for applying human rights treaties in scenarios of armed conflict and occupation. The ILC utilised them as a precedent for applying environmental treaties to such situations as well.

The ILC made other important contributions in relation to this topic, particularly after its three different reports published by the Special Rapporteur in relation to the protection of the environment in times of armed conflict and occupation. The reports clearly supported the view that the protection of the environment at such times goes well beyond IHL and argued for the continued application and operation of IEL treaties to such situations.[121] However, the ILC's reports and its Draft Articles are non-binding documents. Nevertheless, they constitute evidence of support for the continuous application of IEL treaties to such situations.

Regarding the application of the environmental treaties to the occupied territory, there is a group of scholars who have suggested that IEL treaties are not only applicable in peacetime but also continue to be applicable in times of armed conflict and occupation. In particular, this should apply to treaties that aim to protect the environment in the common interest of the whole international community,

117 Sjöstedt, *The Role of Multilateral Environmental Agreements*, 154.

118 Ibid, 152–154.

119 Ibid.

120 VCLT (1969), Article 73: "The provisions of the present Convention shall not prejudge any question that may arise in regard to a treaty from a succession of States or from the international responsibility of a State or from the outbreak of hostilities between States".

121 See ILC, 'First Report', 'Second report', and 'Third report'.

such as the Convention on Biological Diversity.[122] By assuming this assertion is correct, IEL treaties would enhance the general protection of the environment in times of armed conflict and occupation. However, there is still no agreement between international law scholars regarding the issue. For example, there are some who have argued against such an application.[123] They contend that the application of peacetime treaties to situations of armed conflict is a controversial issue, claiming that the law regarding this remains unsettled, chaotic, and far from satisfactory.[124] Furthermore, they have argued that environmental law provisions are not intended to apply in armed conflict situations. Moreover, according to them, some of the environmental treaties advance notification systems and consultation procedures that are often incompatible with armed conflicts scenarios, such as the Kuwait Regional Convention and the United Nations Convention on the Law of the Sea (UNCLOS).[125] They added that the environmental protection provisions under both conventions, therefore, are very unlikely to apply during armed conflict situations.[126] Furthermore, this argument was indirectly implied by the UNSC in its two resolutions 674 and 687 and by a statement forwarded by the United States following the end of the Iraq–Kuwait war.[127] However, for the reasons expounded above, it is not possible, from the author's point of view, to consider that all MEAs are not applicable to situations of armed conflict and occupation based on these arguments, not to mention the fact that this argument is almost three decades old and since then, IEL has developed dramatically and the concerns regarding the protection of the environment during the armed conflict through IEL provisions have received more attention from regional and international courts and state practice as well as international law bodies and scholars.[128]

Furthermore, there are some international law scholars who dismiss the application of MEAs, and instead they concentrate only on the application of customary international environmental law in times of armed conflict and occupation.[129] The dismissal of the application of MEAs to armed conflict situations by scholars is because they believe these treaties are without any clear enforceable content.[130] Furthermore, those scholars consider that MEAs are not able to provide any substantive or prescriptive rule on environmental protection during armed conflict.[131]

122 Vöneky, 'A New Shield for the Environment', 20–32; Patricia Birnie, Alan Boyle, and Catherine Redgwell, *International Law and the Environment* (4th edn, Oxford University Press 2021).

123 Luan Low and David Hodgkinson, 'Compensation for Wartime Environmental Damage: Challenges to International Law after the Gulf War', (1995) 35 *Va J Int'l L* 405, 442–446.

124 Ibid.

125 Ibid.

126 Ibid.

127 Both Resolutions adopted by the UNSC 674 and 687 have not imposed any legal liability on Iraq under International Environmental Law obligations; see footnote number 288 in Low and Hodgkinson, 'Compensation for Wartime Environmental Damage', 445.

128 Dienelt, *Armed Conflicts and the Environment*, 230–232.

129 Sjöstedt, *The Role of Multilateral Environmental Agreements*, 145–146.

130 Ibid.

131 Ibid.

However, it could be argued that IEL treaties have binding legal obligations no less than those of IHL and IHRL; therefore, there is no real or practical reason to rule them out in situations of armed conflict and occupation.[132] Moreover, environmental treaties are the only international law treaties that have been originally drafted to protect the environment as such. Other international law conventions that might indirectly provide protection to the environment come under different bodies of international law, such as IHL and IHRL. Accordingly, it is more sensible to consider their continued application to such situations, rather than dismiss them.

4.1.2.3 The Use of State Practice as Evidence of the Continued Application of MEAs to Situations of Armed Conflict and Occupation

The role of state practice is crucial in determining whether IEL treaties continue to apply in situations of armed conflict and occupation. There have been varied practices by different states in this regard. While some states acknowledge the applicability of environmental treaties in such situations, others oppose or disregard them. Some states remain neutral and suggest that more examination is necessary to determine the application of IEL to situations of armed conflict.[133] This creates a complicated situation, because there is no consensus or shared perspective among states concerning the application of MEAs in situations of armed conflict and occupation. For example, the Gulf Wars and their associated environmental disasters raised concerns about whether IEL treaties could be used to safeguard the environment in such times. During the debate in the UNGA's Sixth Committee between 1991 and 1992, states did not have a unified stance on whether or not IEL should be applied in such circumstances. Some states agreed, such as Iran,[134] while others, such as Brazil,[135] did not, and most states asked for further examination, such as Japan.[136]

There are only a few instances of state practice that could indicate that MEAs remain in force in times of armed conflict and occupation. For example, the practice during the war between Iraq and Iran supports their continued applicability in such situations. Both states continued to co-operate through the Regional Organisation for the Protection of the Marine Environment to implement the 1978

132 Ibid.

133 Sjöstedt, *The Role of Multilateral Environmental Agreements*, 147–148. See also Silja Voneky, 'Peacetime Environmental Law as a Basis of State Responsibility for Environmental Damage Caused by War' in Jay Austin, Carl Bruch (eds), *The Environmental Consequences of War* (Cambridge University Press 2010) 195–196.

134 The Sixth Committee of the UN General Assembly, UN Doc. (A/C.6/ 46/SR.18) (22 October 1991), paras 30–33.

135 The Sixth Committee of the UN General Assembly, UN Doc. (A/C.6/47/SR.9) (6 October 1992), para 13.

136 The Sixth Committee of the UN General Assembly, UN Doc. (A/C.6/47/SR.9) (6 October 1992), paras 67–68. For the summary of the debate see Voneky, 'Peacetime Environmental Law as a Basis of State Responsibility for Environmental Damage Caused by War', 195–196.

Kuwait Regional Convention for Co-operation on the Protection of the Marine Environment from Pollution.[137]

Furthermore, the so-called Oslo Agreements between the Palestine Liberation Organisation (PLO) and Israel include several provisions regarding the environmental cooperation around and protection of forests, nature reserves, parks, water, and agriculture. The Oslo Agreements include several provisions that consider the protection of the environment, which can also be good evidence to show that environmental considerations should be taken into account in such situations, in particular through bilateral agreements between the occupied state and the occupying power.[138] Furthermore, as will be discussed in detail in Section 4.2, the World Heritage Convention is one of a few MEAs that include a provision regarding the operation during armed conflict,[139] which has been active and operational during the armed conflict in the DRC in relation to protecting the environment.

Recently, Azerbaijan invoked the application of the 1979 Convention on the Conservation of European Wildlife and Natural Habitats (Berne Convention)[140] to the previously occupied territories by Armenia and its violations of the Convention, namely to the natural habitats and biodiversity at that time.[141] At the time of writing this book, the arbitral proceedings between the two states are still pending; however, this case is important to support the application of IEL treaties to situations of armed conflict and occupation and whether IEL, namely MEAs, can complement the law of occupation in relation to the protection of the environment in occupied territory and continue to apply during such situations.[142] The Berne Convention places specific and significant legal obligations upon state parties to the Convention to protect, conserve, maintain, and restore wild fauna and flora and their natural habitats.[143] Therefore, the occupying power, if it is a state party to the Berne Convention, has legal obligations to protect and avoid harming wildlife and its natural habitats and the biodiversity of another state party to the Convention. This logic is, indeed, applicable to the case at hand between Azerbaijan and Armenia,

137 Kuwait Regional Convention for Co-operation on the Protection of the Marine Environment from Pollution (adopted 24 April 1978) (entered into force 1 July 1979); Voneky, 'Peacetime Environmental Law as a Basis of State Responsibility for Environmental Damage Caused by War', 195.

138 See e.g., 'The Israeli-Palestinian Interim Agreement On The West Bank and The Gaza Strip Annex III': Protocol Concerning Civil Affairs, Articles 1, 12, 13, 14, 25, 26, 40.

139 The World Heritage Convention, Article 11(4).

140 Council of Europe: Convention on the Conservation of European Wildlife and Natural Habitats (Berne Convention). (adopted 19 September 1979), (entered into force 1 June 1982).

141 Republic of Azerbaijan Ministry of Foreign Affairs, No: 015/23, Press Release on arbitration filed by Azerbaijan against Armenia for widespread environmental destruction. More information available online at: <https://www.mfa.gov.az/en/news/no01523>. Accessed date 4 March 2023.

142 Waad Abualrob, Marco Longobardo, and Ruth Mackenzie, 'Applying International Environmental Law Conventions in Occupied Territory: The Azerbaijan v. Armenia Case under the Bern Convention'. Blog of the European Journal of International Law (2023). Available online at: <https://www.ejiltalk.org/applying-international-environmental-law-conventions-in-occupied-territory-the-azerbaijan-v-armenia-case-under-the-bern-convention>. Accessed date: 21 May 2023.

143 See, for example, the Berne Convention (1979), Articles 2 and 3.

since both countries are parties to the Convention. Thus, it is important to keep a close eye on the results of these arbitral proceedings as they have the potential to establish that IEL treaties complement the law of occupation concerning the protection of the environment in times of occupation.

The proceedings launched by Azerbaijan against Armenia in early 2023 are evidence that the Berne Convention is applicable in occupied territory in relation to Azerbaijan. This constitutes another parcel of state practice that supports the continued application of MEAs to situations of occupation. Therefore, if the legal action launched by Azerbaijan against Armenia leads to a decision by an arbitration tribunal depending on the substance of the matter, this would be a noteworthy precedent that could have significant repercussions in this field.[144]

Furthermore, regarding the ongoing armed conflict and occupation between Russia and Ukraine,[145] the latter has insisted that the former must respect and comply with its obligations under MEAs, such as the Ramsar Convention.[146] A resolution was adopted at the 14th Meeting of the Conference of the Contracting Parties to the Ramsar Convention on Wetlands (Ramsar COP 14/ 2022) concerning "The Ramsar Convention's response to environmental emergency in Ukraine relating to the damage of its Wetlands of International Importance (Ramsar Sites) stemming from the Russian Federation's aggression".[147] The resolution emphasised that "the importance of principles of international cooperation and fulfilment of obligations under the Convention on Wetlands and other multilateral environmental treaties".[148] The resolution called on Russia to fulfil its obligations under the Convention, and it deplored any environmental harm done to the Wetlands of International Importance in Ukraine. It deemed such actions to be a violation of the Ramsar Convention and a serious breach of international law.[149] This resolution is highly significant, because it is acknowledged that the Ramsar Convention, as well as other MEAs, should be taken into account during situations of armed conflict and occupation.

During COP14, the Ukrainian delegation urged the participants to take action against Russia's destruction of wetlands and to condemn Russia's violation of the

144 Abualrob, Longobardo, and Mackenzie, 'Applying International Environmental Law Conventions in Occupied Territory'.

145 Both Russia and Ukraine are parties to the convention, and they have designated several wetlands as Ramsar sites. See the Ramsar Convention: Country Profiles, <https://www.ramsar.org/country-profiles>.

146 United Nations Educational, Scientific and Cultural Organisation: Convention on Wetlands of International Importance, especially as Waterfowl Habitat (Ramsar Convention), (adopted 2 February 1971) (entered into force 21 December 1975).

147 The 14th Meeting of the Conference of the Contracting Parties to the Ramsar Convention on Wetlands, 'Wetlands Action for People and Nature', Geneva, Switzerland, and Wuhan, China, 5–13 November 2022. Resolution (XIV.20), "The Ramsar Convention's response to environmental emergency in Ukraine relating to the damage of its Wetlands of International Importance (Ramsar Sites) stemming from the Russian Federation's aggression".

148 Resolution (XIV.20), para 11.

149 Ibid, paras 12–16.

Ramsar Convention.[150] Ukraine's invocation of the Ramsar Convention at COP14, is, in itself, evidence that it is applicable to Ukraine in such circumstances.

It could be argued that, in the context of the ongoing conflict between Russia and Ukraine, the application of the Ramsar Convention would be essential to protect wetlands, including Ramsar sites, since they are critical habitats for many plant and animal species. Their destruction or degradation will have significant environmental consequences, including a loss of biodiversity and an impact on ecosystem functions.[151] Consequently, regarding the ongoing armed conflict and occupation in Ukraine since 2014, this supports the argument that peacetime treaties, including MEAs, remain applicable in such situations.

It is possible to conclude that, based on the considerable amount of states' practice during times of armed conflict and occupation, there is enough evidence to support the application of MEAs in these situations. That is, it is reasonable to argue that environmental treaties can be applicable in such circumstances, given the perspective of state practice over time.

4.2 The Role of MEAs in Environmental Protection in Times of Armed Conflict and Occupation

This section concentrates on two global MEAs and their role in protecting the environment in times of occupation. These operate on the principle of worldwide collaboration between all countries to preserve and protect the collective well-being and interests of the global community.

4.2.1 Selected MEAs

There are over a thousand MEAs, with each concentrating on a particular environmental issue.[152] Several can be seen as being relevant to protecting the environment in times of armed conflict and occupation. However, the author limited this chapter to examining the application of only two MEAs: one that establishes protection for certain areas/sites, which is the World Heritage Convention; and the other, the Biodiversity Convention, which could enhance the protection of the environment in conflict scenarios by preventing biodiversity loss, which frequently occurs in times of armed conflict and occupation. This selection is based on one main reason, which is that these two conventions have made a significant contribution to conserving biodiversity. The World Heritage Convention, in particular, can preserve biological rich protected "hot-spots" of international importance, which could

150 For more information about the COP14/2022, see Katerina Belousova, 'COP14 participants were Urged to React to Russia's Destruction of International Ecosystems'. Available at: <https://eco-politic.com.ua/en/news/uchasnikiv-cop14-zaklikali-vidreaguvati-na-znishhennya-rosiieju-mizhnarodnih-ekosistem-2/ >. Accessed date: 8 April 2023.

151 See, Dienelt, *Armed Conflicts and the Environment*, 235–237.

152 International Environmental Agreements (IEA) Database Project. Available online at: <https://iea.uoregon.edu/>. Accessed date: 19 August 2023.

include endangered species and rare ecosystems. The Biodiversity Convention was principally drafted to protect biodiversity as such, which could safeguard different types of species. Given the reason explained above, these two MEAs are addressed in detail. Both conventions can be applied to improve the protection of the environment in times of armed conflict and occupation.

4.2.1.1 The Protection of the Environment in Times of Armed Conflict and Occupation under the World Heritage Convention

The World Heritage Convention is the only MEA that includes a provision regarding its application to situations of armed conflict along with several other indicators and practices that confirm a continued application of the Convention under such circumstances. For example, Article 11(4) provides that the "list of World Heritage in Danger" "may include only such property forming part of the cultural and natural heritage as is threatened by serious and specific dangers", "such as the outbreak or the threat of an armed conflict".[153] This statement is also relevant to situations of occupation since belligerent occupation is a type of armed conflict.[154] Article 11(4), therefore, has a clear message that the convention continues to apply to situations of armed conflict. The Operational Guidelines of the Convention confirm that too.[155] The Convention and the Operational Guidelines explicitly refer to an "outbreak or threat of an armed conflict", and thus they apply to such situations.[156]

Furthermore, Article 6(3) of the Convention provides that "Each State Party to this Convention undertakes not to take any deliberate measures which might damage directly or indirectly the cultural and natural heritage referred to in Articles 1 and 2 situated on the territory of other States Parties to this Convention".[157] According to some scholars, Article 6(3) of the World Heritage Convention can be interpreted as that it requires belligerent states to refrain from intentionally attacking cultural, natural, and mixed heritage, including any type of activities that might cause, directly or indirectly, damage to the heritage sites of another state party to the Convention.[158] All this can be considered as a clear indication that the World Heritage in Danger List under Article 11(4) and Article 6(3) of the Convention point to the continued application of the Convention to situations of armed conflict.[159]

153 The World Heritage Convention, Article 11(4).

154 The GCIV, Article 2(2); Longobardo, 'Animals in Occupied Territory', 224.

155 Operational Guidelines for the Implementation of the World Heritage Convention, para 177(b) and para 180(b)(iii).

156 See in general, Karen Hulme, 'Armed Conflict and Biodiversity', in Michael Bowman, Peter Davies, and Edward Goodwin (eds), *Research Handbook on Biodiversity and Law* (Edward Elgar Publishing 2016).

157 The World Heritage Convention, Article 6(3).

158 Nada Al-Duaij, *Environmental Law of Armed Conflict* (Transnational Publishers 2004) 161; Francesco Francioni and Frederico Lenzerini (eds), *The 1972 World Heritage Convention: A Commentary* (OUP 2008), 126.

159 See Sandra Krahenmann, 'Animals as Specially Protected Objects', in Anne Peters, Jérôme De Hemptinne, and Robert Kolb, *Animals in the International Law of Armed Conflict* (Cambridge University Press 2022), 95–96.

Additionally, the World Heritage Convention Committee has confirmed the ongoing validity of the Convention in situations of armed conflict and occupation through various decisions. It has recognised that military activities can cause damage to cultural and natural heritage sites, and that such activities can constitute a violation of the Convention. These decisions have also provided further guidance on the responsibilities of state parties under the Convention to safeguard the integrity of cultural and natural heritage sites during times of armed conflict and occupation.[160] For example, the World Heritage Committee has acknowledged the applicability of both IHL, including the Four Geneva Conventions of 1949, the Hague Convention for the Protection of Cultural Property in the Event of Armed Conflict of 1954, and the World Heritage Convention, in relation to the protection of the cultural heritage of the Old City of Jerusalem in the OPT.[161] This confirmation by the World Heritage Committee supports the continued application of the World Heritage Convention in situations of occupation, alongside IHL, for ensuring the safeguarding of cultural and natural heritage sites in such circumstances.[162]

Furthermore, the Committee has established a system of monitoring and reporting on the state of conservation of World Heritage sites, including those located in areas of armed conflict and occupation.[163] The occupying power should provide reports to the World Heritage Committee on the condition of these sites. This system allows the Committee to assess the state of conservation of these sites and take appropriate measures to protect them, such as placing them on the World Heritage in Danger List.[164] For example, the World Heritage Committee added the Ituri Forest in the Okapi Wildlife Reserve in DRC to the World Heritage in Danger List when the armed conflict started in 1997, along with other natural heritage sites that have been included as well, which are inhabited by many endangered species that are at high risk because of the situation of armed conflict and occupation.[165]

To sum up, the occupying power, if a state party to the World Heritage Convention, must comply with its obligations outlined in the Convention, such as protecting and conserving cultural and natural heritage sites located in the occupied territory from any harm that might affect or change their character.[166]

160 See for example, World Heritage Committee, Decisions Adopted by the 27th Session of the World Heritage Committee in 2003 (WHC-03/27.COM/24) (30 June–5 July 2003), 10, 141; World Heritage Committee, Decisions Adopted at the 31st Session of the World Heritage Committee 2007 (WHC-07/31.COM/24) (23 June–2 July 2007), 11–12, 15, 25–26, 81.

161 Ibid (WHC-07/31.COM/24) (23 June–2 July 2007), 25–26.

162 Ibid, 25–26.

163 Ibid, 11–12, 15, 25–26.

164 Ibid.

165 World Heritage Committee (WHC-03/27.COM/24) (30 June–5 July 2003), 10; World Heritage Committee (WHC-07/31.COM/24) (23 June–2 July 2007), 16; Dienelt, *Armed Conflicts and the Environment*, 243; Krahenmann, 'Animals as Specially Protected Objects', 96.

166 See, for example, Article 4 of the Convention, which states that it is a must that each state party "recognises that the duty of ensuring the identification, protection, conservation, presentation and transmission to future generations of the cultural and natural heritage referred to in Articles 1 and

Furthermore, the occupying power has to consider the decisions adopted by the Committee of the Convention. This includes providing regular reports on the condition of the protected natural and cultural heritage sites located in the occupied territory as well as safeguarding and preserving them from any danger.[167] Furthermore, the occupying power must not take any action that could destroy or harm these heritage sites, nor should it undertake any activities that could change the physical or cultural character of the protected site/s.[168] For example, the occupying power must abstain from using heritage sites located in the occupied territory for military training grounds or as parking spaces for military vehicles.

However, it should be noted that the World Heritage Convention and its list do not protect the environment and its elements as such, but rather only if the environment is considered a part of a protected heritage site included in the Convention's list.[169] For example, there are some cultural landscapes that constitute cultural heritage sites protected under the World Heritage Convention and, at the same time, such protected sites reflect the interaction between the population and its environment, as well as such cultural heritage landscapes. They might also have a special importance value in relation to maintaining healthy ecosystem functions and biological diversity.[170] Therefore, indirect protection of the environment and its elements in situations of armed conflict and occupation under the World Heritage Convention could be provided. For example, endangered species, including insects, birds, and plants, can receive indirect protection through the safeguarding of cultural and natural sites. This is due to the acknowledgement of the interconnection between natural and cultural heritage, including flora and fauna, under the World Heritage Convention.[171] Therefore, the preservation of cultural and natural habitats can contribute to the protection of endangered species, which in turn, enhances the protection of the ecosystem and biodiversity during times of armed conflict and occupation, in accordance with IEL.[172]

---

2 and situated on its territory, belongs primarily to that State. It will do all it can to this end, to the utmost of its own resources and, where appropriate, with any international assistance and co-operation, in particular, financial, artistic, scientific and technical, which it may be able to obtain". This obligation must be also applicable to the occupying power while exercising an effective control over an occupied territory.

167 The World Heritage Convention, Article 29(1) and (2); see, for example, World Heritage Committee (WHC-07/31.COM/24) (23 June–2 July 2007), 12, 15, 25–26.

168 The World Heritage Convention, Article 6(3).

169 Sandra Krahenmann, 'Animals as Specially Protected Objects', 95–99.

170 World Heritage Committee, Report, 16th session, UNESCO Doc. (WHC-92/CONF.002/12), (14 December 1992), 55.

171 The World Heritage Convention, Article 1.

172 Krahenmann, 'Animals as Specially Protected Objects', 95–96.

4.2.1.1.1 THE INTERCONNECTION BETWEEN THE WORLD HERITAGE CONVENTION AND OTHER RELATED RULES UNDER IHL

As mentioned above, the World Heritage Committee affirmed that the World Heritage Convention is applicable in situations of occupation, along with IHL in relation to safeguarding the heritage sites in occupied territory.[173] Accordingly, it is important to consider that the rules of IHL that safeguard cultural property can be understood in conjunction with the rules of IEL that protect cultural heritage. For example, the World Heritage Convention can inform the interpretation of IHL rules and vice versa, with the objective of enhancing the protection provided to the environment in situations of armed conflict and occupation.

The Hague Convention for the Protection of Cultural Property in the Event of Armed Conflict 1954 and the 1999 Second Protocol to the 1954 Hague Convention contain provisions on the protection of cultural property in times of armed conflict.[174] The First Protocol to the 1954 Hague Convention focuses on the protection of cultural property in situations of occupation.[175] Cultural property under the 1954 Hague Convention is protected irrespective of ownership.[176] However, it should be noted that there is some room to consider the natural environment and its elements as cultural property in terms of the categories provided under IHL treaties.[177] IHL treaties that protect cultural property focus on human-made objects and make no reference to any non-human-made ones. However, even though IHL does not really enhance the protection provided to the environment through cultural property rules, it is possible to provide indirect protection of the environment, that is, through the protection provided to cultural heritage sites in particular. They are protected if such sites include a natural environment or they are rich in biodiversity, with several types of rare plants and animals. For example, several types of animals and insects inhabit Angkor Archaeological Park in Cambodia, which is protected as cultural property and granted enhanced protection in times of armed conflict under the 1999 Second Protocol to the 1954 Hague Convention.[178]

From this point of view, it could be argued that, the notion of cultural heritage may be interpreted in a broader sense to include some categories of living creatures, such as endangered species, particularly in light of the World Heritage Convention, since it clearly recognised the links between cultural and natural heritage, including the flora and fauna. According to Article 2 of the World Heritage Convention, natural heritage includes “geological and physiographical formations and precisely delineated areas which constitute the habitat of threatened species of animals and plants of outstanding universal value from the point of view of science

173 World Heritage Committee (WHC-07/31.COM/24) (23 June–2 July 2007), 25–26.

174 The Hague Convention for the Protection of Cultural Property in the Event of Armed Conflict (14 May 1954); Second Protocol to the 1954 Hague Convention (26 March 1999).

175 First Protocol to the 1954 Hague Convention (14 May 1954).

176 The Hague Convention for the Protection of Cultural Property in the Event of Armed Conflict, Article 1.

177 Krahenmann, ‘Animals as Specially Protected Objects’, 93–94.

178 Ibid, 95.

or conservation".[179] Thus, the interpretation of IHL rules on the protection of cultural heritage should consider the developing broader notion of cultural and natural heritage under IEL, namely under the World Heritage Convention. Furthermore, the 2016 UNESCO Military Manual for the Protection of Cultural Property argues that, if a state complies with its obligations under IHL regarding the protection of cultural property that would, at the same time, guarantee its compliance with the obligations under the World Heritage Convention as well. Conversely, a breach of IHL rules "can amount further to a breach of the World Heritage Convention".[180] Furthermore, in favour of including the natural environment under the notion of cultural heritage under IHL, the distinction between natural and cultural heritage has been criticised and described as artificial. That is, immovable cultural heritage sites should be considered as part of a natural context.[181] Boer argued that "The clear and often close links between biological and cultural diversity mean that separating them can be out of the question. These links are encapsulated in the term 'biocultural diversity', which covers biological, cultural, and linguistic diversity".[182] Lixinski contended that the World Heritage Convention "creates a very close relationship by having categories of 'natural' and 'cultural' heritage, a connection that goes back to the original drafting of the treaty".[183] Thus, it could be argued that cultural and natural heritages are interconnected. Despite the apparent limitations of the notion of cultural property under IHL, a progressive interpretation in light of IEL would allow for the inclusion of the environment and its elements, including animals/plants and insects inhabiting or located in cultural heritage sites, under the notion of cultural property of IHL. Hence, the environment could enjoy indirect protection under such a regime.

The parallel application of IHL rules related to the protection of cultural heritage sites and IEL rules concerning these sites is now considered. Both regimes install area-based protection, with states under both having similar, but not identical, legal obligations, relying on commonly shared objectives to protect such heritage sites. In this case, it could be argued that the example of protected sites under IEL and IHL demonstrates harmonisation between both regimes away from the traditional way of treaty interpretation, as mentioned under the ILC's fragmentation report of relying only on treaty interpretation codified under Article 31(3)(c) of the VCLT.[184]

In the case of occupation, the protection of the environment as cultural and natural heritage property could also contribute positively to doing so, not only against destruction but also against any type of acts by the occupying power or

179 The World Heritage Convention, Article 2.

180 Roger O'Keefe et al., *Protection of Cultural Property: Military Manual* (UNESCO 2016), 7.

181 Ben Boer, 'The Environment and Cultural Heritage', in Francesco Francioni and Ana Vrdoljak (eds), *The Oxford Handbook of International Cultural Heritage Law* (Oxford University Press 2020), 319.

182 Ibid.

183 Lucas Lixinski, *International Law for Communities; Exclusion and Re-Imagination* (Oxford University Press 2019), 168.

184 See Dienelt, *Armed Conflicts and the Environment*, 297–298.

even by a third party from the occupied state itself that might harm the environment. However, this protection of the environment is limited to the areas only where they are classified or being added to the world heritage list as cultural and natural heritage sites.

It is important to acknowledge that not all occupied territories have cultural and natural heritage sites. This depends on each individual state's decision to nominate and submit its properties for inclusion on the World Heritage Convention list. Once a site is enlisted, the Committee of the Convention has the authority to make decisions concerning it without the consent of the concerned state party. For example, the Committee can include a site on the list of World Heritage in Danger for receiving enhanced protection if it faces serious and specific threats, including those posed by armed conflict and occupation.[185] The same logic can be applied to IHL as well, since nominating and designating an area and/or site as a cultural property is left to each individual state.[186]

However, sometimes applying the rules to protect cultural and natural heritage sites can be challenging, in particular when the protected areas are huge. For example, in DRC, there are many natural heritage sites and cultural landscapes that are home to several endangered species and are rich in biodiversity.[187] By protecting such large areas during armed conflict and occupation, this can reflect positively on the ecosystem and biodiversity. These areas are not only vast, but also concentrated with numerous endangered species of animals, plants, and insects that are vital for the continuous normal functioning of ecosystem services.

For implementation and compliance purposes, the Committee of the World Heritage Convention would most probably apply a similar process to the so-called "naming and shaming" approach in IHRL in relation to publicly exposing the non-compliant state to the convention along with the reporting system that most MEAs already have.[188]

Summing up, considering the interpretation of IHL rules on cultural property in light of IEL rules on cultural and natural heritage would support the harmonisation and complementarity between both branches of law and how they could inform and influence each other in relation to enhancing the protection provided to the environment in times of armed conflict and occupation. However, cultural property provisions under IHL and under the World Heritage convention do not protect the environment *per se* – only if the natural environment/animals/plants are part of such a protected heritage site. Hence, the World Heritage Convention adopts an area-based approach that protects spaces rather than species.[189]

185 Ibid, 242–245.

186 Krahenmann, 'Animals as Specially Protected Objects', 97.

187 See the World Cultural Heritage in Danger List: UNESCO, International List of Cultural Property under Enhanced Protection (2019).

188 Daniel Bodansky, *The Art and Craft of International Environmental Law* (Harvard University Press 2010), 227; Dienelt, *Armed Conflicts and the Environment*, 245; The World Heritage Convention, Article 29.

189 Dienelt, *Armed Conflicts and the Environment*, 245.

Admittedly, applying the rules designed to protect cultural and natural heritage sites under the World Heritage Convention in times of armed conflict and occupation, with a view to protecting the environment, would definitely enhance the general protection provided to the environment in such situations. It would add extra constraints on the occupying power under its overall legal obligations under public international law, as has been discussed in previous chapters regarding the protection of the environment in such situations.

4.2.1.2 The Protection of the Environment in Times of Armed Conflict and Occupation under the Convention on Biological Diversity

In recent decades, there has been a dramatic increase in human activities that put biodiversity in danger, including situations of armed conflict and occupation. These activities have led to a mass reduction in biodiversity, particularly by destroying plants and animal habitats. The Biodiversity Convention was drafted to address such challenges, and it enjoys an almost universal status.[190] Regarding the Convention's continuous application to armed conflict and occupation situations, it does not include any direct provision that indicates its continuous application. However, the preamble of the Biodiversity Convention expresses the aim of serving the interest and common concern of the whole global community of states.[191] As Dienelt puts it, "the term biodiversity sounds like a global good that requires joint international efforts and close cooperation by all relevant actors".[192] Accordingly, the Biodiversity Convention "protects genetic, species and ecosystem diversity for its intrinsic value but also for economic reasons and for the sake of humankind'.[193] That is, it protects common goods for the whole international community.[194] Therefore, the Biodiversity Convention is one of the MEAs that seek to protect the common good for the whole international community. As noted earlier, this can provide support for the continued application of such a convention to situations of armed conflict and occupation. The reason behind this assumption is that this type of environmental treaty aims to "oblige state parties to protect an environmental good *per se*, and without an immediate advantage resulting from the fulfilment of the obligations for the contracting states".[195] Wolfrum commented on such MEAs that seek to protect the common good, stating that "[t]he essential criterion of the respective treaties is that they oblige the State parties to prohibit or

190 For more information about State Parties to the Convention, the main goals of the conventions, and other key aspects, see Convention on Biological Diversity, <https://www.cbd.int/>. Accessed date: 12 January 2023.

191 The United Nations, the Biodiversity Convention, (adopted 22 May 1992), (entered into force 29 December 1993). Preamble, para 3.

192 Dienelt, *Armed Conflicts and the Environment*, 247.

193 Ibid, 250.

194 The Biodiversity Convention, preamble, para 3.

195 Voneky, 'Peacetime Environmental Law as a basis of State Responsibility for Environmental Damage Caused by War', 213.

to control certain activities within their territories while the measures to be enacted by the states are of essential importance not only for themselves but rather for the state community as a whole as well".[196] Another scholar argued that such MEAs are quite similar to human rights treaties, particularly because they seek to protect the common good in the interest of all humankind and the state community as a whole. Therefore, they should also bind states in times of armed conflict.[197] Furthermore, this argument falls in line with the idea provided by the ILC's Draft Articles as discussed earlier, that is, under Draft Article 6, which mentions that factors depend on the treaty's nature, including its subject matter. When the treaty's subject matter is to protect the common interest of the state parties to the convention, it shall continue to apply during times of armed conflict and occupation. This, indeed, supports the argument that the Biodiversity Convention should continue to apply in times of armed conflict and occupation, because it protects the common good for the entire international community.[198] Notably, in contrast to the World Heritage Convention, the Biodiversity Convention does not follow a listing approach.[199]

The Biodiversity Convention has provisions on *in-situ* and *ex-situ* conservation.[200] The measures to be taken by a state party for the *ex-situ* conservation must be with the purpose of complementing *in-situ* measures.[201] *In-situ* conservation measures aim to establish protected areas in relation to conserving biological diversity.[202] Such protected areas could also include forests, for as is well-known, these can be rich in biodiversity and constitute natural habitats for several kinds of plants, animals, and other species.[203] Arguably, the protection of those protected areas under the Biodiversity Convention, namely *in-situ* conservation, should also be continued in times of armed conflict and occupation, thereby maintaining the biodiversity in such areas protected from the impact of such situations.[204]

It should be noted that Article 8 of the Biodiversity Convention requires state parties to the Convention to take all possible feasible practical measures (as far as possible) and as long as the circumstances allow to protect *in-situ* conservation.[205] This means that the occupying power shall take all possible and appropriate measures to protect and prevent harming the established protected areas under t*in-situ* conservation as long as the circumstances allow it to do that. However, the wording

196 Rudiger Wolfrum, 'Purposes and Principles of International Environmental Law' (1990) 33 *German YB Int'l L* 308, 327.

197 See Voneky, 'Peacetime Environmental Law as a Basis of State Responsibility for Environmental Damage Caused by War', 210–213.

198 Ibid, 210–213.

199 See Philippe Sands and others., *Principles of International Environmental Law* (4th edn, Cambridge University Press 2018), 388–409.

200 The Biodiversity Convention, Articles 8 and 9.

201 Ibid, Article 9(a).

202 Ibid, Article 8(a).

203 Anja Eikermann, *Forests in International Law: Is There Really a Need for an International Forest Convention?* (Springer International Publishing 2015), 99, 103–104.

204 Dienelt, *Armed Conflicts and the Environment*, 248.

205 The Biodiversity Convention, Article 8.

"as far as possible" under Article 8 of the Convention is not an absolute clear-cut binding obligation. For example, in situations of occupation, the occupying power may claim that the circumstances on land would not allow for fulfilling the obligations mentioned under Article 8. The established protected areas might be harmed due to some important necessary military activities or because of other emergency situations that would hinder full compliance with obligations mentioned under such provision. Accordingly, it could be argued that the language used to draw the legal obligations under the Biodiversity Convention, namely "as far as possible", might in some scenarios limit the protection provided to the environment, in particular in situations of armed conflict and occupation. However, that does not mean the Convention is not applicable to such situations but rather that the qualifying language of the Convention's provisions might in some cases limit the scope of state parties' obligations, in particular in situations of armed conflict and occupation.

The conflict clause in Article 22(1) of the convention provides that "the provisions of this Convention shall not affect the rights and obligations of any Contracting Party deriving from any existing international agreement, except where the exercise of those rights and obligations would cause a serious damage or threat to biological diversity".[206] Article 22(1) has been phrased in very broad terms that have been interpreted as supporting the continued application of the Convention to situations of armed conflict.[207] However, the exact meaning of the provision is still disputed.[208] Article 22(1) of the Convention regulates the relationship between the Biodiversity Convention and other international law conventions. It also provides that the Biodiversity Convention, in particular cases, such as those of serious damage or threats to biodiversity, can prevail over other obligations under other conventions. The question is, does this prevalence of the Biodiversity Convention in such certain situations only relate to other MEAs or was it meant to cover all international law conventions, such as IHL? Some have argued that yes, it does prevail in such conditions over IHL.[209] Therefore, it could be argued that the protection provided to the protected areas under *in-situ* conversation under Article 8 of the Biodiversity Convention continues in times of armed conflict and occupation, in accordance with Article 22(1) of the Convention.[210]

It has to be acknowledged that the IHL rules protecting biodiversity are not straightforward or clear. Additionally, as outlined in Chapter 2, the rules that defend the environment under the law of occupation are indirect. Therefore, it is important to read them in light of other more precise MEAs, such as the Biodiversity

206 Ibid, Article 22(1).

207 Dienelt, *Armed Conflicts and the Environment*, 248–250.

208 Richard Caddell, 'The Integration of Multilateral Environmental Agreements: Lessons from the Biodiversity-Related Conventions', (2011) 22 *Yearbook of International Environmental Law* 37, 50–51.

209 See Karen Hulme, 'Armed Conflict and Biodiversity' in Michael Bowman, Peter Davies, and Edward Goodwin (eds), *Research Handbook on Biodiversity and Law* (Edward Elgar Publishing 2016); Dienelt, *Armed Conflicts and the Environment*, 248–249.

210 Dienelt, *Armed Conflicts and the Environment*, 248.

Convention, which has the main aim of conserving biodiversity. For example, Article 55 of the Hague Regulations protects public property in occupied territory, and Article 55 mentions forests as an example of such properties. In this context, Article 8 of the Biodiversity Convention also protects forests, in circumstances where they are part of the established protected areas under the *in-situ* conservation. However, in this scenario, it is safe to assume that there is no normative conflict at all, since the occupying power can comply with both provisions, that is, Article 55 of the Hague Regulations and Article 8 of the Biodiversity Convention, without violating either. It can fulfil its obligations under the Biodiversity Convention by refraining from conducting military operations or any destruction inside the protected area (if the protected area, in this example forests, does not constitute a military objective) and at the same time without breaching its obligation under Article 55 of the Hague Regulations. Accordingly, the occupying power's duty under Article 55 of the Hague Regulations to protect the environment through public property rights rules and its duty under Article 8 of the Biodiversity Convention to protect the established protected areas under the *in-situ* conservation are complementary and support the interpretation and implementation of each other based on the logic of Article 31(3)(c) of the VCLT.

Finally, further support for the proposition that the Biodiversity Convention should apply in times of armed conflict and occupation is Article 4 of the Convention, which regulates its jurisdictional scope and embraces all activities within a state party's national jurisdiction and all activities beyond its territory, but under its "jurisdiction or control" (extraterritorial application of the Convention).[211] This article has significant relevance for situations of occupation, since it stresses that a state party to the Convention holds responsibility for all activities conducted under its control, including those that occur outside of its national territorial jurisdiction.[212] As is well known, in situations of occupation, the occupying power has effective control over the occupied territory.[213] Therefore, it is its responsibility under the Biodiversity Convention to protect the biodiversity of the occupied territory from any activities that could harm it, as long as it retains effective control over the occupied state's territory. However, the occupying power must be a state party to the Convention to have such an obligation. That is, to say that the Convention is applicable to situations of occupation and binds the occupying power, a state must first be a state party to the Convention and in addition, it must be exercising effective control over the other state's territory. Furthermore, it could be argued that the drafters of the Biodiversity Convention used the phrase "or" and not the phrase "and" to show that not only are areas under state party jurisdiction covered by the Convention, but also areas under its control,[214] which, in the case of occupation,

211 The Biodiversity Convention, Article 4(b).

212 Ibid.

213 Dienelt, *Armed Conflicts and the Environment*, 229–230.

214 See, for example, the United Nations Environment Programme, 'Ad Hoc Working Group of Legal and Technical Experts on Biological Diversity: Second Session, Report of the Ad Hoc Working Group of Legal and Technical Experts on Biological Diversity on the Work of its First Session'

might be a territory away from the territorial jurisdiction of the occupying state. Hence, the occupying power, if it is a state party to the Convention, must consider its legal obligations under its provisions when it occupies other states' territories (extraterritorial application).

According to a state of knowledge report published by both the Biodiversity Convention Secretariat and WHO, "Biodiversity plays a critical role in ecosystem functioning and also yields direct and indirect benefits (or ecosystem services) that support human and societal needs, including good health, food and nutrition security, energy provision, freshwater and medicines, livelihoods and spiritual fulfilment".[215] Furthermore, the healthy biodiversity of local animals and plants supports the economic and overall well-being of the population.[216] Damage to the environment, including contamination of water sources and soil, chemical and dangerous waste contamination, air pollution, and any other causes that might lead to ecosystem degradation, will contribute to biodiversity loss and threats to human health and well-being.[217] Accordingly, it could be argued that an occupying power's obligation under the Biodiversity Convention can be interpreted in light of Article 43 of the Hague Regulations, namely its duty to protect and ensure public order, normal and civil life, and the welfare of the occupied population. This is in addition to its obligation under the right to health to ensure that the occupied population are enjoying their right to physical and mental health. Therefore, biodiversity protection can contribute to protecting human health and well-being, whilst at the same time, the duty to protect human health requires protection of the biodiversity (reciprocal relationship). It seems reasonable to conclude that such rules under IEL, IHL, and IHRL can be interpreted in light of each other and that they clearly harmonise with and complement each other in this regard.

To sum up, the Biodiversity Convention protects the environment at all times by addressing biological diversity. That is, it continues to apply during times of armed conflict and situations of occupation. This is clear from its conflict clause under Article 22, its jurisdictional scope under Article 4, and the state parties' obligation to protect the environment for the sake of humankind and the whole international community, as the preamble of the Convention provides. The evidence suggests that the Biodiversity Convention is applicable during times of armed conflict and occupation, playing an important role in enhancing the protection provided to the environment in such situations.

To conclude, it has been explained how both the World Heritage Convention and the Biodiversity Convention could play an important role in enhancing the

(UNEP/Bio.Div/WG.2/1/4/Add.1) (5 February 1991), 2–3, 5, 9–10, 14, 18. All the Preparatory Work Documents of the Biodiversity Convention are available online at: <https://www.cbd.int/history/>. Accessed date: 12 December 2023.

215 Cristina Romanelli and others, 'Connecting Global Priorities: Biodiversity and Human Health: a State of Knowledge Review' (World Health Organisation and Secretariat of the Convention on Biological Diversity, 2015), 26.

216 World Health Organisation, 'Biodiversity and Health' (2015).

217 Ibid.

protection provided to the environment in situations of armed conflict and occupation, in particular through their precise provisions in this regard. The World Heritage Convention is the only MEA that mentioned situations of armed conflict, as such. In contrast, the Biodiversity Convention does not include a direct provision regarding situations of armed conflict; however, that does not mean it is not applicable under such circumstances, since it includes several provisions that have been interpreted as continuing to support the application of the Convention to such situations. Thus, the occupying power has legal obligations under both conventions to consider and respect the environment in occupied territory. This does not mean that other MEAs are not applicable or even less important. For example, the Ramsar and Berne Conventions are also applicable and important, as discussed briefly at the beginning of the chapter. Moreover, the same logic goes for all other MEAs, since each has its scope and its particularities that could enhance the protection of the environment in situations of armed conflict and occupation.

It should be noted, however, that even if MEAs are applicable to occupied territory, their application still meets with some challenges, and some scholars have further criticised their application to situations of armed conflict and occupation for different reasons. These challenges will be discussed in detail in the following section.

4.3 Challenging the Application of IEL to Situations of Occupation

This section addresses the two primary challenges that international law scholars have put forward concerning the continued application of IEL during times of armed conflict and occupation. It considers these challenges with a view to demonstrating that IEL remains applicable in such situations. The two challenges are the following: issues associated with the *lex specialis* rule, and issues connected to the enforceable content of MEAs in times of armed conflict and occupation.

4.3.1 Challenges Related to the Lex Specialis *Rule (IHL) and the Relationship with IEL*

One of the most challenging issues regarding the application of IEL to situations of armed conflict and occupation, as has been raised by international law scholars, is the so-called *lex specialis* rule. This rule, as described in the previous chapter, means that some specific rules may take precedence over other general rules, where these are incompatible. Generally speaking, the *lex specialis* rule applies to solving situations of normative conflicts, when there are two different rules that deal with the same subject matter and are both applicable to the same legal context and to the same time frame. At the same time, both rules show some amount of inconsistency between them, and they cannot apply concurrently.[218] According to this rule, IHL is the *lex specialis* law regulating situations of armed conflict and

218 See generally, Lindroos, 'Addressing Norm Conflicts in a Fragmented Legal System', 39.

occupation, being the specialised legal regime, in relation to other peacetime laws. Some scholars have used this as an argument to deny the application of IEL to armed conflict and occupation or at least to prioritise the application of IHL over other peacetime laws, such as IEL.[219] The ILC, in the 2011 Draft Articles on the Effects of Armed Conflict on Treaties, did not address the interrelation between MEAs and other applicable treaties to armed conflict.[220] According to Voneky, the argument that IHL prevails over peacetime law as *lex specialis* is generally rejected,[221] and the traditional argument about IHL as the *lex specialis* law in times of armed conflict and occupation is dissolving.[222] Some scholars have argued that the choice of what should be considered as a *lex specialis* law relies on from which perspective the issue at hand is being viewed.[223] They added that sometimes to consider that a law prevails over another within a system of unclear rules relations, the decision might be based on political or other considerations, rather than on *lex specialis* rule itself.[224] According to these views, the choice to decide which rule is to be given priority between rules of specialised regimes is a biased decision that depends on other reasoning grounds rather than on legal ones.[225] Such an argument makes the application of the *lex specialis* rule even more uncertain and complex in its application. However, as discussed in Chapter 3, this author believes that using the *lex specialis* rule as an interpretative tool to solve a normative conflict between IHL and other peacetime laws' treaties is the most realistic solution to enhance the protection of the environment in such situations. This confirms the idea that international law works as a cohesive and consistent legal system, where its rules work together in harmony. Therefore, international treaties that are applicable during peacetime, such as MEAs, are generally considered to apply during times of armed conflict and occupation. Hence, the argument that IHL is the *lex specialis* law and overrides peacetime law is no longer persuasive.

If this conclusion is correct, IEL and IHL should be applied in a complementary manner. For example, the protection provided to protected sites and areas under the MEAs introduced above can be safely harmonised with IHL rules, such as those protecting cultural property sites beyond the traditional way of treaty interpretation under Article 31(3)(c) of the VCLT, as long as they share common objectives, and such objectives can be clearly identified. This means that the occupying power

219 See, for example, Wolff Heintschel von Heinegg and Michael Donner, 'New Developments in the Protection of the Natural Environment in Naval Armed Conflicts', (1994) 37 *German YB Int'l L* 281, 295.

220 Sjöstedt, *The Role of Multilateral Environmental Agreements*, 158–159.

221 Voneky, 'Peacetime Environmental Law as a Basis of State Responsibility for Environmental Damage Caused by War', 193.

222 Liesbeth Lijnzaad and Gerard J. Tanja, 'Protection of the Environment in Times of Armed Conflict: The Iraq–Kuwait War', (1993) 40 *NILR* 169, 171–172.

223 Martti Koskenniemi, 'The Fate of Public International Law: Between Technique and Politics', (2007) 70 *The Modern Law Review* 1, 5–7; Lindroos, 'Addressing Norm Conflicts in a Fragmented Legal System', 42, 66.

224 Ibid.

225 Lindroos, 'Addressing Norm Conflicts in a Fragmented Legal System', 66.

could observe its legal obligations under IEL and IHL simultaneously, without violating any of them. It should be noted that there is no focus on environmental issues under IHL, and the existing environmental protection under the API 1977 is vague.[226] Thus, there should be no actual norms conflict between IHL and IEL, since the two regimes do not overlap.[227] However, it could be argued that the reason why the protection of the environment under the rules of the API 1977 is vague is because there is no consensus on how to deal exactly with the environment, as the drafters of the API intentionally left much discretion to the law applier with regard to the environmentally related rules.[228] In other words, there was no consensus between drafters on what exact level of environmental damage is prohibited. For example, no clear clarification or description of the terms of the threshold "widespread, long-term and severe" was given at the ICRC Conference.[229] The term "long-term" was the only one that was defined as a period measuring up to several decades.[230] However, the definition of "long-term" was not even an official position; it was just a view expressed by some delegations at the conference.[231] Moreover, the environmentally related rules under IHL only deal with environmental damage resulting from active hostilities. Other environmental issues related to armed conflict and occupation are not addressed by such rules. One scholar argued that the preparatory work discussion at the ICRC conference regarding the environment was mainly influenced by the Vietnam War and the extensive damage cause by the United States to the environment in this case. Hence, it seems like the intention of the drafters was to forbid similar scenarios in future wars.[232] The author believes that the vagueness under IHL regarding the protection of the environment can be narrowed down with some assistance from the IEL.

226 Sjöstedt, *The Role of Multilateral Environmental Agreements*, 7–8, 67.

227 Ibid, 186.

228 Articles 35 and 55 of the API were negotiated and drafted at the ICRC Conference that took place between 1974 and 1977; Sjöstedt, *The Role of Multilateral Environmental Agreements*, 58; Yves Sandoz, Christophe Swinarski, Bruno Zimmermann (eds), *Commentary on the Additional Protocols of 8 June 1977 to the Geneva Conventions of 12 August 1949* (ICRC 1986), 411–417, 661–664.

229 Official Records of the Diplomatic Conference on the Reaffirmation and Development of International Humanitarian Law Applicable in Armed Conflicts, Geneva, 1974–1977, (Vol. 03: able of amendments: amendments to draft Additional Protocol I), 220–221; (Vol. 05: summary records of the plenary meetings of the Conference: first, second, and third sessions), 139; (Vol. 06: summary records of the plenary meetings of the Conference: fourth session), 99–100, 208–209, 219, 223, 228; (Vol. 14: summary records of Committee III: first and second sessions), 143, 250, 424; (Vol. 15: summary records of Committee III: third and fourth sessions; reports of Committee III), 268–269, 281, 297, 324, 358–360; (Vol. 16: summary records and reports of the Ad Hoc Committee on Conventional Weapons), 271, 283. All the Official Records documents of the API 1977 to the Fourth Geneva Conventions 1945 are available online at: <https://blogs.icrc.org/cross-files/drafting-history-1977-additional-protocols/>. Accessed date: 13 December 2023.

230 Ibid; Sjöstedt, *The Role of Multilateral Environmental Agreements*, 58; Sandoz, Swinarski, Zimmermann, *Commentary on the Additional Protocols of 8 June 1977*, 417.

231 Ibid.

232 Sjöstedt, *The Role of Multilateral Environmental Agreements*, 8.

In the end, it would seem reasonable to conclude that IEL can play an important role in assisting and informing the law applicable to environmental protection in situations of armed conflict and occupation. For example, some MEAs could complement and inform the application of IHL in relation to strengthening and providing more accurate and specific protection to the environment in such situations. As discussed in Chapter 2, IHL contains vague and general provisions regarding environmental protection, and, by allowing MEAs to clarify and complement these vague provisions, this can give more specificity to the rules under IHL, thereby enhancing the overall protection provided to the environment in times of armed conflict and occupation. Thus, applying IEL and IHL together to complement and enhance the protection of the environment at such times should not be considered a biased view but rather a pragmatic application of the rules of international law.

4.3.2 Challenges Related to the Enforceable Content of the MEAs in Times of Armed Conflict and Occupation

The issue of the applicability of MEAs in times of armed conflict and occupation should be kept separate from that of what extent to which they remain effective in such situations. MEAs may enhance environmental protection during these times, but the extent of their effectiveness is uncertain. This has led to some scholars claiming that since their effectiveness is uncertain, they should not apply to armed conflict and occupation. The following paragraphs will delve into this issue and argue that MEAs can provide sufficient and specific protection to the environment under such circumstances.

The question raised here is the extent to which such conventions can be effective or how MEAs could really contribute to enhancing environmental protection in such situations. The effectiveness of IEL conventions in times of armed conflict has been a controversial issue and discussed widely amongst international law scholars, in particular IHL scholars, which has led to many conflicting views in this regard. Furthermore, no such scholars or commentators have explained, in detail, how the MEAs could enhance environmental protection in times of armed conflict and occupation, thus leaving the issue unresolved.[233] For example, Bunker has argued in favour of the applicability of the MEAs to armed conflict, whilst at the same time claiming that the "flexible and ambiguous" loosely worded language in the provisions of IEL treaties does not really help in providing any accurate or effective protection to the environment in situations of armed conflict.[234] She added that the only exception of IEL treaties where its rules can be effective in providing efficient and direct protection to the environment in armed conflict "is the protection of areas of special significance such as World Heritage sites", and "here it is clear that a defined area should be avoided and peacetime protections

233 Sjöstedt, *The Role of Multilateral Environmental Agreements*, 170.

234 Alice Louise Bunker, 'Protection of the Environment During Armed Conflict: One Gulf, Two Wars', (2004) 13 *Rev Eur Comp & Int'l Envtl L* 201, 211.

can be more easily linked to wartime activity".[235] She acknowledged that this is the only obvious way where IEL treaties could have a real impact in such situations.[236] However, some scholars have dismissed the application of the MEAs to situations of armed conflict and occupation for reasons of their being meaningless and unable to provide actual legal obligations upon belligerent states, mainly because of their flexible and loose provisions. In contrast, other scholars have argued in favour of the effectiveness of the MEAs in such situations and confirmed their importance in protecting the environment in situations of armed conflict. Hulme, for example, argued in favour of the application of the MEAs to situations of armed conflict and occupation, providing examples of how the co-application of the World Heritage Convention and the Biodiversity Convention can enhance the protection to the environment in such scenarios.[237] Another scholar claimed that if we could say for a fact that MEAs are applicable to situations of armed conflict, they would definitely have a huge and obvious impact regarding the protection of the environment "compared to the prevailing legal situation".[238]

There are some scholars who seem to have contrasting views on how MEAs could apply in times of armed conflict and how effective they can be. For example, they adopted a very vague view in their work, since, at first, they doubted the application of MEAs to situations of armed conflict and wondered if they could really add any meaningful protection to the environment in times of armed conflict.[239] However, in a footnote in the same article, they mentioned the words of Bunker, where she supports the application of MEAs to situations of armed conflict but at the same time criticises the MEAs' ambiguous language.[240]

It could be argued that MEAs are not meaningless or useless instruments in times of armed conflict and occupation, as some scholars have claimed, but rather they are just constructed and drafted differently compared with the other instruments of IHL and IHRL. MEAs differ from other treaties given their special treaty systems; they are characterised by a dynamic approach, the provisions of which can continuously evolve through their treaty bodies. Hence, even after an environmental treaty text is officially adopted, its provisions could be subject to the further development of its content.[241] However, it could be argued that there is a clear absence

235 Ibid.

236 Ibid.

237 See Karen Hulme, 'Armed Conflict and Biodiversity', in Michael Bowman, Peter Davies, and Edward Goodwin (eds), *Research Handbook on Biodiversity and Law* (Edward Elgar Publishing 2016).

238 Adrian Loets, 'An Old Debate Revisited: Applicability of Environmental Treaties in Times of International Armed Conflict Pursuant to the International Law Commission's "Draft Articles on the Effects of Armed Conflict on Treaties"', (2012) 21 *Review of European Community & International Environmental Law* 127, 128.

239 Michael Bothe et al., 'International Law Protecting the Environment during Armed Conflict: Gaps and Opportunities', (2010) 92 *International Review of the Red Cross* 569, 579, 582.

240 Ibid.

241 Sandrine Maljean-Dubois, 'The Making of International Law Challenging Environmental Protection' in Yann Kerbrat and Sandrine Maljean-Dubois (eds), *The Transformation of International*

of knowledge and misunderstanding among scholars specialising in IHL of how MEAs treaty systems function. MEAs provide platforms for continued dialogue and put an emphasis on the future process of developing the rules. Furthermore, the treaty bodies of MEAs have the authority to develop the content of treaty provisions by adopting new protocols, new recommendations, and new decisions and resolutions, in particular through the Conference of the Contracting Parties (COPs) meetings over time. It should be noted that despite COPs' decisions and resolutions not being legally binding, they are important for tackling new issues that arise and are related to the subject matter of the treaty in question. For example, recently, the COP 14/2022 of the Ramsar Convention adopted a new resolution in relation to response to the environmental situation in Ukraine regarding the damage of Ramsar Sites due to the ongoing armed conflict with and occupation by Russia.[242]

To sum up, the affirmation that MEAs are ineffective in times of armed conflict and occupation is not an accurate perspective. MEAs should be viewed as progressive instruments that aim to protect the environment at all times and are designed to evolve over time within the treaty system to address emerging environmental challenges. Hence, the challenges related to the *lex specialis* rule and the enforceable content and effectiveness of MEAs in times of armed conflict and occupation, which are often raised by IHL scholars, are outdated and subject to unconvincing claims that can be misleading.

MEAs could have a normative impact, since they regulate issues that are not considered or even being addressed by IHL, such as matters related to the protection of world heritage, where IEL, in this case, can inform, complement and enhance the protection provided to the environment in such situations.[243] Thus, there are situations where MEAs could complement and even enrich the obligations under IHL regarding environmental protection in situations of armed conflict and occupation.[244] Therefore, the lack of examination of the MEAs regarding environmental protection at such times could be considered a missed opportunity that, if this were considered carefully, could play an important role to enhancing the protection provided to the environment in such situations. Therefore, the argument that IEL treaties do not apply and/or are not effective to situations of armed conflict and occupation is an outdated view.

4.4 Conclusion

Chapter 4 has discussed the application of IEL, both customary and treaty, to situations of armed conflict and occupation. It has been argued that MEAs that are

Environmental Law (Hart Publishing 2011) 37; Sjöstedt, *The Role of Multilateral Environmental Agreements*, 170–173.

242 See 14th Meeting of the Conference of the Contracting Parties to the Ramsar Convention on Wetlands (Resolution XIV.20).

243 Steenberghe, 'The Interplay between International Humanitarian Law and International Environmental Law', 1128, 1132, 1148–1150.

244 Ibid.

normally applicable in peacetime continue to apply in times of armed conflict and occupation as well.[245] It has also been contended that the application of IEL would enhance the protection provided to the environment under public international law in such situations, in particular that IHL and IEL complement and influence each other, and that they can work together in harmony in relation to protecting the environment.[246] Some scholars have argued against the application of MEAs to situations of armed conflict, but their arguments are not convincing enough to exclude their application in such situations. In contrast, the applicability of MEAs has received extensive support from different international law bodies and scholars.[247] Thus, the view that situations of armed conflict and occupation would entirely displace IEL can be seen as being outdated and misleading.[248]

The application of four environmental treaties – the World Heritage Convention, the Biodiversity Convention, the Ramsar Convention, and the Berne Convention – has been discussed, with a particular focus on the first two. All these conventions are very important for situations of armed conflict and occupation. Their application in such situations would provide extra protection to the environment from any kind of acts that might cause any type of injury to the environment, including the ecosystem and biodiversity. Furthermore, soft law documents, such as the Stockholm and Rio Declarations, serve as good examples explaining how important it is to protect the environment in times of armed conflict and occupation, and how much of their content reflects already customary international law. Therefore, by considering the application of such environmental instruments along with the customary international law related to the protection of the environment, the environment in situations of occupation would enjoy stronger and more specific protection when compared to it being only protected by IHL and IHRL rules.

To sum up, IEL shows the ability to enrich the overall framework regarding the protection of the environment in times of armed conflict and occupation, even though there could be some challenges to such application that require more special examination depending on each situation in question. In sum, and as this chapter has demonstrated, there are no longer valid reasons to exclude the entire application of IEL from situations of armed conflict and occupation.

245 Abualrob, Longobardo, and Mackenzie, 'Applying International Environmental Law Conventions in Occupied Territory'.

246 Steenberghe, 'The Interplay between International Humanitarian Law and International Environmental Law', 1128, 1132, 1148–1150.

247 See, for example, Sjöstedt, *The Role of Multilateral Environmental Agreements*, 173–174; See also, Abualrob, Longobardo and Mackenzie, 'Applying International Environmental Law Conventions in Occupied Territory'.

248 Ibid.

5 General Conclusion

Since it is indisputable that the environment in an occupied territory may be seriously harmed by the occupying power, as stated in the introduction, the primary aim of this study has been to look into the issue and to argue that there is legal protection offered by different rules of international law in times of occupation. The argument relied on a comprehensive examination of a variety of relevant rules and regulations under public international law, including International Humanitarian Law (IHL), International Human Rights Law (IHRL), and International Environmental Law (IEL).

Both international case law and scholarly writings have shown a surprisingly low number of concerns related to the protection of the environment in times of occupation. However, the study tackled the interplay between IHL, IHRL, and IEL applicable to situations of occupation to enhance the protection of the environment in such situations. These frameworks offer an important legal foundation for the protection of the environment, confirming the responsibility of the occupant to protect and conserve that of the occupied territory. However, it is manifest that the existing norms that provide protection to the environment under these laws have some limitations in addressing environmental issues in such territory. To strengthen the protection of the environment in times of occupation, it is essential that environmental considerations are better integrated within the existing legal framework. This implies acknowledging the intrinsic value of the environment and its integral connection to the welfare, well-being, and rights of the occupied population.

In this book, it has been argued that the diversification in public international law serves as a good means to enhance the protection provided to the environment, and the argument supporting the fragmentation of these laws can be said to not be a convincing one anymore. It has been asserted that IHL, IHRL, and IEL regarding environmental protection in occupied territory complement each other, working in harmony and cohesively. However, each law of these international branches has its own particularities and special characteristics, such that there are differences between them, but they are not necessarily incompatible. Each of them provides a different level of protection to the environment in times of occupation, and in the end, all three of them point in the same direction to complement each other in relation to enhancing and enriching the protection provided to the environment in such situations.[1]

1 See Dienelt, *Armed Conflicts and the Environment.*

DOI: 10.4324/9781003518068-5

Chapter 1 introduced the study topic, including the overall structure and scope of the book. The chapter also briefly touched on general environmental problems in several occupied territories worldwide, including Palestine, Georgia, Ukraine, Azerbaijan, Northern Cyprus, East Timor, Western Sahara, Iraq, Kuwait, Egypt, and Estonia. The chapter also explained that the study was aimed at analysing environmental problems and finding legal solutions to them in times of occupation through the lenses of three distinct public international law branches: IHL, IHRL, and IEL.

In Chapter 2, it was argued that IHL, specifically provisions of the law of occupation, can provide protection to the environment in occupied territory. The law of occupation contains no explicit reference to the "environment" *per se*. However, the protection of the environment can still be provided from different perspectives under such law. First, from a property rights perspective, which concerns protecting the environment through the protection provided to public and private property in occupied territory, as the chapter explained, this approach to environmental protection can enhance the protection provided to the environment, in particular through the limitations and obligations imposed on the occupying power, such as the protection provided to public property under Article 55 of the Hague Regulations; Articles 53, 147 of the GCIV; and Article 46(2) of the Hague Regulation regarding private property. Second, the occupying power has the duty under Article 43 of the Hague Regulations and Article 64 of the GCIV to respect the domestic laws of the occupied state. This has been confirmed most recently by the 2022 ILC Draft Principles, which emphasise the occupying power's duty to respect and not to violate the environmental domestic laws and regulations of the occupied state. Chapter 2 also discussed how such protection is vital and that the extent to which the environment can be protected in an occupied state relies on how effectively it is already protected by the domestic environmental laws and regulations in that state. The lack of oversight and/or disrespect of the domestic environmental laws of the occupied state by the occupying power can lead to further environmental consequences, including a negative impact on biodiversity and ecosystem functions, which in turn, will have an impact on the public order, civil life, and welfare of the local people living there.

Furthermore, in Chapter 2, it was argued that there is an obvious mutual relationship between the occupying power's responsibility under the first part of Article 43 of the Hague Regulations to maintain the public order, civil life, and welfare in the occupied state and the protection of the environment, including the stable functioning of the ecosystem and biodiversity during the period of occupation. Therefore, the more the environment is protected, the more stable, normal, and civil life the occupied people can have. Consequently, the more environmental issues are addressed by the occupying power, the more it can comply with its obligations under Article 43 of the Hague Regulations. Therefore, it could be argued that the occupying power has an obligation to protect the environment under Article 43 of the Hague Regulations.

Additionally, Chapter 2 discussed how the obligations of the occupying power under Article 43 of the Hague Regulations and the responsibilities under Article

55 of the same Regulations can be linked to each other. It is clear that both articles provide protection to the environment, particularly by taking into account the interconnection between the welfare and well-being of the local people living in the occupied state under Article 43 and the obligations to respect and protect public immovable property under Article 55, namely by avoiding any unnecessary overexploitation of the natural resources in the occupied state, which could, in turn, cause severe environmental consequences, thereby affecting the lives of the occupied population.

Chapter 2 also explained how the ILC reports and the Draft Principles both reflect an improved approach to enhancing the protection provided to the environment in times of occupation.[2] In particular, this is important since the law of occupation has clear weaknesses in terms of providing sufficient and efficient protection of the environment during such times.[3] Furthermore, it was argued that the environmental obligations might vary depending on the length of occupation, the way that the occupant administers the occupied territory, and the extent to which the occupant considers or complies with its obligations under the norms of the law of occupation, especially the rules of usufruct and the utilisation of natural resources.[4]

Chapter 3 turned to IHRL, where it was argued that there should be its continued application to situations of armed conflict and occupation. It was explained how this can contribute positively to enhancing the protection provided to the environment in such situations. The chapter explained the protection of the environment through different IHRL treaties and documents along with practical examples from situations of occupations in different countries around the world, with a focus on ongoing occupations, such as those of Russia in Ukraine and Israel in Palestine. These examples showed how harming the environment during times of occupation can prevent local populations from exercising and enjoying their basic human rights. It was contended that there are several human rights that are closely related to the environment and that it is impossible to enjoy and exercise these rights without having a safe, clean, sound, and healthy environment. Some of these rights include the right to life, the right to health, and the right to property.

Furthermore, it was reasoned that the harmonisation approach between IHRL and IHL could be the best option to protect the environment through the concurrent application of both laws. Despite the particularities and differences between IHRL and IHL, they are not incompatible. Each of them accords a different level of protection to the environment with respect to situations of occupation. Moreover, the chapter clarified how the provisions of the law of occupation can be interpreted

2 See ILC, 'First Report', 'Second Report', and 'Third Report'; ILC, Draft Principles on Protection of the Environment in relation to Armed Conflicts (2022).

3 ILC, 'First Report', para 8.

4 For further information, see the Proceedings of the Hague Peace Conferences: 'The Conference of 1899', 77, 546. Article 55 of the Hague Regulations was originally adopted and drafted at the Brussels Conference 1874, and it was numbered as Article 7. For the original French text and preparatory work of Article 7, namely, the word "usufruct", see: <https://babel.hathitrust.org/cgi/pt?id=mdp.35112104530417&seq=31&q1=usufruitier>, 27–28, 58–59.

in light of other human rights provisions, such as the duty to ensure public order, civil life, and welfare under Article 43 of the Hague Regulations; and the enjoyment of the right to health and other human rights. Further, how such rules can complement, harmonise, and enrich each other to enhance the protection provided of the environment in times of occupation was explained. For example, damaging and contaminating the environment in occupied territory will constitute a violation of the occupant's legal duty to ensure public health and hygiene and provide the occupied population with an adequate standard of living.[5] This would affect the health, civil life, and welfare of the occupied population, thus constituting a violation of the occupant's obligations under the right to health as well as under Article 43 of the Hague Regulations and Article 56 of the GCIV.

Chapter 3 also discussed the most recent right to a clean, healthy, and sustainable environment adopted by the UNGA in 2022[6] and how such a newly adopted right is a historic landmark move toward more positive protection of the environment under IHRL. However, the UNGA resolutions are non-binding. Hence, the need to adopt an individual self-standing binding right to a healthy environment is indispensable.

Therefore, it is possible to conclude that there is a strong relationship between the enjoyment of human rights and the protection of the environment in times of occupation. Furthermore, the effective implementation of IHRL treaties is impossible without taking into account the protection of the environment, since numerous human rights, if not all of them, cannot fully be enjoyed and exercised by the occupied population while their environment is being harmed and damaged during the time of occupation. Accordingly, the author concludes that the occupying power has a legal obligation under IHRL to consider, respect, and protect the environment in the occupied territory.

Chapter 4 discussed the application of IEL to situations of occupation. The focus was on examining the role of MEAs, such as the World Heritage Convention, the Biodiversity Convention, the Ramsar Convention, and the Berne Convention, and their vital role in providing extra and more specific protection to the environment in such situations. It was argued that the application of MEAs can be compared to the application of IHRL treaties to such situations, since the legal issues at hand are similar to the application of peacetime conventions to situations of armed conflict and occupation. Hence, there is no reason not to apply the same approach to the application of IEL treaties to situations of occupation.

It was contended that the protection provided to cultural and natural heritage sites under the World Heritage Convention can protect the environment through the enhanced protection provided to such sites under the Convention. The national parks in the DRC were cited as an example of how it could protect the natural environment, including endangered species existing in such sites, from any kind of aggression or threat against them. Even if the Convention itself builds on an

5 Aloni, 'Made in Israel: Exploiting Palestinian Land for Treatment of Israeli Waste', 17.

6 United Nations General Assembly, 'The Human Right to a Clean, Healthy and Sustainable Environment' (A/76/L.75) (26 July 2022), 76th session, agenda item 74(b).

area-based approach aimed at protecting cultural or natural heritage sites rather than the environment itself, it can still protect the natural environment and the habitats of the living creatures there under the general protection provided to the protected sites, which, in turn, would protect the biodiversity and the ecosystem function of that area, thereby decreasing the chance of harm being caused to the environment by the occupying power.

In Chapter 4, it was also proposed that some of IHL provisions related to protection of cultural property can be interpreted in light of the obligations set out under the World Heritage Convention, which could help to achieve harmonisation between these rules to overcome the unclarity of the rules of IHL in relation to providing better protection to the environment through that provided to cultural and natural heritage properties/sites.[7] Therefore, the World Heritage Convention has the ability to provide substantial environmental protection in times of armed conflict and occupation. Furthermore, it was argued that the Biodiversity Convention does apply to situations of occupation, and it can provide protection through *in-situ* conservation provisions. This conservation creates protected areas, and the protection of such protected areas continues at all times: in peace and during armed conflict. Thus, the Biodiversity Convention also enriches the general framework of IEL applicable to armed conflict and occupation. Accordingly, IEL can complement and reinforce the protection provided to the environment under IHL and it can be said that it also plays a role in "environmentalising" IHL.[8] Therefore, it would seem that IHL could be interpreted in light of the obligations set out in the World Heritage Convention, the Biodiversity Convention, and/or any other related MEAs, which could help to achieve harmonisation in the application of the overall framework applicable to such situations regarding environmental protection. The interaction between IEL and IHL can be seen as an interesting, albeit controversial, attempt to fill the existing gaps under public international law relating to environmental protection in times of armed conflict and occupation. Thus, it would be instructive to explore how their application alongside each other would, in practice, serve the environment in such situations.

Furthermore, it was explained that, there are some common objectives between IHL, IHRL, and IEL, such as the protection of property. Regarding this, the three branches provide protection to the environment in times of occupation through that provided to property rights under the three regimes: IHL does so through the protection provided to public and private property under provisions of the law of occupation, IHRL does so through the protection provided to the right to property, and IEL achieves this through the protection provided to cultural and natural heritage sites and to protected areas in which such property might be public or private, depending on how it is classified under the national law of each occupied state.[9]

7 Sjöstedt, *The Role of Multilateral Environmental Agreements*, 244–245.
8 Steenberghe, 'The Interplay between International Humanitarian Law and International Environmental Law', 1128.
9 Dienelt, *Armed Conflicts and the Environment*, 242.

Therefore, the protection of property can be considered a commonly shared objective across public international law bodies. Consequently, such a commonly shared objective could facilitate harmonisation and complementation between IHL, IHRL, and IEL, which in turn, would serve to enhance the protection provided to the environment in times of occupation.

The study has made a contribution to knowledge that could enhance the protection provided to the environment in situations of occupation. Specifically, this contribution regards the legal obligations of the occupying power under the domestic environmental laws and regulations of the occupied state. Furthermore, it has been argued that the integration of IHRL and IEL treaties into the domestic environmental laws of occupied states would dramatically enhance the protection provided to the environment. For even if the occupying power has not ratified such treaties, it still, through its duty under the Hague Regulations and GCIV, has to respect such a treaty by considering the domestic environmental laws of the occupied state. Some domestic environmental laws of an occupied state can be very developed and provide effective protection to the environment and its elements, and that would help to make sure the environment is well protected in such situations. As argued throughout the book, the extent to which protection can be provided to the environment in an occupied state relies on how effectively it is already protected by the national environmental laws of that state. The lack of oversight and/or disrespect of the domestic environmental laws of the occupied state by the occupying power can lead to further environmental consequences, including a negative impact on biodiversity and ecosystem functions. Moreover, this will be detrimental to the public order, civil life, and welfare of the local people living in the occupied state, thereby affecting the ability of the occupied population to fully enjoy their human rights. Therefore, this argument can contribute to strengthening the protection provided to the environment through the national environmental laws of the occupied state. Furthermore, the current book is the first scholarly work considering the application of both IHRL and IEL to situations of occupation and arguing in favour of such application.

To the best of this author's knowledge, this study is important since there has been no other comprehensive study that has been written in English and in Arabic regarding the topic in question. In particular, this research is the first to examine the protection of the environment in situations of occupations in relation to the occupying power's obligations under the domestic environmental laws of occupied states. Furthermore, the environmental situation in different occupied territories worldwide has been examined. This is especially relevant, since there has been no academic research investigating the environmental situation in such occupied territories in detail from the public international law perspective.

To sum up, public international law plays a vital role in providing protection to the environment in times of occupation. This protection is not limited just to IHL; IHRL and IEL are also relevant and applicable. IHL, IHRL, and IEL complement and harmonise with each other regarding the protection of the environment in times of occupation. Therefore, the occupying power has a legal obligation under public international law to protect and conserve the environment in the occupied territory.

This obligation remains as long as the occupying power maintains control over such territory. Failure to fulfil this obligation will result in the occupying power being held legally liable for violating its environmental obligations in times of occupation under public international law.

Bibliography

Case Law

Al-Adsani v. The United Kingdom, the ECtHR, (App No. 35763/97), (21 November 2001)
Al-Jedda v. the United Kingdom, Grand Chamber, the ECtHR, (App No. 27021/08), (2011)
Al-Skeini and Others v. the United Kingdom, the ECtHR, (App. No. 55721/07), (7 July 2011)
Armed Activities on the Territory of the Congo (*Democratic Republic of the Congo v. Uganda*), Judgment, I.C.J. Reports (2005)
Armed Activities on the Territory of the Congo (*Democratic Republic of the Congo v. Uganda*), the ICJ, Judgment of (09 February 2022)
Ayub et al. v. Minister of Defense et al., (H.C.J 606/78) and (H.C.J 610/78), (15 March 1979)
Bataafsche Petroleum v. The War Damage Commission, (1956), 22 Malayan Law Journal 155, Court of Appeal, Singapore, (13 April 1956)
Budayeva and Others v. Russia, the ECtHR, (App No. 15339/02, 21166/02, 20058/02, 11673/02 and 15343/02), Judgment of (22 March 2008)
Chiragov and Others v. Armenia, the ECtHR, Judgment (Merits), (App. No.13216/05), Judgment of (16 June 2015)
Coard et al. v. United States, Report N. 109/99 - Case 10.951, Inter-American Commission on Human Rights (IACHR), (29 September 1999)
Council of the European Union v. Front Polisario, The Court of Justice of the European Union, (C-104/16 P), (21 December 2016)
Cyprus v. Turkey, the ECtHR, (Appl. No. 25781/94), Judgment of (10 May 2001)
Dimitar Yordanov v. Bulgaria, the ECtHR (App. No. 3401/09), Judgment of (06 December 2018)
Dweikat et al v. Government of Israel et al, H.C.J 390/79, (Judgment of the Israeli Supreme Court, 22 October 1979), known as: *(Elon Moreh case*)
Ecuador v. Colombia, Inter-state Petition IP-02 Admissibility Franklin Guillermo Aisalla Molina, Report No. 112/10, Inter-American Commission on Human Rights (IACHR), (21 October 2011)
El Nazer et al. v. Commander of Judea and Samaria et al., (HCJ 285/81), (13 IYHR 368) (1983)
Front populaire pour la libération de la saguia-el-hamra et du rio de oro (Front Polisario) v. Council of the European Union, The Court of Justice of the European Union, Judgment of the General Court (Eighth Chamber), (Case T-512/12), (10 December 2015)
Gabčíkovo-Nagymaros Project (*Hungary v. Slovakia*), Judgment, I. C. J. Reports (1997)
Georgia v. Russian Federation, (Application of the International Convention on the Elimination of All Forms of Racial Discrimination), Preliminary Objections, Judgment, I.C.J. Reports (2011)
Hassan v the United Kingdom, the ECtHR, (App. No. 29750/09), (16 September 2014)
Hatton and Others v. the United Kingdom, the ECtHR, Judgment (App. No. 36022/97), (8 July 2003)

Legal Consequences of the Constriction of a Wall in the Occupied Palestinians Territory, Advisory Opinion. I.C.J. Reports (2004)
Legality of the Threat or Use of Nuclear Weapons, Advisory Opinion, I. C.J. Reports 1996
Loizidou v Turkey, (merits), Reports of Judgments and Decisions 1996-VI, (18 December 1996)
Loizidou v. Turkey, the ECtHR, (App. No. 40/1993), (435/514), Preliminary Objection of (23 February 1995)
Lopez Ostra v. Spain, the ECtHR/Court (CHAMBER) (App. No. 16798/90), (09 December 1994)
Marangopoulos Foundation for Human Rights (MFHR) v. Greece, European Committee of Social Rights, (Complaint No. 30/2005). Decision on the Merits: (Adoption: 6 December 2006)
Nicaragua v. United States of America, Merits, Judgment. I.C.J. Reports (1986)
National Movement Ekoglasnost v. Bulgaria, the ECtHR, (App. No. 31678/17), (15 December 2020)
Öneryıldız v. Turkey, the ECtHR, (App. No. 48939/99), Judgment, (30 November 2004)
Prosecutor v. Delalic et al. (ICTY, Trial Chamber, 1998), (Case No.: IT-96-21-T)
Prosecutor v. Fofana and Kondewa (Appeals Judgment), (Special Court for Sierra Leone) (Case No. SCSL-04-14-A), (28 May 2008) (*CDF Case*)
Prosecutor v. Mladen Naletilic aka "Tuta", Vinko Martinovic aka "Stela" (Trial Judgment), International Criminal Tribunal for the former Yugoslavia (ICTY), (IT-98-34-T), (31 March 2003)
Serrano Cruz v. El-Salvador, Preliminary Objections, the IACtHR, (23 November 2004)
Society Lawfully Registered v. Commander of the IDF, CA 393/82, 37(4) PD 785, (1983)
Tatar v. Romania, the ECtHR, (App No. 67021/01), (27 January 2009)
The Afro-descendant Communities Displaced from the Cacarica River Basin (Operation Genesis) v. Colombia, the IACtHR, Judgment of (20 November 2013)
The Demopoulos and others v. Turkey, (App. No. 46113/99), Eur. Ct. H.R (2010)
The Jerusalem District Electricity Company Ltd v. (a) Minster of Energy and Infrastructure, (b) Commander of the Judea and Samaria Region, 35(23), (H.C 351/80), 35(2) Piskei Din 673
The Queen (on the Application of Mazin Mumaa Galteh Al-Skeini and Others) v. The Secretary of State for Defence, [2005] EWCA Civ 1609, United Kingdom: Court of Appeal (England and Wales), (21 December 2005)
The Santo Domingo Massacre v. Colombia, the IACtHR, Judgment of (30 November 2012)
Trial of the Major War Criminals before the International Military Tribunal, Nuremberg, (14/November/1945- 01/October/1946), Vol. I, Nuremberg, pp. 238–239 (1947)
Trials of the Major War Criminals before the International Military Tribunal, Nuremberg, Vol. XXII
Trials of War Criminals Before the Nuremberg Military Tribunals Under Control Council Law No. 10. (Volume XIV), (Nuremberg 1949) '*The Ministries Case*'
Ukraine v. Russian Federation, the ICJ, (Application of the International Convention for the Suppression of the Financing of Terrorism and of the International Convention on the Elimination of All Forms of Racial Discrimination)

Books

Al-Duaij N, *Environmental Law of Armed Conflict* (Transnational Publishers 2004)
Al-Salem R, *Security, Rights and Law: The Israeli High Court of Justice and Israeli Settlements in the Occupied West Bank* (Routledge 2019)
Alan Boyle and Michael Anderson (eds), *Human Rights Approaches to Environmental Protection* (OUP 1996)
Alston P (ed), *Peoples' Rights* (OUP 2005)

Arai-Takahashi Y, *The Law of Occupation: Continuity and Change of International Humanitarian Law, and Its Interaction with International Human Rights Law* (Martinus Nijhoff Publishers 2009)
Austin J and Bruch C (eds), *The Environmental Consequences of War: Legal, Economic, and Scientific Perspectives* (Cambridge University Press 2000)
Austin J and Bruch C (eds), *The Environmental Consequences of War* (Cambridge University Press 2010)
Bantekas I and Oette L, *International Human Rights Law and Practice* (3rd edn, Cambridge University Press 2020)
Bashir H and Sbeita A, *The Occupation of Iraq and Violations of the Environment and Cultural Property* (Al Manhal/The National Centre for Legal Issues 2013)
Benvenisti E, *The International Law of Occupation* (2nd edn, OUP 2012)
Birnie P, Boyle A and Redgwell C, *International Law and the Environment* (4th edn, OUP 2021)
Bodansky D, Brunnée J, and Hey E (eds), *The Oxford Handbook of International Environmental Law* (OUP 2008)
Bodansky D, *The Art and Craft of International Environmental Law* (Harvard University Press 2010)
Bowman M, Davies P, and Goodwin E (eds), *Research Handbook on Biodiversity and Law* (Edward Elgar Publishing 2016)
Boyd D, *The Environmental Rights Revolution: A Global Study of Constitutions, Human Rights, and the Environment* (UBC Press 2012)
Buffard I, Crawford J, Pellet A, and Wittich S (eds), *International Law Between Universalism and Fragmentation* (Martinus Nijhoff 2008)
Chircop A, McDorman T, and Rolston S (eds), *The Future of Ocean Regime-Building: Essays in Tribute to Douglas M. Johnston* (Brill Nijhoff 2009)
Clapham A and Gaeta P (eds), *The Oxford Handbook of International Law in Armed Conflict* (OUP 2015)
Clapham A, Gaeta P, and Sassoli M (eds), *The 1949 Geneva Conventions: A Commentary* (OUP 2015)
Coomans F and Kamminga M (eds), *Extraterritorial Application of Human Rights Treaties* (Intersentia-Antwerp 2004)
Cuyckens H, *Revisiting the Law of Occupation* (Brill Nijhoff 2018)
Doswald-Beck L, Chowdhury A, and Bhuiyan J (eds), International *Humanitarian Law: An Anthology* (LexisNexis Butterworths 2009)
Dejeant-Pons M, Pallemaerts M, and Fioravanti S, *Human Rights and the Environment: Compendium of Instruments and Other International Texts on Individual and Collective Rights Relating to the Environment in the International and European Framework* (Council of Europe Publishing 2002)
Dienelt A, *Armed Conflicts and the Environment: Complementing the Laws of Armed Conflict with Human Rights Law and International Environmental Law* (Springer International Publishing 2022)
Dinstein Y, *The Conduct of Hostilities Under the Law of International Armed* Conflict (3rd edn, Cambridge University Press 2016)
Dinstein Y, *The International Law of Belligerent Occupation* (2nd edn, Cambridge University Press 2019)
Dupuy P-M and Viñuales J, *International Environmental Law* (2nd edn, Cambridge University Press 2018)
Eikermann A, *Forests in International Law: Is There Really a Need for an International Forest Convention?* (Springer International Publishing 2015)
Evans M, *International Law Documents* (13th edn, OUP 2017)
Fleck D (ed), *The Handbook of International Humanitarian Law* (2nd edn, OUP 2009)
Fleck D (ed), *The Handbook of International Humanitarian Law* (4th edn, OUP 2021)

Fraenkel E, *Military Occupation and the Rule of Law* (OUP 1944)
Francioni F and Lenzerini F (eds), *The 1972 World Heritage Convention: A Commentary* (OUP 2008)
Francioni F and Vrdoljak A (eds), *The Oxford Handbook of International Cultural Heritage Law* (OUP 2020)
Garner J, *International Law and the World War* (Longmans, Green and Company 1920)
Gilbert J, *Natural Resources and Human Rights: An Appraisal* (OUP 2018)
Grear A and Kotzé L (eds), *Research Handbook on Human Rights and the Environment* (Edward Elgar 2015)
Gross A, *The Writing on the Wall: Rethinking the International Law of Occupation* (Cambridge University Press 2017)
Graber D, *The Development of the Law of Belligerent Occupation 1863–1914: A Historical Survey* (Columbia University Press 1949)
Henckaerts J and Doswald-Beck L, *Customary International Humanitarian Law* (Cambridge University Press 2009)
Hesham B and Sbeita A, *The Occupation of Iraq and Violations of the Environment and Cultural Property* (Al Manhal/The National Centre for Legal Issues 2013)
Hulme K, *War Torn Environment: Interpreting the Legal Threshold* (Brill Publisher 2004)
Humphreys S (ed), *Human Rights and Climate Change* (Cambridge University Press 2009)
Hunter D, Salzman J, and Zaelke D, *International Environmental Law and Policy* (5th edn, Foundation Press 2015)
Hupkes D, *What Constitutes Occupation? Israel as the Occupying Power in the Gaza Strip After the Disengagement* (E.M. Meijers Instituu 2008)
Jabbra J and Jabbra N (eds), Challenging *Environmental Issues: Middle Eastern Perspectives* (Brill 1997)
Jayawickrama N, *The Judicial Application of Human Rights Law: National, Regional, and International Jurisprudence* (Cambridge University Press 2002)
Jensen D and Lonergan S (eds), *Assessing and Restoring Natural Resources in Post-Conflict Peacebuilding* (Routledge 2012)
Kalandarishvili-Mueller N, *Occupation and Control in International Humanitarian Law* (Taylor & Francis 2021)
Kalin W (ed), *Human Rights in Times of Occupation: The Case of Kuwait* (Law Books in Europe LBE 1994)
Kassim T and Barceló D (eds), *Environmental Consequences of War and Aftermath* (Springer-Verlag Berlin Heidelberg 2009)
Kerbrat Y and Maljean-Dubois S (eds), *The Transformation of International Environmental Law* (Hart Publishing 2011)
Kiss A and Shelton D, *Guide to International Environmental Law* (Martinus Nijhoff Publishers 2007)
Kolb R and Gaggioli G (eds), *Research Handbook on Human Rights and Humanitarian Law* (Edward Elgar 2013)
Kolb R and Hyde R, *An Introduction to the International Law of Armed Conflicts* (Hart Publishing 2008)
Kretzmer D and Ronen Y, *The Occupation of Justice: The Supreme Court of Israel and the Occupied Territories* (OUP 2021)
Lepard B, *Customary International Law: A New Theory with Practical Applications* (Cambridge University Press 2010)
Ling C, *The Rio Declaration on Environment and Development: An Assessment* (Third World Network 2012)
Lixinski L, *International Law for Communities; Exclusion and Re-Imagination* (OUP 2019)
Longobardo M, *The Use of Armed Force in Occupied Territory* (Cambridge University Press 2018)
Lieblich E and Benvenisti E, *Occupation in International Law* (OUP 2022)

McDougal M and Feliciano F, *Law and Minimum World Public Order: The Legal Regulation and International Coercion* (Yale University Press 1961)
McGoldrick D, *The Human Rights Committee: Its Role in the Development of the International Covenant on Civil and Political Rights* (Clarendon Press 1991)
Meron T, *Human Rights in Internal Strife: Their International Protection* (Cambridge University Press 1987)
Milanovic M, *Extraterritorial Application of Human Rights Treaties: Law, Principles, and Policy* (OUP 2011)
Moeckli D, Shah S, and Sivakumaran S (eds), *International Human Rights Law* (3rd edn, OUP 2018)
Murray D, *Practitioners' Guide to Human Rights Law in Armed Conflict* (OUP 2016)
Musgrave T, *Self-Determination and National Minorities* (OUP 1997)
Mustafa W, *Natural Resources in Palestine: Determinants of Exploitation and Mechanisms for Maximizing Benefit* (MAS/The Palestinian Economic Policy Research Institute 2016)
O'Keefe R, et al., *Protection of Cultural Property: Military Manual* (UNESCO 2016)
Oberleitner G, *Human Rights in Armed Conflict: Law, Practice, Policy* (Cambridge University Press 2015)
Oppenheim L, *International Law. A Treatise, Volume II. War and Neutrality* (2nd edn, Longmans, Green and Co 1912)
Pauwelyn J, *Conflict of Norms in Public International Law: How WTO Law Relates to other Rules of International Law* (Cambridge University Press 2003)
Peters A, De Hemptinne J, and Kolb R, *Animals in the International Law of Armed Conflict* (Cambridge University Press 2022)
Platsas A, *The Harmonisation of National Legal System: Strategic Models and Factors* (Edward Elgar 2017)
Playfair E (ed), *International Law and the Administration of Occupied Territories: Two Decades of Israeli Occupation of the West Bank and Gaza Strip* (OUP 1992)
Provost R, *International Human Rights and Humanitarian Law* (Cambridge University Press 2002)
Rogers A, *Law on the Battlefield* (2nd edn, Manchester University Press 2004)
Rajamani L and Peel J (eds), *The Oxford Handbook of International Environmental Law* (OUP 2021)
Ramcharan B (ed), *The Right to Life in International Law* (Martinus Nijhoff 1985)
Sands P and Others., *Principles of International Environmental Law* (4th edn, Cambridge University Press 2018)
Sabel R, *International Law and the Arab-Israeli Conflict* (Cambridge University Press 2022)
Saul B and Akande D (eds), *The Oxford Guide to International Humanitarian Law* (OUP 2020)
Sayapin S and Tsybulenko E (eds), *The Use of Force against Ukraine and International Law: Jus Ad Bellum, Jus In Bello, Jus Post Bellum* (Asser Press 2018)
Schabas W, *The Customary International Law of Human Rights* (OUP 2021)
Schrijver N, *Sovereignty over Natural Resources: Balancing Rights and Duties* (Cambridge University Press 2008)
Shaw M, *International Law* (9th edn, Cambridge University Press 2021)
Shehab M, *Studies in International Humanitarian Law* (The Arab Future Publishing House, Cairo 2009)
Siegrist M, *The Functional Beginning of Belligerent Occupation* (Geneva Graduate Institute 2011)
Singh N (ed), *The Human Right to Water: From Concept to Reality* (Springer International Publishing Switzerland 2016)
Sjöstedt B, *The Role of Multilateral Environmental Agreements: A Reconciliatory Approach to Environmental Protection in Armed Conflict* (Hart Publishing 2021)
Stahn C, Iverson J, and Easterday J (eds), *Environmental Protection and Transitions from Conflict to Peace: Clarifying Norms, Principles, and Practices* (OUP 2017)

Sandoz Y, Swinarski C, and Zimmermann B (eds), *Commentary on the Additional Protocols of 8 June 1977 to the Geneva Conventions of 12 August 1949* (ICRC 1986)
Taylor P, A *Commentary on the International Covenant on Civil and Political Rights: The UN Human Rights Committee's Monitoring of ICCPR Rights* (Cambridge University Press 2020)
Tobin J, *The Right to Health in International Law* (OUP 2011)
Trachtman J, *The Future of International Law: Global Government* (Cambridge University Press 2013)
UK Ministry of Defence, *The Manual of the Law of Armed Conflict* (OUP 2004)
Vagias M, *The Territorial Jurisdiction of the International Criminal Court* (Cambridge University Press 2014)
Viñuales J (ed), *The Rio Declaration on Environment and Development: A Commentary* (OUP 2015)
Von Glahn G, *The Occupation of Enemy Territory: A Commentary on the Law and Practice of Belligerent Occupation* (The University of Minnesota Press 1957)
Wilmshurst E and Breau S (eds), *Perspectives on the ICRC Study on Customary International Humanitarian Law* (Cambridge University Press 2007)
Wolfrum R and Matz N, *Conflicts in International Environmental Law* (Springer Verlag 2003)

Journal Articles

Abdul Hadi A, 'The Iraqi Aggression against the Environment in the State of Kuwait in Light of the Provisions of International Law' (1991) 15 *The Law Journal, Kuwait University -Academic Publication Council* 237
Abouali G, 'Natural Resources Under Occupation: The Status of Palestinian Water under International Law' (1998) 10 *Peace International Law Review* 411
Abu-Eid A, 'Water as a Human Right: The Palestinian Occupied Territories as an Example' (2007) 23 *International Journal of Water Resources Development* 285
Akande D, 'Nuclear Weapons, Unclear Law? Deciphering the Nuclear Weapons Advisory Opinion of the International Court' (1998) 68 *BYBIL* 165
Alaani S, Savabieasfahani M, Tafash M, and Manduca P, 'Four Polygamous Families with Congenital Birth Defects from Fallujah, Iraq' (2011) 8 *International Journal of Environmental Research and Public Health* 89
Alston P and Quinn G, 'The Nature and Scope of States Parties' Obligations Under the International Covenant on Economic, Social and Cultural Rights' (1987) 9 *Human Rights Quarterly* 156
Atapattu S, 'The Right to a Healthy Life or the Right to Die Polluted?: The Emergence of a Human Right to a Healthy Environment Under International Law' (2002) 16 *Tulane Environmental Law Journal* 65
Babin B, Chvaliuk A, and Plotnikov O, 'Attempted Annexation of Crimea and Maritime Environment Legal Protection' (2021) 7 *Lex Portus* 31
Bakhshiyeva Y, 'Threats and Provocations Originating from The Republic of Armenia Towards The Water Resources of The Republic of Azerbaijan' (2019) 40 *Review of Armenian Studies* 113
Bannelier-Christakis K, 'International Law Commission and Protection of the Environment in Times of Armed Conflict: A Possibility for Adjudication?' (2013) 20 *Journal for International Cooperation Studies* 129
Bentwich N, 'The Legal Administration of Palestine under the British Military Occupation' (1920–1921) 1 *British Yearbook of International Law* 139
Ben-Naftali O and Shany Y, 'Living in Denial: The Application of Human Rights in the Occupied Territories' (2003) 37 *Israel Law Review* 17
Bethlehem D, 'The Relationship Between International Humanitarian Law and International Human Rights Law in Situations of Armed Conflict' (2013) 2 *Cambridge Journal of International and Comparative Law* 180

Beyerlin U and Stoutenburg J, 'Environment, International Protection' (2013) *Oxford Public International Law*

Boon F K, 'The Rio Declaration and Its Influence on International Environmental Law' (1992) *Singapore Journal of Legal Studies* 347

Bothe M et al., 'International Law Protecting the Environment during Armed Conflict: Gaps and Opportunities' (2010) 92 *International Review of the Red Cross* 569

Boyd D, 'The Constitutional Right to a Healthy Environment' (2012) 54 *Environment: Science and Policy for Sustainable Development* 3

Brown G and Calas G, 'Environmental Mineralogy – Understanding Element Behavior in Ecosystems' (2011) 343 *Comptes Rendus Geoscience* 90

Bunker A-L, 'Protection of the Environment During Armed Conflict: One Gulf, Two Wars' (2004) 13 *Review of European, Comparative & International Environmental Law* 201

Caddell R, 'The Integration of Multilateral Environmental Agreements: Lessons from the Biodiversity-Related Conventions' (2011) 22 *Yearbook of International Environmental Law* 37

Chekera Y and Nmehielle V, 'The International Law Principle of Permanent Sovereignty over Natural Resources as an Instrument for Development: The Case of Zimbabwean Diamonds' (2013) 6 *African Journal of Legal Studies* 69

Clagett B and Johnson O, 'May Israel as a Belligerent Occupant Lawfully Exploit Previously Unexploited Oil Resources of the Gulf of Suez?' (1978) 72 *AJIL* 558

Dam-de Jong D, 'Enhancing Environmental Protection in Relation to Armed Conflict: An Assessment of the ILC Draft Principles' (2021) 44 Loyola of Los Angeles International and Comparative Law Review 129

Dam-de Jong D, 'International Law and Resource Plunder: The Protection of Natural Resources During Armed Conflict' (2008) 19 *Yearbook of International Environmental Law* 27

Dennis M, 'Application of Human Rights Treaties Extraterritorially in Times of Armed Conflict and Military Occupation' (2005) 99 *American Journal of International Law* 119

Dinstein Y, 'The International Law of Belligerent Occupation and Human Rights' (1978) 8 *IYHR* 104

Domb F, 'Judgments of the Supreme Court of Israel Relating to the Administered Territories' (1981) 11 *Israel Yearbook on Human Rights* 344

Doswald-Beck L, 'The Right to Life in Armed Conflict: Does International Humanitarian Law Provide All the Answers?' (2006) 88 *International Review of the Red Cross* 881

Doswald-Beck L, 'International Humanitarian Law and the International Court of Justice on the Legality of the Threat or Use of Nuclear Weapons' (1997) 37 *International Review of the Red Cross* 35

Droege C, 'The Interplay Between International Humanitarian Law and International Human Rights Law in Situations of Armed Conflict' (2007) 40 *Israel Law Review* 310

Gasser HP, 'International Humanitarian Law and Human Rights Law in Non-International Armed Conflict: Joint Venture or Mutual Exclusion' (2002) 45 *The German Yearbook of International Law* 149

Gupta S, 'Iraq's Environmental Warfare in the Persian Gulf' (1993) 6 *Georgetown Environmental Law Review* 251

Haugen H, 'The Right to Self-Determination and Natural Resources: The Case of Western Sahara' (2007) 3 *Law Environmental Development Journal (LEAD)* 70

Heintschel von Heinegg W and Donner M, 'New Developments in the Protection of the Natural Environment in Naval Armed Conflicts' (1994) 37 *The German Yearbook of International Law* 281

Hulme K, 'Enhancing Environmental Protection During Occupation Through Human Rights' (2020) 10 *Goettingen Journal of International Law* 203

Kaplan L, 'International Responsibility of an Occupying Power for Environmental Harm: The Case of Estonia' (1999) 12 *Transnat'l Law* 153

Koskenniemi M, 'The Fate of Public International Law: Between Technique and Politics' (2007) 70 *The Modern Law Review* 1

Koutroulis V, 'The Application of International Humanitarian Law and International Human Rights Law in Situation of Prolonged Occupation: Only a Matter of Time?' (2012) 94 *International Review of the Red Cross* 165

Lee J, 'The Underlying Legal Theory to Support a Well-Defined Human Right to a Healthy Environment as a Principle of Customary International Law' (2000) 25 *Columbia Journal of Environmental Law* 283

Lijnzaad L and Tanja G, 'Protection of the Environment in Times of Armed Conflict: The Iraq-Kuwait War' (1993) 40 *NILR* 169

Lindroos A, 'Addressing Norm Conflicts in a Fragmented Legal System: The Doctrine of *Lex Specialis*' (2005) 74 *Nordic Journal of International Law* 27

Loets A, 'An Old Debate Revisited: Applicability of Environmental Treaties in Times of International Armed Conflict Pursuant to the International Law Commission's "Draft Articles on the Effects of Armed Conflict on Treaties"' (2012) 21 *Review of European Community & International Environmental Law* 127

Longobardo M, 'The Palestinian Right to Exploit the Dead Sea Coastline for Tourism' (2015) 58 *The German Yearbook of International Law* 317

Longobardo M, 'State Responsibility for International Humanitarian Law Violations by Private Actors in Occupied Territories and the Exploitation of Natural Resources' (2016) 63 *NILR* 251

Longobardo M, 'The Duties of Occupying Powers in Relation to the Prevention and Control of Contagious Diseases Through the Interplay Between International Humanitarian Law and the Right to Health' (2022) 55 *Vanderbilt Journal of Transnational Law* 757

Longobardo M, 'The Relevance of the Concept of Due Diligence for International Humanitarian Law' (2019) 37 *Wisconsin International Law Journal* 44

Low L and Hodgkinson D, 'Compensation for Wartime Environmental Damage: Challenges to International Law After the Gulf War' (1995) 35 *Virginia Journal of International Law* 405

Lubell N, 'Human Rights Obligations in Military Occupation' (2012) 94 *International Review of the Red Cross* 317

Lubell N, 'Challenges in Applying Human Rights Law to Armed Conflict' (2005) 87 *International Review of the Red Cross* 737

Modirzadeh N, 'The Dark Sides of Convergence: A Pro-Civilian Critique of the Extraterritorial Application of Human Rights Law in Armed Conflict' (2010) 86 *U.S. Naval War College International Law Studies (Blue Book) Series* 349

Müller A, 'Limitations to and Derogations from Economic, Social and Cultural Rights' (2009) 9 *Human Rights Law Review* 557

Müller A, 'The Right to Health and International Humanitarian Law: Parallel Application for Building Peaceful Societies and the Prevention of Armed Conflict' (2015) 32 *Wisconsin International Law Journal* 416

Orakhelashvili A, 'The Post-War Settlement in Iraq: The UN Security Council Resolution 1483 (2003) and General International Law' (2003) 8 *Journal of Conflict & Security Law* 307

Prud'homme N, 'Lex Specialis: Oversimplifying a More Complex and Multifaceted Relationship' (2007) 40 *Israel Law Review* 356

Roberts A, 'What Is a Military Occupation?' (1985) 55 *British Yearbook of International Law* 249

Roberts A, 'The Applicability of Human Rights Law during Military Occupations' (1987) 13 *Review of International Studies JSTOR* 39

Robinson G, 'The Politics of Legal Reform in Palestine' (1997) 27 *Journal of Palestine Studies* 51

Saul B 'The status of Western Sahara as Occupied Territory Under International Humanitarian Law and the Exploitation of Ntural Resources' (2015) 27 *Global Change, Peace & Security* 301

Schindler D, 'The International Committee of the Red Cross and Human Rights' (1979) 19 *International Review of the Red Cross* 3

Schwenk E, 'Legislative Power of the Military Occupant Under Article 43 Hague Regulations' (1945) 54 *The Yale Law Journal* 393

Shelton D, 'Human Rights, Environmental Rights, and the Right to Environment' (1991) 28 *Stanford Journal of International Law* 103

Shelton D and Cutting I, 'If You Break It, Do You Own It? Legal Consequences of Environmental Harm from Military Activities' (2015) 6 *Journal of International Humanitarian Legal Studies* 201

Smith J, 'The Taking of the Sahara: The Role of Natural Resources in the Continuing Occupation of Western Sahara' (2015) 27 *Global Change, Peace & Security* 263

Smith HA, 'The Government of Occupied Territory' (1944) 21 *BYBIL* 151

Sprankling J, 'The Global Right to Property' (2014) 52 *Columbia Journal of Transnational Law* 464

Steenberghe R, 'The Interplay Between International Humanitarian Law and International Environmental Law: Towards a Comprehensive Framework for a Better Protection of the Environment in Armed Conflict' (2022) 20 *JICJ* 1123

Arai-Takahashi Y, 'Preoccupied with Occupation: Critical Examinations of the Historical Development of the Law of Occupation' (2012) 94 *International Review of the Red Cross* 51

Verwey W, 'Protection of the Environment in Times of Armed Conflict: In Search of a New Legal Perspective' (1995) 8 *LJIL* 7

Vité S, 'The Interrelation of the Law of Occupation and Economic, Social and Cultural Rights: The Examples of Food, Health and Property' (2008) 90 *International Review of the Red Cross* 629

Vöneky S, 'A New Shield for the Environment: Peacetime Treaties as Legal Restraints of Wartime Damage' (2000) 9 *Review of European Community & International Environmental Law* 20

Wilde R, 'Human Rights Beyond Borders at the World Court: The Significance of the International Court of Justice's Jurisprudence on the Extraterritorial Application of International Human Rights Law Treaties' (2013) 12 *Chinese Journal of International Law* 639

Wolfrum R, 'Purposes and Principles of International Environmental Law' (1990) 33 *The German Yearbook of International Law* 308

Zwanenburg M, Bothe M, and Sassòli M, 'Is the Law of Occupation Applicable to the Invasion Phase?' (2012) 94 *International Review of the Red Cross* 29

The United Nations Documents

The United Nations: "Draft Articles on the Effects of Armed Conflicts on Treaties", with Commentaries. Adopted by the International Law Commission at Its Sixty-Third Session, in 2011, and Submitted to the General Assembly as a Part of the Commission's Report Covering the Work of that Session UN Doc (A/66/10)

The Charter of the United Nations, (Signed on 26 June 1945), (into Force on 24 October 1945)

Declaration of the United Nations Conference on the Human Environment: *'Stockholm Declaration'* (1972)

The United Nations: International Convention on the Protection of the Rights of All Migrant Workers and Members of Their Families. (Adopted by General Assembly Resolution 45/158 of 18 December 1990)

The United Nations: Jaquet J, Harayama A, Kaeser D, 'Desk Study on the Environment in the Occupied Palestinian Territories' (The United Nations Environmental Programme 2003)

The United Nations: Report of the Secretary-General, UN Doc (A/49/323), (19 August/1994)

Sloan B, The United Nations: General Assembly: Economic and Social Council, 'Implications, Under International Law, of the United Nations Resolutions on Permanent Sovereignty Over Natural Resources, on the Occupied Palestinian and Other Arab Territories and on the Obligations of Israel Concerning Its Conduct in These Territories: Report of the Secretary-General' (A/38/265) (E/1983/85) (21 June 1983)

The ILC Draft Principles on Protection of the Environment in Relation to Armed Conflicts, with Commentaries (2022)

The Second Optional Protocol to the International Covenant on Civil and Political Rights, Aiming at the Abolition of the Death Penalty, (Adopted and Proclaimed by General Assembly Resolution 44/128 of 15 December 1989)

The Sixth Committee of the UN General Assembly, UN Doc. (A/C.6/ 46/SR.18), (22 October 1991)

The Sixth Committee of the UN General Assembly, UN Doc. (A/C.6/47/SR.9), (6 October 1992)

The UN Committee on Economic, Social and Cultural Rights, General Comment No. 14: The Right to the Highest Attainable Standard of Health (Art. 12). Adopted at the Twenty-second Session of the Committee on Economic, Social and Cultural Rights, on (11 August 2000) (Contained in Document E/C.12/2000/4)

The United Nations Conference on Environment and Development: *'The Rio Declaration'* (1992)

The United Nations Convention on the Rights of the Child, (Adopted and Opened for Signature, Ratification, and Accession by General Assembly Resolution (44/25) of 20 November 1989, Entry into Force 2 September 1990)

The United Nations Economic Commission for Europe (UNECE), Convention on Access to Information, Public Participation in Decision-Making and Access to Justice in Environmental Matters (Aarhus Convention), (25 June 1998)

The United Nations Educational, Social, and Cultural Organisation (UNESCO): General Conference; 30th Session, The Declaration of Bizkaia on the Right to the Environment, (30C/INF.11), (24 September 1999)

The United Nations Environment Programme, 'Desk Study on the Environment in Iraq' (2003)

The United Nations Environment Programme (UNEP), 'Environment in Iraq: UNEP Progress Report' (2003)

The United Nations Environmental Programme, 'Environmental Assessment of the Gaza Strip, Following the Escalation of Hostilities in December 2008–January 2009' (2009)

The United Nations Environmental Programme, 'Protecting the Environment During Armed Conflict: An Inventory and Analysis of International Law' (2009)

The United Nations Environmental Programmes (UNEP) at:<www.ecolex.org>

The United Nations General Assembly, 'The Human Right to a Clean, Healthy and Sustainable Environment' (A/76/L.75), (26 July 2022). Seventy-Sixth Session, Agenda Item 74 (b)

The United Nations General Assembly, Official Records, 'Annotations on the Text of the Draft International Covenants on Human Rights (Prepared by the Secretary-General)', Agenda Item 28 (Part II), Document: A/2929, (New York 1955)

The United Nations General Assembly: Universal Declaration of Human Rights, G.A. res. 217A (III), U.N. Doc A/810 at 71 (1948)

The United Nations, 'Interim Report of the Panel of Experts on the Illegal Exploitation of Natural Resources and Other Forms of Wealth of DR Congo' (S/2002/565) (22 May 2002)

The United Nations, Convention on the Elimination of All Forms of Discrimination against Women, Committee on the Elimination of Discrimination against Women, General Recommendation No. 30 on Women in Conflict Prevention, Conflict and Post-Conflict Situations, (CEDAW/C/GC/30), (18 October 2013)

The United Nations, Economic and Social Council, Committee on Economic, Social and Cultural Rights, 'Consideration of Reports Submitted by States Parties Under Articles 16 and 17 of the Covenant: Concluding Observations of the Committee on Economic, Social and Cultural Rights (Israel)' (E/C.12/1/Add.90), (26 June 2003)

The United Nations, Environment Assembly of the United Nations Environment Programme: Resolution on Environment and Health, (UNEP/EA.3/Res.4), (30 January 2018)

The United Nations, Final Act of the International Conference on Human Rights, (Tehran 1968)

The United Nations, International Covenant on Civil and Political Rights, Human Rights Committee, 'Views Adopted by the Committee Under Article 5 (4) of the Optional Protocol, Concerning Communication No. 2751/2016'. (CCPR/C/126/D/2751/2016), (20 September 2019)

The United Nations, International Law Commission, <https://legal.un.org/ilc/>

The United Nations: 'Report of the International Law Commission on the Work of Its Seventy-First Session' (2019) UN Doc (A/74/10)

The United Nations: 'Report of the United Nations Water Conference' Mar del Plata Declaration, Resolution X, 'Water Policies in Occupied Territories' (Mar del Plata, 14–5 March 1977), (E/CONF/70/29)

The United Nations: Convention on Environmental Impact Assessment in a Transboundary Context- the 'Espoo (EIA) Convention'. (Adopted in 1991 and Entered into Force on 10 September 1997)

The United Nations: Economic and Social Council, 'Question of the Violation of Human Rights and Fundamental Freedoms in Any Part of the World, with Particular Reference to Colonial and Other Dependent Countries and Territories. Situation of Human Rights in Occupied Kuwait'. (E/CN.4/1992/26), (16 January 1992)

The United Nations: Economic and Social Council, 'Report of the Situation of Human Rights in Kuwait Under Iraqi Occupation / Prepared by Mr. Walter Kälin, Special Rapporteur of the Commission on Human Rights, in Accordance with Commission Resolution (1991/67)'. (E/CN.4/1992/26), (16 January 1992)

The United Nations: Economic and Social Council, 'Report of the Special Rapporteur of the Commission on Human Rights, John Dugard, on the Situation of Human Rights in the Palestinian Territories Occupied by Israel Since 1967, Submitted in Accordance with Commission Resolution 1993/2 A' (E/CN.4/2004/6), (8 September 2003)

The United Nations: Economic and Social Council, 'The Right to Food', Report by the Special Rapporteur, Jean Ziegler: Mission to the Occupied Palestinian Territories. (E/CN.4/2004/10/Add.2), (31 October 2003)

The United Nations: Food and Agriculture Organisation of the United Nations, "What Are MEA's?"

The United Nations: General Assembly 'The World Charter for Nature' (1982)

The United Nations: General Assembly, 'Effects of Armed Conflicts on Treaties' (18 December 2017), (A/RES/72/121)

The United Nations: General Assembly, 'Fragmentation of International Law: Difficulties Arising from the Diversification and Expansion of International Law: Report of the Study Group of the International Law Commission'. (A/CN.4/L.702), (18 July 2006)

The United Nations: General Assembly, 'Human Rights Obligations Relating to the Enjoyment of a Safe, Clean, Healthy and Sustainable Environment' (A/73/188), (19 July 2018)

The United Nations: General Assembly, 'Permanent Sovereignty of the Palestinian People in the Occupied Palestinian Territory, Including East Jerusalem, and of the Arab Population in the Occupied Syrian Golan Over Their Natural Resources' (A/RES/70/225), (23 February 2016)

The United Nations: General Assembly, 'Permanent Sovereignty Over National Resources in the Occupied Arab Territories, (A/RES/3175 (XXVIII), (17 December 1973)
The United Nations: General Assembly, 'Question of Western Sahara', Res. (34/37), (21 November 1979)
The United Nations: General Assembly, 'Report of the International Law Commission', "ILC Draft Commentary", Seventy-First Session, (29 April–7 June and 8 July–9 August 2019) (A/74/10) (20 August 2019)
The United Nations: General Assembly, 'Report of the Special Committee to Investigate Israeli Practices Affecting the Human Rights of the Palestinian People and Other Arabs of the Occupied Territories' (A/58/311), (22 August 2003)
The United Nations: General Assembly, "Report of the Secretary-General on the Protection of the Environment in Times of Armed Conflict", (A/48/269), (29 July 1993)
The United Nations: General Assembly, Human Rights Council, 'Human Rights Situation in Palestine and Other Occupied Arab Territories: Israeli Settlements in the Occupied Palestinian Territory, Including East Jerusalem, and the Occupied Syrian Golan'. (A/HRC/34/39), (16 March 2017)
The United Nations: General Assembly, Human Rights Council, 'Report of the Special Rapporteur on the Issue of Human Rights Obligations Relating to the Enjoyment of a Safe, Clean, Healthy and Sustainable Environment' (A/HRC/37/59), (24 January 2018)
The United Nations: General Assembly, Human Rights Council, 'Report of the Special Rapporteur on the Implications for Human Rights of the Environmentally Sound Management and Disposal of Hazardous Substances and Wastes' (A/HRC/33/41), (2 August 2016)
The United Nations: General Assembly, Human Rights Council, 'Resolution Adopted by the Human Rights Council on 22 March 2018: Human Rights and the Environment, (A/HRC/RES/37/8)
The United Nations: General Assembly, Human Rights Council, 'The Human Right to a Safe, Clean, Healthy and Sustainable Environment' (A/HRC/48/L.23/Rev.1), (5 October 2021)
The United Nations: General Assembly, Human Rights Council, Human Rights Situation in Palestine and Other Occupied Arab Territories, 'Right of the Palestinian People to Self-Determination, (A/HRC/RES/49/28), (11 April 2022)
The United Nations: General Assembly, Human Rights Obligations Relating to the Enjoyment of a Safe, Clean, Healthy and Sustainable Environment: 'Report of the Special Rapporteur on the Issue of Human Rights Obligations Relating to the Enjoyment of a Safe, Clean, Healthy and Sustainable Environment' (A/73/188), (19 July 2018)
The United Nations: General Assembly, International Covenant on Economic, Social and Cultural Rights (ICESCR), (Adopted 16/ Dec/1966), (in force: 3 January 1976)
The United Nations: General Assembly, International Law Commission, 'Protection of the Environment in Relation to Armed Conflicts: Text and Titles of the Draft Principles Provisionally Adopted by the Drafting Committee on First Reading' (A/CN.4/L.937). (6 June 2019)
The United Nations: General Assembly, International Law Commission, 'Report of the Study Group of the International Law Commission: Finalized by Martti Koskenniemi,' 'Fragmentation of International Law: Difficulties Arising from the Diversification and Expansion of International Law'. (A/CN.4/L.682), (13 April 2006)
The United Nations: General Assembly, International Law Commission: 'Protection of the Environment in Relation to Armed Conflicts: Text and Titles of the Draft Principles Provisionally Adopted by the Drafting Committee on First Reading' (A/CN.4/L.937), (6 June 2019)
The United Nations: General Assembly, Preparatory Committee for the United Nations Conference on the Human Environment, (A/CONF.48/PC/17), (15 March 1972)

The United Nations: General Assembly, Res. 2106 A (XX). International Convention on the Elimination of All Forms of Racial Discrimination (A/RES/20/2106), (21 December 1965)

The United Nations: General Assembly, Res. 2200A (XXI). International Covenant on Economic, Social and Cultural Rights, International Covenant on Civil and Political Rights and Optional Protocol to the International Covenant on Civil and Political Rights. (A/RES/21/2200), (16 December 1966)

The United Nations: General Assembly, (Res. 2398) (XXIII) (3 December 1968).

The United Nations: General Assembly, (Res. 34/180). Convention on the Elimination of All Forms of Discrimination against Women. (A/RES/34/180), (18 December 1979), (Entry into Force 3 September 1981)

The United Nations: General Assembly, (Res. 44/25) Convention on the Rights of the Child (A/RES/44/25), (5 December 1989)

The United Nations: General Assembly, Resolution (46/216) (1991)

The United Nations: General Assembly, Resolution (47/151) (A/RES/47/151) (1992)

The United Nations: General Assembly, Resolution adopted by the General Assembly on the Report of the Sixth Committee (A/49/737), (A/RES/49/50) (1995)

The United Nations: General Assembly: 'The International Covenant on Civil and Political Rights, (ICCPR), (Adopted in 16 December 1966, in force in: 23 March 1976)

The United Nations: General Assembly: Human Rights Council, 'Human Rights Situation in the Occupied Palestinian Territory, Including East Jerusalem, with a Focus on Access to Water and Environmental Degradation: Report of the Special Rapporteur on the Situation of Human Rights in the Palestinian Territories Occupied Since 1967'. (A/HRC/40/73), (30 May 2019)

The United Nations: General Assembly: International Law Commission,' First Report on Protection of the Environment in Relation to Armed Conflicts by Marja Lehto, Special Rapporteur' (A/CN.4/720) (30 April 2018)

The United Nations: General Assembly: International Law Commission, 'Second Report on Protection of the Environment in Relation to Armed Conflicts by Marja Lehto, Special Rapporteur' (A/CN.4/728) (27 March 2019)

The United Nations: General Assembly: International Law Commission, 'Third Report on Protection of the Environment in Relation to Armed Conflicts, by Marja Lehto, Special Rapporteur' (A/CN.4/750) (16 March 2022)

The United Nations: General Assembly: Resolution 1803 (XVII) of (14 December 1962)

The United Nations: General Assembly: Summary Record of the 29th Meeting (A/C.6/73/SR.29) (10 December 2018)

The United Nations: General Assembly: Summary Record of the 30th Meeting (A/C.6/73/SR.30) (6 December 2018)

The United Nations: Human Rights Council, 'Report of the Special Rapporteur on the Situation of Human Rights in the Palestinian Territories Occupied Since 1967' (A/HRC/40/73), (15 March 2019)

The United Nations: International Covenant on Civil and Political Rights, 'Consideration of Reports Submitted by States Parties Under Article 40 of the Covenant: Concluding Observations of the Human Rights Committee. (Israel)'. (CCPR/C/ISR/CO/3), (3 September 2010)

The United Nations: Office of the United Nations High Commissioner for Human Rights: Special Procedures of the United Nations Human Rights Council. "Mapping Human Rights Obligations Relating to the Enjoyment of a Safe, Clean, Healthy and Sustainable Environment: Individual Report on the International Covenant on Civil and Political Rights" (Report No.2), (December 2013)

The United Nations: Office of the United Nations High Commissioner for Human Rights, Special Procedures of the United Nations Human Rights Council, 'Mapping Human Rights Obligations Relating to the Enjoyment of a Safe, Clean, Healthy and Sustainable

Environment: Individual Report on the United Nations Convention on the Elimination of All Forms of Discrimination against Women' (Report No.4), (December 2013)

The United Nations: Office of the United Nations High Commissioner for Human Rights, 'Mapping Human Rights Obligations Relating to the Enjoyment of a Safe, Clean, Healthy and Sustainable Environment: Individual Report on the International Covenant on Economic, Social and Cultural Rights' (Report No.1), (December 2013)

The United Nations: Reports of International Arbitral Awards, 'Eritrea Ethiopia Claims Commission, Final Award- Pensions: Eritrea's Claims 15, 19& 23' (19 December 2005), vol. XXXVI,

The United Nations: Security Council, Resolution (S/RES/1483)/ adopted by the Security Council at Its 4761st Meeting, on (22 May 2003)

The United Nations: Security Council, (SC Res. 1546) Adopted by the Security Council at its 4987th Meeting, on 8 June 2004 of 8 June 2004

The United Nations: Security Council, Resolution 687 Iraq- Kuwait (1991)

The United Nations, The Biodiversity Convention, (Adopted: 22 May 1992), (into Force: 29 December 1993)

The United Nations: The General Assembly, Human Rights Council, 'Annual Report of the United Nations High Commissioner for Human Rights and Reports of the Office of the High Commissioner and the Secretary-General': Analytical Study on the Relationship Between Human Rights and the Environment: Report of the United Nations High Commissioner for Human Rights' (A/HRC/19/34), (16 December 2011)

The United Nations: The United Nations Compensation Commission (UNCC), <https://uncc.ch/home>

The United Nations: United Nations Environment Programme (UNEP): 'Protecting the Environment During Armed Conflict: An Inventory and Analysis of International Law' (United Nations 2009)

The United Nations: Commission on Human Rights, Human Rights and the Environment, (E/CN.4/RES/1991/44), (5 March 1991)

The United Nations: Committee on the Rights of the Child (CRC), General Comment No. 15 (2013) on the Right of the Child to the Enjoyment of the Highest Attainable Standard of Health (art. 24), (17 April 2013), (CRC/C/GC/15)

The United Nations: Committee on the Rights of the Child (CRC), General Comment No. 16 (2013) on State Obligations Regarding the Impact of the Business Sector on Children's Rights, (17 April 2013), (CRC/C/GC/16)

The United Nations: Committee on the Rights of the Child (CRC), General comment No. 6 (2005): Treatment of Unaccompanied and Separated Children Outside their Country of Origin, (1 September 2005), (CRC/GC/2005/6)

The United Nations: Human Rights Committee (HRC), CCPR General Comment No. 26: Continuity of Obligations, (8 December 1997), (CCPR/C/21/Rev.1/Add.8/Rev.1)

The United Nations: Human Rights Committee (HRC), General Comment No. 31 [80], The Nature of the General Legal Obligation Imposed on States Parties to the Covenant, (26 May 2004), (CCPR/C/21/Rev.1/Add.13)

The United Nations: General Assembly, (41st sess. 1986–1987), (A/RES/41/132)

The United Nations: UNESCO, International List of Cultural Property under Enhanced Protection (2019)

United Nations Educational, Scientific and Cultural Organisation: Convention on Wetlands of International Importance Ēspecially as Waterfowl Habitat, (Ramsar Convention). (Adopted 2 February 1971) (Entered into Force 21 December 1975)

United Nations: General Assembly, 'Fragmentation of International Law: Difficulties Arising from the Diversification and Expansion of International Law: Report of the Study Group of the International Law Commission'. (A/CN.4/L.702), (18 July 2006)

United Nations: General Assembly: United Nations Declaration on the Rights of Indigenous Peoples, (UNDIPR), (61/295), (13 September 2007)

United Nations: Human Rights Office of the High Commissioner: International Covenant on Civil and Political Rights, <https://indicators.ohchr.org/>

The UN Committee on the Rights of the Child, 'General Comment No. 26 (2023) on Children's Rights and the Environment with a Special Focus on Climate Change' (22 August 2023), (CRC/C/GC/26)

UNGA, Resolution 3314 (XXIX), 14 December 1974

WHO, Official Records of the World Health Organization No.2: Proceedings and Final Acts of the International Health Conference Held in New York from 19 June to 22 July 1946 (UN WHO Interim Commission June 1948)

Other Sources: (Reports, Treaties, Websites)

Abu Amr A, "The Israeli Occupation and Environmental Degradation in Palestine", *Ro'ea Magazine* 8 (2001)

Abualrob W, Longobardo M, and Mackenzie R, 'Applying International Environmental Law Conventions in Occupied Territory: The Azerbaijan v. Armenia Case under the Bern Convention, Blog of the European Journal of International Law (2023) <https://www.ejiltalk.org/applying-international-environmental-law-conventions-in-occupied-territory-the-azerbaijan-v-armenia-case-under-the-bern-convention> accessed 21 May 2023

Abualrob W, 'Environmental Racism in Situations of Occupation', International Law Blog (2023) <https://internationallaw.blog/2023/07/10/environmental-racism-in-situations-of-occupation/> accessed 19 August 2023

Abualrob W, 'The Protection of the Environment in Situations of Occupation under the Rome Statute', International Law Blog (2023) <https://internationallaw.blog/2023/12/11/the-protection-of-the-environment-in-situations-of-occupation-under-the-rome-statute/#_ftn2> accessed 4 April 2024

Administrative Department of the President of the Republic of Azerbaijan: Presidential Library, 'Armenia-Azerbaijan Nagorno-Karabakh Conflict' <http://files.preslib.az/projects/azerbaijan/eng/gl7.pdf> accessed 17 December 2020

African Commission on Human and Peoples' Rights: African Charter on Human and Peoples' Rights (into force: 21 October 1986)

Ahmed K, Gayle D, Mousa A, ''Ecocide in Gaza': does scale of environmental destruction amount to a war crime?', The Guardian (2024) <https://www.theguardian.com/environment/2024/mar/29/gaza-israel-palestinian-war-ecocide-environmental-destruction-pollution-rome-statute-war-crimes-aoe> accessed 15 April 2024

Al-Haq Defending Human Rights Organisation, 'ILC Draft Principles on the Protection of the Environment in Relation to Armed Conflicts, (25 July 2019) <http://www.alhaq.org/advocacy/14746.html> accessed 22 February 2020

Al-Haq Organization, 'Environmental Rights Case Succeeds in Holding Israel Accountable for Illegal Hazardous Waste Dumping in Palestine, (25 August 2016)

Aloni A, 'Made in Israel: Exploiting Palestinian Land for Treatment of Israeli Waste' (B'tselem December 2017)

Azimzade A, 'Armenia Plundering Natural Resources in Occupied Azerbaijani Territories'. <https://irs-az.com/new/files/2019/247/2954.pdf> accessed 20 September 2020

Berlin Rules on Water Resources: International Law Association: Berlin Conference 2004: Water Recourses Law

Birzeit University, Institute of Law, 'Legal Status in Palestine: Palestinian Judicial System: Historical Evolution of the Palestinian Legal System' <http://lawcenter.birzeit.edu/lawcenter/en/homepage/legal-status-in-palestine> accessed 25 August 2021

Belousova K, 'COP14 Participants Were Urged to React to Russia's Destruction of International Ecosystems' <https://ecopolitic.com.ua/en/news/uchasnikiv-cop14-zaklikali-vidreaguvati-na-znishhennya-rosiieju-mizhnarodnih-ekosistem-2/> accessed 8 April 2023

Caliva S, 'Chernobyl 2.0 –The Crimean Ecological Disaster' (30 September 2018) <https://www.vocaleurope.eu/chernobyl-2-0-the-crimean-ecological-disaster/> accessed 28 June 2021

Commission for Reception, Truth and Reconciliation in East-Timor, Final Report, January 2006

Committee on the Rights of the Child: Report of the 2016 day of General Discussion: Children's Rights and the Environment, (2016)

Conflict and Environment Observatory: Country brief: Iraq, (Published: March 16, 2018) <https://ceobs.org/country-brief-iraq/> accessed 8 October 2020

Convention Concerning the Protection of the World Cultural and Natural Heritage (the World Heritage Convention), (Adopted 23/November/1972), (Entered into force 15 December 1979)

Council of Europe: Chart of Signatures and Ratifications of Treaty 009, Protocol to the Convention for the Protection of Human Rights and Fundamental Freedoms (ETS No. 009) <https://www.coe.int/en/web/conventions/full-list?module=signatures-by-treaty&treatynum=009>

Council of Europe: Convention on the Conservation of European Wildlife and Natural Habitats (Berne Convention). (Adopted: 19 September 1979) (Entered into force: 1 June 1982)

Council of Europe, Department for the Execution of Judgments of the European Court of Human Rights, Environment: Thematic Factsheet, (October 2020)

Council of Europe, The European Convention on Human Rights, 'Preparatory work'. <https://www.coe.int/en/web/human-rights-convention/preparatory-works> accessed 6 December 2023

Crimean Tatar Resource Center, 'Contributions for the Study on Indigenous Peoples' Rights in the Context of Borders, Migration and Displacement' (No. 26/02), (1 February 2019)

Crimean Tatar Resource Center, 'Contributions for the study on Right to Land under the UNDRIP: A Human Rights Focus' (No.01/02), (15 January 2020)

Dinstein Y, 'Legislation Under Article 43 of the Hague Regulations: Belligerent Occupation and Peacebuilding' (2004), (Occasional Paper Series, No.1), (Program on Humanitarian Policy and Conflict Research (HPCR)/ Harvard University)

European Court of Human Rights, 'Environment and the European Convention on Human Rights' (Press Unit 2022)

Feilchenfeld E, The International Economic Law of Belligerent Occupation, (Monograph Series of the Carnegie Endowment for International Peace, Division of International Law, No. 6. Washington 1942)

Ferraro T, 'Occupation and other Forms of Administration of Foreign Territory' (ICRC 2012)

Final Record of the Diplomatic Conference of Geneva of 1949 (Berne, 1950) Vol. II-A

Final record of the Diplomatic Conference of Geneva of 1949. Vol: III, Annexes,

Final Record of the Diplomatic Conference of Geneva of 1949, Vol: I; Final Record of the Diplomatic Conference of Geneva of 1949, Vol: II-A, Final Record of the Diplomatic Conference of Geneva of 1949, Vol: II-B, ; Final Record of the Diplomatic Conference of Geneva of 1949, Vol: III, All Volumes are <https://www.loc.gov/item/2011525350/> accessed 2 December 2023

First Protocol to the 1954 Hague Convention, (14 May 1954)

Gabčíkovo-Nagymaros Project (Hungary/Slovakia), Judgment, I.C.J. Reports 1997, p.7. Separate Opinion of Vice-President Weeramantry

Geneva Convention (IV) relative to the Protection of Civilian Persons in Time of War. Geneva (12 August 1949)

Hague Convention for the Protection of Cultural Property in the Event of Armed Conflict, (14 May 1954)

Hareuveni E, 'By Hook and by Crook: Israeli Settlement Policy in the West Bank' (B'Tselem 2010)

Hareuveni E, 'Foul Play: Neglect of Wastewater Treatment in the West Bank' (B'Tselem 2009)

Human Rights in Armed Conflicts. Resolution XXIII adopted by the International Conference on Human Rights, Teheran (12 May 1968) <http://hrlibrary.umn.edu/instree/1968a.htm> accessed 20 March 2022

ICRC Commentary to Additional Protocol I

ICRC, 'Contemporary challenges to IHL - Occupation: Overview' (11 June 2012)

ICRC, 'Convention (I) for the Amelioration of the Condition of the Wounded and Sick in Armed Forces in the Field. Geneva, 12 August 1949', Commentary of 2016: Article 2: Application of the Convention

ICRC, 'Customary IHL', "Rule 54. Attacks against Objects Indispensable to the Survival of the Civilian Population"

ICRC, 'Treaties, States Parties and Commentaries': Protocol Additional to the Geneva Conventions of 12 August 1949, and Relating to the Protection of Victims of International Armed Conflicts (Protocol I), 8 June 1977. "Commentary of 1987: Article 54: 'Protection of Objects Indispensable to the Survival of the Civilian Population'

ICRC, Guidelines for Military Manuals and Instructions on the Protection of the Environment in Times of Armed Conflict, 30-04-1996 Article, International Review of the Red Cross, No. 311

ICRC, Interpretive Guidance on the Notion of Direct Participation in Hostilities Under International Humanitarian Law, Geneva, May 2009 <https://casebook.icrc.org/case-study/icrc-interpretive-guidance-notion-direct-participation-hostilities> accessed 29 November 2023

ICRC: 'The Relevance of Preparatory Work and Archival Materials in Updating the ICRC Commentaries' (2017)

ICRC, International Humanitarian Law Databases, 'Protocol Additional to the Geneva Conventions of 12 August 1949, and Relating to the Protection of Victims of International Armed Conflicts (Protocol I), 8 June 1977: Commentary of 1987, Article 1 - General Principles and Scope of Application: Paragraph 2' <https://ihl-databases.icrc.org/en/ihl-treaties/api-1977/article-1/commentary/1987?activeTab=undefined> accessed 8 December 2023

International Law and Policy Institute, Protection of the Natural Environment in Armed Conflict: An Empirical Study (2014), 29–30

Isaac J and Rishmawi K, *Status of the Environment in the State of Palestine – 2015* (The Applied Research Institute (ARIJ) – Jerusalem 2015)

IUCN Draft International Covenant on Environment and Development (IUCN Draft Covenant)

International Environmental Agreements (IEA) Database Project. <https://iea.uoregon.edu/> accessed 19 August 2023

Jaquet J, Harayama A, and Kaeser D, *Desk Study on the Environment in the Occupied Palestinian Territories* (The United Nations Environmental Programme 2003)

Kriebaum U, and Reinisch A, 'Property, Right to, International Protection' (Max Planck Encyclopedias of International Law (MPIL) 2019)

Kuwait Regional Convention for Co-operation on the Protection of the Marine Environment from Pollution (Adopted 24 April 1978), (Entered into force 1 July 1979)

Law of Georgia on Environmental Protection, (No. 519), of (1996)

Laws and Customs of War on Land (The Hague, IV), (Convention Signed at The Hague October 18, 1907), (Entered into Force: 26 January 26 1910)

League of Arab States, Arab Charter on Human Rights, 15 September 1994

Lindén O, Jernelöv A, and Egerup J, 'The Environmental Impacts of the Gulf War 1991', IIASA Interim Report, April 2004

Manna A, 'The Duties of the Occupant in Protecting the Natural Resources of the Occupied Territory Under International Humanitarian Law', University of Palestine, Majallat Jamiat Filastin lil-Abḥath (2015)

Manual on Human Rights and the Environment (2nd edn, Council of Europe Publishing 2012)

Médecins Sans Frontières, 'The Practical Guide to Humanitarian Law: Fundamental Guarantees' <https://guide-humanitarian-law.org/content/article/3/fundamental-guarantees/> accessed 3 December 2023
McArdle M, 'How Property Rights Could Help Save the Environment' (29 May 2012)
Operational Guidelines for the Implementation of the World Heritage Convention
Oslo Accords, 'The Israeli-Palestinian Interim Agreement On The West Bank and The Gaza Strip Annex III': Protocol Concerning Civil Affairs
Official Records of the Diplomatic Conference on the Reaffirmation and Development of International Humanitarian Law Applicable in Armed Conflicts, Geneva, 1974–1977; (Vol. 15: Summary Records of Committee III: Third and Fourth Sessions; Reports of Committee III) <https://library.icrc.org/library/docs/CD/CD_1977_ACTES_ENG_15.pdf>; <https://library.icrc.org/library/search/Notice/2374> accessed 4 December 2023
Official Records of the Diplomatic Conference on the Reaffirmation and Development of International Humanitarian Law Applicable in Armed Conflicts, Geneva, 1974 – 1977, (Vol. 03: Table of Amendments: Amendments to Draft Additional Protocol I); (Vol. 05: Summary Records of the Plenary Meetings of the Conference: First, Second and Third Sessions); (Vol. 06: Summary Records of the Plenary Meetings of the Conference: Fourth Session); (Vol. 14: Summary Records of Committee III: First and Second Sessions); (Vol. 15: Summary Records of Committee III: Third and Fourth Sessions; Reports of Committee III); (Vol. 16: Summary Records and Reports of the Ad Hoc Committee on Conventional Weapons) <https://blogs.icrc.org/cross-files/drafting-history-1977-additional-protocols/> accessed 13 December 2023
Palestinian Environmental Law, Law No. (7) of (1999)
Pictet J, The Geneva Conventions of 12 August 1949, Commentary: IV Geneva Convention relative to the Protection of Civilian Persons in Time of War, (International Committee of the Red Cross 1958)
PLO/Palestine, 'Israel's Belligerent Occupation of the Palestinian Territory, Including Jerusalem and International Humanitarian Law': 'Paper Presented to the Conference of the High Contracting Parties to the Fourth Geneva Convention on Measures to Enforce the Convention in the Occupied Palestinian Territory, including Jerusalem' (15 July 1999)
Pontin B, De Lucia V, and Rus J, *Environmental Injustice in Occupied Palestinian Territory: Problems and Prospects* (Al-Haq Organization 2015)
Power S and Weir D, 'Stress-testing the ILC's Draft Principles on Environmental Protection During Occupation': 'The Revisions to the Draft Principles on Environmental Protection in Situations of Occupation Have Improved Them Considerably but Gaps Remain That Should Be Addressed'. (19 September 2018)
Project of an International Declaration Concerning the Laws and Customs of War. Brussels, 27 August 1874
Protocol Additional to the Geneva Conventions of 12 August 1949, and Relating to the Protection of Victims of International Armed Conflict (Protocol I)
Qupty M, 'The Application of International Law in the Occupied Territories as Reflected in the Judgments of the High Court of Justice in Israel'
Ramsar Convention: Country Profiles <https://www.ramsar.org/country-profiles>
Rayfuse R and Sjöstedt B, *Workshop on the Protection of the Environment in Relation to Armed Conflict* (Lund University 2012)
Reeh G, 'Human Rights and the Environment: The UN Human Rights Committee Affirms the Duty to Protect', *Blog of the European Journal of International Law* (2019)
Republic of Azerbaijan Ministry of Foreign Affairs, No:015/23, Press Release on Arbitration Filed by Azerbaijan against Armenia for Widespread Environmental Destruction. More Information <https://www.mfa.gov.az/en/news/no01523> accessed 4 March 2023
Republic of Azerbaijan: Environmental Protection Law (No. 678–IQ) of (1999)

Romanelli C and Others, *Connecting Global Priorities: Biodiversity and Human Health: A Sate of Knowledge Review* (World Health Organization and Secretariat of the Convention on Biological Diversity 2015)
Rome Statute of the International Criminal Court, 'Official Records of the Assembly of States Parties to the Rome Statute of the International Criminal Court (ICC-ASP/1/3 and Corr.1)' (First Session, 3–10 September 2002)
Sassòli M, 'Article 43 of the Hague Regulations and Peace Operations in the Twenty-First Century' (International Humanitarian Law Research Initiative) (2004)
Second Protocol to the 1954 Hague Convention, (26 March 1999)
Statute of the International Court of Justice, (Adopted on: 26 June 1945), (into Force: 24 October 1945)
The 14th Meeting of the Conference of the Contracting Parties to the Ramsar Convention on Wetlands, 'Wetlands Action for People and Nature' Geneva, Switzerland, and Wuhan, China 5–13 November 2022. Resolution XIV.20, 'The Ramsar Convention's Response to Environmental Emergency in Ukraine Relating to the Damage of Its Wetlands of International Importance (Ramsar Sites) Stemming from the Russian Federation's Aggression'
The Basel Convention on the Control of Transboundary Movements of Hazardous Wastes and Their Disposal: Parties to the Basel Convention on the Control of Transboundary Movements of Hazardous Wastes and Their Disposal (Adopted 22 March 1989, entered in Force 5 May 1992)
The European Court of Human Rights, 'Guide to the Case-Law of the European Court of Human Rights- Environment' (Council of Europe 2022)
The European Parliament, 'The Universal Declaration of Human Rights and its relevance for the European Union'
Human Rights Committee, 'General Comment No. 36 on Article 6 of the International Covenant on Civil and Political Rights, on the Right to Life' (CCPR/C/GC/36), (3 September 2019)
Human Rights Committee, *Sergio Euben Lopez Burgos v. Uruguay*, Communication No. R.12/52, U.N. Doc. Supp. No. 40 (A/36/40) at 176 (1981)
The International Committee of the Red Cross, 'Treaties, States Parties and Commentaries: Convention (IV) Respecting the Laws and Customs of War on Land and Its Annex: Regulations Concerning the Laws and Customs of War on Land. The Hague, (18 October 1907)
The Iraqi Law of Protection and Improvement of the Environment No. (3) of the Year 1997.
(Iraqi Law of Protection and Improvement of the Environment, (No. 27) of (2009), the Law Repeals the Law No. 3 of 1997 on the Protection and Improvement of the Environment)
The Laws of War on Land. (Oxford Manual), Oxford, (9 September 1880)
The Proceedings of the Hague Peace Conferences. Translation of the Official Texts, Prepared in the Division of International Law of the Carnegie Endowment for International Peace, Under the Supervision of James Brown Scott. The Conference of 1899 <https://ogc.osd.mil/Portals/99/proceedings_of_the_hague_peace_conferences_the_conference_of_1899%20%281%29.pdf> accessed 7 December 2023
Ticehurst R, "The Martens Clause and the Laws of Armed Conflict" <https://www.onlinelibrary.iihl.org/wp-content/uploads/2021/07/Martens-Clause-LOAC.pdf> accessed 8 December 2023
The Preparatory Work Documents of the Biodiversity Convention <https://www.cbd.int/history/> accessed 12 December 2023
The Preparatory Works of the (ICCPR) and (ICESCR), See: UN Human Rights Treaties: *Travaux Préparatoires*, (ICCPR) and *Travaux Préparatoires*, (ICESCR)
The Proceedings of the Hague Peace Conferences. Translation of the Official Texts, Prepared in the Division of International Law of the Carnegie Endowment for International Peace, Under the Supervision of J.B. Scott. The Conference of 1907. (Vol. i–iii. v.3). The Conference of 1907, Meetings of the Second, Third and Fourth Commissions. (OUP 1921) <https://babel.hathitrust.org/cgi/pt?id=hvd.hnyamj&seq=9> accessed 1 December 2023
The US Military Manual, 'The law of Land Warfare' (FM- Field Manual No. 27-10, 1956)

Ukraine Crisis Media Center, ‘Environmental Disaster in Crimea: Key Things to Know’ (8 September 2018). <https://uacrisis.org/en/68485-environmental-disaster-crimea> accessed 20 June 2021

UN Human Rights Council: ‘Iraq: Grave Human Rights Violations During the War and Occupation in Iraq’, 22nd Regular Session (25 February–22 March 2013)

United Nations, ‘Universal Declaration of Human Rights’ <https://www.un.org/en/about-us/universal-declaration-of-human-rights>

Vienna Convention on the Law of Treaties (1969), (Adopted on 23 May 1969, into Force 27 January 1980)

Warsaw Institute, ‘Ecological Disaster in the Crimea’ (7 September 2018) <https://warsawinstitute.org/ecological-disaster-crimea/> accessed 21 June 2021

World Conference on Human Rights, Vienna Deceleration and Programme of Action, (A/CONF.157/23), (12 July 1993)

World Health Organisation, ‘Biodiversity and Health’ (2015)

World Heritage Committee, Decisions Adopted at the 31st Session of the World Heritage Committee 2007, (WHC-07/31.COM/24), (23 June–2 July 2007)

World Heritage Committee, Decisions Adopted By the 27th Session of the World Heritage Committee in 2003, (WHC-03/27.COM/24), (30 June–5 July 2003)

World Heritage Committee, Report, 16th Session, UNESCO Doc. (WHC-92/CONF.002/12), (14 December 1992)

Weizman E and Others, ‘‘No Traces of Life’: Israel’s Ecocide in Gaza 2023–2024’ <https://forensic-architecture.org/investigation/ecocide-in-gaza> accessed 2 May 2024

Wrange P, ‘Occupation/Annexation of a Territory: Respect for International Humanitarian Law and Human Rights and Consistent EU Policy’, Directorate General for External Policies/ Policy Department, (European Union 2015)

Z. Brophy and Isaac J, ‘The Environmental Impact of Israeli Military Activities in the Occupied Palestinian Territory’ (Applied Research Institute – Jerusalem 2009)

Zoria Y, ‘What Caused the Environmental Disaster in Occupied Crimea? A Chemist Explains’ (21 September 2018)

<u>Sources in other languages</u>

مركز الامارات للدراسات والبحوث الاستراتيجية، " الحروب والبيئة: حالة العراق والخليج العربي".
(UAE, 2004 31 مايو)

Lakhdar N, ‘Preserving the Environment in Times of Armed Wars in the light of International Humanitarian Law’ (2023) 16 *Journal of Law & Humanities Sciences, University of Djelfa, Algeria* 1163–1179

نقيش لخضر، "المحافظة على البيئة في أوقات الحروب المسلحة على ضوء ما قرره القانون الدولي الإنساني"،مجلة الحقوق والعلوم الإنسانية، المجلد16/ العـــدد:01، (2023)،ص1163-1179

Bougalim Y, *Accountability for Environmental Crimes Under International Law* (Arab Studies Centre for Publishing 2015)

(يوسف بوغالم، *المساءلة عن الجرائم البيئية في القانون الدولي* (مركز الدراسات العربية للنشر والتوزيع، مصر ٢٠١٥

Actes de la Conférence de Bruxelles de 1874 sur le projet d’une convention internationale concernant la guerre (1874) <https://babel.hathitrust.org/cgi/pt?id=mdp.35112104530417&seq=5&q1=./>accessed 2 December 2023. For the English Language translation of the Brussels Conference of 1874 and other related information see: ICRC: IHL Databases: Project of an International Declaration concerning the Laws and Customs of War. Brussels, 27 August 1874 <https://ihl-databases.icrc.org/en/ihl-treaties/brussels-decl-1874?activeTab=undefined>

Index

FSC
www.fsc.org
MIX
Papier | Fördert
gute Waldnutzung
FSC® C083411

Kolibri 360 GmbH
Ferdinand-Jühlke-Straße 7
99095 Erfurt, Deutschland
produktsicherheit@kolibri360.de